THE Bed & Breakfast
COOKBOOK

THE Bed & Breakfast COOKBOOK

Great American B&Bs and Their Recipes from All Fifty States

MARTHA W. MURPHY

Drawings by Amelia Rockwell Seton

To Gail —
of "GALE WINDS" @ Bristol Point Road,
with best wishes !

Martha W Murphy

12·3·01

Stemmer House
PUBLISHERS, INC.
Owings Mills, Maryland

FRONTISPIECE: *Bridgeford Cottage* (page 58)
is in the quaint old resort town of Eureka
Springs, Arkansas.

Inquiries should be directed to
Stemmer House Publishers, Inc.
2627 Caves Road
Owings Mills, Maryland 21117

A Barbara Holdridge book
First printing 1991
Second printing 1997

Printed and bound in Hong Kong

Designed by John Beck of The Bookmakers, Incorporated, with
Barbara Holdridge

Composed in Garamond No. 49 by the Bookmakers, Incorporated,
Wilkes-Barre, Pennsylvania

Printed on 75-pound Korean gloss acid-free paper and bound in .012
coated artboard by Everbest Printing Company, Hong Kong / Four
Colour Imports, Ltd., Louisville, Kentucky

Library of Congress Cataloging in Publication

Murphy, Martha W., 1951-
    The Bed & Breakfast cookbook : great America B & Bs and their
recipes from all fifty states / by Martha W. Murphy.
      p. cm.
    "A Barbara Holdridge book"—T.p. verso.
    Includes bibliographical references and index.
    ISBN 0-88045-047-9 (paper cover : alk. paper) : $19.95
    1. Breakfasts. 2. Cookery, American. 3. Bed and breakfast
accommodations—United States—Guide-books. I. Title. II. Title:
Bed and breakfast cookbook.
TX733.M78   1991
641.5′2—dc20   91–9701
                          CIP

TO MY PARENTS

Contents

Author's Note ... ix

What Is a Bed & Breakfast? ... 3

Beverages ... 7

Fruit & Cereals ... 19

Pancakes, Waffles, French Toast & Crepes ... 43

Eggs, Omelets, Soufflés & Quiches ... 75

Seafood ... 107

Breakfast Meats ... 115

Vegetables & Side Dishes ... 127

Muffins, Biscuits & Scones ... 139

Coffeecakes, Quickbreads & Unyeasted Pastries ... 163

Yeasted Rolls, Breads & Pastries ... 199

Jams, Jellies & Sauces ... 211

Afternoon Tea: Sandwiches & Sweets ... 227

Metric Conversion Tables ... 253

Featured B&Bs by State ... 255

B&B Reservation Agencies ... 261

B&B Guidebooks ... 265

B&B Index ... 266

General Index ... 269

*The Bufflehead Cove Inn overlooks the
Kennebunk River (see page 63).*

Author's Note

*T*HE IDEA FOR THIS BOOK originated in 1986, during my second season of running a bed and breakfast. Looking at my menus for Murphy's B&B of Narragansett, Rhode Island, I realized I was serving the same breakfast fare over and over. Although the dishes were good, I needed some new ideas and recipes. I decided to find out what other B&Bs were serving their guests. After asking around a little bit, I came to believe that a collection of recipes from a variety of bed and breakfasts around the country could become a useful book, one that would be appreciated by many B&B hosts.

At first, I thought such a book would appeal only to B&B proprietors. But as more and more guests asked for copies of my recipes to take home, I realized that B&B travelers would also enjoy a Bed and Breakfast cookbook, so that their houseguests and family could share these special treats.

I began by sending letters to five hundred B&Bs, located in all fifty states, to ask if they would be interested in submitting recipes to be used in a Bed and Breakfast cookbook. I asked for their best, favorite, most requested recipes for dishes served at breakfast, brunch or afternoon tea: "original, unusual or favorite old-standards, as long as you feel the recipe is special and delicious." The response was tremendous. Everyone who wrote was enthusiastic about having such a book available. In compiling my list, I limited invitations to what I consider to be true B&B establishments: private homes that are lived in by the hosts, generally offering from two to ten guestrooms for overnight accommodation. All offer breakfast in the morning—and quite often afternoon tea—included in the price of the room, but most do not offer any other meal, although some B&Bs offer box lunches or dinner by prior arrangement.

Eventually I corresponded with about twelve hundred American B&Bs. Of course, not everyone responded, but hundreds of letters and phone calls later, I finally had what I felt was both a good representation of the states and a special collection of recipes: 315 recipes from 146 B&Bs located in all 50 states. I do think they give a fair and accurate picture of what the American B&B is all about. I was able to include almost every B&B that submitted a recipe, barring a handful that sent items based primarily on box mixes or other commercially prepared foods which did not meet my standards for this book. I have tested all the recipes myself and included tips on preparing them, both in the chapter introductions and in the recipe directions. For the most part, I am happy to say, B&B hosts are revealed here to be good cooks, serving delicious breakfasts of fresh, innovative, varied and healthy fare.

As I worked on the book, recipes and anecdotes continued to arrive. It soon became clear that I was receiving more than the components of a standard cookbook. Hosts were including much more than recipes: interesting information about their houses, their locales and what there was for visitors to see and do. The book thus grew to include a glimpse into each B&B—the style and location of the house, where and how breakfast is served and any pertinent anecdotes—as well as the recipes and menus for the breakfasts. As I read the submissions, I felt I was taking a tour of America, with all its regional accents.

For anyone who enjoys traveling, and all the good eating that can accompany the exploration of new places, I hope this book will act as a pleasurable guide to B&Bs all over America. For those who have not yet tried an American B&B, I hope this book will be an appealing invitation.

For prospective B&B hosts (anyone toying with the idea of starting a B&B) *The Bed & Breakfast Cookbook* can provide a glimpse of the breakfast part of bed and breakfast. Even the B&Bs that offer only a continental breakfast recognize the importance of doing this well.

The generous responses of the B&B hosts who contributed to this book are a good indication of the spirit of the American B&B. I hope that as you use this book, the contributors will come to seem like friends and tempt you to be more than an armchair traveler. From all the hosts and me, therefore, happy travels and *bon appetit!*

Acknowledgments

First of all, I must thank all the B&B hosts and hostesses who so generously and enthusiastically participated in making this book. Without them, it would not be. Second, I want to thank the two people who helped me gather hundreds of B&B addresses: my sister Lucia Watson, and my sister-in-law Karen Murphy. I must also thank Heather Blair and the ladies at Sheila Sussman's Letter Perfect, for their help in typing and retyping the early pages, and Lisa Wilkinson du Hamel, for her help in transcribing and organizing. Triona Quinlan was a big help in testing the recipes; as were Trevor Bishop, Tom and John Morris and Rob Wykoff in tasting the recipes.

The illustrations throughout the book—photographs and sketches, both professional and amateur—were largely supplied by the B&B hosts. For this, I am extremely grateful; without their help I could not have obtained so much good work. Elsewhere the book is enhanced by the original art of Amelia Rockwell Seton, whose whimsical drawings perfectly capture the spirit of the book. I am grateful for her participation.

My thanks to all my B&B guests over the years whose constant requests for recipes continually renewed my enthusiasm for this lengthy project. My sister Jane Wykoff and her husband Jim and my brother John Watson and his wife Debbie offered comments, criticisms and unflagging support as well. I thank John Beck and the crew at The Bookmakers Incorporated and Barbara Holdridge of Stemmer House, who turned the manuscript into the beautiful book that it is. And last but never least, I thank my husband Kevin, who believed in this project from the start, and who kept me believing in it too.

Gingerbread Mansion recalls that splendid period of opulence known as the Gilded Age (see page 71).

Picture Acknowledgments

Decorative illustrations throughout the book are the work of Amelia Rockwell Seton. All other pictures, both photographs and drawings, have been supplied by the featured B&Bs themselves and grateful acknowledgment is made of their help and cooperation. The following list acknowledges the professional photographers who generously lent their work for this book.

Page vi, Bufflehead Cove Inn, Suzanne Stohlman, photographer; pp. x–xi, The Gingerbread Mansion, Bob von Norman, photographer; p. 2, The Captain Jefferds Inn, Patrick Grace, photographer; pp. 6–7, The Bells Bed & Breakfast, Ron Paula, photographer; pp. 15 and 42, The Captain Jefferds Inn, courtesy *Country Inns Magazine,* Dan Gair, photographer; p. 18, Carter House, Will Faller, photographer; p. 30, The Carriage House, Ralph Starkweather, photographer; pp. 34–35, Carter House, Will Faller, photographer; p. 62, Casa de Solana, Henry Hird, photographer; p. 123, Murphy's B&B, Nancy Truszynski, photographer; pp. 126–127, Manor House, Ruth Mari Einstein, photographer; p. 131, Barrow House, David B. Nicolay, photographer; p. 162, Carter House, Doug Plummer, photographer; p. 170, Manor House, Ruth Mari Einstein, photographer; p. 222, Barrow House, David B. Nicolay, photographer.

THE Bed & Breakfast
COOKBOOK

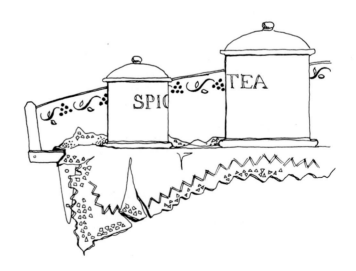

What Is a Bed & Breakfast?

POPULAR AS Bed & Breakfasts have become in this country, many people are still unfamiliar with them. I am often asked, "What is a B&B?" I have heard them referred to as "bread and breakfast," "bed and bath," "bed and bread" and the list goes on.

B&B always stands for bed & breakfast. Simply put, a B&B is a private home that takes in overnight guests and serves breakfast, which is included in the price of the room. The variations on this theme range widely, as you will see. Both the name and the concept of the B&B have been imported and adapted from Great Britain and Ireland, where B&B accommodations have long been popular. Almost without fail, travelers there can find B&B signs in the windows of any number of houses in most cities and towns. Almost any energetic housewife with an attractive house and a spare bedroom or two can found a profitable little home business in this way. Travelers to the British Isles find, particularly as they leave the cities, that B&Bs are more common than hotels or motels.

In the United States, B&B lodgings are a more recent phenomenon, but they are growing rapidly in both number and popularity. At least a dozen guidebooks offer nationwide B&B listings and there are countless regional publications. Reservation services for B&Bs are popping up in every state, and tourism brochures from most chambers of commerce now include B&B listings along with hotels and motels.

Although each B&B is unique (this indeed is part of their collective charm), a certain distinctive style is emerging in the United States. Many B&Bs are historically or architecturally interesting houses. As you will find, their hosts, who have often restored their original splendor from a condition of neglect, are usually delighted to point out these items of interest. Most often, the hosts have also decorated their antique houses with appropriate furnishings from the appropriate period. Sometimes a host proudly explains that the old house is furnished with pieces of all kinds collected during years of world travel.

LEFT: *The exterior of the Captain Jefferds Inn (see page 16) in Kennebunkport, Maine, is matched by its handsomely appointed interior. The old mansion, built in 1804, has been refurbished from stem to stern by two former antiques dealers who have made sure its furniture and bric-a-brac are worthy of the building.*

RIGHT: *The restoration at Barrow House (see page 207) in St. Francisville, Louisiana, includes furniture like this old fourposter with a canopy and a lace bedspread.*

3

Not every B&B is an old building; some are new or relatively new and don't possess any outstanding architectural feature. Their special appeal lies in their locations—offering a lovely view of the ocean or the mountains or the desert or simply a large, well-landscaped back yard where guests are welcome to relax.

Guest accommodations vary as widely as the type and style of B&Bs themselves, ranging from almost palatial suites that include a bedroom and a sitting room as well as a private bath, to small but cozy bedrooms with a shared bath. Most fall somewhere in between, offering good-sized, comfortably furnished bedrooms, with private or guest-only semiprivate bathrooms. Guidebooks and B&B brochures provide this kind of information in detail, and of course hosts are happy to answer any questions when potential guests call. Whether extravagant or simple, what all guest rooms should have in common are comfort, cleanliness, privacy and a sense of hominess. The host's caring touch should everywhere be evident, from a vase of fresh flowers on the dresser to potpourri in the closet, an extra blanket on the foot of the bed or perhaps a generous supply of reading materials on the bedside table.

However much thought, energy and money the hosts put into their homes to make them lovely and comfortable, breakfast is the time when most hosts (certainly all those in this book) shine their brightest. After all (according to my husband) to the travel-weary tourist, the bed comes as a great relief, but the breakfast makes the day! Hosts go all out to make their breakfasts special. Many happily tell you that they themselves grow the herbs, vegetables, berries, or fruit they combine in varied breakfast dishes. Some even serve fresh eggs or dairy products from their own small farms or from neighboring ones. And the morning aroma at most B&Bs leaves no doubt that the coffee was freshly ground and the pastries baked that morning.

Breakfasts offered in B&Bs range from the simple and satisfying to the elaborately replete, along the following lines:

Continental—coffee, juice and some kind of breakfast roll or muffin
Continental Plus—coffee, juice, baked goods and perhaps a selection of cereals, fruit and cheese
Full—coffee, juice, baked goods, bacon or sausage and a choice of eggs, pancakes or French toast
Gourmet—coffee, juices, fruit dishes, baked goods and a main dish of crepes, quiche, eggs Benedict or the like
Gourmet Brunch—champagne cocktails or bloody marys, coffee, juices, fruit dishes, cheeses and baked goods, with a main dish such as lobster quiche, fruit filled crepes or shrimp omelet

Information about the types of breakfast is available in guidebooks and B&B brochures or from the hosts; and of course, the elaborateness of the breakfast is reflected in the price of the accommodations.

Besides offering good food, most hosts make a point of serving breakfast in an attractive manner. Tables are set carefully and artistically. Descriptions of the B&Bs in this book often mention antique sterling silver, heirloom china, crisp linen or lace tablecloths, cut crystal, and (almost always) an arrangement of fresh flowers—often from the host's own garden. Some B&Bs serve breakfast in a formal dining room, some offer breakfast in bed, some serve breakfast in a garden or on a patio, some serve their guests in a country kitchen with a fire crackling in the fireplace. The variety of settings is almost endless.

Breakfast is a time when guests can chat with their hosts and with their fellow guests. Travel information shared around the breakfast table is always worthwhile, and the conversation is interesting and often educational. In this respect, B&Bs share the heritage of the convivial roadside inns of times past. B&B hosts all seem to share a certain spirit of adventure. Some are young couples just starting out, perhaps using their B&B to pay for renovating an old mansion they are restoring; some are retired couples with an empty nest and a desire to stay put while remaining active and meeting new people. Most hosts have other jobs besides running their B&B, but some devote themselves entirely to their business. B&B hosts come from all kinds of backgrounds and professions—some are engineers, artists, teachers or physicians. Most have traveled widely and enjoy meeting other travelers; they find that the opportunity to do this is the best part of running a B&B.

As you read the B&B descriptions in this book, the different personalities and voices of the hosts come through, each charmingly individual. Though varied in ages, occupations and reasons for running a B&B, all hosts have in common an enthusiasm for life and a desire to extend their gracious hospitality.

If charming homes and hearty breakfasts were not enticing enough, the other feature helping B&Bs become popular in America is their price, which is almost always lower that that of any local hotels or motels, often substantially so. And hotels and motels, of course, do not serve up home-cooked breakfasts at no extra charge.

If you are just becoming familiar with B&Bs in America and wonder where you can find them, the answer is almost anywhere, as you can see by browsing through this book. There are B&Bs in all fifty states. Of course, some states and regions draw more tourists and therefore have more B&Bs to meet the demand. At the end of this book is a bibliography of good guidebooks and a list of reservation services to help the interested traveler.

The United States is a spectacular country. One of the most enjoyable ways of touring it and meeting its most colorful people—whether your tastes run to backroads and small towns or boulevards and large cities—is to sample the wonderful variety of American Bed and Breakfasts.

With this book, your introduction to the infinite variety of American B&Bs is a close as your own kitchen. There you can recreate the excellent dishes listed in this book and sample B&B fare from all fifty states. Just add your own touches in table decor, genuine hospitality and pleasure in your own home and family and savor the results.

After a day spent outdoors or at a performance of the Oregon Shakespearean festival, guests at Hersey House (page 54) gather in the main parlor for a social hour.

Beverages

ORANGE JULIUS   9
The Bells Bed & Breakfast

ORANGE JULIUS SPRITZER   10
Dunbar House, 1880

MIMOSAS   11
Madewood Plantation House

CRANAPPLE TEA   12
Morton Street Bed & Breakfast

LEMONADE   13
Murphy's B&B

COFFEE MOCHA
    CONTINENTAL   13
Holland House

TOM'S TREAT II   14
Barnard–Good House

CRANBERRY BANANA FRAPPÉ   14
Grant Corner Inn

HOT MULLED WINE   15
The Captain Jefferds Inn

HOT SPICED CIDER   16
Britt House

HOT CHOCOLATE MIX   16
Britt House

HOT CHRISTMAS WASSAIL   17
The Pullman Inn B&B

LEFT: *The Bells (see page 9), in Bethlehem, New Hampshire, was a gift to the builder's son, a missionary to the Far East, thus explaining the architect's quaintly oriental gestures. The photograph captures the old house just at the moment when the cold light of a winter sky balances the glow of the building's lights, with their promise of warmth and good cheer within.*

COFFEE IS PROBABLY the most popular morning drink among Americans, and often it is the first thing they consume. It would be a mistake to underestimate its impact and the wide range in quality that is available. I recommend that you grind your own beans fresh, just before brewing your coffee. This approach guarantees the freshest-tasting and most aromatic and flavorful brew. You will soon find canned coffee seems almost flavorless—certainly not within the same realm as freshly ground coffee. Tea is also a popular breakfast beverage. For instructions on making and presenting an excellent pot of tea, see "Afternoon Tea," page 228.

You are likely to find that you can combine a supermarket brand of coffee beans with those from a gourmet shop. Experiment with a few different blends or roasts of beans until you find your favorite; this can become your own "house blend." There are other ways to change the flavor of coffee; for instance, try adding a litte ground cinnamon or a vanilla bean to your coffee beans for an interesting variation. Keep coffee beans in an air-tight container in the refrigerator.

Always start with fresh, cold water. If the tap water in your area is not good enough to drink by the glass and you keep bottled water for drinking, use the bottled water for making coffee, too. This can make quite a difference in taste. If you are making drip coffee manually, pour the water over the coffee *just before it reaches a boil*. Letting the water bubble away in the kettle reduces the amount of oxygen it contains and makes coffee taste flat. A good rule of thumb in making coffee is to use two level tablespoons of ground coffee to every cup of water. You may find that you prefer your brew weaker or stronger, but with a little experimentation, you will reach just the right proportions.

Once coffee is brewed, it should be served right away. Do not let coffee sit on a warming plate for an hour before serving. When coffee sits too long (30 minutes is the maximum), it becomes bitter and tastes burned. Even the color changes; it loses its translucent quality and becomes opaque. When you're looking forward to that first invigorating cup of coffee in the morning, there is nothing more disappointing than being handed a cup of old, overheated coffee.

How else can you improve your coffee? Here are just a few more pointers. Have pitchers of cream, not milk, on the breakfast table for the coffee. I find that half & half is best, a blend of half whole milk and half cream. Do not put out a pitcher of the skim milk you may offer with cereal. This can destroy the taste of an otherwise good cup of coffee. Have a bowl of granulated sugar or of sugar cubes— possibly brown demerara as well as white—on the table. In addition, it's wise to keep a supply of artificial sweetener on hand for the sake of guests who can't (or won't) use sugar.

This chapter offers a dozen good recipes for drinks that are a little out of the ordinary. The blender drinks are fun and a refreshing change from just plain orange juice, especially during hot weather. Served in tall goblets, they add beauty to the breakfast table. The hot drinks are well suited for fall and winter, particularly as afternoon refreshments. Don't be afraid to improvise, especially with blender drinks. Substitute your own favorite juice or fruit to come up with a variation. If you want to liven up a Sunday brunch, break out the champagne—many of the B&Bs in this book do. And use your imagination!

The Bells Bed & Breakfast

Bethlehem, New Hampshire

ACCORDING TO ONE SCHOLAR, Bethlehem, New Hampshire, has a greater variety of architectural styles than any other town in New England. The Bells certainly contributes to this distinction. Built in 1892 as a summer "cottage," it is a fascinating Victorian structure with a pagoda-like roof. More than a hundred wooden and tin bells hanging from the eaves give it its name. The original owner had the house built for his son, a missionary to the Far East. When the Simses purchased the house, they found its original nameplate—written in Japanese—among the antiquities in the basement.

The house is furnished and decorated with antiques and collectibles. Louise Sims says, "We have tried to keep the interior as eclectic as the exterior. Guests have commented that we should charge admission just to see the furnishings." Louise and Bill have, in fact, recently opened their own antiques shop in a guest house on the property.

Set in the heart of the White Mountains, Bethlehem was a popular summer resort for the well-to-do in the late 1800s. Famous for its pollen-free air, the town at one point had thirty resort hotels—with seven trains a day from Boston or New York stopping during the season. Nowadays, Bethlehem is a popular resort again, but this time a year-round one.

Guests at The Bells are within walking distance of Bethlehem's two golf courses, as well as the tennis courts and some delightful antiques shops. Summer theatre, fishing, boating and endless hiking opportunities are some of the activities that occupy visitors from spring through fall. In the winter, there is excellent cross-country and downhill skiing available; Cannon Mountain and Bretton Woods are nearby.

A full breakfast is served in the dining room at an eight-foot mahogany table artistically set with sterling silver and antique china. Although breakfast varies daily, it is always substantial. Besides a variety of fruit dishes, baked goods and unusual hot entrees, Louise Sims likes to serve a dessert with breakfast. "No lunch required after breakfast at The Bells," she says.

The Bells Bed & Breakfast
Strawberry Hill, P.O. Box 276
Bethlehem, New Hampshire 03574
(603) 869-2647

Bill and Louise Sims

ORANGE JULIUS

SERVES 6.

"This beverage is juice, milk, dessert and table decoration all in one when served in an oversized red-wine glass and garnished with an orange slice and sprig of mint," says Louise Sims.

6 oz. frozen orange juice concentrate
1 cup milk
1 cup water
½ cup sugar
1 tsp. vanilla
12 ice cubes, crushed

Place all ingredients in a blender and process at high speed for 30 seconds. Serve immediately.

OPPOSITE: *With its tiled roof and stucco walls, Grant Corner Inn (page 154) is characteristic of the Southwestern style.*

BELOW: *Under its Oriental veneer, The Bells is a comfortable Victorian "cottage."*

Dunbar House, 1880
Murphy's, California

WILLIS DUNBAR BUILT this house for his bride in 1880. It is set in the heart of the Southern Mother Lode region of California, in a town that is one of the best preserved of the early mining towns of Calaveras County and the Mother Lode region.

Carefully restored, the house is furnished with the Costa family collection of antiques. Lace from Ireland and Germany hangs at the windows. Guests are welcome to relax in the century-old garden; Barbara thinks it's most lovely in spring when the lilacs are in bloom. Calaveras Big Tree State Park, the famous Mercer Caves and the Stevenot Winery are all close by, making for interesting day trips from Dunbar House.

A generous continental breakfast is served in the dining room, with a fire crackling in the fireplace on cool mornings. On warmer mornings, guests may choose to breakfast on the porch or in the garden. Another option is to have a full country breakfast delivered to a guest's room in a picnic basket—the last word in room service.

Dunbar House, 1880
271 Jones Street
Murphy's, California 95247
(209) 728–2897

Bob and Barbara Costa

ORANGE JUICE SPRITZER

SERVES 4.

This is marvelously refreshing during hot weather. An alternative to iced tea or lemonade at afternoon tea in the summer, it is also appropriate for a brunch.

1 6-oz. can frozen orange juice concentrate, thawed
1 cup cold water
1 Tbs. lemon juice
1½ cups bitter lemon or bitter orange (carbonated soft drink)
1 orange, sliced
1 lime, sliced

In a large pitcher combine the orange juice concentrate with the water and lemon juice. *Just before serving,* slowly add the bitter lemon. Pour into ice-filled, tall glasses and garnish each serving with a slice of orange and lime.

LEFT: *With its Italianate touches, the Dunbar House is a typical American Victorian residence. Willis Dunbar and his bride, Ellen Roberts Dunbar, a local girl from Douglas Flat, raised five sons here.*

OPPOSITE: *The great high ceilings and overhanging porticos of plantation houses like Madewood were not only breathtakingly beautiful but practical. In the hot Louisiana summers, they helped keep the house as cool and shaded as possible.*

Madewood Plantation House
Napoleonville, Louisiana

BUILT IN 1846, Madewood is an exquisite Southern plantation mansion. At the front of the house, a wide lawn flanked by magnolias and liveoaks sweeps up to the handsome central portico, which is supported by six massive Ionic columns. Stepping inside, one faces an unsupported stairway ascending from the grand entry hall to the second floor.

The period furnishings, the carved cypress mantels and the floor-to-ceiling windows (fourteen to twenty feet high) create an ambiance that often makes guests feel as if they had stepped back in time. "But this is, after all, a home, and guests are made to feel welcome here," Millie Marshall notes.

Wake-up coffee is brought to the guests' rooms in the morning. Then a full Southern-style breakfast is served either in the dining room or on the back porch. The breakfast menu might include mimosas, eggs Florentine, baked ham, cheese grits, pumpkin laFourche, French bread, homemade pear and fig preserves, fresh fruit compote and chicory coffee.

After breakfast, guests may tour the extensive grounds before setting off for a day of sightseeing in this historic and lovely region of Louisiana.

Madewood Plantation House
Highway 308
Napoleonville, Louisiana 70390
(504) 369-7151

Keith and Millie Marshall

MIMOSAS

SERVES 6 to 8.

A festive beverage for a special brunch.

1 liter dry champagne, well chilled
1 quart fresh-squeezed orange juice,
    well chilled

Combine the champagne and orange juice in a large pitcher just before serving. Pour into champagne flutes; *serve immediately.*

Morton Street Bed and Breakfast Homes
Shipshewana, Indiana

AS ITS NAME IMPLIES, Morton Street Bed and Breakfast Homes is actually three houses, standing side by side on a tree-lined street in this charming old town. Each house has been restored, and each is furnished with a different theme: one is Shaker, one Victorian and one country antiques.

Shipshewana is located in the midst of the second-largest Amish community in the United States. Its restored houses, well-kept farms and horse-drawn buggies combine to make it an especially charming place. Known for its craft and antiques shops, the town is also home of the renowned Shipshewana Auction and Flea Market—an enormous country sale with a thousand vendors and a dozen auctioneers going at the same time. This event draws people from hundreds of miles away.

Guests at Morton Street Bed and Breakfast simply walk next door to the Buggy Wheel Restaurant (also owned by Joel and Esther Mishler), to enjoy a full home-cooked breakfast. B&B guests have their choice from the menu. The restaurant is also open to the general public, serving lunch and dinner as well. The Mishler's Bread Box Bake Shop, next door to the restaurant, is a stop most visitors find hard to resist. With a full day of sightseeing ahead, its fresh breads, pies, cookies and cakes can provide the essentials of a picnic lunch or midmorning snack.

Morton Street Bed and Breakfast Homes
P.O. Box 775
Shipshewana, Indiana 46565
(219) 768-4391

Joel and Esther Mishler

OPPOSITE: *The wide front porch at Murphy's B&B, furnished with French café tables and chairs and cooled by sea breezes, is a popular spot for afternoon tea.*

BELOW: *The Morton Street Bed and Breakfast Homes include the B&B itself, a restaurant and a bakery.*

CRANAPPLE TEA

MAKES 3½ quarts.

This treat is made in a coffee percolator, the kind many of us have long since tucked away in the back of a kitchen cupboard. It's well worth pulling out for this tangy tea. As it perks, a wonderful aroma fills the air. This tea has become a special favorite at the annual open house held every November at the Morton Street Bed and Breakfast Homes. Perfect for a crisp fall day.

2½ qts. cranapple juice
1 qt. apple juice
½ cup brown sugar
4 sticks cinnamon
2 tsp. whole cloves

Optional
6 lemons or oranges
 whole cloves

Pour the cranapple and apple juices into a 30-cup percolator. Place the sugar and spices in the percolator basket. Brew just as you would when making coffee.

When the pot has finished percolating, the tea is ready to be served. Serve piping hot in large mugs or cups and saucers.

If desired, garnish each serving with a thin slice of lemon or orange studded with 3 whole cloves.

Murphy's B&B
Narragansett, Rhode Island

BUILT IN 1894 as a summer house, Murphy's B&B is a comfortable Victorian restored with care. The antique furnishings, original oak parquet floors, massive fieldstone fireplace in the living room and restored woodwork and brass hardware are some of its special features. Its restful, serene atmosphere, along with the big breakfasts and attention to detail, keeps guests returning year after year.

Situated on a tree-lined residential street a block from the ocean, Murphy's makes the perfect base for an enjoyable stay in southern Rhode Island. Narragansett Beach and the many other beaches in the area are among the region's finest. Historic Newport and idyllic Block Island are popular day trips; the University of Rhode Island is just six miles away; and one of New England's most famous summer theatres—Theatre by the Sea—is a few miles down the road. Wineries and vineyards, antiques shops, galleries and museums, and restaurants featuring the fresh seafood caught by Narragansett's own commercial fishing fleet are some highlights of a stay here. The list of activities and points of interest is extensive, so Martha and Kevin Murphy, who are both avid travelers, keep their desk well stocked with maps and brochures to be certain guests get the most from their visit.

A full breakfast is served in the elegant dining room, with its original wainscot and its wall sconces of Waterford crystal. From July through September, colorful arrangements from Martha Murphy's cutting garden appear on the table. Breakfast varies daily, but it always includes fresh fruit in season; homebaked goods; and a changing selection of egg dishes, pancakes, waffles and the like; along with juice and freshly ground coffee. Afternoon tea is available daily, served in the living room or on the front porch.

Murphy's B&B
43 South Pier Road
Narragansett, Rhode Island 02882
(401) 789–1824

Kevin and Martha Murphy

LEMONADE

MAKES 2 quarts.

There's nothing so refreshing as a tall, icy glass of homemade lemonade on a hot summer afternoon. Once you try it, you'll never want it any other way.

    juice of 9 lemons
1½ cups sugar, or to taste
  7 cups water

Combine all ingredients in a large pitcher and blend well. Cover and refrigerate for at least 60 minutes.

Stir the mixture before serving and pour into tall glasses filled with ice. Garnish with a sprig of fresh mint or a wedge of lime.

Note: I like very tart lemonade. This may be too tart for some. If so, just increase the amount of sugar and water.

COFFEE MOCHA CONTINENTAL
Holland House (p. 70)

MAKES 4 servings.

A refreshing beverage to offer as an alternative to hot coffee during the summer months, this is appropriate at breakfast, at afternoon tea or after dinner.

2 cups freshly brewed coffee, chilled
2 cups cocoa (prepared as beverage), chilled
1 cup whipped cream
  cinnamon, as a garnish

Combine the coffee and cocoa in a large pitcher. Pour into tall, iced-filled glasses. Top each serving with whipped cream and a dash of cinnamon. Serve immediately.

Barnard–Good House
Cape May, New Jersey

SET IN PICTURESQUE Cape May, Barnard–Good House is a turn-of-the-century Victorian. The exterior is painted rosy pink, with white gingerbread trim and burgundy shutters. The town of Cape May itself is a national historic landmark city, with street after street of beautifully restored Victorian and Colonial houses. Long, white, sandy beaches and fine dining with an emphasis on fresh seafood — landed by Cape May's own commercial fishing fleet — make this a bustling town in the summer. Spring and fall find the pace a little slower, giving the visitor a chance to explore the antiques shops, art galleries and boutiques without all the crowds.

Breakfast at Barnard–Good House can be the highlight of the day for guests, no matter what else is on their agenda. Nan and Tom Hawkins set a beautiful table in the dining room and serve an elaborate breakfast. A sample menu might begin with Tom's Treat II and go on to apple cider soup, shellfish crepe pie, sweet potato pancakes, cottage cheese pan rolls, and prune tart — with, of course, plenty of freshly ground coffee and a selection of teas. The Hawkinses are devoted to fresh ingredients; living near the produce growers of the Garden State, they serve seasonal fruits and vegetables to keep menus varied and at their best. "Everything is homemade, and never repeated during a guest's stay," according to Nan Hawkins.

Barnard–Good House
238 Perry Street
Cape May, New Jersey 08204
(609) 884–5381

Nan and Tom Hawkins

TOM'S TREAT II

SERVES 4 to 6.

This pale green drink — served icy cold in elegant long-stemmed glasses — looks as frothy and refreshing as it tastes. A perfect way to start breakfast on a summer morning, this is indeed a treat any time of the year.

  1 6-oz. can frozen pineappple juice
  1 10-oz. bottle white grape juice
      juice of 2 limes
1½ cups chopped ice
      fresh mint leaves

Combine the pineapple, grape and lime juices in a blender with the chopped ice and blend thoroughly. Pour into chilled, long-stemmed glasses; garnish with fresh mint. Serve immediately.

CRANBERRY BANANA FRAPPÉ
Grant Corner Inn (p. 154)

SERVES 6.

Delicious and easy. A refreshing change from orange juice.

  2 cups cranapple juice
  1 cup fresh-squeezed orange juice
 ¼ cup whipping cream
  1 Tbs. lemon juice
  2 bananas
 ¾ cup crushed ice
      fresh mint leaves for garnish

Combine all the ingredients, except the mint leaves, in a blender. Process on high speed for 1 minute. Serve in frosted, stemmed goblets, garnished with fresh mint leaves.

The Captain Jefferds Inn
Kennebunkport, Maine

THE PROSPEROUS SEA CAPTAIN who built this mansion in 1804 probably never guessed that many years later it would become an inn named for him. A striking example of federal-style architecture, it has been lovingly and authentically restored. Warren Fitzsimmons is a former antiques dealer, as is evident from the fine collection throughout the house.

Set back from the street on a well-kept lawn enclosed by an antique spindle fence, the house is only five hundred feet from the harbor. A short walk away, a visitor finds Dock Square, with its many shops, galleries and restaurants. This picturesque town was once a thriving seaport, home to many prosperous seafarers in the 1800s. Street after street of handsome houses, many topped with captain's watches—a glassed-in observation room on the roof—stand as a testament to that time.

Guests at the Captain Jefferds are treated to breakfast in the formal dining room at a table set with crystal and china. The menu varies each day; fresh fruit in season is followed by one of the favorites such as eggs Benedict, blueberry crepes or ham and cheese quiche. The meal always ends with a homebaked pastry. During the cooler months, afternoon tea is available.

The Captain Jefferds Inn
Pearl Street, Box 691
Kennebunkport, Maine 04046
(207) 967-2311

Warren Fitzsimmons

HOT MULLED WINE

SERVES 12.

This makes a wonderful treat on a fall or winter afternoon. It is served on special occasions at the Captain Jefferds Inn.

 1 8-inch square of cheesecloth
10 cinnamon sticks
24 whole cloves
12 whole allspice berries
24 sprigs fresh lemon thyme (available from herb nurseries)
 2 bottles red wine, each 1½ liters (claret is best)
 1 cup sugar
 2 lemons, sliced thin

Place the cinnamon sticks, cloves, allspice and *half* the lemon thyme on the square of cheesecloth and make a pouch, securing it with a string.

Place the wine in a large pot and add the sugar. Stir over medium-high heat until the mixture reaches a boil. Add the pouch of spices and the lemon slices to the wine. Simmer for 30 minutes. Remove the pouch from the wine. Serve hot, and garnish each serving with a sprig of the remaining fresh lemon thyme.

LEFT: *The dining room at the Captain Jefferds Inn, here decked out for Christmas, is appointed with carefully selected antiques.*

OPPOSITE: *Built by the Barnards and later owned by the Goods, this fine old house, with its Mansard roof and wraparound porch, is one of many immaculately maintained Victorian buildings in Cape May.*

Britt House
San Diego, California

BUILT IN 1887 for the Britt family, Britt House is a lovely Victorian, carefully restored to its original elegance. This imposing turretted structure is a fine example of the fancy shinglework popular at the turn of the century. Balconies, large windows and wide verandahs keep the house light and graceful.

   The beautifully kept grounds include a formal garden where guests are welcome to relax and enjoy the almost constant southern California sunshine. Along with colorful flower beds that include hibiscus and hollyhock, Daun Martin grows her own strawberries. Freshly picked at the peak of ripeness, these jewels show up in fresh strawberry shortcake, trifle, puddings and more.

   Nearby, Balboa Park, the San Diego Zoo (one of the country's finest), Embarcadero Square, the Maritime Museum, several art museums and a variety of shops and restaurants offer the visitor more than enough to do. The Pacific Ocean is just a short drive away, and the beaches here are spectacular.

   One of the highlights of a stay at Britt House is the food. Everything is fresh and homemade, prepared with skill and care. A full breakfast is served in the parlor or, if preferred, in a guest's own room. A substantial afternoon tea is served daily. It includes tea sandwiches made with bread baked on the premises, a large selection of home-baked goodies and sweets, and of course hot tea, as well as homemade California lemonade.

Britt House
406 Maple Street
San Diego, California 92103
(619) 234-2962

Daun Martin

HOT SPICED CIDER

MAKES 1 gallon.

This is well received at breakfast or afternoon tea during the fall and winter.

1 gallon apple cider
3 oranges, seedless
4 cinnamon sticks
2 tsp. whole cloves

Place the cider in a large, heavy pot over medium-high heat. Slice the oranges thinly and add to the cider, along with the cinnamon sticks. Place the cloves in a tea infusor or make a cheesecloth pouch for them, and add to the cider. Simmer for at least 60 minutes. Serve hot, and if desired garnish each serving with a fresh orange slice.

HOT CHOCOLATE MIX

MAKES approximately 3 quarts of cocoa.

This is a handy item for a busy hostess who caters to families with children.

   Mix
1 ½ cups cocoa
2 ¼ cups sugar
       dash salt
   3 cups dry milk

Place all ingredients in a large bowl and combine well. Store in an airtight container and use as needed.

   1 Serving
½ cup dry cocoa mix
1 cup boiling water
½ tsp. vanilla

Place ½ cup of the mix in a large mug. Add 1 cup boiling water and mix well. Stir in the vanilla. Serve immediately.

The Pullman Inn Bed and Breakfast
Provo, Utah

WITH SUCH A MAGNIFICENT Victorian house, the owners of the Pullman Inn named it after the luxurious Pullman railroad cars of the same era. Built in 1898, the old manse everywhere shows careful attention to detail. One of its most stunning features is the graceful staircase that winds through a two-story turret. Stained glass windows, hand-carved woodwork and antique period furnishings add to the grace of the interior.

The historic Town Square is nearby, home to an interesting variety of shops and restaurants. Within a short drive, a visitor finds Brigham Young University, the Sundance Ski Resort and Summer Theatre, Timpanogos Cave and the breathtaking Bridal Veil Falls.

A full breakfast—including a variety of egg dishes, homebaked goods, fresh fruit, juices and freshly ground coffee—is served in the elegant dining room under a crystal chandelier.

The Pullman Inn Bed and Breakfast
415 South University Avenue
Provo, Utah 84601
(801) 374–8141

Dennis Morganson

HOT CHRISTMAS WASSAIL

MAKES about 8 quarts.

"The weekend following Thanksgiving we host our annual 'Old Fashioned Christmas' open-house here at the Pullman Inn. We truly deck the halls and then open our inn to the public, for all to enjoy the warmth of the season in our restored Victorian mansion. We always have a large kettle of Hot Christmas Wassail on the stove."—DENNIS MORGANSON

Note: this recipe is meant for a large gathering. For smaller parties, the recipe can be cut to one-half or even one-quarter.

 4 quarts water
 6 large cinnamon sticks
¼ cup whole cloves
 3 16-oz. cans frozen concentrate orange juice
 4 16-oz. cans frozen concentrate apple juice
 2 quarts grapefruit juice
 4 cups sugar

Place the water, cinnamon sticks and cloves in a large pot over high heat. Bring to a boil, reduce the temperature and simmer for 15 minutes. Remove the cinnamon and cloves and add the rest of the ingredients. Heat to almost boiling, stirring well. Serve hot.

To make this a more spirited drink, add a shot of rum to each serving.

LEFT: *Among the furnishings of the opulent Pullman Inn is this ornate headboard.*

OPPOSITE: *Britt House is high Victorian splendor at its best.*

Fruit & Cereals

GRAPEFRUIT WITH
STRAWBERRIES   21
The Capers-Motte House

FAVORITE FRUIT SUNDAE   22
The Parsonage 1901

GALLIANO FRUIT CUPS   23
Rogers House B&B

GOLDEN FRUIT CUP   24
Cedar Knoll Farm

GRAPEFRUIT AMBROSIA   25
Barley Sheaf Farm

MICHIGAN SESQUICENTENNIAL
FRUIT AND YOGURT   26
The House on the Hill

FRIED NECTARINES   27
The Voss Inn B&B

ELLEN'S BLUEBERRY DELIGHT   28
Kenniston Hill Inn

SAUTÉED APPLES   29
Little Piney Canoe Resort

HOT SPICED FRUIT   30
The Carriage House

BAKED APPLES   31
Glendeven

APPLE COMPOTE   32
Phoenix House

SCRUBBED & TUBBED, BOILED,
BAKED & GLAZED ORANGES   33
The Bells Bed & Breakfast

PUMPKIN MADEWOOD
LAFOURCHE   33
Madewood Plantation House

BAKED PEARS HERSEY   33
Hersey House

PEARS POACHED IN WINE
SAUCE   34
Carter House

BAKED APPLES IN CARAMEL
SAUCE   35
Carter House

NORWEGIAN FRUIT SOUP   36
Canterbury Inn

BANANA BISQUE WITH
CINNAMON CROUTONS   37
The Southern Hotel

SUMMER FRUIT SOUP   37
The Victorian Inn

APPLE CIDER SOUP   37
Barnard–Good House

HOT APPLE CEREAL   38
Small Wonder B&B

HOMESTYLE GRANOLA
CEREAL   39
Small Wonder B&B

BAKED OATMEAL   40
Hollinger House

BREAKFAST PARFAIT   41
Starr Cottage Inn

Through the dining room window of Carter House (see page 34), a visitor can contemplate the Victorian charm of Eureka, California, with its many fine Victorian buildings. The town reached its zenith as a lumber capital more than a century ago.

*A*S I COMPILED the recipes contributed to this book, I was happy to discover that a fruit course is a standard part of breakfast at most B&Bs. Many of my guests tell me that they seldom bother to prepare or serve fruit for themselves at home—at breakfast or any other time. They usually say this as they dig enthusiastically into the fruit course and ask for the recipe.

Following the seasons when you buy fruit or decide on a recipe is a good strategy for two reasons: seasonal fruit is both better tasting and less expensive. If you live in New England, don't buy strawberries in November. They may be red on the outside, but they will be white and flavorless inside. In fact, if you indulged yourself with strawberries when they were in season—May, June and July—you should be eager to move on to the fruits in season for fall: apples, pears, pumpkins, cranberries and the like. By following the seasons, you will not only enjoy each fruit at its peak, but also experience a greater variety of fruits. Of course, some fruits, notably bananas, lemons, oranges and grapefruits, are available in tasty condition all year round—although grapefruits are at their best during the winter months.

The fruit recipes in this chapter offer a wide variety of dishes, hot and cold, that should get any American through the four seasons. Don't feel limited by the twenty-one recipes here; use your imagination and improvise. Use the perpetually available banana as a backdrop to fruit in season, and top it off with a little creme fraiche (page 221) and brown sugar. A dish of sliced bananas—topped with ripe strawberries, raspberries or pitted and halved ripe cherries—makes a simple yet delicious combination. A carefully sectioned, ripe, juicy half-grapefruit is a perennial favorite at breakfast; serve it chilled in summer or broiled with a little brown sugar in winter. When melons are in season, make a three-melon salad with balls of watermelon, cantaloupe and honeydew. Top with Lime Ice (page 221) and a sprig of fresh mint, and you have a fruit dish as pretty as it is refreshing. Once you get into the habit of carefully buying fresh fruit in season, you will find yourself coming up with your own combinations. Many of the fruit recipes in this chapter also make excellent desserts.

With so many people concerned about weight, fiber and fat intake, and good health in general, cereal is frequently the breakfast of choice. Cereal can be both high in fiber and low in fat, sugar and salt, while the milk poured over it supplies calcium. Topped with a little fresh fruit, a bowl of cereal served with low-fat milk is a nutritious light breakfast. As many B&B hosts point out, business travelers usually prefer light breakfasts, cereal being high on their list of preferred victuals.

This chapter also offers four recipes for homemade cereal, two cold and two hot. They are healthful as well as tasty. The granola recipes may be made in a double or triple batch, since they can be stored well in airtight containers.

The Capers–Motte House
Charleston, South Carolina

A BEAUTIFUL PRE-REVOLUTIONARY MANSION, built in the 1730s, the Capers–Motte House is recorded by the Historic American Buildings Survey of the Department of the Interior. One of the grand old houses of this grand old city, it stands within the original walled-city district. The spacious second-floor drawing room, with its original cypress panelling and Adam mantels, offers a magnificent view of Church Street—sometimes said to be the most interesting street in America.

Excellent walking tours of Charleston are conducted by guides familiar with the history of the city, and the Marshalls gladly help their guest make arrangements for them. Fort Sumter, one of the most famous landmarks of this waterfront city, is accessible by boat; and indeed sunset cruises are an especially beautiful way to see the city. Fine restaurants, antiques shops, museums and a lively cultural scene round out a stay here.

Guests at the Capers–Motte House are served a full breakfast in the dining room, after which they are well prepared for a day in this fascinating city.

The Capers–Motte House
69 Church Street
Charleston, South Carolina 29401
(803) 722-2263

Jessica C. Marshall

GRAPEFRUIT WITH STRAWBERRIES

SERVES 6.

A refreshing fruit dish as pretty as it is delicious. Make this when strawberries are in season.

3 large grapefruits
1 pint strawberries
¼ cup sugar

Cut the grapefruits in half; section, and remove sections to individual footed glass dishes (½ grapefruit per person). Cover and refrigerate.

Squeeze the grapefruit juice from the rinds into a saucepan. Add the sugar and, stirring constantly, heat over medium heat until the sugar is dissolved. Remove from heat and set aside.

Clean and hull the strawberries; cut into quarters. Add the berries to the sugar/juice mixture and stir well. Cover and refrigerate until well chilled, at least 2 hours.

When ready to serve, spoon the strawberries and juice over the chilled grapefruit sections. Serve immediately.

OPPOSITE: *Kenniston Hill Inn (page 28) was built in Boothbay, Maine, more than two centuries ago.*

LEFT: *In any eighteenth-century city, a canny homebuilder put the public rooms on the second floor and the bedrooms on the third to avoid the noise and smell of the street. These are no longer problems in present-day Charleston, but the beautiful drawing room of the Capers–Motte House remains on the second floor, where it has been for more than two hundred years.*

The Parsonage 1901
Gig Harbor, Washington

ORIGINALLY A METHODIST-EPISCOPALIAN PARSONAGE, this charming Victorian house gives the year of its construction in its name. Sheila and Edward Koscik have turned it into a B&B partly because they greatly enjoy being hosts. "Our guests enrich our lives, and the B&B brings people from all over the world to our door."

Gig Harbor is within walking distance of the Parsonage. Here visitors find a harbor full of sailboats, and a quaint village with interesting shops and cafes. Guests may also choose to spend an afternoon relaxing in the Kosciks' yard. Edward is an avid gardener, and in spring and summer there are strawberries and blackberries to pick. The fresh berries often show up at breakfast: in a fruit salad, in the homemade muffins or in preserves—just part of the full breakfast served at the Parsonage 1901.

A native of Belfast, Ireland, Sheila is carrying on the long tradition of gracious Irish hospitality: "We have a Claddagh door-knocker on our front door. It represents our heart, hands and loyalty. We hope we are achieving our goals by offering a sincere welcome."

The Parsonage 1901
4107 Burnham Drive
Gig Harbor, Washington 98335
(206) 851-8654

Sheila and Edward Koscik

FAVORITE FRUIT SUNDAE

SERVES 4.

4 Tbs. honey (approx.)
1 pint strawberries
1 cantaloupe melon
2 seedless oranges
2 bananas

Coat the insides of 4 individual serving dishes with approximately ½ tablespoon of honey each. Set aside.

Follow the directions on preparing each fruit. As each step is completed, layer the fruit evenly in each dish.

To prepare the fruit:

1. Clean, hull and quarter the strawberries
2. Halve and seed the melon; scoop out all the meat with a melon baller
3. Halve and section the oranges
4. Peel and slice the banana in ¼"–½" slices

Spoon the remaining honey over the top of each serving. Cover and let sit at room temperature for 10 minutes to enhance the flavor before serving.

Optional: Garnish with shredded coconut, chopped nuts, or granola.

LEFT: *During July and August, when melons are at their peak, the breakfast menu at Murphy's B&B (page 13) often includes a chilled dish of three-melon salad—honeydew, cantaloupe and watermelon, topped with fresh lime juice—as refreshing as it is pretty.*

OPPOSITE: *The living room of the Rogers House shows the spacious comfort characteristic of the whole house—and of the Near South District of Lincoln where it stands.*

The Rogers House Bed and Breakfast
Lincoln, Nebraska

THIS HANDSOME IVY-COVERED BRICK MANSION is named for the banker who built it in 1914. A local historic landmark, Rogers House is situated in the fashionable Near South neighborhood of Lincoln, just a short walk from downtown. The interior is graced with windows of leaded and beveled glass, French doors, polished hardwood floors, three sunrooms, a library and a mahogany-paneled dining room. The furnishings are antique.

Because the University of Nebraska is just two blocks away, visitors there find this a good base for combining business with pleasure. The city of Lincoln, with a number of interesting museums, historic landmarks and fine restaurants, is, as Nora Houtsma says, "a welcome stopping place for travelers from all points."

In the morning, guests are served a full breakfast that includes a specially prepared hot entrée, fresh fruit, pastry, fresh-squeezed orange juice and specially blended coffee. Breakfast is served in one of three sunporches or in the formal dining room. Room service is also available. A breakfast buffet is also an option for guests who rent the house as a group.

"Whether time is spent in solitude, perhaps with a Willa Cather book from the many volumes in the guest library, or spent in shared company before the fireplace or within one of the sunrooms, Rogers House offers a very special and unique place of lodging," says Nora Houtsma.

The Rogers House Bed and Breakfast
2145 B. Street
Lincoln, Nebraska 68502
(402) 476–6961

Nora Houtsma

GALLIANO FRUIT CUPS

SERVES 6.

An elegant treat! You may want to make the sauce the evening before so it can chill overnight. This is served as a fruit course for breakfast at the Rogers House, but it can also be an excellent dessert.

1 10-oz. package of 6 frozen pastry shells
1½ cups fresh fruit, such as strawberries, blueberries, or peaches

Sauce
3 egg yolks
⅓ cup confectioners sugar
   dash salt
¼ cup dry white wine
2 Tbs. Galliano

Bake the pastry shells according to directions. Remove the tops and cool on a rack.

Use a fresh fruit in season, cleaning, peeling, slicing and preparing as necessary. Place in a bowl, cover and chill.

To make the sauce, place the egg yolks in the top of a double boiler, beating until thick and lemon colored. Gradually beat in the sugar and salt. Place the top of the double boiler over simmering but not boiling water. Gradually beat in the wine and liqueur, beating until the sauce is thickened, about 5 minutes. Remove from heat and chill thoroughly.

To serve, fill each pastry shell with fruit and top with sauce.

Cedar Knoll Farm
Good Thunder, Minnesota

SPRAWLING OVER 138 ACRES, Cedar Knoll is a working farm in rural Minnesota. Guests are encouraged to wander anywhere they like; the Christensens happily share the natural beauty and tranquillity of the spot, their own "peaceable kingdom."

Nearby attractions include skiing in winter, golfing, antiques shops, all and any water sports and everywhere "vistas across the magnificent abundance of lakes."

Breakfast is served either in the large country kitchen or in the formal dining room, depending on which the hostess thinks guests will most enjoy. Mavis Christensen, who comes from a long line of farm wives, has inherited the knack of cooking substantial meals for large crowds, along with some great old farm recipes. The morning meal consists of hearty country fare: ham, eggs, homefries, hotcakes, apple pie, homemade jams or a "lighter" menu of muffins, pastries, fruit and omelets, "all served with pitchers and pots of juice, milk and coffee or tea."

Cedar Knoll Farm
Route 2, Box 147
Good Thunder, Minnesota 56037
(507) 524–3813

Mavis Christensen

GOLDEN FRUIT CUP

SERVES 6.

This light and refreshing fruit cup offers an interesting variety of flavors and textures. Because it is refrigerated overnight, the cook has more free time in the morning.

2 apples, peeled, cored and chopped
2 seedless oranges, sectioned
⅓ cup sugar
2 Tbs. cornstarch
¾ cup pineapple juice
1 Tbs. lemon juice
    grated zest and juice of 1 orange
2 bananas, sliced just before serving

Place the chopped apples and orange sections in a bowl; cover and set aside. In a small saucepan mix the sugar and cornstarch; stir in the pineapple juice, lemon juice and orange zest and juice. Cook over medium heat, stirring constantly, until the mixture thickens and boils. Boil and stir for 1 minute. Remove from the heat and pour over the apple and orange sections. Gently toss the fruits; cover and refrigerate overnight.

Just before serving, slice the bananas, add to the apple/orange mixture and toss gently. Serve immediately in individual footed compote dishes.

LEFT: *Above all else Cedar Knoll Farm offers homey, unpretentious comfort. Visitors to this working farm get all the country food they can eat and all the peace and quiet they can handle.*

OPPOSITE: *It is said that critic Alexander Woollcott spent a weekend being obnoxious at Barley Sheaf Farm when it was the country retreat of playwright George S. Kaufman. "Good Lord," said coauthor Moss Hart, "what if he broke his leg and had to stay for a month?" "Just imagine," said George, as he uncovered the typewriter. And thus was born* The Man Who Came to Dinner.

Barley Sheaf Farm Bed and Breakfast
Holicong, Pennsylvania

THE OLDEST PART of Barley Sheaf Farm Bed and Breakfast dates from 1740. The old farm, which has been designated a National Historic Site, is situated on thirty peaceful acres in Bucks County, Pennsylvania. The barn, swimming pool, pond and especially the majestic old trees round out a beautiful setting.

This was once the home of noted playwright George S. Kaufman, and weekend guests included Lillian Hellman, the Marx brothers, Alexander Woollcott, S. J. Perelman and a host of other notables. To-day, this working farm is also a Bed & Breakfast. The eggs and honey served as part of an abundant and varied breakfast are the farm's own. Seated at long harvest tables on an enclosed sun porch, guests are treated to a view of rolling meadows—snow covered in winter, bright with wildflowers in summer—crossed by a stream that spills into a duck pond. The antics of the ducks, especially of the duck-lings in the spring, are a never-ending source of delight.

Within a short distance of the farm there are activities and points of interest for all: antiquing, historic sites, museums, parks, flea markets, canoeing and a variety of charming restaurants on both sides of the Delaware River. Don and Ann Mills say, "We can't promise that the serenity won't occasionally be broken by the 'baa' of the sheep in the meadow or the call of the Canada geese, but we can promise a warm and friendly atmosphere."

Barley Sheaf Farm Bed and Breakfast
Box 10
Holicong, Pennsylvania 18928
(215) 794-5104

Don and Ann Mills

GRAPEFRUIT AMBROSIA

SERVES 6.

This pretty fruit dish is refreshing, light and tangy.

  3 large grapefruits
¼ cup honey
  1 pint strawberries
¼ cup shredded coconut

Halve and section the grapefruits. Remove the sections over a bowl, being sure to catch all the juices. Squeeze the grapefruit rinds hard to get all the juice after the sections have been removed. Add the honey and toss gently. Cover with plastic wrap and chill.

Hull the strawberries and cut into quarters. Just before serving, gently toss the strawberries and coconut with the chilled grapefruit. Serve immediately in footed compote dishes.

The House on the Hill

Ellsworth, Michigan

LOCATED NEAR THE quiet village of Ellsworth on the beautiful chain of lakes in the resort region of the Mackinac Straits, the House on the Hill is an ideal base for outdoor enthusiasts. This Victorian farmhouse is set on 55 acres of meadows, with woods and trails intersected by creeks and brooks. One can go no more than six miles in any direction without coming upon a lake. Lake Michigan is five miles away, a favored spot for swimming and boating. In the winter, ice-skating and ice-fishing are popular here; and within a thirty-mile radius there are three ski areas, offering excellent downhill and cross-country skiing.

Two world-class restaurants, reviewed with praise in national publications, are within walking distance of the House on the Hill. Julie Arnim is proud of her area and boasts that visitors here enjoy the peace and quiet of the farm setting, year-round outdoor recreation and dining as superb as that found in any major city.

Guests are treated to a full farm breakfast featuring fresh Michigan produce.

The House on the Hill
Box 206, Lake Street
Ellsworth, Michigan 49729
(616) 588–6304

Julie Arnim

MICHIGAN SESQUICENTENNIAL FRUIT AND YOGURT

SERVES 6.

Julie Arnim created this special recipe in celebration of Michigan's 150th birthday. She serves it on heirloom Cobalt and Ruby china. It is a pretty red, white and blue fruit dish that I have served on the Fourth of July to everyone's delight. A cool, creamy summer treat—make this when blueberries and raspberries are at their peak.

1 pt. vanilla yogurt
5 tsp. sugar
1 tsp. vanilla
1 pt. blueberries
1 pt. red raspberries

In a medium sized bowl, blend the yogurt with the sugar and vanilla. Set aside.

Clean and divide the blueberries and raspberries into 6 equal portions of each fruit. In parfait glasses make three layers, blueberries on the bottom, yogurt mixture in the center and raspberries on top. Serve cold.

At the left end of its immense porch, The House on the Hill has a round observation area with a conical roof—an ideal spot for absorbing the quiet of rural Michigan.

The Voss Inn B&B

Bozeman, Montana

THIS LOVINGLY RESTORED brick house, more than a century old, is comfortably furnished with antiques. The house sits on a large lawn set back from one of the main streets. Guest bedrooms are large enough to hold small breakfast tables and chairs, as well as other standard furnishings, allowing guests to enjoy breakfast in the privacy of their rooms.

The seasonal attractions for visitors to the Voss Inn include hiking, white-water rafting, cross-country and downhill skiing, and trout fishing. A visit to the Museum of the Rockies is always in season. Among other displays, the museum features a fascinating exhibit of North American dinosaurs.

Hosts Bruce and Frankee Muller describe their breakfast: "Each morning help yourself to fresh, homemade breakfast rolls from the unique built-in warmer in our 1880s ornate radiator. A delicious full breakfast is prepared for you to enjoy in the comfort of your room."

The Voss Inn B&B
319 South Willson
Bozeman, Montana 59715
(406) 587–0982

Bruce and Frankee Muller

FRIED NECTARINES

SERVES 4.

This recipe is so simple it belies the delicious results. The nectarines release an exquisite nectar, which enhances their tart flavor. The peel is left on in this recipe, and sautéed, it adds a slightly chewy texture that rounds out the dish. This is always a hit at breakfast, and I often serve it as a dessert as well.

6 nectarines
3 Tbs. butter
6 Tbs. brown sugar
  cinnamon to taste
  heavy cream to taste

Wash and slice the nectarines, but do not peel them. In a large skillet over medium-high heat, sauté them in the butter until tender, but not mushy, approximately 10 minutes. Stir in the brown sugar and cinnamon, and leave over the heat until the sugar has completely melted. Serve immediately, topped with a dollop of fresh heavy cream.

The solid simplicity of the old brick Voss Inn house ideally complements the rugged simplicity of the state of Montana, with its vast plains and soaring mountains.

Kenniston Hill Inn

Boothbay, Maine

DAVID KENNISTON, a prominent shipbuilder and landowner, built this mansion in 1786. The stately white clapboard house stands on a knoll between Boothbay and Boothbay Harbor. The old house is carefully decorated, furnished with antiques, handmade quilts and fresh flowers. A huge open-hearth fireplace in the living room provides a welcome setting for reading, chatting or playing board games.

The harbor is just down the road; the ferry for Monhegan Island leaves from here, as do whale-watching and sightseeing cruise boats. The picturesque old town, which can be comfortably seen on foot, offers a variety of shops, galleries and cafés. In the summer, there is also a famous dinner theatre nearby.

Guests are served a full country breakfast in the dining room, which looks out over gardens and fields. On chilly mornings, the fireplace is put to good use. In warmer weather, breakfast is served in the courtyard or on the front porch. Ellen and Paul Morissette owned a restaurant in Vermont for many years before they became B&B hosts. As avid chefs, they take pride in serving fresh, unusual and well-prepared dishes.

Kenniston Hill Inn
Route 27
Boothbay, Maine 04537
(207) 633-2159

Ellen and Paul Morissette

ELLEN'S BLUEBERRY DELIGHT

SERVES 6.

This recipe should be made a day ahead. The caramelized topping of this cool, creamy fruit dish is unusual and delicious. The variations listed at the end of the recipe make this a good dish all summer long.

3 cups fresh blueberries
1 cup sour cream
1 tsp. vanilla extract
1 cup brown sugar, firmly packed

Preheat oven to Broil.
Divide the blueberries evenly among 6 serving-size ramekins or custard dishes. Set aside.
In a small bowl combine the sour cream and vanilla. Pour over the fruit. Sprinkle evenly with the brown sugar. Broil until the sugar caramelizes. Watch carefully! The sugar needs to melt but not burn.
Cover and refrigerate several hours or overnight before serving.
Variations: This recipe may be made with seedless green grapes, peaches or strawberries.

The flag on the porch of the Kenniston Hill Inn at one time had thirteen stars, for the old house was already standing proudly when George Washington took the oath of office. Of course, at that time, Maine was still part of Massachusetts, and statehood would not come for several years.

Little Piney Canoe Resort
Newburg, Missouri

OVERLOOKING THE LITTLE PINEY RIVER, one of the fastest-moving rivers in Missouri, Little Piney Canoe Resort, a converted barn, is both rustic and comfortable. The Davises offer a canoe-rental service, making it easy for guests to do some boating during their stay, a particularly good way to enjoy the scenery.

Guests are served a full breakfast in one of two locations; on the deck overlooking the river, weather permitting, or in the country kitchen with a view of the hills and garden. The full, homecooked breakfast features fresh ingredients, such as freshly squeezed orange juice, fresh eggs from the Davises' own laying hens, apples from their orchard and maple syrup from a neighbor, all served with freshly ground coffee or a choice of herbal teas.

The Davises prefer to list themselves with a reservation service, Bed & Breakfast of St. Louis. Their address and phone number are given below.

Little Piney Canoe Resort
Newburg, Missouri
Joan Davis
c/o Bed & Breakfast of St. Louis
1900 Wyoming Street
St. Louis, Missouri 63118
(314) 965–4328

Mike Warner

SAUTÉED APPLES

SERVES 4.

Simple but delicious. With so few ingredients, this dish is handy for serving unexpected guests. The Davises use apples from their own trees.

  4   tart apples
  4   Tbs. butter
  2   cups water
  8   Tbs. sugar
  1   tsp. cinnamon
  ½   cup heavy cream

Peel, core and slice the apples. Melt the butter in a skillet over medium-high heat and add the apples, stirring quickly. When the apples brown a little on the edges, add the water, sugar and cinnamon. Stir until the ingredients are well combined, being careful not to mash the apples. Lower the heat to medium-low and steam uncovered until the apples are tender.

Serve in footed compote dishes with a little heavy cream, whipped if preferred.

The Carriage House
Laguna Beach, California

THE CARRIAGE HOUSE is one of Laguna Beach's designated historical landmarks. Located in the heart of the village, the colonial-style Carriage House is within pleasant walking distance of a variety of unique shops and galleries, as well as a number of cafés and restaurants. The Pacific Ocean is just a few houses away.

The house is furnished with antiques, and all rooms face a secluded brick courtyard filled with tropical plants and comfortable furniture. The courtyard makes an especially inviting place to read and relax.

Guests are welcomed to their suites with a bottle of California wine and fresh fruit. A full breakfast is served in the dining room or, if preferred, in the courtyard.

The Carriage House
1322 Catalina Street
Laguna Beach, California 92651
(714) 494–8945

Dee Taylor

HOT SPICED FRUIT

SERVES 4.

Tangy and flavorful, this is especially good in fall or winter.

3 cooking apples
3 Tbs. water
1 can whole cranberry sauce
2 cinnamon sticks
    dash nutmeg
    heavy cream (optional)

Core the apples, and cut into chunks. Place the apple chunks in a saucepan with the water, cover, and cook over medium-high heat until the apples are slightly tender. Add the cranberry sauce, cinnamon and nutmeg. Stir and continue cooking, uncovered, until the apples are tender and the mixture is thoroughly hot, approximately 5 to 10 minutes. Remove the cinnamon sticks before serving. Serve hot, plain or with a splash of heavy cream.

The Carriage House is built in a neo-Colonial style. Like the dining room, the entire house is furnished with an eclectic array of antiques. Photo by Ralph Starkweather.

Glendeven

Little River, California

A FINE EXAMPLE OF Maine-style architecture, this handsome farmhouse, built in 1867, is set back on a headland meadow with the bay of Little River in the distance. Fern Canyon below is a popular place for walking or jogging. The sounds of the surf and the smell of the salt air combine with the rural setting and lovely surroundings of Glendeven to provide a most peaceful, relaxing environment.

The historic and colorful town of Mendocino is just a mile and a half from here, and the rugged Mendocino coastline is spectacularly beautiful. Glendeven sits on two acres of tended grounds with room to spread a blanket for a picnic, read quietly in the shade of a tree or enjoy the sunshine on the brick patio. The house is furnished with a mix of antiques and contemporary pieces.

A generous breakfast of fresh juice, fruits in season, homebaked breads and locally roasted coffee or a selection of teas is served in the sunny sitting room. If preferred it can also be brought to a guest's room. In the evening, wine and sherry are offered in the sitting room, where a fire takes the chill off cool evenings, and a fine piano awaits the impulse!

Glendeven
Little River, California 95456
(707) 937–0083

Jan and Janet DeVries

BAKED APPLES

SERVES 4.

Baked apples are always a favorite at breakfast. These make a delicious dessert, too.

4 Pippin or Granny Smith apples
4 Tbs. brown sugar
1 tsp. cinnamon
1 tsp. grated orange zest
4 tsp. currants
4 Tbs. butter
1 Tbs. honey or maple syrup
   whipped cream or creme fraiche
      to taste

Preheat oven to 400°F.

Clean and core the apples; set aside. In a small bowl mix together the brown sugar, cinnamon, grated orange rind and currants. Fill the apples with this mixture, packing it in if necessary. Set the apples in an oven-proof glass baking dish. Carefully pour about ½" of cold water into the dish. Top each apple with a tablespoon of butter and drizzle the honey or maple syrup over the butter.

Bake for about 30 to 40 minutes. The apples should be cooked thoroughly but should not rupture. Serve hot, with whipped cream or creme fraiche.

Although well into its second century, the Glendeven farmhouse is maintained in perfect repair. Perhaps the house was built by a transplanted New Englander. Certainly it would be as at home on the coast of Maine as on the coast of California.

Phoenix House
Minocqua, Wisconsin

PHOENIX HOUSE is situated on forty acres, fronting on two-hundred-acre White Fish Lake. The lake is clear and fresh, perfect for swimming, fishing and boating. The Prudhoms have rowboats and a sailboat that they make available to guests. During the summer, early risers often like to go for a swim in the lake before breakfast.

Minocqua, a small town with antiques shops and a variety of restaurants, is just eight miles away. But the primary reason visitors come here is to enjoy the natural beauty and outdoor activities. The surrounding countryside is dotted with lakes, rivers and streams, making water sports such as canoeing, sailing, waterskiing and swimming prime activities. In the winter, this area is known for excellent cross-country skiing and ice-skating.

A stay includes a full breakfast served at a table set with linen and rose-colored glassware. In the cooler months, breakfast is served in the dining room with a fire crackling in the fireplace; during summer, breakfast is served on the porch overlooking the lake.

Phoenix House
1075 Highway F
Minocqua, Wisconsin 54548
(715) 356–3535

Odeen and Fred Prudhom

APPLE COMPOTE

SERVES 6.

"For this apple dish I use apples from my tree, called 'Duchess of Oldenburg.' This apple originated in Russia and was brought to this country by way of England over 150 years ago. Extremely hardy and unexcelled for pies and sauce."
—ODEEN PRUDHOM

8	tart apples
2½	cups water
4	Tbs. lemon juice
¾	cup sugar
6	Tbs. red currant jelly
	grated zest of 2 lemons
2	cinnamon sticks
½	cup walnut pieces
½	cup raisins

Peel and core the apples; cut into chunks. Place the apples in a saucepan with the water and lemon juice; simmer until just tender. Using a slotted spoon, remove the apples and set aside in a bowl. Add the sugar, jelly, lemon zest and cinnamon sticks to the water in the saucepan. Bring to a boil, stirring constantly, and then simmer until a syrup forms. Pour the syrup over the apple chunks, add the walnuts and raisins and toss gently. Remove the cinnamon sticks.

Serve warm or cold in individual compote dishes. May be served plain or topped with a dollop of whipped cream.

SCRUBBED & TUBBED, BOILED, BAKED & GLAZED ORANGES
The Bells B&B (p.9)

SERVES 8.

"This is a wonderful edible garnish. You may eat the whole thing, skin and all. It looks festive served on a green of some kind, garnished with a cherry and sprig of parsley or mint. Would be lovely surrounding a pork roast. I use it on my breakfast plate. A guest suggested adding Grand Marnier to the syrup and serving it with ice cream as a dessert."—LOUISE SIMMS, hostess at The Bells.

I love these. The variations Louise Simms suggests are all excellent. —MWM

  4 oranges, thin skinned, seedless variety
  1 cup sugar
  ½ cup orange juice
  2 Tbs. butter

Preheat oven to 400°F.
  Wash the oranges. Place whole in a saucepan and cover with water. Bring to a boil, reduce to simmer and simmer for 30 minutes. Using a slotted spoon, remove the oranges from the water and set them on a plate to cool.
  In a small saucepan, combine the sugar and orange juice. Bring to a boil, stirring constantly, and cook for about 5 minutes, until a syrup forms.
  Halve the oranges, and trim the bottoms so that they will sit evenly in an oven-proof dish. Dot with butter. Pour the syrup over the oranges and bake at 400° for 30 minutes. Serve warm.

PUMPKIN MADEWOOD LAFOURCHE
Madewood Plantation House (p.11)

SERVES 12 to 20.

The pumpkin makes a pretty serving bowl at the table, and the flavor of the fruit mix inside is rich and smooth.

  2 large pumpkins
 12 apples
  ¾ cup honey
  1 tsp. cinnamon
  1 tsp. nutmeg
  2 cups raisins
  ¼ cup butter

Preheat oven to 275°F.
  Select the prettier of the two pumpkins and wash the outside well. Grease with vegetable oil and place whole in a large baking pan. Bake at 275° for about 60 minutes, until the pumpkin is still firm, but slightly soft to the touch. (This pumpkin will be used as a server so don't let it get too soft.) Set aside to cool.

While the whole pumpkin is in the oven, peel, seed and chop the other pumpkin. Place in a large pot with a little water and cook until soft. Peel, core and slice the apples. Place the apples in a separate saucepan and cover with water. Cook until soft and all the water is evaporated.
  In a large pot, mix the cooked apple with the cooked pumpkin; add honey and spices. Stir in the raisins and butter and cook over low heat for about 30 minutes, stirring occasionally.
  When the baked pumpkin is cool, cut off the top to make a lid, and scoop out the seeds. Place the hot pumpkin/apple mixture in the pumpkin and cover with the lid. (There should be enough to fill the pumpkin a second time.) Serve hot.
  Note: When finished with the serving pumpkin, peel and dice it, then freeze to use as a filling the next time you make this recipe.

BAKED PEARS HERSEY
Hersey House (p.54)

SERVES 8.

Baked Pears Hersey take advantage of the local fruit, and are very popular with guests. This dish may be served at breakfast or as an elegant light dessert after a rich dinner.

  4 pears, halved, cored and peeled
  ¼ tsp. cinnamon
  ⅛ tsp. nutmeg
  4 Tbs. butter, softened
  4 Tbs. brown sugar
  2 cups heavy cream, whipped, or vanilla yogurt (optional)

Preheat oven to 350°F.
  Place the pear halves in a greased pie plate, arranged like spokes with the narrow ends pointed towards the center. Sprinkle the pears with the cinnamon and nutmeg. Cover and set aside.
  In a small bowl combine the butter and brown sugar thoroughly, and then carefully spread the mixture over the pears.
  Bake at 350° for 20 to 25 minutes. Serve warm. Top with whipped cream or vanilla yogurt if you like.

Carter House
Eureka, California

LOOKING AT CARTER HOUSE, it is hard to believe that this Victorian fantasy was built in the 1980s. But it is Mark Carter's stunning, meticulous realization of plans originally drawn in the 1880s. The exterior features fancy shingle-work and handsome masonry chimneys. The interior is bright with marble floors, polished oak and redwood wainscot. In the evening, the Carters offer hors d'oeuvres and cocktails over which they are happy to share information about their town.

The charming Victorian town of Eureka, set on the rugged northern California coast, offers visitors a wealth of activities in addition to the opportunity to just enjoy the natural beauty of the area. Sequoia Park and Zoo—fifty-four acres of virgin redwoods—is nearby; it includes picnic areas, a children's playground, duck ponds, gardens and a petting zoo. Eureka is also home to the most photographed Victorian house in America, the Carson Mansion. The Clarke Memorial Museum has an impressive collection of Northwest California Indian basketry and regalia, and other exhibits include local history and Victorian decorative arts. The oldest part of town, easily viewed on a walking tour, is the waterfront section, along Humboldt Bay. The Humboldt Bay Maritime Museum both displays the maritime heritage of the area and operates harbor cruises.

A full breakfast is served in the dining room of Carter House at tables set with linen, crystal and china. As a former restaurant owner, Christie Carter takes pride in her impressive breakfast menus.

Carter House
1033 3rd Street
Eureka, California 95501
(707) 445-1390

Mark and Christie Carter

PEARS POACHED IN WINE SAUCE

SERVES 8 or 16 (1 whole or ½ pear per person).

Although the sauce for this delicious recipe has a sweet and tangy flavor, it does not taste like red wine. Excellent as the fruit course at breakfast or brunch, it is also suitable as an elegant dessert after a rich dinner.

    8   pears, ripe but firm
    2   cups burgundy wine
    2   Tbs. lemon juice
    1   cup sugar
    2   tsp. cinnamon
        grated zest of 1 lemon
    1   tsp. vanilla extract
    ½   cup whipping cream, whipped
        fresh mint leaves

Peel the pears, cut in half and core. Place the pears in a deep saucepan; cover and set aside. In another large saucepan combine the wine, lemon juice, sugar, cinnamon, lemon zest and vanilla, and bring to a boil. Pour the liquid over the pears and simmer slowly until the pears are tender, 10 to 20 minutes. Using a slotted spoon, carefully remove the pears from the liquid and place in individual serving dishes. Then, boil the liquid until it is reduced by half. Pour the wine sauce over the pears, top each serving with a dollop of whipped cream and garnish with a fresh mint leaf.

LEFT AND OPPOSITE: *With its intricate cedar millwork, elaborate shingle patterns and brick panelwork, Carter House is an amazing and authentic recreation of a Victorian house.*

BAKED APPLES IN CARAMEL SAUCE

SERVES 4 or 8 (1 whole apple or ½ apple per person).

Apples
4 Granny Smith apples
½ cup butter, melted
¾ cup granulated sugar

Caramel Sauce
⅔ cup sugar
3 Tbs. cold water
2 Tbs. hot water
¾ cup cream
1 Tbs. butter
1 tsp. vanilla

whipped cream & fresh mint leaves
  for garnish

Start with the sauce: in a heavy sauce-pan, combine the sugar and cold water. Bring the mixture to a boil, stirring constantly. When the mixture begins to brown, remove the saucepan from the heat. Add the hot water carefully, as the mixture may splatter. Quickly add the cream, stirring briskly. Return the pan to a medium-low heat, whisk in the butter and add the vanilla. Continue cooking over medium-low heat, stirring constantly, until the mixture thickens. Reduce heat.

Turn the oven on at broil when you begin to prepare the apples.

Peel and core the apples, cut them in half and lightly score the tops. Roll each apple-half in melted butter, then in the sugar. Cover a baking sheet with foil and place the apples on the foil. Broil the apples for about 10 minutes or until the tops are nicely browned. Keep an eye on the apples as they broil; don't let them scorch.

Remove the apples from the baking sheet and transfer them to dessert plates or footed compote dishes. Drizzle with the caramel sauce, top with whipped cream and garnish with mint sprigs.

Canterbury Inn

Rochester, Minnesota

A RESTORED VICTORIAN BUILT IN 1890, Canterbury Inn was Rochester's first B&B. It is located just three blocks from the famous Mayo Clinic and St. Mary's Hospital, making it an especially good base for business travelers. The ambiance here is gracious and comfortable, and the rooms glow with the warmth of hand-carved woodwork. Guests are welcome to use the living room, which is supplied with a wealth of books and magazines, writing materials, board games and music. A special feature of Canterbury Inn is tea time, when guests are invited to join the hosts each afternoon from 5:30 to 7:30 for wine, canapés and conversation.

In the morning, guests enjoy a full homecooked breakfast, served either in the dining room or in their bedrooms.

Canterbury Inn
723 Second Street S.W.
Rochester, Minnesota 55902
(507) 289-5553

Mary Martin and Jeffrey Van Sant

NORWEGIAN FRUIT SOUP

SERVES 12.

"This is one of our guests' favorites. It is particularly winning when served as a first course, followed by eggs Benedict or Grand Marnier French Toast."—MARY MARTIN

This must be started a day in advance.

2 cups pitted prunes
1½ cups dried apricots
1 cup golden raisins
1 cup currants
1 cup dried tart cherries
1 lemon, sliced thin
4 sticks cinnamon
½ cup pearl tapioca
¾ cup apple juice
1 cup fresh or frozen raspberries
whipped cream (optional)

Place the first 5 ingredients in a large pot. Add fresh cold water just to cover. *Allow to soak overnight.*

The next day, place the pot of soaked fruit over medium heat, add the lemon and cinnamon and simmer gently. Meanwhile, in a small bowl soak the tapioca in the apple juice; let sit for 30 minutes. Continue to simmer the fruit mixture, stirring occasionally. Add the tapioca, and continue to cook for another 15 minutes. Remove from the heat; stir in the raspberries. Serve hot or cold, plain or with a dollop of whipped cream.

The Canterbury Inn is a fine example of the late-Victorian shingle style, with unusual triple gables.

BANANA BISQUE WITH CINNAMON CROUTONS

The Southern Hotel (p. 95)

SERVES 4.

"Soup for breakfast? An unusual experience to be sure! We serve this bisque in small Ste. Genevieve pattern glass bowls. A freshly baked croissant, dripping with honey butter, fresh ground coffee, iced fruit juice, squares of Miss Dodie's Eggs and you're ready for your walking tour of historic Ste. Genevieve."— BARBARA HANKINS

Bisque
3 cups sliced bananas (about 4 large bananas)
3 cups light cream, well chilled
¼ tsp. cinnamon
4 perfect, ripe strawberries

Blend the bananas, cream and cinnamon in a food processor until smooth. Serve in small glass bowls topped with croutons and one perfect strawberry in each.

Croutons
1 loaf 2-day-old French bread
6 Tbs. butter, melted
½ tsp. cinnamon

Preheat oven to 400°F.
Cut the bread into ½" slices; remove crusts and cut into small cubes. Place the bread in a large bowl and drizzle with the melted butter, stirring well. Spread the bread cubes on a cookie sheet and bake at 400° until golden brown, about 10 minutes. Remove from the oven and while hot sprinkle with the cinnamon. Let cool completely before using in the bisque.

SUMMER FRUIT SOUP

The Victorian Inn (p. 246)

SERVES 12.

This chilled soup is a refreshing way to start the morning.

3 cantaloupes
1 honeydew melon
2 13-oz. cans peaches
2 qts. apricot nectar
¼ cup honey
½ cup brown sugar
3 cups sour cream
2 tsp. cinnamon
   fresh mint leaves for garnish

Halve and seed the melons. Separate the melon from the rind and cut into chunks. Place the chunks of the cantaloupe and honeydew melons in a food processor. Add the peaches, undrained, and puree, but leave a little chunky. (You will probably need to do this step in two or three stages, depending on the capacity of your food processor.)
In a large bowl, blend the pureed fruit with the rest of the ingredients, combine thoroughly. Cover and chill for at least 2 hours.
Serve well chilled in small glass bowls; garnish each serving with a fresh mint leaf.
Note: I generally prefer to use only fresh fruit, but I found the canned peaches to be fine. If you prefer, use 6 fresh peaches that have been properly poached and peeled, adding the liquid as well.

APPLE CIDER SOUP

Barnard–Good House (p. 14)

SERVES 4 to 6.

Soup
¼ cup rice, uncooked
¾ cup fresh cider
2 cooking apples, peeled, cored and chopped
½ cup raisins
¼ cup water
2 Tbs. apple schnapps or applejack
¼ tsp. cinnamon
¼ tsp. nutmeg
1 Tbs. brown sugar

Croutons
3 slices white bread
3 Tbs. butter

Topping
½ cup heavy cream or sour cream
1 tsp. sugar
¼ tsp. vanilla

To make the soup: Combine all the ingredients in a large pot and place over high heat. Stirring well, bring to a boil. Stir at a boil briefly, then cover tightly and reduce to simmer. Simmer for 30 minutes.
To make the croutons: Trim crusts from bread and cut into cubes. Sauté diced bread with the butter in a large frying pan over medium heat, turning frequently until golden brown. Drain on paper towels.
To make the topping: Whip the cream with the sugar and vanilla until it holds firm peaks; or if using sour cream, mix the 3 ingredients together and chill well.
Serve hot or cold. Top each serving with a few croutons and a dollop of the cream topping.

Small Wonder Bed & Breakfast
Wilmington, Delaware

A MODIFIED CAPE COD COTTAGE, Small Wonder Bed & Breakfast is located in suburban Wilmington, convenient to the uniquely varied setting of the Delaware Valley. Many historical points of interest lie in the area—Revolutionary War battlefields, old statehouses, the seventeenth-century Swedish and Dutch heritage exemplified by Old New Castle, nineteenth-century powder mills, and vast stretches of marshland.

Small Wonder also offers a good location for the business traveler, with quick access to Interstate 95. Downtown Wilmington is just minutes away, and Philadelphia is only a twenty-seven-mile drive. Whether on business or pleasure, all guests at Small Wonder enjoy the award-winning landscaping of the backyard, which includes a pool.

The full breakfast served here might include bacon, sausage or scrapple; a choice from such entrees as waffles, pancakes, French toast, quiche or eggs; all this accompanied by pastries, fruit juices, hot or cold cereals, coffee and tea.

Small Wonder Bed & Breakfast
213 West Crest Road
Wilmington, Delaware 19803
(302) 764–0789

Dorothy Brill

HOT APPLE CEREAL

SERVES 6 to 8.

This is a delicious, hearty treat on a cold morning, perfect for fall and winter. Topped with fresh summer fruit, it is also good on a cool summer morning.

 4 cups milk
 ½ cup brown sugar
 ½ tsp. salt
 ½ tsp. cinnamon
 2 cups rolled oats
 2 cups chopped apples, peeled and cored
 1 cup chopped walnuts
 1 cup raisins
 1 cup wheat germ

Preheat oven to 350°F.

In a saucepan combine the milk, brown sugar, salt and cinnamon. Scald and set aside. In a large bowl combine the other ingredients. Pour the scalded milk over the oat mixture and stir well. Pour into a greased 2-qt. casserole and cover with foil.

Bake, covered, at 350° for 45 minutes, stirring several times during the baking period. Serve hot, with a splash of heavy cream.

LEFT: *A new cottage, the Small Wonder B&B emphasizes comfort rather than antiquities.*

OPPOSITE, TOP: *Among its amenities is a swimming pool.*

HOMESTYLE GRANOLA CEREAL

SERVES 8.

"Here at Small Wonder B&B we offer our guests a wide choice of breakfast entrées, including some hearty items like waffles, pancakes, quiche and hot muffins. But some guests, particularly the business person, like a lighter fare. Of the lighter fare, two of our guests' favorites are the Homestyle Granola and Hot Apple Cereal."—DOROTHY BRILL

¼ cup honey
¼ cup vegetable oil
½ cup water
4 cups rolled oats
1 cup wheat germ
¼ cup chopped walnuts
¼ cup slivered almonds
2 Tbs. sesame seeds
2 Tbs. raw bran
2 Tbs. raisins
2 Tbs. chopped dates
2 Tbs. dried coconut

Make this cereal at least one day in advance.

Preheat oven to 225°F.

In a small saucepan combine the honey, oil and water. Heat slightly; set aside. In a large bowl combine the rest of the ingredients and mix well. Pour the honey mixture over the dry ingredients and blend thoroughly. Spread the mixture into a large baking pan and bake at 225° for 2 hours, turning and stirring every 15 minutes.

Cool completely before serving. Can be stored indefinitely in an airtight container.

Hollinger House
Lancaster, Pennsylvania

DURING THE GILDED AGE, the Hollinger family won an international reputation for the excellence of its harness leather. They built their mansion near their tannery in 1870. Today the tannery no longer stands, but the gracious old house still sits on five peaceful acres crossed by a woodland stream. Guests are welcome to stroll the grounds or to take in the view while relaxing on the wrap-around porches.

Lancaster is the heart of the Pennsylvania Dutch country, an area rich in lush farmland and home to some of the country's best antiques shops. Jean Thomas, who has led tours in both the city and the countryside, knows the area well. She is happy to answer questions and help guests plan a day of exploring. There are wineries that offer tours and tastings, old county stores (one has been in business since 1779), and picturesque Amish farms. Craft shops—filled with handmade patchwork quilts, baskets, pewter and glass—are another special feature of a visit here.

In the morning, guests at Hollinger House are offered a choice of a light continental breakfast or a full Lancaster-style breakfast of eggs with bacon or scrapple, accompanied by coffee, juice, biscuits, and jam.

Hollinger House
2336 Hollinger Road
Lancaster, Pennsylvania 17602
(717) 464–3050

Leon and Jean Thomas

BAKED OATMEAL

SERVES 4.

A delicious hot treat on a cold morning, this dish is easy to prepare and a nice change from ordinary cooked oatmeal.

> 2 cups oatmeal
> 1½ tsp. baking powder
> ½ tsp. salt
> 1 cup milk
> 2 eggs
> ¼ cup oil
> ½ cup brown sugar
>
> *Topping*
> 1 cup vanilla yogurt

Preheat oven to 325°F.

In a large bowl combine the oatmeal, baking powder and salt. In a blender mix the milk, eggs, oil and brown sugar. Add the liquid ingredients to the oatmeal mix and stir well. Allow to sit for 5 minutes. Stir and pour into a greased casserole dish. Bake at 325° for 45 minutes. Serve hot, topping each serving with vanilla yogurt.

LEFT: *Although built in 1870, Hollinger House displays a style more associated with 1807, perhaps reflecting the innate conservatism of the Pennsylvania Dutch community in which it stands.*

OPPOSITE: *In contrast, Starr Cottage, built in 1883, is undoubtedly an artifact of the Gilded Age, as are the many Victorian "cottages" of Narragansett.*

Starr Cottage Inn
Narragansett, Rhode Island

LISTED ON THE National Register of Historic Places, Starr Cottage was built in 1883. A large, shingle-style house with a wide verandah, it is a fine example of the abundant architectural heritage of Narragansett. With the oak parquet floors, birds-eye maple paneling in the dining room, and a ballroom hung with chandeliers, it is noteworthy for the elegance of its interior.

Located in the historic district of Narragansett, Starr Cottage is just two blocks from the beach. A mile long, the sandy beach is inviting year-round for a leisurely stroll or for jogging. In the summer, the swimming and surfing are excellent. Sports fishing and charter sailing are also available in the area, and fine restaurants and interesting boutiques are within walking distance. Guests are served a continental-plus breakfast in the dining room or on the front porch, depending on the weather. Breakfast consists of home-baked goods, fresh fruit dishes, juices, freshly ground coffee and a selection of herbal teas.

Starr Cottage Inn
68 Caswell Street
Narragansett, Rhode Island 02882
(401) 783-2411

Gail Charren

BREAKFAST PARFAIT

SERVES 6 to 8.

This breakfast dish is pretty as well as healthful. The granola must be made at least a day in advance. If you want to serve this without homemade granola on hand, Quaker 100% Natural is an excellent brand and a fine substitution.

Granola
4 cups rolled oats
½ cup brown sugar
½ cup shredded coconut
½ cup sunflower seeds
½ cup chopped cashews
½ cup slivered almonds
½ cup chopped dates
½ cup honey
¼ cup oil

Preheat oven to 325°F.
Mix the oats, brown sugar, coconut, sunflower seeds, nuts and dates. In a small saucepan heat the honey and oil until very warm. Pour over the oat mixture and stir well. Spread the mixture over a lightly oiled cookie sheet. Bake at 325° for 10 minutes. Remove from oven and place the cookie sheet on a cooling rack. *Cool completely before using.* Store in an airtight container.

Parfait
7 cups Granola
1 qt. yogurt, plain or lemon
4 ripe bananas, sliced, or other
   fresh fruit

Using 8 parfait glasses, layer the granola with the yogurt and sliced banana, repeating the layers 3 times, beginning with the granola and ending with the fruit.
Substitute strawberries, raspberries, blueberries or peaches for the bananas, using whatever is in season.

Pancakes, Waffles, French Toast & Crepes

BUTTERMILK PANCAKES 45
  Murphy's B&B

SOURDOUGH HOTCAKES 45
  Crondahl's B&B

GINGERBREAD PANCAKES 45
  Hersey House

BUTTERMILK PANCAKES
WITH BLUEBERRIES 46
  Maplecrest Farm

PEARL'S PRIZE-WINNING
PANCAKE MIX 47
  Bed 'n' Breakfast–Still Country

SWEDISH PANCAKES 48
  Skoglund Farm B&B

SOUR CREAM PANCAKES 48
  Aldrich Guest House

FRUIT PANCAKES 49
  Old Pioneer Garden

PUMPKIN RAISIN PANCAKES 49
  Grant Corner Inn

THREE-GRAIN GRIDDLE
CAKES 49
  Little Piney Canoe Resort

OATMEAL PANCAKES 50
  Milburn House

PANCAKES SUPREME 51
  Tree House in the Park

APPLE PANCAKE 52
  Country House Inn

BAKED APPLE PANCAKE 53
  River Song

PUFFED PEAR PANCAKES 54
  Hersey House

COTTAGE CHEESE HOTCAKES 55
  Log Castle

AEBLESKIVERS 56
  Marjon Bed & Breakfast

DUTCH BABIES WITH APPLES 57
  Elizabeth Street Guest House

APPLE FRITTERS 58
  Bridgeford Cottage

OUTLAW WAFFLES 59
  Savery Creek Thoroughbred
  Ranch

HILLCREST HOUSE WAFFLES 60
  Hillcrest House

CHOCOLATE WAFFLES 61
  Murphy's B&B

ORANGE WAFFLES 61
  Manor House

PUMPKIN WAFFLES 61
  Longswamp Bed & Breakfast

LOST BREAD 62
  Casa de Solana

GREEN APPLE STUFFED
FRENCH TOAST 63
  The Bufflehead Cove Inn

DOVER TOAST 64
  The Fowler House

APPLE FRENCH TOAST WITH
COTTAGE CHEESE 65
  The Dove Inn

BAKED TOAST ALMONDINE 66
  Williams House B&B

SKIERS FRENCH TOAST 67
  The Pentwater Inn

FRENCH TOAST PUFF 68
  Victorian Bed & Breakfast Inn

PEACHES-AND-CREAM
FRENCH TOAST 69
  Kenniston Hill Inn

SUPER FRENCH TOAST
A L'ORANGE 69
  The Inn at Mitchell House

NIGHT-BEFORE FRENCH
TOAST CASSEROLE 70
  Holland House

BLUEBERRY CREPES 71
  The John Palmer House

BLUEBERRY-SAUCED BLINTZES 72
  Richards' Bed & Breakfast

BLINTZ CASSEROLE 72
  The Bells Bed & Breakfast

CHEESE BLINTZES 73
  The House on the Hill

The dining room at the Captain Jefferds Inn (see page 15), is full of winter warmth.

SIXTEEN PANCAKE RECIPES are offered in this section, ranging from the plain to the sublime. Some call for fresh fruit, some for puréed fruit, some for whole wheat flour or other grains, some for spices, and so on. Some are sweet, and some have no sugar at all.

Pancake batter should be prepared the morning it is to be used. The best utensil for cooking pancakes is a cast-iron skillet or griddle. Whatever you use, the surface should be lightly oiled and hot enough that a drop of water sizzles on it. Ladle the batter onto the hot skillet or griddle and watch as bubbles appear on the top of the batter. When the batter is well covered with bubbles, flip the pancake. The cooked side should be golden. If it is too dark, the heat is too high; and if it is too light, the pan is not hot enough. Cook until the pancake is golden on both sides, flipping the pancake *only once,* and serve immediately. Serve with soft or melted butter, real maple syrup or fruit syrups, and jams and jellies for those who do not like syrup. Following the pancake recipes are three recipes that cannot quite be called pancakes, but which certainly fit into this category. They are Aebleskivers (a Scandinavian "pancake"), Apple Fritters and Dutch Babies (a baked "pancake").

The five waffle recipes offered here supply five very different flavors. As with pancakes, the batter should be made fresh the morning it is to be used. You may use an electric waffle iron or a stove-top waffle iron. The surface should be lightly oiled and hot enough that a drop of water sizzles on it. Serve waffles hot, right out of the waffle iron. If you're cooking for a large crowd, cooked waffles may be kept on a plate in a warm oven as you cook enough to serve everyone at once. Waffles should be accompanied by a choice of syrups—maple and fruit—jams and butter. Waffles topped with fresh fruit in season and whipped cream make an elegant and memorable breakfast.

The ten French toast recipes given here also range from the simple to the complex. I have included a couple of simple recipes, because they are good and because they are useful; but beyond that, the recipes are downright sinful. Some are stuffed with fresh fruit or fruit preserves, some are topped with toasted nuts, some are flavored with liqueurs, others are baked in a caramel glaze.

Last in this section come four recipes for crepes and blintzes. A crepe is a very thin, eggy pancake, cooked quickly and lightly on both sides and then stuffed, usually with a fruit filling, and topped with a sauce. A blintz is a crepe cooked on only one side, stuffed and rolled or folded leaving the uncooked side facing out, lightly fried, and then topped with a sauce or syrup. If you have never made crepes before, don't be intimidated by the process: you can easily master the technique. Although the recipes for crepes and blintzes are the most complicated in this chapter, many would undoubtedly consider them the most elegant.

You can buy a special crepe pan at a kitchen supply shop, but you may also use your favorite small (5″ to 6″) skillet. The skillet should be lightly oiled, with a little butter sizzling in the bottom, and it should be fairly hot. The trick is to pour in very little batter and then, by manipulating the pan, swirl the batter (which is quite runny) over the bottom of the pan. Cook very lightly; crepes should be pale in color, not the rich golden color of a pancake. Crepes are usually cooked one at a time; stack the cooked crepes on sheets of waxed paper until you are ready to fill them. If you are making blintzes, the crepes may be made a day ahead and refrigerated, then filled and fried in the morning.

BUTTERMILK PANCAKES
Murphy's B&B (p. 13)

SERVES 6.

I have used this recipe for years, and it's still one of my favorites. These pancakes are light and fluffy and always get rave reviews. Try them with the suggested variations for a change of pace.

2½ cups flour
4 Tbs. sugar
4 tsp. baking powder
1 tsp. salt
6 Tbs. oil
1⅓ cups buttermilk
1 cup milk
2 eggs

In a large bowl mix together the flour, sugar, baking powder and salt. In a separate bowl beat together the oil, milk and eggs. Add the wet ingredients to the dry and mix well. Ladle the batter onto a hot, lightly oiled griddle and cook until pancakes are golden on both sides. (For more specific directions on cooking pancakes, see the introduction to this section.) Serve hot, with butter and maple or fruit syrup.

Variations

Banana Pancakes. Immediately after ladling batter onto the griddle, place a few slices of banana in the batter. Cook by the standard method.

Cherry Pancakes. Stir 1 cup of fresh cherries (pitted and quartered) into the batter. Cook in the standard manner.

SOURDOUGH HOTCAKES
Crondahl's Bed & Breakfast (p. 142)

BATCH serves 6.

Judy Crondahl explains, "Sourdough was one of the foods of the gold rush; it is said that the miners used to sleep with their sourdough pot to keep it warm, and that a good cook could make bread with only the sourdough, flour and water."
   Start this recipe a day or more before you serve the hotcakes. Judy likes to make a very thin batter, as this makes for lighter hotcakes. Vary the proportion of flour to water to get the kind of batter you prefer. Because of the baking soda and all the beating, these hotcakes are very light and airy; yet at the same time, they have a rich and delicious flavor.

Sourdough Starter
1 pkg. dry yeast
1½ cups warm water
2 cups flour

In a large bowl mix the yeast with the water and let stand in a warm place for about 10 minutes. Then add the flour gradually, mixing well until it forms a thick batter. Cover and let stand in a warm, draft-free place for 24 hours. (I find that setting the covered bowl on top of the refrigerator is the perfect spot in my kitchen.)

Batch of Hotcakes
2 cups sourdough starter
1 egg
2 Tbs. sugar
4 Tbs. oil
1 tsp. baking soda

Combine the sourdough starter with the rest of the ingredients in a large bowl and beat well. (If the batter is too thick, thin with a little water.) Beat until the batter doubles in volume. Ladle onto a hot, well-oiled griddle and cook until golden on both sides. Serve hot.
   Note: Use only glass, crockery, plastic or wooden containers and utensils, never metal, when making sourdough starter.

GINGERBREAD PANCAKES
Hersey House (p. 54)

SERVES 6.

2½ cups flour
5 tsp. baking powder
1½ tsp. salt
1 tsp. baking soda
1 tsp. cinnamon
½ tsp. ginger
¼ cup molasses
2 cups milk
2 eggs
6 Tbs. butter, melted
1 cup raisins

In a large bowl sift together the flour, baking powder, salt, baking soda and spices. In a separate bowl combine the molasses and milk; beat in the eggs and the melted butter. Add to the flour mixture and stir until just moistened; stir in the raisins. Ladle the batter onto a hot, lightly oiled griddle and cook until golden on both sides. Serve hot, with butter and syrup.

Maple Crest Farm
Cuttingsville, Vermont

SPREADING OVER FOUR HUNDRED acres set in the heart of the Green Mountains, Maple Crest Farm is located in the town of Shrewsbury. The handsome, classically proportioned house was built in 1808, and until recently its acreage was a dairy farm. The Smiths still operate a maple syrup-making venture, and keep some cattle. Guests are welcome to roam all over the farm; and in spring, they can see how maple syrup is made. Most take home a supply of this special product.

The Green Mountains are a year-round resort area. In the winter, downhill and cross-country skiing are excellent. Spring and summer offer endless hiking and boating opportunities. And in the fall, the spectacular Vermont foliage sets the hills on fire. Whatever the season, just touring the back roads of the area is a scenic adventure.

In the morning, guests at Maple Crest Farm are served a full, home-cooked breakfast in the dining room.

Maple Crest Farm
Box 120
Cuttingsville, Vermont 05738
(802) 492–3367

William and Donna Smith

BUTTERMILK PANCAKES WITH BLUEBERRIES

SERVES 4 to 6.

This is a classic blueberry pancake recipe. The hosts at Maple Crest Farm serve these with their own maple syrup.

        2 cups flour
        1 Tbs. baking powder
        1 tsp. baking soda
        2 tsp. salt
        3 Tbs. sugar
        2 eggs
        6 Tbs. oil
     2¼ cups buttermilk
        1 cup blueberries

In a large bowl sift together the flour, baking powder, baking soda, salt and sugar. In a separate bowl beat the eggs, oil and buttermilk. Add to the dry ingredients and beat well. Lightly fold in the blueberries.

Ladle the batter on to a hot, lightly oiled skillet and cook until golden on both sides. (For more specific directions on cooking pancakes, see the introduction to this section.) Serve hot with butter and syrup.

LEFT: *Built in 1808, Maple Crest Farm promises snugness and warmth in the chill of a winter landscape after a day of trekking in the woods or skiing.*

OPPOSITE: *Flowers add brightness to a sunny corner at Murphy's B&B (see page 13).*

Bed 'n' Breakfast–Still Country
Wakefield, Kansas

IN THE PEACEFUL town of Wakefield (population 800), Bed 'n' Breakfast–Still Country sits on eighty acres, largely planted in orchards. The house offers vistas of Milford Lake stretching for twenty-three miles. Clay County Park is also nearby, offering seventy-five acres of woods and walking trails. Clearly, Pearl Thurlow had good reason to name her B&B "Still Country."

Abilene, just twenty-five miles to the southwest, provides an interesting day trip—there are historic mansions open for touring and the National Greyhound Hall of Fame. The nearby town of Riley is known for its fine antiques shops; and Fort Riley has an Indian reservation, with buffalo on the range to view. Kansas State University, in Manhattan, is only twenty miles away, making Still Country a good location for those who want or need to see the campus.

Pearl Thurlow's guests enjoy down-home hospitality and excellent home cooking served in generous farm portions.

Bed 'n' Breakfast–Still Country
Route 1, Box 297 / 206 6th Street
Wakefield, Kansas 67487-9629
(913) 461–5596

Pearl Thurlow

PEARL'S PRIZE-WINNING ORIGINAL PANCAKE MIX

MAKES 12 cups of dry mix (2 cups needed for 1 batch).
BATCH serves 4 to 6.

In 1951 this recipe won first prize in a contest featured by *Country Gentleman* magazine. Pearl Thurlow originally made it with wheat flour she ground herself, but now she gets it fresh from a local farmer's market. She still uses applesauce made from her own trees.

The dry master mix keeps well in the refrigerator, and pancakes can be prepared quickly for unexpected guests. The wholesome ingredients give these pancakes a hearty texture and flavor.

Master Mix
6 cups whole wheat flour
4 cups cornmeal
2 cups rolled oats
¼ cup baking powder
2 Tbs. baking soda
¼ cup salt
½ cup sugar

Mix together all ingredients. Store in refrigerator in an airtight container, and only use as much as you need. Keeps for weeks.

Batch of Pancake Batter
2 eggs
1 cup applesauce
1 cup milk
3 Tbs. melted butter
2 cups master mix

In a blender combine the eggs and applesauce. Add the milk and butter, then the dry mix. Mix well.

Make pancakes in the standard way. Serve hot with butter, syrup and jam.

Skoglund Farm Bed & Breakfast
Canova, South Dakota

HOME TO CATTLE, chicken, geese, ducks, peacocks, ostriches and horses, Skoglund Farm Bed & Breakfast is part of a family farm stretching over South Dakota prairie. Guests can roam over the farm on horseback or on foot. They can just as easily take in the peaceful setting and do nothing more strenuous than reading.

Some nearby attractions include the "Little House on the Prairie" at De Sonet (made famous by American writer Laura I. Wilder), the Corn Palace and Doll House at Mitchell, Prairie Village at Madison, and a variety of museums, zoos and lakes.

Guests at Skoglund Farm are served a full farm breakfast made from home-grown or local ingredients. A sample menu might consist of orange juice or home-canned tomato juice, fresh fruit in season, Swedish pancakes with homemade raspberry syrup and coffee or tea.

Skoglund Farm Bed & Breakfast
Route 31, Box 45
Canova, South Dakota 57321
(605) 247-3445

Delores Skoglund

SWEDISH PANCAKES

SERVES 2 to 4.

These are very good and call for no oil or butter, making this recipe a good choice for those watching their fat intake.

2 eggs
1 cup milk
½ tsp. vanilla
1 tsp. sugar
¼ tsp. salt
1 cup flour

In a large bowl beat the eggs. Add the milk and vanilla and beat well. Mix in the sugar, salt and flour. Ladle onto a hot, well-oiled griddle and cook until golden on both sides. Serve hot, with butter and syrup.

SOUR CREAM PANCAKES
Aldrich Guest House (p. 98)

SERVES 2.

These are an interesting change from a standard pancake. They are less sweet, lighter and slightly cheesy.

2 eggs
½ cup cottage cheese
¾ cup sour cream
¾ cup flour
¾ tsp. salt
½ tsp. baking soda

Combine all ingredients in a large bowl and mix well. (Batter will be slightly lumpy because of the cottage cheese.) Ladle onto a hot, lightly oiled griddle. Cook until golden on both sides. Serve hot with warm maple syrup or apple-sauce.

FRUIT PANCAKES
Old Pioneer Garden (p. 131)

SERVES 4.

Moist, flavorful and grainy, these pancakes are a delicious way to use fresh fruit in season.

2 cups corn flour
2 tsp. baking powder
1 tsp. baking soda
1 tsp. salt
1 egg
2 cups buttermilk
1 cup sliced fresh fruit or berries

In a large bowl combine the flour, baking powder, baking soda and salt. In a separate bowl beat the egg with the buttermilk; add to the dry ingredients and blend well. Gently stir in the fruit. Ladle onto a hot, well-oiled griddle and cook until golden on both sides. Serve hot, with maple syrup and sour cream.

For the fruit, use almost any ripe fruit: peaches (peeled and sliced thin), blueberries, raspberries, bananas or strawberries, to name a few.

PUMPKIN RAISIN PANCAKES
Grant Corner Inn (p. 154)

SERVES 6.

These rich, delicious pancakes are especially good for a fall or winter breakfast.

1½ cups flour
3½ tsp. baking powder
1 tsp. cinnamon
1 tsp. salt
1 tsp. nutmeg
1 tsp. allspice
1¼ cups canned or fresh puréed pumpkin
3 eggs
1 cup sugar
1 cup milk
¾ cup oil
1 tsp. vanilla
1 cup raisins

In a large bowl sift together the flour, baking powder, cinnamon, salt, nutmeg and allspice; set aside. In a separate bowl beat together the pumpkin and eggs; add the sugar, milk, oil and vanilla, beating well. Add the dry ingredients and blend thoroughly. Stir in the raisins.

Ladle the batter on to a hot, well-oiled griddle. Cook until golden on both sides. Serve hot, with warmed maple syrup.

THREE-GRAIN GRIDDLE CAKES
Little Piney Canoe Resort (p. 29)

SERVES 6 to 8.

These wholesome, not-too-sweet pancakes have a good grainy texture and flavor. For those concerned about it, this recipe calls for no oil or butter. The Davises serve these griddle cakes with maple syrup from a neighbor's tree.

1 cup cornmeal
1 cup wholewheat flour
1 cup unbleached white flour
6 tsp. baking powder
6 Tbs. sugar
1½ tsp. salt
3 eggs
1½ cups milk

In a large bowl mix together all the dry ingredients. In a separate bowl beat together the eggs and milk. Stir the wet ingredients into the dry. Ladle onto a hot, well-oiled griddle and cook until golden on both sides. Serve hot with butter and maple syrup.

Note: the dry ingredients may be mixed and stored in the refrigerator in an airtight container. To make a small batch of pancakes, mix 1 cup of the dry mix with 1 beaten egg and ½ cup milk. This will serve 1 or 2 people.

OPPOSITE: *This fanciful rendering of the Skoglund Farm Bed & Breakfast suggests the openness of the Dakota prairie and hints at the varied menagerie assembled by Delores Skoglund.*

Milburn House
Bristol, Indiana

A STRIKING ITALIANATE Victorian house, Milburn House was built sometime between 1876 and 1879. The large, gracious rooms—restored to their original beauty by the current owners—give a sense of having stepped back to a more leisurely time.

Pauline Mihojevich recommends that guests explore Crystal Valley, where Amish horse-drawn buggies ramble from town to town on narrow country roads. This area is home to historic Bonneyville Mill Park, where tours of the fully operational grist mill are available. Visitors may also choose to see cheese made on a tour of the Deutsch Käse Haus cheese factory. The restored Bristol Opera House is known for excellent theatre, and this area is rich in antiques and Amish handiwork shops.

Breakfast at Milburn House, served in the lovely formal dining room, always includes fresh home-baked goods.

Milburn House
707 East Vistula
Bristol, Indiana 46507
(219) 848-4026

Pauline Mihojevich

OATMEAL PANCAKES

SERVES 2 to 4.

Another tasty variation on the standard pancake. The oatmeal gives these a good texture and a hearty flavor.

½ cup flour
1 tsp. baking powder
½ tsp. baking soda
½ tsp. salt
½ cup quick-cooking oatmeal
1 Tbs. sugar
¾ cup buttermilk
¼ cup milk
2 Tbs. oil
1 egg

Combine all the dry ingredients in a large bowl. In a separate bowl beat together the buttermilk, milk, oil and egg. Add the wet ingredients to the dry and beat well. Ladle onto a hot, well-oiled griddle and cook until puffed, and golden on both sides. Serve hot with butter and syrup.

LEFT AND OPPOSITE: *A modern house, Tree House in the Park stands on posts that lift it fifteen feet above the ground. From its windows are views like these. The Louisiana bayou country possesses marshes and swamps in abundance, with an austere beauty all their own.*

Tree House in the Park

Port Vincent, Louisiana

BUILT HIGH AMONG THE TREES, Tree House in the Park is a Cajun cabin set in the Louisiana swampland, offering a setting of privacy and tranquility.

Nearby are many points of interest. Antebellum plantation houses stand just thirty minutes to the west; the state capital of Baton Rouge is forty-five minutes to the north and New Orleans one hour to the south.

Guests at the Tree House enjoy breakfast in one of three settings: a sunlit room with picture windows high among the tree tops, the upper deck where cypress trees branch overhead or the lower deck by the pool. Breakfast is served on bright yellow ceramic dishes that hostess Fran Schmieder throws and fires herself. "We have traveled the world, and now let the world beat a path to our door," she says.

Although Tree House in the Park is located in Port Vincent, the Schmieder's mailing address is Prairieville.

Tree House in the Park
16520 Airport Road
Prairieville, Louisiana 70769
(504) 622–2850

Fran and Julius Schmieder

PANCAKES SUPREME

SERVES 4.

These unusual pancakes, not too sweet, have a nutty whole-grain flavor, wholesome and hearty.

    1 cup whole wheat flour
    ½ cup rolled oats
    1 tsp. baking powder
    ½ tsp. cinnamon
    ¼ tsp. nutmeg
    1½ cups milk
    1 egg
    2 Tbs. oil
    2 Tbs. honey
    1 apple (peeled, cored, and chopped
        fine or grated)
    ¼ cup pecans, chopped

In a large bowl mix together the flour, oats, baking powder, cinnamon and nutmeg. In a separate bowl beat the milk, egg, oil and honey; stir into the dry ingredients. Add the apple and pecans. Mix well.

Cook the pancakes in a lightly oiled, hot skillet, until golden on both sides. Serve hot, with butter and honey.

Country House Inn
Templeton, California

THE LITTLE TOWN of Templeton is part of an historic county. It was once the southern terminus of the Southern Pacific Railroad; to go farther south in the days of the Old West, travelers were obliged to take the stagecoach. Among the beautifully restored antique buildings that attest to the town's early origins and rich history is the Country House Inn—built in 1896 by the founder of the town. Dianne Garth, its proprietor, is a member of the committee to start a historic museum in Templeton.

The region is now a rich wine-growing area, with vineyards open for touring and wine tasting. The wine served at one of the 1989 presidential inaugural balls was produced by a winery here—Creston Manor. High Country Horseback Adventures, just a ten-minute drive from Templeton, offers trail rides through the hills, and even overnight rides going as far as the coast. Lovely Cambria Beach is just a scenic half-hour drive away. A forty-minute drive up the coast brings visitors to the famous and spectacular Hearst Castle in San Simeon.

The Country House Inn offers a full breakfast in the formal dining room, at a table set with china, silver and linen. The twelve-foot ceiling, chandelier and French doors opening out to the garden make this a delightful setting in which to enjoy Dianne Garth's excellent cooking.

Country House Inn
91 Main Street
Templeton, California 93465
(805) 434-1598

Dianne Garth

APPLE PANCAKE

SERVES 2.

This is a quick, easy pancake to prepare, but always impressive. It is delicious as is or served with maple syrup.

2 green apples, peeled, cored and
   sliced thin
2 Tbs. butter
3 eggs
½ cup milk
½ cup flour
¼ cup melted butter
½ cup sugar
2 Tbs. cinnamon

Preheat oven to 500°F.

Sauté the apples in the butter in a 10" ovenproof skillet until they are soft but not mushy. Remove from heat and set aside. In a bowl, beat together the eggs, milk and flour. Pour the batter into the skillet, over the apples, and bake at 500° for 10 minutes, or until the pancake puffs up and browns around the edges. *Watch carefully*. Pour the melted butter over the top of the pancake. Mix the sugar and cinnamon and sprinkle over the top. Return to the oven for another 5 minutes or until the sugar melts. Cut in half and serve immediately.

Note: You may make this dish in individual servings by using two 5" or 6" skillets, simply dividing the ingredients between the two. The puffed apple pancakes will slip right out of the pan on to a plate.

LEFT: *The Country House Inn is a reminder of California's unhurried days of agriculture.*

OPPOSITE: *Built during prohibition by a millionaire who wanted isolation to throw parties right out of* The Great Gatsby, River Song *remains a secluded hideaway.*

River Song
Estes Park, Colorado

SET ON TWENTY-SEVEN wooded acres nestled at the foot of Giant Track Mountain, River Song offers travelers a quiet respite where they can enjoy panoramic views of snow-capped mountains and a rushing stream with glimpses of wildlife such as deer, elk, eagles and owls.

There are year-round activities in Rocky Mountain National Park: skiing, hiking or participation in the Rocky Mountain Nature Association summer seminars. Some of the special events held throughout the year include the Scottish Festival, Aspenfest, the Estes Park Spring Snow Festival and the Coors International Bicycle Classic.

A full breakfast is offered in the sunny octagonal dining room at a table set with heirloom silver in a blue-and-white color scheme. A wood-burning stove keeps the room warm and cozy, while the large windows provide views of the wooded hillsides.

River Song
P.O. Box 1910
Estes Park, Colorado 80517
(303) 586-4666

Gary and Sue Mansfield

BAKED APPLE PANCAKE

SERVES 4.

Pancake
3 cups apples, peeled, cored and chopped fine
¼ cup lemon juice
grated zest of 1 orange
¼ cup butter
½ cup and 1 Tbs. flour
½ tsp. baking powder
¼ tsp. salt
6 eggs, separated
¾ cup sugar
½ cup and 1 Tbs. milk
1 tsp. vanilla extract

Topping
¼ cup sugar
1 Tbs. cinnamon

Preheat oven to 375°F.

Prepare the apples; place them in a large bowl, add the lemon juice and orange zest, toss and set aside.

Prepare the topping by mixing the sugar and cinnamon together; set aside.

Melt butter in a 12″ cast-iron skillet, coating pan well. Remove from heat.

In a large bowl sift together the flour, baking powder and salt; set aside.

In a separate bowl beat the egg whites until stiff, gradually beating in the sugar; set aside.

In another bowl beat the egg yolks until thick; blend in the milk and vanilla extract. Add the egg yolk mixture to the flour mixture and beat until smooth. Fold in the beaten egg whites, then fold in the apple mixture.

Pour the batter into the prepared skillet and sprinkle with the topping. Bake at 375° for 15 minutes or until set. Cut into 4 portions and serve immediately, with butter and maple syrup.

Hersey House

Ashland, Oregon

NAMED FOR THE FIVE GENERATIONS of Herseys who lived here from 1916 to 1974, Hersey House is a comfortable arts-and-crafts building dating from 1904. The house has been a B&B since 1983, when two sisters who summered in Ashland as young girls decided to buy it. The house is furnished with period pieces, and its large porch is graced with wicker. Offering a lovely view of the Rogue Valley with its abundant orchards that supply pears to the whole country, the porch is a popular spot for guests during fine weather.

Ashland's plaza, three theatres and lush Lithia Park are all just a short walk away. The famous Oregon Shakespearean Festival, which draws visitors from across the country, is held here every summer. The valley vineyards, the historic mining town of Jacksonville and the beautiful blue Crater Lake are just a few of the other special spots nearby. Outdoor activities abound: golf, tennis, horseback riding, biking, hiking, fishing and boating keep the sports-minded visitor well occupied.

Guests at Hersey House relish a full breakfast that includes freshly ground coffee, freshly squeezed orange juice and home-cooked delights that change daily.

Hersey House
451 N. Main Street
Ashland, Oregon 97520
(503) 482-4563

Gail E. Orell

PUFFED PEAR PANCAKES

SERVES 8.

Gail Orell created this recipe to take advantage of the fabulous pears available in her area—home to the country's largest pear orchards. These are some of the best pancakes I've ever had. Use only top quality, ripe pears; they will melt in your mouth.

    6 whole eggs
    ¾ cup sugar
    2 cups flour
    1½ tsp. cinnamon
    1 tsp. salt
    5 cups finely chopped pears (ripe,
         peeled and cored—about 5 pears)
    6 egg whites

In a large bowl beat 6 whole eggs with the sugar until the mixture is lemon yellow. Add the flour, cinnamon and salt; beat until smooth. Fold in the pears. In a separate bowl, beat the 6 egg whites until stiff; fold into the batter. Spoon the batter onto a hot, lightly oiled griddle. Cook until golden on both sides. Serve hot, sprinkled with powdered or brown sugar.

Note: Golden Delicious apples may be substituted for the pears. I was certain I had some pears in the pantry one morning when I started putting this recipe together, only to find at the last minute that I did not. I improvised with the apples I had on hand, and the results were a success.

Hersey House itself is a fine, well-maintained old house. In the summertime its greatest feature is the abundant flower garden that surrounds it.

Log Castle
Langley, Washington

WHIGBEY ISLAND, with its secluded beach and breathtaking view of Mt. Baker and the Cascade Mountains, is the site of Log Castle. The logs for the lodge were felled on the property, and Senator Jack Metcalf built his keep between sessions of the Washington State Senate. A guest bedroom in the turret, with its five large windows, offers a panoramic view of water, beach and surrounding mountains and pasture.

Always a conversation piece, the dining table is an end-cut of a Douglas fir with "FW" branded every few inches around the edge. In the lumber business, logs are branded for ownership as cattle are branded in ranching; and it is a crime of some magnitude to steal one. Many years ago when a log boom broke up during a storm on Puget Sound it was quite common for owners of small mills to go out and steal the logs. They first had to destroy the evidence by sawing off the branded ends and setting them afloat before making off with their booty. Norma Metcalf's father-in-law retrieved one such branded discard from a beach forty-five years ago and stored it in his basement, someday to be made into a table. From its growth rings, he saw that the tree was more than three centuries old. It was already a sapling when the Pilgrims landed.

After a full breakfast around this table, guests can stroll along the beach or through the quiet woods where some of the oldest trees on the island still grow. The quaint village of Langley is only a short walk away. Of course, they can also stay put and curl up with a good book in front of the large stone fireplace.

Log Castle
3273 East Saratoga Road
Langley, Washington 98260
(206) 321–5483

Jack and Norma Metcalf

COTTAGE CHEESE HOTCAKES

SERVES 2.

These light, tasty hotcakes are a pleasant change from the sweeter variety. Delicious for breakfast, they also make a meal with a garden fresh salad in the summer months when light dinners are desirable.

    3 eggs, separated
    ¾ cup cottage cheese
    ⅓ cup flour
    ¼ tsp. salt

Beat the egg whites until stiff; set aside. In a separate bowl beat the egg yolks until thick. Add the cottage cheese to the yolks and beat well. Stir in the flour and salt. Fold in the beaten egg whites. Drop by spoonfuls on a well-oiled, hot griddle. (Make them 4″ in diameter so they are easy to turn.) Cook until golden on the outside, and dry and fluffy inside. Serve immediately, topped with a dab of sour cream and raspberry jam.

Washington State Senator Jack Metcalf built the Log Castle with his own hands between sessions of the Washington legislature. Situated on an isolated island, the castle offers superb views of Mt. Baker and other mountains of the Cascade Range.

Marjon Bed & Breakfast

Leaburg, Oregon

MARJON BED AND BREAKFAST is located on the bank of the McKenzie River in Leaburg, just twenty-four miles east of Eugene. The house is set on two acres of landscaped grounds planted with hundreds of azaleas and rhododendrons, with three levels of lawns sweeping down to the river. The architect made the most of this setting with windows that are virtually walls of glass. Margaret Von Retzlaff Haas writes that although each season here has its own special charm, springtime is especially beautiful.

The countryside surrounding this idyllic setting offers many year-round activities: trout fishing, boating, golfing, water and snow skiing, mountain climbing and hiking over seemingly endless trails.

A full breakfast is served either in the dining room, with its glass wall affording a splendid view of the river, or (in warm weather) on the terrace, which also overlooks the river.

Marjon Bed & Breakfast
44975 Leaburg Dam Road
Leaburg, Oregon 97489
(503) 896–3145

Countess Margaret Olga Von Retzlaff Haas

Situated on the bank of a river on two acres of its own, Marjon Bed & Breakfast is magnificently landscaped, with vistas that can be enjoyed from every window of the house.

AEBLESKIVERS

SERVES 4.

A traditional Scandinavian recipe. You will need an aebleskiver pan, which you can probably find at a well-stocked kitchen shop.

1½ cups flour
2 tsp. baking powder
½ tsp. salt
3 eggs
1 cup milk
3 Tbs. butter, melted
1 large ripe banana

Peel the banana and cut into ¼" slices.

In a large bowl sift together the flour, baking powder and salt. In a separate bowl beat the eggs; blend in the milk and butter. Add this to the flour mixture; beat until thoroughly blended.

Lightly oil an aebleskiver pan. Heat over medium-high heat until a drop of water sizzles when dropped into one of the wells. Ladle a little batter into each well, filling it halfway. Place a slice of banana in the batter of each aebleskiver.

After 2 to 3 minutes of cooking over medium-high heat (small bubbles will be forming around the edge of the batter), gently give the aebleskiver a half turn with a fork. As you turn the aebleskiver, it will begin forming a sphere with a golden crust. Turn gently with the fork until a sphere is formed (the top of the sphere will be thoroughly cooked—this was the bottom of the batter first poured into the pan), and cook an additional 2–3 minutes. You should have crisp golden spheres, that are dry and fluffy inside. Serve immediately, dusted with powdered sugar. Accompany with butter, jams and maple syrup.

Variation: Instead of the banana slices, use thin, small chunks of peeled apple.

Elizabeth Street Guest House
Ft. Collins, Colorado

BUILT IN 1905, Elizabeth Street Guest House is a handsome American four-square brick house. Completely restored by John and Sheryl Clark, the house is furnished with family antiques. The original leaded windows and oak woodwork always draw comments.

As ten-year residents of Fort Collins, the Clarks are glad to share maps and information about the area with visitors. They are just one block east of Colorado State University. A few blocks away is the restored Old Town square. The surrounding countryside is popular for hiking, swimming and boating. The entrance to the Rocky Mountain National Park is only thirty miles away; Denver is sixty-five miles to the south.

A full breakfast, including homemade muffins, pastries and jams, is served in the dining room at a table set with linen and silver.

Elizabeth Street Guest House
202 E. Elizabeth Street
Ft. Collins, Colorado 80524
(303) 493–BEDS

Sheryl Clark

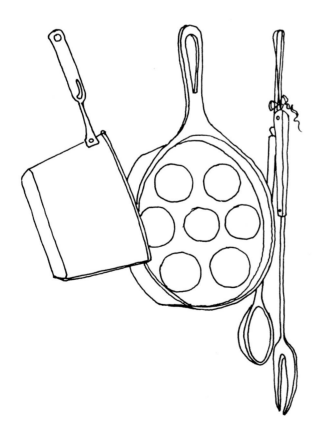

DUTCH BABIES WITH APPLES

SERVES 8.

Dutch Babies
6 Tbs. butter
5 eggs
1¼ cups milk
1½ cups flour

Preheat oven to 400°F.

Put butter in a 3-quart baking dish (a dutch oven is best), and place in oven long enough for the butter to melt. While the butter is melting, place the eggs in a blender at high speed. Add the milk and flour and blend until smooth. Pour this batter into the baking dish with the melted (but not sizzling) butter. *Do not stir.* Return the dish to the oven and bake at 400° for 20 minutes. The batter will puff up while baking and fall immediately when removed from oven.

Cut into 8 portions and serve topped with Hot Apples.

Hot Apples
1 qt. canned apples
or
8–10 apples, peeled, cored and sliced
¾ cup apple juice
1 tsp. cinnamon
2 Tbs. butter
½ cup sugar
2 Tbs. cornstarch
¼ cup cold water

Place canned apples or fresh apples in a large saucepan. Add the juice, cinnamon, butter and sugar, and cook over high heat, stirring, for about 5 minutes. In a small glass mix the cornstarch with the cold water; add to the apples and cook for another 2 minutes to thicken. Serve hot over the Dutch Babies.

Bridgeford Cottage
Eureka Springs, Arkansas

BUILT IN 1884, Bridgeford Cottage is a Victorian cottage in the heart of the Eureka Springs historic district. The comfortable front porch, decorated with wicker furniture and hanging ferns, is a good spot for watching the activity of Spring Street. Horse-drawn carriages amble by, as do trollies and pedestrians, all enjoying the view of stately Victorian houses that line the street. Although situated on one of the most famous streets in Eureka Springs, Bridgeford Cottage is far enough away from the hustle and bustle of downtown to ensure that guests enjoy a stay of "peaceful calm and quiet entertainment."

A popular resort at the turn of the century, the town is known for its hot mineral springs. Today the old spa is enjoying a rebirth, and downtown boasts a variety of stylish and unusual shops, boutiques and cafes.

Guests are served a full breakfast that gives them, according to Nyla Sawyer, "just the right send-off for a pleasant day in one of America's most charming and unusual cities."

Bridgeford Cottage
263 Spring Street
Eureka Springs, Arkansas 72632
(501) 253-7853

Ken and Nyla Sawyer

APPLE FRITTERS

SERVES 4.

These fritters have a sugary crust, reminiscent of a glazed doughnut, and a hot fluffy inside chock full of apples. You may want to make a double batch—these go fast!

1 cup flour
1 tsp. baking powder
¼ tsp. salt
3 Tbs. sugar
1 egg
¼ cup milk
1 cup apples, peeled, cored and chopped fine

In a large bowl sift together the flour, baking powder, salt and sugar. In a separate bowl beat together the egg and milk; gradually add to the flour mixture, beating well. Stir in the chopped apple.

In a large skillet heat about 1″ of oil until it is hot but not smoking. Dip a large spoon into the hot oil, and then into the batter. Drop spoonfuls of the batter into the hot oil, and cook 1 to 2 minutes on each side, or until golden. Remove from skillet with a slotted spoon and place on paper toweling to drain for a moment. While still hot, quickly roll each fritter in granulated sugar. Serve immediately.

Cooking tips: The oil must be hot enough for the batter to begin to form a crust as soon as it hits the oil. But if it is too hot, the fritters will brown too quickly, and the insides will not be cooked.

Savery Creek Thoroughbred Ranch
Savery, Wyoming

SOUTHERN WYOMING is noted for its rushing streams and old copper mines, but most of all for its wildlife. Savery Creek Thoroughbred Ranch borders Medicine Bow National Forest—an area rich in deer and elk; and twenty miles to the west lies the Red Desert, home to wild horses and antelope.

The ranch house is surrounded by lawns and cottonwood trees; in the evening deer can be seen grazing across Savery Creek. In the house Navajo rugs combine with paintings and antiques gathered during fourteen years in Spain, England and Ireland to provide striking furnishings. More than three thousand books, as well as periodicals like the *New Yorker* and the *Wall Street Journal,* are available to guests. Joyce Saer also maintains an antiques shop on the property. Although remote, this small, select horse-ranch is easy to reach.

Tennis, fly-fishing, hiking, painting, photography, fossil collecting, swimming in the creek and "just loafing" are some of the favorite activities; but the ranch caters most to horseback riders. English or western tack is available, and the trails for riding are virtually unlimited. Joyce Saer writes, "My horses are the BEST, and even the gentle ones are not nags." Local rodeos, including a cowboy roping practice every Thursday night, are other attractions for the horse enthusiast. Winters are cold and snowy, a time for cross-country skiing, snow shoeing, sleighing and skating.

"Many years ago a cowboy bitterly complained to the cook, 'I caint ride all day 'thout taters for breakfast'—with this in mind breakfasts are *hearty.*" Because the ranch is so isolated, lunch and dinner are also part of a stay here, featuring homegrown vegetables, ranch lamb, beef or chicken and a selection of wines.

Savery Creek Thoroughbred Ranch
Box 24
Savery, Wyoming 82332
(307) 383–7840

Joyce Saer

OPPOSITE: *A century ago, Eureka Springs was one of the famous Arkansas watering places. Although visitors no longer "take the waters" for health purposes, the old town is enjoying a revival as a well-preserved Victorian spa. Bridgeford Cottage is part of this renaissance.*

OUTLAW WAFFLES

SERVES 4 to 6.

A delicious and pretty treat. Make the topping *before* cooking the waffles.

Waffles
3 ½ cups flour
2 tsp. baking soda
2 tsp. baking powder
½ tsp. salt
4 Tbs. sugar
2 cups buttermilk
2 cups milk
⅔ cup oil
4 eggs

In a large bowl sift together the flour, baking soda, baking powder, salt and sugar; set aside. In a separate bowl beat together the buttermilk, milk, oil and eggs. Add to the dry ingredients and blend thoroughly.

Ladle the batter into a hot, well-oiled waffle iron. Cook until golden. Serve hot, with fruit topping (see below). Top each serving of waffles with a ring of whipped cream. Fill the ring with a generous spoonful of the prepared fruit. Serve immediately.

Topping
1 pint fresh blueberries or raspberries
½ cup confectioners' sugar
1 cup whipping cream

Clean and sort the berries and place in a bowl. Add all but 1 ½ Tbs. of the sugar to the fruit. Mash *slightly,* to release some of the juices, and stir. Cover and let sit.

Whip the cream, and when it is almost stiff add the remaining 1 ½ Tbs. sugar. Beat until stiff.

Hillcrest House
Chapel Hill, North Carolina

HILLCREST HOUSE IS located in a quiet, wooded neighborhood a mile from the University of North Carolina. Duke University is fifteen miles away, and the state capital at Raleigh is only thirty miles away. Whether you visit Chapel Hill on business or solely for pleasure, you will find it diverting to allow time in the evening to take advantage of the many cultural events available: plays, concerts, lectures, exhibits and films, among other happenings almost daily.

Breakfast at Hillcrest House is served either in the kitchen, the dining room or on the secluded brick patio. Betty York notes, "A typical breakfast for our guests might include waffles, poached eggs on corned beef hash, or omelets with buttermilk biscuits and bran muffins—all made from family recipes."

Hillcrest House
209 Hillcrest Road
Chapel Hill, North Carolina 27514
(919) 942-2369

Betty and James York

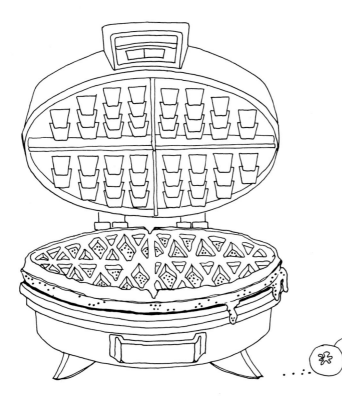

HILLCREST HOUSE WAFFLES

SERVES 2 to 4.

A plain but delicious waffle, well complemented by fresh fruits and syrups.

    1 cup flour
1 ½ tsp. baking powder
    1 Tbs. sugar
    2 eggs, separated
    1 cup milk
    4 Tbs. butter, melted

In a large bowl sift together the flour, baking powder and sugar. In a separate bowl beat the egg yolks until lemon-colored; add milk and melted butter, beat well. Add this to the dry ingredients and blend thoroughly. Beat the egg white until firm but not dry; fold into the batter. Allow batter to rest for a few minutes before spooning into a hot, well-oiled waffle iron. Serve waffles immediately, with pitchers of melted butter and maple syrup.

CHOCOLATE WAFFLES
Murphy's B&B (p. 13)

SERVES 4.

Chocolate in the morning may sound odd to some, but I love these as one item for a special brunch. They are always a big hit with guests.

Waffles
½ cup butter, melted
¾ cup sugar
2 eggs, separated
½ tsp. vanilla
3 oz. bittersweet chocolate, melted and cooled
1½ cups flour
2 tsp. baking powder
¼ tsp. salt
2 tsp. instant coffee
½ cup milk

Topping
whipped cream
fresh fruit in season

In a large bowl beat together the butter and sugar; add the egg yolks, vanilla and chocolate. Beat well. In a separate bowl sift together the flour, baking powder, salt and instant coffee. Add this to the chocolate mixture, alternately with the milk, blending well after each addition. Beat the egg whites until stiff; fold into the batter.

Ladle batter into a hot, well-oiled waffle iron and bake until crisp outside, dry inside. Serve topped with a dollop of whipped cream and fresh fruit in season.

Strawberries or peaches make excellent toppings. To prepare, peel or hull and slice the fruit, then sprinkle lightly with confectioners' sugar.

ORANGE WAFFLES
Manor House (p. 171)

SERVES 6.

These delicious waffles, with a subtle orange flavor, are crisp outside, fluffy inside. Wonderful for breakfast, but also suitable as a dessert waffle.

2 cups flour
3 tsp. baking powder
2 Tbs. sugar
½ tsp. salt
4 eggs
1 cup milk
4 Tbs. butter, melted
3 Tbs. finely grated orange zest

In a large bowl sift together the flour, baking powder, sugar and salt. In a separate bowl combine the eggs, milk and butter; beat well. Add the orange zest to the egg mixture; pour this into the flour mixture, one half at a time, beating well after each addition until the batter is smooth.

Ladle into a hot, well-oiled waffle iron, and cook until waffles are golden. Keep waffles warm in the oven while making the rest. Serve hot, with butter, jams and syrup.

PUMPKIN WAFFLES
Longswamp Bed & Breakfast (p. 249)

SERVES 4.

These rich waffles are perfect for a fall or winter breakfast.

1 cup flour
1½ tsp. baking powder
¼ tsp. salt
½ tsp. pumpkin pie spice
2 eggs
2 Tbs. brown sugar
1 cup half-and-half
4 Tbs. butter, melted
½ cup canned pumpkin
¼ cup finely chopped apple, peeled and cored
⅓ cup ground toasted walnuts or pecans

In a large bowl sift together the flour, baking powder, salt and spices; set aside. In a separate bowl beat together the eggs and brown sugar. Add the half-and-half, butter and pumpkin; beat well. Add this to the flour mixture and stir until just blended. Fold in the apples and nuts.

Ladle the batter into a hot, well-oiled waffle iron and cook until done. Serve hot with butter and warmed maple syrup.

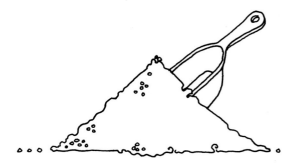

Casa de Solana

St. Augustine, Florida

FOUNDED IN 1598, St. Augustine is the oldest city in the United States. When Don Manuel Solana built his *casa*, or house, in 1763, Florida was still part of the Spanish Empire. The old mansion has thick coquina-shell walls, high ceilings with dark, hand-hewn beams, hand-pegged floors, marble hearths and cut glass chandeliers. Faye McMurry has furnished the house with antiques, and many of the rooms are graced with balconies offering views over the gardens to Matanzaz Bay.

A true "down-home, Southern breakfast," complete with grits and homemade banana-nut bread, is served in the formal dining room. The impressive mahogany table, ten feet long, is set with china, crystal and flatware that has been in the McMurry family for generations. In the center of the table, a basket brims over with freshly gathered flowers.

Casa de Solana
21 Aviles Street
St. Augustine, Florida 32084
(904) 824–3555

Faye McMurry

BELOW: *The views from the balconies and fine old arched windows of the Casa de Solana are among the finest in St. Augustine.* Photo by Henry Hird.

OPPOSITE: *The Bufflehead Cove Inn lies in complete seclusion along the banks of the Kennebunk River, where guests may enjoy bird-watching with their breakfast. The town of Kennebunkport is about a mile away.*

LOST BREAD

SERVES 2.

"This recipe was given to us several years ago by a Sarasota client who had become intensely interested in New Orleans cuisine. Its name, 'lost bread,' refers to the fact that it was a way to use stale bread. He said he did not know of any New Orleans restaurants that now serve it. We once saw a reference to lost bread in a culinary article about New Orleans, but it was described as plain French toast. The real secret of this recipe seems to be that the frying process caramelizes the strawberry preserves." —FAYE MCMURRY

4 slices French bread
2 Tbs. strawberry preserves
2 eggs
2 Tbs. half-and-half
    drop of vanilla extract
    confectioners' sugar

Using 1"-thick slices of French bread, cut the crust off the bottom and cut a pocket into the bread. Fill each pocket with preserves and then press the pocket closed.

In a shallow, wide bowl, beat the eggs with the half-and-half and vanilla. Soak the jam-filled bread in the egg mixture until it is completely absorbed.

Heat a little butter in a lightly oiled skillet until it sizzles. Place the bread in the pan and cook over medium heat as you would any French toast, turning when the bottom is golden and cooking until golden on both sides. Remove from the pan, drain briefly on paper toweling, sprinkle with confectioners' sugar and serve immediately.

Note: If you are preparing this for a large crowd, keep cooked bread warm in the oven and sprinkle with sugar *only just before* serving.

The Bufflehead Cove Inn
Kennebunkport, Maine

NAMED FOR the Arctic birds that winter in this area, The Bufflehead Cove Inn is a large, comfortable house built in 1910 along the banks of the Kennebunk River. Porches and decks overlook the water and the woods beyond. The river and cove are home to an ever-changing variety of birds, and the Gotts enjoy identifying them for guests.

Furnished largely with antiques, the house abounds with cozy window seats. On cold days, with a fire glowing in the living room fireplace, they are an invitation to curl up with one of the many books on Maine the Gotts have collected. Although only a mile from the town of Kennebunkport, guests enjoy a remote and idyllic setting.

Kennebunkport itself is known for its beautifully restored captains' mansions from the nineteenth century. The town also offers fine antiques shops and art galleries, live theatre in the summer and whale-watching excursions. There are also excellent golf courses to enjoy during spring, summer and fall.

Guests at the Bufflehead Cove Inn are served a full breakfast either in the dining room or (in warm weather) on the front porch overlooking the river. Harriet Gott varies the menu every day. "My breakfasts are usually at least three courses, so there's room for variety." Breakfast includes fresh fruit dishes, fresh juice, coffee and a selection of teas, and choices from a variety of egg dishes, pancakes, French toast, waffles, quiches and even lobster Newburg.

The Bufflehead Cove Inn
Gounitz Lane, P.O. Box 499
Kennebunkport, Maine 04046
(207) 967-3879

Harriet Gott

GREEN-APPLE STUFFED FRENCH TOAST

SERVES 8 to 10.

This is one of my favorite French toast recipes for fall and winter. The recipe requires a number of steps and is a little more time-consuming than some, so you may want to start some of the steps ahead of time.

      3 Tbs. dark rum
      4 Tbs. apple jelly
  1 ½ cups ricotta cheese
      ½ cup cream cheese
      1 cup grated Monterey jack (cheese)
      ½ cup apple butter
      2 Granny Smith apples, peeled, cored and chopped fine
      1 large loaf Italian bread, day old
      8 eggs
  1 ½ cups cream
      ¼ tsp. nutmeg

Preheat oven to 375°F.

Combine the rum and jelly in a small saucepan and heat to boiling. Remove from heat and let cool. In a large bowl combine the ricotta cheese, cream cheese, grated cheese and apple butter. Blend thoroughly. Stir in the apples. Slice the loaf into 1″ slices. Make a cut in the bottom of each slice, creating a pocket. Stuff the pocket with the cheese-apple mixture and press the opening closed. Place the bread in a large baking pan. In a bowl beat the eggs, cream and nutmeg; pour over the bread and let soak for one hour.

Cook the French toast in a little butter in a hot skillet until golden on both sides. Place in a baking pan, and pour on the rum glaze. Bake at 375° for 15 minutes. Serve immediately with warm maple syrup.

The Fowler House
Moodus, Connecticut

THIS EXQUISITIVE EXAMPLE of the Queen Anne style was built in 1890 as a private residence for Dr. Frank C. Fowler. Set facing the town green, the house is endowed with stained glass windows and skylights, hand-carved woodwork, elegant wallcoverings and fireplaces set with Italian tiles.

The quaint old Goodspeed Opera House and Goodspeed at Chester—both offering fine professional theatre—are just minutes away from the Fowler House in historic East Haddam, where antiques shops, fine restaurants and a variety of boutiques also await the visitor. In the summer, swimming, hiking, golfing and boating are available in the surrounding area. Ice-skating and cross-country skiing are popular in the winter.

The full breakfast at the Fowler House might include orange juice, broiled grapefruit, homemade granola, German apple pancakes, lemon yogurt bread and crumb cake muffins with homemade jams, coffee and assorted teas. Breakfast is served in the dining room around a common table with "plenty of good conversation." Room service is also available.

The Fowler House
P.O. Box 432, Plains Road
Moodus, Connecticut 06469
(203) 873-8906

Penny and Arnie Davidson
Barbara and Paul Ally

DOVER TOAST

SERVES 6.

This simple recipe is surprisingly delicious. It calls for ingredients that most households have on hand, making it a good dish to serve to unexpected guests when there is no time to run to the market.

3 eggs
1 cup cream
1 tsp. vanilla
1 tsp. cinnamon or 1 tsp. grated
   orange zest
6 English muffins
   fresh fruit for garnish

Beat the eggs; add the cream, vanilla and cinnamon or orange zest, beating well. Set aside. Split the English muffins with a fork. Prick each half with the fork and soak well in the egg mixture. Place a little butter (2 Tbs.) in a lightly oiled, hot skillet. When the butter is melted and just sizzling, place the muffin halves in the pan and cook over medium-low heat, so that the muffins cook through *slowly. Do not flatten with a spatula.* Turn once, cooking until golden on both sides.

Serve each person 2 halves; garnish with fresh fruit. Serve immediately with fruit syrups and butter.

LEFT: *In the nineteenth century, the coastal towns of eastern Connecticut were bustling ports. Today they bask in relative tranquility. Graceful mansions like the Fowler House are wonderful reminders of the past.*

OPPOSITE: *Built a year before the Fowler House, in a very different milieu, the Dove Inn is modeled on an English country villa.*

The Dove Inn

Golden, Colorado

CONVENIENTLY NEAR the historic district of downtown Golden, the Dove Inn is a restored Victorian villa built in 1889. The Colorado College of Mining—one of the oldest in the country—is nearby, Golden itself being the oldest mining town in the foothills of the Rocky Mountains. The Colorado Railroad Museum (one of the best in the country), the Golden Gate Canyon State Park and the Buffalo Bill Grave and Museum are other points of interest.

Once the territorial capital of Colorado, Golden is rich with history; and visitors can take the Golden Walk, which covers a mile and a half of the historic district and includes a stop at the Golden DAR Pioneer Museum—filled with memorabilia from the days of the gold rush through the 1930s. The Coors Brewery is also in Golden, and tours are available. Horseback-riding stables in the area provide an interesting way to see the countryside. Cattle-ranching land is found on the outskirts of town, and Denver is just twelve miles away.

Guests at the Dove Inn enjoy a full, hearty breakfast, served with "true Western hospitality."

The Dove Inn
711 14th Street
Golden, Colorado 80401
(303) 278–2209

Ken and Jean Sims

APPLE FRENCH TOAST WITH COTTAGE CHEESE

SERVES 6.

    6 apples, tart (Granny Smith, Pippin
       or the like)
    4 Tbs. butter
    6 Tbs. brown sugar
    1 tsp. cinnamon
 1½ cups cottage cheese at room
       temperature
    1 loaf day-old Italian bread
    8 eggs
  ½ cup milk

Core and slice, but do not peel, the apples. Sauté in the butter until slightly soft but still crunchy. Sprinkle with brown sugar, adjusting for desired tartness. Add the cinnamon; stir and cook until well blended. Leave over lowest heat while making the French toast.

Slice a loaf of slightly stale Italian bread into ½" to ¾" slices (this should give you 12 slices). Beat together the eggs and milk; soak the bread in the egg batter. Place a little butter in a well-oiled, hot skillet. When the butter sizzles add the slices of soaked bread and cook until golden on both sides.

To serve: Top each portion with a generous dollop of cottage cheese, and on top of that spoon the hot apple mixture. Serve immediately, with a selection of warm syrups.

Williams House Bed & Breakfast

Hot Springs National Park, Arkansas

A WONDERFUL EXAMPLE of American eclectic architecture, Williams House combines neoclassical, Gothic revival and arts and crafts elements into a delightful hodge-podge. With broad porches on both the first and second floors, it is set on a large, well-groomed yard with towering shade trees. The interior features some of the best of the craftsmanship available when it was built a century ago, and for this reason the house is on the National Register of Historic Places. Beautifully furnished with period antiques, the house is as comfortable as it is elegant. Williams House is centrally located in this historic town, within walking distance of downtown and the famous Bathhouse Row.

A full breakfast is served in the dining room with its oak wainscot. The table is set with linen, china and antique cut glass. The three different selections offered daily might include whole wheat pancakes, pecan waffles, create-your-own omelets, quiches, eggs benedict, homemade muffins and jams or french toast, to name just a few. According to Mary Riley, "People do not normally have a tendency to spoil themselves with a fancy breakfast, so we add special touches to complement the breakfast plates and to *look* extra-appealing. We will cater to special diets upon request. We use salt-free seasonings and quality ingredients at all times."

Williams House Bed & Breakfast
420 Quapaw
Hot Srings National Park, Arkansas 71901
(501) 624–4275

Mary and Gary Riley

BAKED TOAST ALMONDINE

SERVES 4.

Another variation on French toast. The topping is rich and delicious.

3 Tbs. butter
6 eggs
8 Tbs. cream
8 thick slices Italian bread, day-old

Preheat oven to 450°F.

Melt the butter and pour into a 9″ × 13″ baking pan; set aside. In a wide, shallow bowl, beat the eggs and cream. Soak the bread in the egg mixture, and then place in the prepared baking pan. Pour any remaining egg batter over the bread. Bake at 450° for 10 minutes, turn the slices over and bake for an additional 10 minutes.

While the bread is in the oven, make the topping.

Topping
4 Tbs. butter
1 cup sliced almonds
1¼ cups brown sugar
1 tsp. almond extract

Sauté the almonds in the butter until golden brown. Add the brown sugar and almond extract. Stir well and leave over low heat.

When the French toast has finished baking, spoon a little topping over each serving. Serve immediately.

LEFT: *With its stained glass and panelled wainscoting, the dining room at Williams House epitomizes the formality of an earlier time.*

OPPOSITE: *The Pentwater Inn is at its most welcoming in a winter landscape.*

The Pentwater Inn Bed & Breakfast
Pentwater, Michigan

THE STATELY OLD Pentwater Inn is a big clapboard-covered frame house built in 1880. Set among mature plantings on a generous lawn, the building has unusual second-story porches. The interior, furnished with antiques, is brightened by the many windows. The inn is located in a quiet neighborhood of old houses only two blocks from downtown Pentwater.

The town itself is home to a variety of interesting shops and restaurants. For lovers of outdoor activities, this area offers all kinds of water diversions—the inn is just a five-minute walk away from the beach—and in the winter, cross-country skiing is popular.

Dick and Sue Hand serve a continental-plus breakfast during the week, and on Sundays they go all-out with a full breakfast. The recipe for Skiers' French Toast was inherited from Janet Gunn, previous owner of this B&B, who like the Hands found it to be one of her most popular recipes.

The Pentwater Inn Bed & Breakfast
180 East Lowell Street
Pentwater, Michigan 49449
(616) 869–5909

Dick and Sue Hand

SKIERS FRENCH TOAST

SERVES 6 to 8.

This makes a delicious French toast casserole, particularly suitable for winter as its name implies. Busy cooks will like the fact that the recipe must be assembled in advance and refrigerated overnight, to be baked in the morning. As with all French toast recipes, use a good bakery or home-baked loaf of white bread.

      2 Tbs. corn syrup (light or dark, or a combination)
    ½ cup butter
      1 cup brown sugar, packed
      1 loaf white bread, thickly sliced
      5 eggs
  1 ½ cups milk
      1 tsp. vanilla
    ¼ tsp. salt

In a small saucepan combine the syrup, butter and brown sugar; simmer until syrupy. Pour this mixture into a 9″ × 13″ baking pan. Set aside.

Slice the loaf into thick slices, remove the crusts, and place on the syrup in the baking pan. You will have 2 even layers.

In a large bowl, beat together the eggs, milk, vanilla and salt. Pour evenly over the bread. *Cover and refrigerate overnight.*

In the morning leave the casserole at room temperature while the oven preheats. Bake at 350°, uncovered, for 45 minutes. Cut into squares and serve immediately. Serve with butter and a selection of syrups.

Victorian Bed & Breakfast Inn
Avoca, Iowa

THE EXTERIOR OF this Queen Anne house is entirely covered in fishtail shakes. In addition, the house has gables, dormers, a turret, fancy metalwork on the roof and a pedimented front porch. The house was constructed in 1904 by a leading builder of the time, who saw to it that the interior was every bit as fancy, with handcarved southern yellow pine woodwork throughout. The furnishings are comfortable Midwestern antiques, and the overall effect is bright and cheery.

Avoca is a peaceful farming community in southwestern Iowa, forty-five miles east of Omaha, Nebraska. The town annually hosts the National Old Time Country Music Contest, as well as the Pottawattamie County Fair. Avoca's lovely park is also home to a restored one-room schoolhouse, built in 1858—a delightful piece of Americana.

Guests at the Victorian Bed & Breakfast Inn receive a full breakfast in the formal dining room. Some of the specialties include eggs Benedict, a variety of quiches, pancakes and French toast, to name a few, accompanied by ham, bacon or sausage, and always juice, coffee and coffeecake.

Victorian Bed & Breakfast Inn
425 Walnut Street
Avoca, Iowa 51521
(712) 343–6336

Jan and Gene Kuehn

FRENCH TOAST PUFF

SERVES 4.

"This is an absolute favorite at the Inn."—JAN KUEHN.

An unusual variation on French toast. The bread is encased in a batter that frys up puffy and golden. This delicious treat is a hit every time I serve it.

2 cups flour
2 Tbs. sugar
1 Tbs. baking powder
   pinch of salt
2 eggs
1 cup milk
1 tsp. vanilla
8 thick slices of day-old white bread
   (homemade or bakery)

In a large bowl combine the flour, sugar, baking powder and salt; set aside. In a separate bowl beat the eggs, milk and vanilla; add to the flour mixture and beat well.

Dip the bread in the batter, coating well and evenly.

Heat a little (about 1/2") cooking oil in a skillet. When the oil is hot but not smoking, place batter-coated slices of bread in the oil. Lower the heat if necessary, so that the batter does not burn or brown too quickly; if the batter cooks too quickly, the bread inside will not be hot.

Cook until golden on both sides, remove from the skillet with a slotted spoon, and drain briefly on paper toweling. Sprinkle with confectioners' sugar and serve immediately. Accompany with butter and maple syrup.

The Victorian Bed & Breakfast Inn is a first-rate example of the restrained late-Victorian shingle style.

PEACHES-AND-CREAM FRENCH TOAST

Kenniston Hill Inn (p. 28)

SERVES 6.

This is an absolutely delicious recipe. Once tried, it quickly became a favorite in my house. Very pretty on the plate and a wonderful way to use summer peaches, this recipe is also good for a busy hostess, as it must be assembled the day before.

12 slices Italian bread, cut diagonally, ¾" thick
 6 eggs
 2 cups light cream
 4 Tbs. peach preserves
 1 tsp. nutmeg
 6 ripe peaches, peeled and sliced
 ¾ cup confectioners' sugar

Arrange the bread in a single layer in a large baking pan. Place the eggs, cream, preserves and nutmeg in a blender and process until well beaten; pour over the bread, turning the slices to coat evenly. *Cover and refrigerate overnight.*

The following morning, let the pan of soaked bread sit at room temperature while you prepare the peaches. Leave the prepared peaches covered and at room temperature, ready on a plate while you cook the French toast. Melt a little butter in a hot skillet, and cook the soaked bread until golden and hot—a few minutes on each side. Place 2 slices of French toast on each plate, top with 8 peach slices (one peach per person) attractively fanned out over the bread, and sprinkle with confectioners' sugar. Serve immediately.

Note: To make this recipe properly, you *must* peel the peaches. This may seem like a troublesome step, so here is a tip on how to do it easily and quickly. It *really* does make a difference; slices of peeled, ripe peach seem to melt in your mouth.

To peel a peach: Start with high-quality, ripe peaches. Cut the peach in half, going through the stem end. Pull the two halves apart; the pit should come out easily if the peach is ripe. Now cut each half in half again, again going the long way. Then, using a good paring knife, start at what was the stem end and just *lift* the skin off, pulling downwards. If the peach is ripe, you should be removing only skin, and no fruit.

Once you are in the habit of peeling peaches, you will never want to serve them with the skin again. Somehow the flavor is enhanced, and the fruit becomes a confection.

SUPER FRENCH TOAST À L'ORANGE

The Inn at Mitchell House (p. 130)

SERVES 4.

According to Tracy Stone, this is a "wonderful brunch item served with mimosas." This fabulous French toast recipe, with its rich orangey flavor, is a big hit every time I serve it. Must be assembled a day ahead.

 6 eggs
 ⅔ cup orange juice
 ⅓ cup orange liqueur
     (Grand Marnier)
 ⅓ cup milk
 3 Tbs. sugar
 ¼ tsp. vanilla
 ¼ tsp. salt
     finely grated zest of 1 orange
12 thick slices of day-old
     French bread

In a large bowl beat the eggs; add the orange juice, liqueur, milk, sugar, vanilla, salt and orange zest. Mix well. Dip the bread in the egg mixture and transfer to a large baking dish, in one layer. Pour the remaining egg mixture evenly over the bread in the pan. *Cover and refrigerate overnight.*

Let the soaked bread sit at room temperature for 15 minutes before cooking.

Melt a little butter in a large skillet. Add the bread and cook until golden brown on both sides. Serve 3 slices per person, topped with a generous sprinkle of powdered sugar. Serve immediately, accompanied by maple syrup.

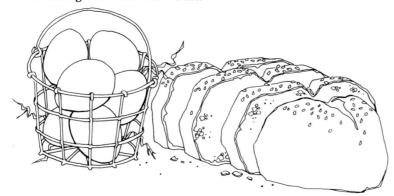

Holland House
Berlin, Maryland

BUILT AROUND 1900, Holland House is an unpretentious but solid and welcoming structure. Naming the house for the man who built it, Jim and Jan Quick have restored it with care and furnished it with a lovely collection of antiques. The house affords views of the yard, with its well-established plantings and gardens, where guests are always welcome to stroll and enjoy the setting.

Berlin is a small town just seven miles from the ocean. Holland House is located in a restored section in the center of town, an historic district that invites walking tours. Quaint antiques shops abound in this area, and many a "find" is waiting to be found. Nearby Assateague Island, a state and national seashore park, should be included in an exploration of the coast. Ocean City, golf courses, horse racing, diverse shopping and a wide range of restaurants are among the other attractions of the area.

In the morning a full breakfast is served in the dining room.

Holland House
5 Bay Street
Berlin, Maryland 21811
(301) 641–1956

Jim and Jan Quick

NIGHT-BEFORE FRENCH TOAST CASSEROLE

SERVES 6 to 8.

This is simple to make and calls for just a few basic ingredients; ideal for a hostess surprised by unexpected guests. Since it must be assembled the night before, the cook is free to do something more creative with a fruit dish or beverage in the morning. It comes out of the oven puffy and golden and is also well suited for a buffet-style breakfast.

1 loaf French or Italian bread, cut into 1" slices
3 eggs
3 cups milk
4 tsp. sugar
¾ tsp. salt
1 Tbs. vanilla
2 Tbs. butter, cut into small pieces
1 tsp. cinnamon

Grease a 13" × 9" × 2" baking pan. Arrange the bread in the pan. Beat together the eggs, milk, sugar, salt and vanilla. Pour over the bread evenly. *Cover and refrigerate overnight.*

Before baking, uncover and dot the top with the butter; sprinkle with the cinnamon. Bake at 350° for 45 minutes. Cut into squares and serve immediately with warmed maple syrup.

LEFT: *Holland House offers quiet elegance in a historic setting.*

OPPOSITE: *At Hersey House (see page 54), when the garden beckons, blueberry crepes are served outdoors.*

The John Palmer House
Portland, Oregon

BUILDER AND CONTRACTOR John Palmer clearly spared no expense when he put up his own house. In 1890, this meant turned or cut filigree on every gable, pediment, soffit or balustrade. The exterior also features an inviting wrap-around porch and second-story galleries. Resplendent in tan and brown, the old house is truly a "painted lady." The interior is decorated with comfortable antiques, wallpapers and fabrics of the late Victorian period. There are even a horse and buggy to take guests on a tour of the town.

Guests at the John Palmer House are served a full, gourmet breakfast in the lovely dining room. The table is set with antique silver and china, and blown and pressed glass. There is always a colorful centerpiece of fresh flowers. Mary Sauter gets some of her recipe and menu ideas from her son, a professional chef. Her Blueberry Crepes accompany fresh muffins, bacon, orange juice and coffee. "Quality is always important to us and the food we serve must be fresh, tasty and high in visual appeal," says Mary.

The John Palmer House
4314 N. Mississippi Avenue
Portland, Oregon 97217
(503) 284–5893

Mary Sauter

BLUEBERRY CREPES

SERVES 2.

Made with no flour, this is an "egg crepe."

  1 tsp. cornstarch
  ¼ cup water
  2 cups fresh or frozen blueberries
  ¼ cup sugar
  4 eggs
  8 Tbs. cottage cheese

Dissolve the cornstarch in the water. Place the blueberries in a saucepan and add the cornstarch mixture. Cook over medium heat until the berries are heated and a syrup begins to form. Add the sugar and continue cooking, stirring constantly, until the mixture has thickened. Leave over the lowest possible heat while you prepare the crepes.

Work with one egg at a time. Beat an egg well, and pour into a hot 6" skillet that has a small amount of melted butter in it. Tilt the pan so that the egg covers the entire bottom. Cook over medium-high heat until the egg is set in the center.

Remove the pan from the heat, place 2 Tbs. of cottage cheese in the center of the crepe, and fold the sides of the crepe over the cottage cheese. Slip off onto a heated plate. (Do not attempt to move crepes onto another plate after removing from the pan.)

Continue to cook each crepe in this manner; it will not take long. Allow 2 crepes per person, topped with a large spoonful of the blueberry topping. Serve immediately.

Note: You will have more blueberry sauce than you need to serve 2. Refrigerate and save the leftover sauce to serve over ice cream, French toast, pancakes or waffles.

BLUEBERRY-SAUCED BLINTZES

Richards' Bed & Breakfast (p. 87)

SERVES 8.

I put off trying this recipe because I thought it looked too time-consuming; but it really isn't, especially if it is started and partially assembled the day before. Rich and impressive, this recipe is well worth the effort.

Crepes
4 eggs
¾ cup water
¾ cup milk
2 Tbs. sugar
3 Tbs. triple sec or brandy
½ tsp. salt
3 Tbs. butter, melted

Filling
1 lb. ricotta cheese
1 egg, beaten
1 tsp. sugar
⅛ tsp. nutmeg

Blueberry Sauce
1 pint blueberries
1 tsp. water
½ cup sugar
½ tsp. grated orange zest
1 pint sour cream, for topping

To make the crepes: Combine all the ingredients in a food processor and blend completely. Let the batter rest for at least 1 hour before cooking the crepes. Then, pour a *little* batter into a hot 5" or 6" skillet that has a little butter sizzling in it. Quickly tilt the pan so that the batter covers the entire bottom.

Cook over medium heat until just set. The crepe will be pale; do not overcook. Cook the crepes one at a time (this recipe makes 16); and as they are done, set them on waxed paper.

To make the filling: Place all ingredients in a large bowl and blend well.

To fill the blintzes: Place a generous tablespoon of the filling in the center of each crepe. Overlap two opposite sides atop the filling. Then turn the ends over to form a pillow.

At this point, the filled blintzes may be covered and refrigerated over night. In the morning, make the blueberry sauce, and then fry the blintzes.

To make the sauce: Rinse and sort the blueberries. Place half the blueberries in a saucepan with the water and sugar; cook over medium-high heat, stirring, until the sugar dissolves and the sauce is thick. Add the rest of the blueberries and the orange zest, stir, and lower the heat to the lowest setting.

To fry the blintzes: Heat 3 Tbs. butter in a large skillet until it sizzles. Place the blintzes, seam side down, in the skillet and cook over medium-high heat until golden. Turn carefully, and continue cooking until golden on both sides.

Serve 2 blintzes per person, seam side down, topped with blueberry sauce and a dollop of sour cream.

BLINTZ CASSEROLE

The Bells Bed & Breakfast (p. 9)

SERVES 8.

Filling
1 lb. cottage cheese, drained
1 8 oz. pkg. cream cheese, softened
2 egg yolks
1 Tbs. sugar
1 tsp. vanilla

Batter
1½ cups sour cream
½ cup orange juice
6 eggs
¼ cup butter
1 cup flour
⅓ cup sugar
2 tsp. baking powder
½ tsp. cinnamon

Topping
sour cream
apricot preserves

To make the filling: Using an electric beater or food processor, mix all the ingredients; set aside.

To make the batter: Gradually add all the ingredients in a blender, in the order given. Pour half the batter into a greased 9" x 13" baking dish. Gently spread the filling over the batter; it will mix a little. Pour the rest of the batter over the filling. *Cover and refrigerate overnight.*

In the morning, bake at 350°, uncovered, for 50 to 60 minutes. The casserole will be sightly puffed and golden in color. Set on a rack to cool; then cut into squares, top each portion with a dollop of sour cream and preserves and serve immediately.

House on the Hill
High Falls, New York

BUILT IN 1825, House on the Hill is an eyebrow house (so named because of the narrow horizontal lights atop the windows), located in the historic hamlet of High Falls, New York. Set predictably enough on a hill, surrounded by a wrought iron fence, this handsome home offers the traveler a respite from the modern world.

The famous Mohonk Mountain House is nearby, as are Lake Minnewaska and Williams Lake. Part of the "snow belt," this area is a skier's paradise in winter with miles of cross-country ski trails, as well as plentiful ice-skating areas. Spring, summer and fall bring their own attractions, such as boating, hiking and foliage viewing. The roads wind among the hills, offering panoramic views at every turn. First-time visitors are sometimes surprised to find fine antiques shops and gourmet restaurants in this rural area, but they too are part of its appeal.

Guests at the House on the Hill are served a full breakfast in either the large kitchen, with its views of the pond and woods, or in the keeping room with its fine fireplace. A favorite winter menu is hot spiced cider, homemade pumpkin bread, freshly brewed coffee or tea, cheese blintzes with homemade sausage patties and red grapefruit.

House on the Hill
Box 86
High Falls, New York 12440
(916) 687–9627

Shelly and Sharon Glassman

CHEESE BLINTZES

SERVES 6.

Crepes
1 cup flour
⅛ tsp. salt
3 eggs
1½ cups milk
2 Tbs. oil

Filling
1 lb. cottage cheese
1 egg, beaten
1 tsp. sugar
8 saltine crackers, crushed

To make the crepes: Sift together the flour and salt. Beat in the eggs, one at a time. Gradually add first the milk and then the oil. Beat to a smooth consistency. Let stand at room temperature for 1 hour. Pour a *little* batter into a hot 6″ skillet, well coated with melted butter. Tilt the pan to cover the entire bottom. Cook for about 45 seconds, flip and cook the other side for about 10 seconds. Set on waxed paper until all 12 crepes are cooked and cooled.

To make the filling: Drain the cottage cheese so that it is dry. Add the egg and beat well. Mix in the sugar and cracker crumbs and blend thoroughly.

To assemble the blintzes: Put 1 heaping tablespoon of filling in each crepe and fold into a square. *May now be covered and refrigerated overnight.*

To cook: Sauté the blintzes in butter starting with the seam side down. Turn and continue cooking until golden on both sides. Serve 2 per person, topped with a dollop of sour cream.

The House on the Hill, located in an area noted for its unusual rock formations, abundant mountain laurel and picturesque trails, photographed during an equally picturesque snowstorm.

Eggs, Omelets, Souffles & Quiches

CREAMY SCRAMBLED EGGS 77
Spahn's Big Horn Mountain B&B

FANCY EGG SCRAMBLE 78
Pleasant View B&B

CHEESY SCRAMBLED EGGS IN PUFFY SHELL 79
Robin's Nest Inn

ZUCCHINI FRITTATA 80
The Captain Jefferds Inn

VOSS INN BAKED EGGS 80
Voss Inn B&B

AVOCADO OMELET 80
Hersey House

BAKED HERB CHEESE EGGS 81
The Fleming Jones Homestead

GARDEN SCRAMBLE 81
The Dove Inn

JANA'S KÄSE UND EIEER 81
The Rogers House B&B

SOUTH-OF-THE-BORDER SCRAMBLED EGGS 82
The Boyer YL Ranch

FRESH VEGETABLE & HERB OMELET 83
Fala Bed & Breakfast

SCOTCH EGGS 84
Elizabeth Street Guest House

SCOTCH EGGS 84
The Heartstone Inn

EGG STRATA 84
O'Connors Guest House

EGGS BENEDICT 85
Murphy's B&B

EGGS BENEDICT 85
Williams House B&B

EGGS PAULA 86
Toccoa River Hideaway

EGGS FLORENTINE 87
Richards B&B

EGGS JERUSALEM IN AN ORANGE CHAMPAGNE SAUCE 88
Carter House

CHIPPED BEEF AND EGG BAKE 88
The Bells Bed & Breakfast

BAKED HAM AND CHEESE SANDWICH 89
The Bells Bed & Breakfast

HAM AND EGGS AU GRATIN 89
Radcliffe Cross

HAM AND CHEESE SOUFFLÉ 89
Phoenix House

SAUSAGE SOUFFLÉ 90
The Old Talbott Tavern

AUNT MARIE'S CHEESE SOUFFLÉ 91
The Heirloom

CHEESE SOUFFLÉ 92
The Stagecoach Stop

BRUNCH EGG CASSEROLE 93
MacMaster House

ENGLISH HOUSE 24-HOUR SOUFFLÉ 94
The English House B&B

MISS DODIE'S EGGS 95
The Southern Hotel

POACHED EGGS WITH LEMON-CHIVE SAUCE 96
Manor House

EGG SOUFFLÉ 96
Hersey House

QUICHE LORRAINE 96
Hersey House

SAUSAGE MUSHROOM QUICHE 96
Lafayette House

TEXAS HAZLEWOOD QUICHE 97
Hazlewood House

SAUSAGE BREAKFAST CASSEROLE 98
Aldrich Guest House

CATLIN-ABBOTT BREAKFAST BAKE 99
The Catlin-Abbott House

SAUSAGE AND EGG BRUNCH CASSEROLE 100
Lafayette House

REUBEN BRUNCH CASSEROLE 101
The Inn on Kelley's Island

CREPE CUPS 102
Holden House

SAUSAGE-FILLED CREPES 103
The Frederick Fitting House

HOT CHICKEN SALAD CREPES 104
Robin's Nest Inn

ZUCCHINI CRESCENT PIE 104
Bridgeford Cottage

ITALIAN SPINACH PIE 105
The River Street Inn

The Aldrich House in Galena, Illinois (see page 98) began as a one-room dwelling in 1845. After several enlargements, it achieved its present size and its Italianate trim in the 1880s. During this period, President Grant was a frequent visitor.

WAYS OF PREPARING eggs range from the simple to the complex—this section offers more than twenty-five ways to serve eggs (not counting the recipes for casseroles, quiches and crepes). to the more complicated. Using the recipes in this section in rotation with those in "Pancakes, Waffles, French Toast and Crepes," and those in "Seafood," a host or hostess can serve a different main course at breakfast every day for more than three months without repeating once. The four recipes for crepes are for dishes both more substantial and less sweet than those given in the previous section.

The basic techniques for cooking eggs given here are intended both to help the novice and to add to the knowledge of any cook unsure of the best way to poach or boil an egg. Have eggs at room temperature for best results.

Sunny-side up. Use 1 tablespoon of butter or bacon drippings per egg. Heat the butter in a lightly oiled skillet until it sizzles. Then crack the egg with a single sharp rap against the edge of the pan and break the egg into the pan. (Some people prefer to break the egg into a saucer or shallow dish first and then slip it into the hot butter, to replace it if yolk is broken and to avoid any pieces of shell.) Cook the egg over medium heat, basting the top with the hot butter until the white is completely cooked and the yolk is set. (The more the yolk cooks, the paler yellow it becomes. Firm or runny yolk is a matter of personal preference.) Serve immediately.

Over easy. Much the same as cooking sunny-side up, except that the egg is flipped so it fries on both sides. There is no need to baste an egg if you are going to flip it. Use 1 tablespoon of butter or bacon drippings per egg and break the egg into the skillet when the butter sizzles. When the white is mostly but not completely done, flip the egg with a wide spatula, being careful not to break the yolk. Continue cooking over medium-high heat until the yolk is as set as desired. Serve immediately.

Scrambled. Allow 2 eggs and 1 tablespoon of cream per person. Break the eggs into a bowl; add the cream and beat with a fork. Melt 1 to 2 tablespoons of butter in a lightly oiled skillet; and when the butter is just sizzling, pour in the beaten eggs. Cook over medium heat, moving the eggs with a spatula so that the uncooked egg runs to the bottom of the pan to cook. Cook until just set and then remove from pan and serve immediately. For people who prefer dry scrambled eggs, just cook the eggs longer, continuing to move them around the pan with the spatula. If desired, you may season the beaten eggs and cream with a little salt and pepper (or with a choice of herbs or spices such as dill, sage or chives if you are so inclined).

Poached. Fill a lightly oiled skillet with fresh cold water. Heat the water until it is just about to boil, then lower the heat, and gently crack in the number of eggs you want to poach (my 8-inch skillet easily poaches 4 eggs at a time). If you prefer, you may have the eggs already broken into saucers. Once the eggs are in the water, adjust the heat so that the water is just simmering. If the water is boiling, the egg whites will swirl away from the egg yolk in strands. Once you master the correct water temperature, you will find that the eggs stay together in a nice cohesive shape. Allow the eggs to cook 3 to 5 minutes. Lift them out of the water with a slotted spoon and place them on toasted English muffins, or crisp-fried corned beef hash or whatever you have chosen. Serve immediately.

Soft boiled. Place eggs in a pan and cover with cold water. Bring the water to a boil, then immediately cover the pan and remove it from the heat. Let the eggs sit for 3 to 5 minutes. Using a slotted spoon lift the eggs from the water and put them in egg cups, narrow end up. Serve immediately.

Hard boiled. Place the eggs in a pan and cover with cold water. Bring the water to a boil, then immediately cover the pan and remove it from the heat. Let the eggs sit for 10 minutes. Place the eggs in a colander and rinse with cool water. Let the eggs sit for a few minutes before shelling.

As part of a full breakfast, the recipes given here would generally follow the fruit course. Two later sections, "Breakfast Meats" (page 115) and "Vegetables & Side Dishes" (page 127) present side-dishes that can be used to complement these recipes, adding color to the plate as well as flavor to the meal.

Spahn's Big Horn Mountain Bed & Breakfast

Big Horn, Wyoming

A HUNDRED MILES of view and a million acres of public forest land surround Spahn's Big Horn Mountain Bed and Breakfast, which is situated on the side of Big Horn Mountain. This setting offers plenty of peace and quiet and breathtaking scenery; deer, wild turkeys, moose and sometimes bears or mountain lions can be seen from Spahn's. There are miles of walking trails for hikers and excellent cross-country skiing in the winter.

The large log house, built by Ron Spahn and his wife Bobbie, seems right at home among the towering evergreens. The living room has a cathedral ceiling and open fireplace, and guests are welcome to use the library and piano.

A full breakfast that includes fresh fruit in season, eggs, sausage and cinnamon rolls baked in a wood-fired kitchen range send guests off ready to make the most of the day. In warm weather, breakfast is served on the deck, with its incredible view.

Spahn's Big Horn Mountain Bed & Breakfast
P.O. Box 579
Big Horn, Wyoming 82833
(307) 674–8150

Ron and Bobbie Spahn

CREAMY SCRAMBLED EGGS

SERVES 4.

    8 eggs
 ¼ cup milk
 ¼ tsp. salt
    dash of freshly ground pepper
    2 Tbs. butter
    8 oz. cream cheese, cut in ½" cubes
    1 Tbs. chopped fresh chives
    1 tsp. chopped fresh parsley for
       garnish

In a large bowl beat together the eggs, milk, salt and pepper. In a large, lightly oiled skillet, heat the butter to sizzling. Pour in the egg mixture. When the eggs just begin to set on the bottom, run a spatula underneath, lifting up the cooked egg and letting the uncooked egg flow to the bottom of the pan. Sprinkle in the cream cheese pieces and the chopped chives. Continue cooking in the standard manner for scrambled eggs. When the eggs are set, the cheese will be melted. Serve immediately, garnished with the chopped parsley.

An artist's rendering of the Big Horn Mountain Bed & Breakfast emphasizes the great log building's isolation from people and its closeness to the forest.

Pleasant View B&B

Regent, North Dakota

BUILT AS A farmhouse in 1914, Pleasant View B&B today combines the artifacts of an earlier era with today's conveniences. During the warm months, for example, guests are invited to use the heated pool, play a lively game of volleyball or take on a slow-paced but hotly contested game of croquet. The neighboring town has not only public tennis courts, but also a lovely city park and the county museum, which includes a drugstore that has been named to the National Register of Historic Places.

The hosts at Pleasant View B&B also maintain accommodations on Lake Sakakawea and will make arrangements for a fishing trip there. The famous Badlands are only a few miles away.

Guests enjoy a hearty breakfast at the kitchen table. Through generous windows, they enjoy a view of the fields and woods where deer often graze.

Pleasant View B&B
Box 211
Regent, North Dakota 58650
(701) 563–4542

Marlys Prince

FANCY EGG SCRAMBLE

SERVES 8.

This must be assembled the night before, refrigerated and baked in the morning.

½ cup butter
1 cup chopped ham
½ cup chopped green onion
½ cup chopped green pepper
½ cup chopped mushrooms
12 eggs, beaten
3 Tbs. flour
½ tsp. salt
⅛ tsp. pepper
2 cups milk
1 cup grated cheddar cheese
3 slices white bread, trimmed and cubed
⅛ tsp. paprika

Sauté the ham, onions, peppers and mushrooms in 3 tablespoons of the butter. Add the beaten eggs and scramble. Remove from the heat and put in a large mixing bowl.

In a saucepan melt 3 tablespoons of butter. Blend in the flour. Add the milk and stir until bubbly. Add the cheese, stirring until melted. Remove from heat and pour into the scrambled egg mixture. Stir until well combined and then spoon into a greased 11" × 7" × 2" baking dish. Distribute the bread cubes evenly over the top of the eggs. Melt the remaining 2 tablespoons of butter and drizzle over the bread cubes. Sprinkle with paprika. *Cover and refrigerate overnight.*

Remove from the refrigerator 45 minutes before baking. Bake uncovered at 350° for 30 to 40 minutes. Remove from oven, cut into squares and serve hot with biscuits.

Robin's Nest Inn

Council Bluffs, Iowa

A PROSPEROUS FAMILY of Polish immigrant grocers built this Italianate Victorian, with its gingerbread porch and gallery and its French doors, in the 1880s. The interior still contains the original gas and electric light fixtures. With its soaring ceilings, pocket doors, pressed tin cornices and authentic stenciled walls, it is a fragment of an earlier time. The decorations include many family heirlooms.

Points of interest in the area include the Lincoln Monument, the Lewis and Clark Monument, the Henry Doorly Zoo, the Desoto Bend Wildlife Refuge and Lake Manawa. The house is within walking distance of historic Haymarket Square, a commercial area recently listed on the National Register of Historic Places.

A full breakfast is served in the sunny dining room.

Robin's Nest Inn
327 9th Avenue
Council Bluffs, Iowa 51503
(712) 323–1649

Dorothea Smith and Wendy Storey

Like other Victorian villas, Robin's Nest Inn offers an abundance of airiness and light.

CHEESY SCRAMBLED EGGS IN PUFFY SHELL

SERVES 6.

Pastry Shell
¼ cup butter
½ cup water
½ cup flour
½ tsp. baking soda
½ tsp. baking powder
    dash salt
2 eggs

Preheat oven to 400°F.

Place the butter and water in a saucepan. Bring to a boil. Add the flour, baking soda, baking powder and salt. Stir just until the mixture forms a ball. Remove from heat. Add the eggs one at a time, beating well after each addition. Spread the dough evenly in a greased 9″ pie plate. Bake at 400° for 15 to 18 minutes, or until puffed and golden.

Scrambled Eggs
¼ cup chopped green onion
¼ cup chopped green pepper
¼ cup chopped mushrooms
8 eggs
1½ cups grated cheddar cheese
6 pieces of crisp bacon

Sauté the vegetables in a little butter. Beat the eggs and add the sautéed vegetables. Scramble the eggs in a skillet with a little butter heated to sizzling. Cook, stirring gently to scramble, just until set.

When the pastry shell has finished baking, fill it with the scrambled egg mixture. Sprinkle the cheese evenly over the top. Lower oven temperature to 350° and return dish to oven for a few minutes, until the cheese melts.

Cut into 6 portions and top each with a piece of bacon. Serve immediately.

ZUCCHINI FRITTATA

The Captain Jefferds Inn (p. 15)

SERVES 10.

This popular breakfast item at the Captain Jefferds Inn is a great way to use overabundant summer zucchini—often a challenge to the New England gardener!

  6 medium-size zucchini
  2 cloves garlic
⅓ cup olive oil
20 eggs
¾ cup milk
  1 Tbs. salt
  1 tsp. freshly ground pepper
½ cup fresh sweet basil, chopped
½ cup parmesan cheese
    paprika
10 fresh basil leaves

Preheat oven to broil.
   Slice the zucchini into ½″ sections and chop coarsely. Heat 1 Tbs. of the olive oil in a 12″ skillet, add the zucchini and garlic (minced or pressed) and sauté until almost soft. Remove from pan and set aside.
   In a large bowl beat the eggs, milk, salt, pepper and chopped basil. Add the remainder of the olive oil to the pan, heat, and pour in the egg mixture. Cook over moderate heat until fluffy, add the zucchini-garlic and cook until semi-firm. Top with cheese, paprika and basil. Place until broiler for a few minutes until slightly brown. Slice as a pie and serve immediately.

VOSS INN BAKED EGGS

The Voss Inn (p. 27)

SERVES 1.

These are easy to prepare and so rich that one per person is plenty.

1 slice Canadian bacon
1 Tbs. sour cream
1 egg
2 Tbs. grated cheddar cheese
1 tsp. chopped green onion

Preheat oven to 350°F.
   Place slice of Canadian bacon in greased ramekin. Spread sour cream over bacon. Break egg into ramekin. Top with grated cheddar cheese mixed with green onion.
   Place the ramekin in a pie plate with a little water in the bottom. Bake at 350° for 15 to 20 minutes, or until set. Run a knife around the edge of the ramekin and carefully slip the baked egg onto a slice of toast or a toasted English muffin.
   Variation: A piquant salsa may be substituted for the sour cream. At the Voss Inn, they use La Victoria Salsa Suprema.

AVOCADO OMELET

Hersey House (p. 54)

MAKES 2 omelets.

I served this one morning to guests who said they didn't think they liked avocado but were willing to try something new. They loved this tangy dish and wanted the recipe. Make sure the avocados are ripe.

   1 medium-sized, ripe avocado
1½ Tbs. mayonnaise
   1 Tbs. fresh lemon juice
   1 Tbs. red onion, finely chopped
     salt and pepper to taste
   4 eggs
   2 Tbs. cream
   2 Tbs. butter
     sour cream
     Mexican hot sauce (salsa)

Halve, pit and peel the avocado. Chop it into small bits; combine in a bowl with mayonnaise, lemon juice and chopped onions. Mash slightly and stir together thoroughly. Season to taste with salt and pepper. Set aside.
   Beat the eggs and cream together. Using 2 skillets over medium high heat, melt 1 Tbs. butter in each and pour ½ the egg mixture into each. When the eggs are nearly set but still moist on top, spoon half of the avocado mixture onto each omelet. Fold one side over the other and leave each in its pan over low heat for another minute or two. Slide onto warm plate. Top with a dollop of sour cream and Mexican hot sauce. Serve immediately.

BAKED HERB CHEESE EGGS

The Fleming Jones Homestead (p. 122)

SERVES 1.

This is a delicious way to serve eggs, so rich that one egg per person is plenty.

1 Tbs. melted butter
1 egg
1 Tbs. half and half
1 Tbs. grated sharp cheddar cheese
  pinch Italian herbs
  parsley
  ground black pepper
  parmesan cheese
  paprika

Preheat oven to 350°F.

Pour melted butter into an individual serving-size ramekin or custard dish. Break the egg into the dish. Pour in the half and half. Sprinkle the grated cheese over the half and half. Sprinkle herbs, a pinch of parsley, a shake of parmesan cheese, a little ground black pepper and paprika over top. Place ramekin in a baking dish; carefully add water until the ramekin is sitting in about 1" of water. Bake at 350° for 20 minutes.

To serve, run a knife around the edge of the ramekin, drain off any excess liquid, and slip the baked egg onto a toasted English muffin half. Serve immediately.

Variation: The baked egg may be served on a muffin topped with Canadian bacon, a thick slice of ripe tomato, or 2 pieces of crisp bacon.

GARDEN SCRAMBLE

The Dove Inn (p. 65)

SERVES 4.

"This one is always a hit. We have a garden in the summer and use our own homegrown vegetables in this"—JEAN SIMS.

8 pieces of bacon
1 small summer squash, or zucchini, sliced thin
1 clove garlic, crushed
4 scallions, chopped
8 eggs
2 Tbs. cream
½ cup parmesan cheese, grated

Fry bacon until crisp, drain on paper toweling, and set aside.

Sauté together the squash, scallions and garlic in a little butter until just tender and golden. (The squash should still be a little crunchy, and the garlic should not burn).

Beat the eggs with the cream, and pour over the sautéed vegetables in the hot skillet. Sprinkle with ¼ cup parmesan and stir mixture as if making scrambled eggs.

When done, remove to plates and sprinkle top with remaining parmesan and crumbled bacon (2 slices per serving).

JANA'S KÄSE UND EIEER

The Rogers House Bed & Breakfast (p. 23)

SERVES 8.

A unique and simple egg and cheese dish that is always a hit at the Rogers House.

½ cup butter
12 eggs
1 lb. Monterey jack cheese, grated
1 pint small curd cottage cheese
½ cup flour
1 tsp. baking powder
2 cups finely chopped ham (optional)

Preheat oven to 400°F.

Melt the butter and pour into a 9" × 13" baking pan, making sure the bottom of the pan is coated. In a large bowl beat the eggs slightly, and stir in the cheeses. Combine the flour and baking powder and add to the egg/cheese mixture, blending thoroughly. If desired, add the chopped ham. Pour into the baking pan, and bake at 400° for 15 minutes. Lower the oven temperature to 350° and continue baking for another 20 minutes. Cut into squares and serve hot.

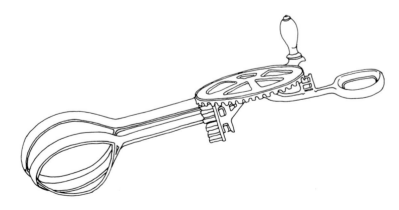

The Boyer YL Ranch

Savery, Wyoming

FOUNDED BY Jack and Mary Boyer in 1910, Boyer YL Ranch was, and still is, a large sheep, cattle and horse ranch. Located about nine miles from Savery (population twenty-five), the ranch house, guest cabins, barns, saddle house, blacksmithy and corrals are nestled among huge cottonwood trees. Hay meadows border the entrance road. Jack Boyer's old polo field sits directly in front of the ranch-house. Nearby, Savery Creek meanders on its way to the Little Snake River, beckoning to the trout fisherman or inviting the swimmer in for a dip on a hot summer day.

Part of the ranch borders on Medicine Bow National Forest, which abounds with wildlife, ghost towns and old mines, as well as Battle Lake. A few miles to the west lies the Red Desert, with its fossils, formations, badlands, Indian arrowheads and wild horses and antelope. This area is also home to a wide range of birds, including bald eagles, hummingbirds, sharptail grouse and sand hill cranes.

The ranch caters to people looking to "get away from it all"; there's fishing, horseback riding, tennis, swimming and just plain "loafing" available. The large and eclectic library in the ranch house should suit just about all tastes. The expansive lawns, bordered with flower beds, are an inviting spot to relax. The ranch house, which is maintained much as it was fifty years ago, contains original hand-hewn beds and claw-foot bath tubs.

A full breakfast is served in the Roundup Room off the ranch house kitchen. Orange juice, hot coffee or tea, bacon and eggs or waffles with butter and syrup are the most popular choices. After breakfast "you may want to watch the horses being saddled, or help with same, or sit in the sunlight on the front lawn with a last cup of coffee."

The Boyer YL Ranch
Box 24, Savery, Wyoming 82332
(307) 383-7840

Joyce Saer, caretaker

SOUTH-OF-THE-BORDER SCRAMBLED EGGS

SERVES 4.

A spicy variation on scrambled eggs.

8 eggs
¼ cup cream
2 cups salsa
3 Tbs. butter

In a large bowl beat together the eggs and cream. Stir in the salsa. Heat the butter in a large skillet until it sizzles, then pour in the egg mixture and scramble in the standard manner. Serve hot, with crisp bacon and fresh biscuits.

Fala Bed & Breakfast
Hyde Park, New York

NAMED FOR FDR's famous "little dog," Fala Bed and Breakfast is in a charming town on the Hudson River about a two-hour drive north of New York City. Franklin and Eleanor Roosevelt lived in the Roosevelt family mansion in Hyde Park, now open to the public for tours, and both are buried on the grounds. One of the Vanderbilt mansions is also here, likewise open for tours. Vassar College and Marist College are both nearby, and the Culinary Institute of America is three miles away.

Guests at Fala B&B stay in a cottage furnished with wicker and antiques, located behind the Martinez home. In the morning they walk down the short path to the solarium for breakfast. The herbs used in the omelets at Fala B&B come from the Martinez herb garden, picked and chopped daily. Any vegetables ripe in their garden (zucchini, tomatoes, swiss chard, spinach and the like) are also harvested for breakfast omelets. The fresh fruits served—including strawberries, raspberries, blueberries and apples—always come from local "U-Pick" farms.

Fala Bed & Breakfast
East Market Street
Hyde Park, New York 12538
(914) 229-5937

Maryann Martinez

FRESH VEGETABLE & HERB OMELET

SERVES 2.

Omelets are always popular at breakfast and this one is very good. The green spinach and red tomato make for a pretty presentation. Make this when tomatoes are in season.

```
 4  large eggs
¼  cup milk
¼  cup grated cheddar cheese
    fresh ground black pepper
 1  ripe tomato, chopped
½  cup fresh spinach, cleaned and
        chopped
½  tsp. each of these fresh herbs,
        finely chopped:
        basil
        rosemary
        chives
        parsley
```

Melt 2 Tbs. butter in a skillet. With a whisk blend eggs, milk, pepper and cheese. Pour into the hot skillet. Allow the omelet to cook about half way, then add the fresh tomato and spinach. Sprinkle with herbs. Carefully fold omelet in half. Continue cooking for another minute or two. Serve immediately.

LEFT: *With sauce and garnish, eggs Benedict appeal to the eyes as well as the palate. This is how they are served at Barrow House (page 207).*

OPPOSITE: *Flowers can be expensive to buy, but they cost almost nothing to grow. Even a small bouquet in a simple vase or pot can bring a room to life. These come from the cutting garden at Murphy's B&B (page 13).*

SCOTCH EGGS

Elizabeth Street Guest House (p. 57)

SERVES 6.

"This always gets raves! Guests want to know how the eggs get in there. I'm happy to share the secret." —SHERYL CLARK, hostess of the Elizabeth Street Guest House

Dijon mustard and Parmesan cheese add a delicious tangy flavor. This recipe is made a day in advance.

    6 hard-boiled eggs, cooled
         and shelled
    1 lb. bulk sausage, uncooked
    3 tsp. Dijon mustard
    ¾ cup bread crumbs
    ¾ cup parmesan cheese

Oven temperature: 350°F.
    Cut sausage into 6 equal portions. Mold each sausage portion around a boiled egg completely covering the egg. Brush with Dijon mustard. Combine the bread crumbs and parmesan cheese; roll the eggs in this, covering them thoroughly. *Refrigerate overnight.* Next morning, bake on cookie sheet at 350° for 20 to 25 minutes until sausage is thoroughly cooked. Cool 3 to 5 minutes, slice in half and serve.

SCOTCH EGGS

The Heartstone Inn (p. 160)

SERVES 4.

These are a delicious change from standard breakfast egg preparations. The recipe may be prepared a day in advance and refrigerated, then baked in the morning. Scotch Eggs are rich; one per person is plenty.

    1 egg, beaten.
    1 lb. bulk sausage meat, uncooked
    4 hard-boiled eggs, shelled
    ¾ cup bread crumbs

Preheat oven to 375°F.
    Mix the egg and the sausage meat together. Divide the mixture into four equal parts. Mold each sausage portion around a shelled hard-boiled egg, completely covering the egg. Roll each in the bread-crumbs until well coated. The eggs should have a well-shaped, even covering of sausage and bread crumbs.
    Place in a baking pan and bake at 375° for 45 minutes. Serve hot.

EGG STRATA

O'Connor Guest House Bed & Breakfast (p. 190)

SERVES 8 to 10.

This is a tasty breakfast casserole, ideal for a large crowd. It comes out of the oven puffy and golden. Since it is assembled the day before, it eliminates standing over a hot stove in the morning.

    12 slices bread (a good white bread
          is best)
    ½ cup chopped onion
    ½ cup chopped mushrooms
    10 strips bacon
    1 cup grated Swiss or cheddar
          cheese
    12 eggs
    4 cups milk

Oven temperature: 350°F.
    Cut crusts from the bread. Butter on both sides and place 6 slices in the bottom of a 9" × 12" pan. Keep the other 6 slices aside.
    Sauté the onions and mushrooms. Set aside.
    Cook the bacon until crisp. Drain on paper towling. Crumble. Set aside.
    Spoon half the mushrooms, onions and bacon over the bread, covering evenly. Cover this with half the grated cheese. Repeat the layers again, starting with a layer of bread and ending with the grated cheese.
    Beat together the eggs and milk and pour over the casserole. *Cover and refrigerate overnight.*
    Bake at 350° for 30 minutes, covered; then for 30 minutes uncovered. Cut into squares and serve hot.

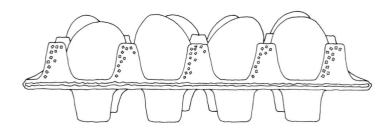

EGGS BENEDICT
Murphy's B&B (p. 13)

SERVES 4.

Bacon, Eggs, and Muffins
4 or 8 poached eggs (1 or 2 per person)
4 slices Canadian bacon, grilled
4 English muffins, split and grilled

Hollandaise Sauce
3 egg yolks
2 Tbs. fresh lemon juice
¼ tsp. white pepper
½ cup butter, melted
1 Tbs. fresh chopped chives

For directions on poaching eggs, turn to the beginning of this chapter.

You may toast the English muffin halves, but a tip from my brother-in-law, Brad Murphy, is to grill them. Grilled muffins stay hot longer than toasted and thus keep the whole dish hot longer.

Put the egg yolks, lemon juice and pepper in a blender and process for a minute. With the blender running, pour in the melted butter, sizzling hot, in a slow, steady stream. Continue blending until the sauce is the desired thickness, usually a couple of minutes.

Because this sauce is prepared so quickly and served hot, have the poached eggs, Canadian bacon and muffins ready before you make the sauce.

Top the English muffins with the Canadian bacon, then the poached eggs, and cover with Hollandaise Sauce. Sprinkle a few fresh chives over the Hollandaise. Serve hot.

If desired, garnish each serving with 2 stems of freshly steamed asparagus or ripe tomato wedges.

EGGS BENEDICT
Williams House Bed & Breakfast (p. 66)

SERVES 4.

Eggs Benedict is a classic breakfast or brunch dish. This sauce recipe is a little more complicated than the one given in the preceding recipe, but it is delicious and worth the effort. I usually find that one egg per person is fine, since this is such a rich dish, but you may increase that to two. You will have enough sauce.

Eggs, Ham and Muffins
4 poached eggs
4 English muffins, split, toasted and buttered
4 slices baked ham, warmed

Sauce
3 Tbs. white wine vinegar
1 Tbs. water
1 bay leaf
several peppercorns
3 egg yolks
1½ sticks butter
dash cayenne pepper
1 tsp. salad herbs
1 tsp. dry mustard

To make the sauce: Assemble the sauce before poaching the eggs. Keep warm on the back of the stove; do *not* overcook.

Combine the vinegar, water, bay leaf and peppercorns in a small pan. Boil until reduced to 1 Tbs. of liquid. Strain and set aside to cool. Place the egg yolks and 1 Tbs. butter in the top of a double boiler and heat slowly, whisking constantly. Add the vinegar mixture, and the remaining butter, 1 Tbs. at a time. Add the cayenne pepper, salad herbs and dry mustard, whisking constantly over low heat until it thickens.

To poach the eggs: Fill a well-oiled skillet with cold water. Bring to a boil. Reduce the heat, and when the water stops boiling, give each egg a firm rap against the edge of the skillet and break open the shell, being careful not to break the yolk, and carefully slip the eggs into the water. Cook the eggs over medium high heat (the water should be just shy of boiling), until the whites are done and the yolk has turned an opaque yellow color around the edges. How firm or runny you prefer your poached eggs is a personal choice. Most people like the yolk to be slightly runny in the very center but done around the edges.

While the eggs are poaching, toast the English muffins.

To serve: Lift the poached eggs from the water with a slotted spoon and place each on top of a toasted and buttered English muffin already covered with a slice of ham. Top with sauce and serve immediately.

Variation: Substitute a thick slice of garden-fresh tomato for the ham.

Toccoa River Hideaway

Blue Ridge, Georgia

A PRIVATE RETREAT beside a beautiful river, nestled in a peaceful valley, Toccoa River Hideaway provides the visitor a base from which to explore the Blue Ridge Mountains. Lake Blue Ridge is two miles away, offering beach swimming, boating and waterskiing. The Occoee River, just fifteen minutes away, is popular for white-water rafting. The Chattahoochee National Forest has a wide range of hiking trails, and the surrounding area is known for its lakes and scenic countryside. Other attractions include bluegrass and country music festivals, antiques and craft shops, the mining museum, horseback riding and touring restored historic buildings.

Charles Hay tells this story about the accompanying recipe: "One Easter we were faced with quite a dilemma. Our larder contained only two dozen eggs, some leftover boiled rice, and a half bottle of white wine. We live in an isolated mountain community and, of course, no stores were open on Easter Sunday. What to serve for breakfast? Some fast thinking led to the following recipe, which we call Eggs Paula after the guest we first served it to."

Breakfast at Toccoa River Hideaway is fresh and wholesome. Among other treats are homemade apple butter, freshly churned butter, homemade apple cider and homemade breads. "We feel this combination is full of the flavors of the apple-growing region and also gives our guests a sense of the history of our valley," notes Charles Hay.

Toccoa River Hideaway
P.O. Box 300
Blue Ridge, Georgia 30513
(404) 632-2411

Charles Hay

EGGS PAULA

SERVES 6.

Rice Cakes
2 cups cooked rice, cold
3 eggs, beaten
½ cup self-rising flour

Combine the rice with the beaten eggs. Add flour and mix but do not beat. Heat a generous layer of oil in a large cast-iron skillet. Drop tablespoons of the batter into the hot oil and flatten them gently with a spatula. Cook until golden brown on both sides. This should make 12 rice cakes. Place the cooked rice cakes on paper toweling and keep in a warm (200°) oven.

Sauce Bearnaise
¼ cup white wine
2 Tbs. vinegar
1 Tbs. tarragon
1 Tbs. minced onion
3 egg yolks
¾ cup butter, melted and cooled
2–3 drops Tabasco sauce

Combine the wine, vinegar, tarragon and onion in a saucepan and bring to a boil. When reduced to about 2 Tbs. liquid, remove from the heat and let cool. Place in a double boiler over medium heat and beat in the egg yolks until the mixture thickens. Remove from the heat and beat in the butter, a tablespoon at a time. Add the Tabasco sauce. Cover the sauce and keep warm while the eggs are poaching.

Eggs
12 eggs, poached

To serve: Place 2 rice cakes on each plate, top each rice cake with a poached egg and cover with Sauce Bearnaise. Serve immediately. Grilled Canadian bacon goes well with this dish.

Richards' Bed & Breakfast
Narragansett, Rhode Island

DURING THE nineteenth century, the Hazard family was well known in southern Rhode Island both for skill in building with granite and for civic generosity. They donated several buildings, including a library, to towns in the area. One member of the Hazard clan claimed to be a follower of the Druids, through whose intervention the entire design for the house came to him in dreams. He built the house in 1884, calling it Druid's Dream, a name that can still be seen carved in the granite lintel above the front door.

Today, as Richards' Bed & Breakfast, this handsome stone house — surrounded by the lawns, gardens and woods of this twenty-acre estate — is a peaceful, private refuge only a few minutes from the center of town.

The house has a forty-foot entry hall, eleven fireplaces and French doors opening onto the south lawn. Steven and Nancy Richards have restored the house with great care; furnishings are antique.

Narragansett Beach, one of New England's finest, is about a mile away. Opposite the beach, the center of town has a small cluster of specialty shops, boutiques and cafes. Other points of interest nearby include the University of Rhode Island, historic Newport and the bustling fishing port of Galilee.

Nancy Richards is a skillful cook, and her guests are treated to a full breakfast served in the elegant dining room. The entrées are out of the ordinary and vary daily.

Richards' Bed & Breakfast
144 Gibson Avenue
Narragansett, Rhode Island 02882
(401) 789–7746

Steven and Nancy Richards

EGGS FLORENTINE

SERVES 8.

My guests love this dish, and it is one of my favorites too. Impressive but quite easy to make, it emerges from the oven puffed up like a soufflé, with a flavor that is out of this world.

  1 pkg. frozen chopped spinach
  8 eggs
½ cup butter, melted
½ lb. swiss cheese, grated
½ lb. feta cheese, crumbled
⅛ tsp. nutmeg

Preheat oven to 350°F.

Cook the spinach according to the directions. Drain well in a colander, then squeeze in paper toweling to remove all moisture. Set aside. In a large bowl beat the eggs well. Add the melted butter, cheeses and nutmeg and stir well. Add the spinach and blend thoroughly. Pour into a greased 9″ × 12″ baking dish or individual ramekins and bake at 350° for 30 minutes. Cut into squares or release from ramekins and serve immediately.

OPPOSITE: *Deep in the mountains of northern Georgia, the Toccoa River Hideaway provides rural solitude overlooking a quiet river.*

LEFT: *Antique lace festoons the canopy of one of the beds in Richards' Bed & Breakfast.*

EGGS JERUSALEM WITH ORANGE CHAMPAGNE SAUCE

Carter House (p. 34)

SERVES 2.

Clearly, this recipe is somewhat time consuming. But don't be put off by it. Read it carefully before beginning and organize as much as possible in advance. You are likely to be delighted with the results. This is an elegant, rich dish, suitable for a special, intimate brunch.

Eggs Jerusalem
2 large artichokes
1 lemon, halved
2 small carrots
   salt and pepper to taste
2 eggs
1 tsp. chopped chives

Cut the stems off the artichokes and rub the bottoms with the halved lemon. Cut off the top leaves just above the choke and discard them. Rub the tops also with lemon. Squeeze the remaining lemon juice into a large pot of boiling water; add the artichokes and boil for about 25 minutes or until the bottoms can be easily pierced with a knife.

Cool the cooked artichokes under running water. Drain in a colander. Remove the remaining leaves and the chokes; trim the hearts to a nice round shape. Gently push the bottom of the artichoke hearts flat; place the hearts on a plate and transfer to a warm oven.

While the artichokes are cooking, make the carrot puree. Cook the carrots in lightly salted water until tender. Drain and process in a food processor until smooth.

Spoon the carrot puree on to the artichoke hearts; leave in warm oven while poaching the eggs.

While the carrots are cooking, get a pan of water ready to poach the eggs. When the eggs are poached, remove from the water with a slotted spoon and place on the artichoke hearts topped with carrot puree. Pour orange champagne sauce over this and garnish with chives. Serve immediately.

Orange Champagne Sauce
½ cup freshly squeezed orange juice
½ cup champagne
½ cup unsalted butter

You can make the sauce while the carrots are cooking. In a saucepan combine the orange juice and champagne over medium-high heat. Cook and reduce until it becomes a glaze. Remove pan from heat and whisk in 2 Tbs. of butter. Return to the heat and whisk in the remaining butter. When all the butter is incorporated, the sauce will have the consistency of Hollandaise.

CHIPPED BEEF AND EGG BAKE

The Bells Bed & Breakfast (p. 9)

SERVES 8 to 10.

This hearty casserole is a substantial breakfast dish. At the Bells it is served with fruit compote, biscuits and sweet rolls.

4 slices bacon, diced
1 5-oz. pkg. dried chipped beef
½ cup butter
1 cup sliced mushrooms
½ cup flour
4 cups milk
   freshly ground pepper
16 eggs
1 cup evaporated milk

Sauté the bacon; do not drain. Add the beef, torn into small pieces, the butter and the mushrooms. Cook briefly. Sprinkle with flour and continue cooking. Stir in the milk and continue cooking over medium-high heat until thickened. Season liberally with pepper. Remove from heat and set aside.

Beat together the eggs and evaporated milk. In the top of a double-boiler melt the remaining ¼ cup of butter. Add the egg-and-milk mixture, cooking until soft-set, stirring frequently. Remove from heat.

Starting with the egg mixture, layer with the beef mixture in a 2-quart, greased casserole. Make 6 alternating layers. *Cover with plastic wrap and refrigerate overnight.* Bake at 300° for 1 to 1¼ hours. Cool on a rack for a few minutes before serving.

BAKED HAM AND CHEESE SANDWICH

The Bells Bed & Breakfast
(p. 9)

SERVES 6.

Sandwiches
12 slices white sandwich bread
   (Pepperidge Farm is good)
½ lb. muenster cheese, grated
1 ½ cups chopped boiled ham
2 eggs
1 ½ cups milk

Remove the crusts from the bread and butter on one side. Lay 6 pieces of the bread, buttered side down, in a greased 9″ × 13″ glass baking dish. Sprinkle the grated cheese and chopped ham evenly over the bread. Cover with the remaining 6 slices of bread, buttered side up. Beat together the eggs and milk. Pour over the sandwiches. *Cover and refrigerate overnight.* Remove from refrigerator 30 minutes before baking. Bake, uncovered, at 325° for 1 hour. While the sandwiches are baking, make the sauce.

Sauce
1 cup sliced mushrooms
1 Tbs. butter
1 Tbs. flour
1 cup milk
   salt and pepper to taste
1 tsp. sherry (optional)

Sauté the mushrooms in the butter. Add the flour and stir over medium heat until well mixed. Add the milk and cook, stirring, until thickened. Season with salt and pepper. If desired, stir in the sherry.
To serve: Place one sandwich per person on a plate and top with sauce.

HAM AND EGGS AU GRATIN

Radcliffe Cross (p. 223)

SERVES 4 to 6.

This is a rich egg dish, well suited for a large crowd at breakfast or brunch. Much of the preparation can be done ahead of time.

6 hard-boiled eggs
4 Tbs. butter
4 Tbs. flour
2 cups milk
1 ½ tsp. Worcestershire sauce
½ tsp. prepared mustard
1 cup grated cheddar cheese
½ lb. cooked ham, coarsely
   chopped
¾ cup fine bread crumbs

Hardboil 6 eggs; when cool, shell and run through an egg slicer. Set aside. Melt the butter in a saucepan and mix in the flour to form a smooth paste. Add the milk slowly, stirring constantly, and simmer for 3 minutes.
   Preheat the oven to Broil. To the sauce add Worcestershire sauce, mustard and cheese; heat until cheese melts, continuing to stir. Add ham and eggs, heating thoroughly. Turn into a greased casserole, and sprinkle with bread crumbs.
   Broil until lightly browned. Serve immediately over split biscuits or toasted English muffins.

HAM AND CHEESE SOUFFLÉ

Phoenix House (p. 32)

SERVES 6.

This is always well liked by my guests, and I like it because it is assembled the day before, freeing me for other tasks in the morning.

8 slices white bread
1 ½ cups ham, chopped
1 ½ cups cheddar cheese, grated
1 small onion, minced
   salt and pepper to taste
10 eggs
1 ½ cups milk
½ cup butter, melted
2 tsp. dry mustard
½ cup parmesan cheese
   paprika

Remove the crusts from the bread and cut into cubes. In a buttered 10″ soufflé dish, make a layer of ⅓ of the bread; cover with half of the ham, half of the cheese, and half of the onion. Repeat this, and top with the remaining third of the bread.
   In a large bowl beat the eggs well. Add the milk, butter (cooled) and dry mustard, and blend well. Pour this over the soufflé. Sprinkle with the parmesan and a little paprika. *Cover with plastic wrap and refrigerate overnight.*
   In the morning, bring the soufflé to room temperature while the oven heats and bake at 350° for about 50 minutes. Serve immediately.

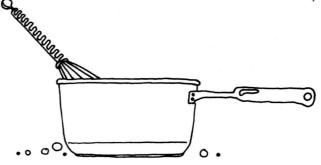

Old Talbott Tavern
Bardstown, Kentucky

THE OLD TALBOTT TAVERN is a handsome stone structure dating from 1779. The original stonework is a unique example of Flemish bond stone construction. Each stone was faced by more than two-hundred hand-chiseled marks. Originally built as an all-purpose public house, Old Talbott Tavern is the oldest western stagecoach stop in America. As such, it has been witness to a parade of famous and infamous men and women throughout the decades. In 1797, before setting out to see the western frontier of the New World (which at that time began in this part of Kentucky), exiled French King Louis Phillippe and his two brothers stayed here.

A member of the royal party painted the murals that are still on the walls of one of the upstairs rooms. Legend has it that Jesse James later used them for target practice. Whether this is true or not, the bullet holes are undoubtedly there. Abraham Lincoln stayed here with his family as a young boy; Daniel Boone was a frequent patron. General George Rogers Clark, Revolutionary War leader, used the tavern as a recruiting base. Other famous guests include John Fitch, inventor of the steamboat, Stephen Foster, John J. Audubon, Queen Marie of Rumania and General George Patton.

The Tavern prides itself on its cooking: "Our menu and style of cooking is still done with the same old-fashioned spirit and atmosphere as in the past, as we served statesmen, generals, artists, inventors, and countless other members of the general public."

Old Talbott Tavern
107 West Stephen Foster
Bardstown, Kentucky 40004
(502) 348–3494

Jim Kelley

SAUSAGE SOUFFLÉ

SERVES 10 to 12.

This tasty, savory dish is always a crowd pleaser; and because it must be assembled a day ahead, it allows the cook a relaxed morning.

½ lb. hot sausage, bulk
½ lb. mild sausage, bulk
12 slices white bread
2 cups grated sharp cheddar cheese
8 eggs
4 cups milk
¼ cup Worcestershire sauce
1 tsp. salt
1 tsp. dry mustard

Cook the sausage, stirring it as necessary to crumble, until done. Drain on paper toweling.

Remove the crusts from the bread and cut into cubes. Sprinkle half the cubed bread into a greased 3-quart casserole. Cover with 1 cup of the cheese. Cover this with the sausage, and follow this layer with the rest of the bread, ending with the cheese.

In a large bowl beat together the eggs, milk, Worcestershire sauce, salt and mustard. Pour over the casserole; *cover and refrigerate overnight.*

In the morning let the casserole sit at room temperature while the oven is heating. Bake uncovered at 325° for 45 minutes to 1 hour. Let cool briefly on a rack; cut into squares and serve hot.

Since 1779 the venerable Old Talbott Tavern has been receiving visitors, including President Lincoln, General Patton and (according to legend at least) Jesse James.

The Heirloom

Ione, California

THIS PLANTATION-STYLE brick house was built in 1863. It sits on an acre and a half of well-planted grounds, complete with gazebo. Porches on both the first and second stories overlook the gardens.

Thirty miles from Sacramento, the Heirloom is near wineries, interesting antiques shops and a variety of restaurants.

A full breakfast is served in a number of locations: before a warm fire in the cozy dining room, on a private balcony among the wisteria vines, at umbrella tables in the garden or, if desired, in bed.

The Heirloom
P.O. Box 322
Ione, California 95640
(209) 274-4468

Mellissande Hubbs

AUNT MARIE'S CHEESE SOUFFLÉ

SERVES 6.

A classic soufflé—pretty, puffy, light. This is appropriate for brunch, lunch or a light dinner. Be prepared to serve it as soon as it comes out of the oven.

      3 Tbs. butter
      4 Tbs. flour
    ½ tsp. salt
      1 cup milk
      1 cup grated sharp cheddar cheese
    ⅛ tsp. cayenne pepper
    ¾ tsp. dry mustard
  1½ tsp. sugar
      2 tsp. water
      3 eggs, separated

Preheat oven to 350°F.

In a saucepan, melt butter over medium-high heat. Stir in the flour and salt. Slowly add the milk, whisking to make a sauce. Add cheese, stir until melted. In a small bowl mix cayenne pepper, mustard and sugar in the water to dissolve. Add to sauce and stir in. Remove from heat. Add egg yolks and beat in well. In a separate bowl beat the egg whites until peaks form, Fold into sauce. Pour into ungreased 2-quart soufflé dish. Set in baking pan with enough water in the bottom to cover 1½" of sides of soufflé dish.

Bake at 350° for 40 minutes, or until nicely puffed. Serve immediately.

When the weather is appropriate, the Heirloom offers breakfast at umbrella tables in the garden, surrounded by lush vegetation.

The Stagecoach Stop
Lamont, Michigan

THE STAGECOACH STOP is a commodious carpenter Gothic building located halfway between Grand Rapids and Grand Haven in the picturesque Grand River village of Lamont. The large, two-story house stands handsomely at one end of a boulevard lined with majestic pines and historic houses. Built in 1859 by Cyrus Dudley, this house has played an important role in Lamont's history. In the old days, travelers rested here while stagecoach repairs were made by the smithy. Local legend suggests that slaves, too, found shelter in this home along the Underground Railroad route.

Centrally located in western Michigan, the Stagecoach Stop provides travelers with a base for exploring an area full of history or for just enjoying the scenic countryside. The inn itself offers a spectacular view of the surrounding countryside, and Grand Rapids and the lake communities of Grand Haven, Muskegon and Holland (home of the famous Holland Tulip Festival) are only minutes away.

Guests enjoy a hearty, continental-plus breakfast that includes fresh rolls, fruit and coffee.

The Stagecoach Stop
0–4819 Leonard Road West
Lamont, Michigan 49430
(616) 677–3940

Marcia Ashby

One of the oldest houses in central Michigan, the Stagecoach Stop is still the welcoming haven that travelers enjoyed in its colorful past.

CHEESE SOUFFLÉ

SERVES 8 to 10.

This soufflé comes out of the oven puffy and golden. It is crusty outside, creamy inside. It is not baked in the traditional soufflé dish, which makes it easier to serve as a breakfast or brunch item.

    4 eggs
    3 cups milk
    1 tsp. salt
    2 cups flour
    ½ lb. cheddar cheese, grated
    ½ cup chopped onion
    ½ cup chopped mushrooms
    ½ cup butter, melted

Preheat oven to 400°F.

In a large bowl mix together eggs, milk, salt and flour. Stir in the cheese, onions, mushrooms and melted butter. Pour the mixture into a greased 9" × 13" pan. Bake at 400° for 35 to 45 minutes or until sides puff up brown. Cut into squares and serve immediately.

Note: The onions and mushrooms may be sautéed in a little butter if desired, before being added to the recipe.

MacMaster House
Portland, Oregon

IN 1885, when William MacMaster came from England to manage the investments of the Dundee Land Company, he built this house on prestigious King's Hill. A classic colonial revival, it features a colossal portico with Doric columns, a lovely Palladian window with leaded glass, seven fireplaces and bright, spacious rooms. MacMaster House is furnished with many European antiques and an eclectic collection of works by Oregon artists.

Beautiful Washington Park is two blocks away, with its famous Japanese and Rose Gardens, its zoo, jogging trails, tennis courts and concerts in summer. MacMaster House is also convenient to the financial district, the Portland Art Museum and the Oregon Historical Society. Also nearby is the Uptown Shopping Center with boutiques, pastry and wine shops, markets, antiques and art galleries, and several of Portland's favorite restaurants.

A full breakfast, varied daily, is served in the dining room. Picnic baskets are also available upon request.

MacMaster House
1041 SW Vista Avenue
Portland, Oregon 97205
(503) 223–7362

Cecilia Murphy

With its stately Doric columns, MacMaster House exemplifies the hospitality associated with such elegant nineteenth-century houses.

BRUNCH EGG CASSEROLE

SERVES 8 to 10.

This recipe is from Maisie MacMaster Oldenborg Barber, an heir of William MacMaster. She and her husband spent a few days at MacMaster House with Cecilia Murphy, pored over old scrapbooks and exchanged information. She sent this recipe of her grandmother's to Cecilia, noting that her grandmother had been a good friend of James Beard, who spoke wonderfully of her culinary expertise and beautiful presentation.

This casserole may be made a day in advance. It is a meal in one dish, helpful when serving a large crowd.

¼ cup butter
½ cup flour
2 cups milk
¼ tsp. thyme
¼ tsp. basil
¼ tsp. marjoram
½ cup chopped fresh parsley
18 hard-boiled eggs, shelled and sliced
1 lb. sharp cheddar cheese, grated
1 lb. bacon, fried and crumbled.

Preheat oven to 350°F.

Make a white sauce by melting the butter, stirring in the flour, and then whisking in the milk over medium-high heat until thickened. Season with the herbs. Mix in the eggs, cheese and bacon. Pour into a greased 2-quart casserole dish, or 9" x 13" pan, and bake at 350° for 30 minutes. Serve hot over toasted and buttered English muffins.

The English House Bed and Breakfast
Andover, New Hampshire

THE ENGLISH HOUSE Bed and Breakfast is a large, comfortable shingle-style house in the center of the picturesque town of Andover. This area of the country is known for its excellent downhill and cross-country skiing in winter, and guests of the English House can enjoy cross-country skiing right from the premises. Hiking, canoeing, fishing and swimming are popular in spring and summer in the surrounding hills, lakes and rivers. Golf and tennis facilities are also close by. In fall, the foliage is spectacular, and many travel to the area just to enjoy the brilliant show of color. There is a wonderful range of excellent restaurants in the area, and because of the proximity to Concord, New London and Hanover—home to Dartmouth College—theatre, museums and cultural activities abound.

Gillian and Ken Smith came from England; and in keeping with English tradition, they offer afternoon tea daily at 4:00 PM. A full breakfast, which includes fresh home-baked goods, fresh fruit in season, homemade cereal and selections from a variety of main course dishes is meant to see guests through most, if not all, of a day's activities.

The English House Bed and Breakfast
Route 4 & 11, P.O. Box 162
Andover, New Hampshire 03216
(603) 735-5987

Gillian and Ken Smith

ENGLISH HOUSE 24-HOUR SOUFFLÉ

SERVES 12 to 16.

This is a popular breakfast dish at the English House, well suited for a large crowd. The salami adds a marvelous flavor to this hearty dish.

    1 loaf Italian bread, day old
    6 Tbs. butter, melted
    9 thin slices Genoa salami
    ¾ lb. Swiss cheese, grated
    ½ lb. Monterey jack cheese, grated
   16 eggs
 3¾ cups milk
    ½ cup dry white wine
    4 scallions
    1 Tbs. German mustard
    ½ tsp. black pepper
    ⅛ tsp. cayenne pepper
 1½ cups sour cream
    1 cup parmesan cheese, grated

Oven temperature: 325°F.

Chop or break the bread into small pieces, and distribute evenly between 2 greased 9″ × 13″ baking pans. Drizzle with the melted butter. Chop the salami, and distribute evenly over the bread. Sprinkle the grated Swiss and Monterey jack cheeses over the salami.

In a large bowl beat together the eggs, milk and wine. Chop the scallions, and stir into the egg mixture along with the mustard and peppers. Pour this over the casseroles, cover with foil and *refrigerate overnight*.

Remove from refrigerator 30 minutes before baking. Bake, covered, at 325° for about 1 hour or until set. Uncover and carefully spread with the sour cream. Sprinkle the parmesan cheese over the sour cream. Return to the oven and bake uncovered for 10 minutes. Cut into squares and serve immediately.

The Southern Hotel
Ste. Genevieve, Missouri

AS EARLY AS 1812, the Southern Hotel was known for the finest accommodations between Natchez and St. Louis. It was famous for its fine food, and its bustling gambling rooms included the first pool hall west of the Mississippi. This gracious old federal-style building sat neglected and empty from 1981 until 1986 when Mike and Barbara Hankins bought it and restored it to its current splendor.

Historic Ste. Genevieve sits on the banks of the Mississippi River, just one hour south of St. Louis. Visitors can enjoy a walking tour of the city or a paddle-boat ride on the river.

To prepare them for the day, guests are treated to a full breakfast served in the dining room. Menus change every day. "We want our guests to have an out-of-the ordinary experience while they are with us, and the cook doesn't want to be bored either," says Barbara Hankins.

The Southern Hotel
146 South Third Street
Ste. Genevieve, Missouri 63670
(314) 883-3493

Mike and Barbara Hankins

MISS DODIE'S EGGS

SERVES 4.

A light and fluffy egg dish, this is always a hit at the Southern Hotel, where they top it with a thin ribbon of hot maple syrup.

3 eggs
1 cup milk
1 cup grated cheddar cheese
1 cup shredded bread
1 tsp. dry mustard
 salt and pepper to taste

Preheat oven to 350°F.

Beat the eggs. Add the milk and beat well. Stir in the cheese, shredded bread, mustard and a little salt and pepper. Pour into an 8"-square greased baking dish and bake at 350° for 30 minutes. Let cool for 10 minutes before cutting into squares. Serve topped with a thin ribbon of hot maple syrup, if desired.

OPPOSITE: *Although its architecture is no more British than that of any other New Hampshire country house, the English House observes the graciousness of an English household.*

LEFT: *With a tradition of hospitality that goes back nearly two centuries, the Southern Hotel is one of the oldest buildings in Missouri.*

POACHED EGGS WITH LEMON-CHIVE SAUCE
Manor House (p. 171)

SERVES 4.

Eggs and Muffins
8 eggs, poached
4 English muffins, split and
    toasted

Sauce
⅓ cup butter
2 Tbs. finely chopped chives
1 Tbs. lemon juice
1 tsp. grated lemon zest
½ tsp. salt
    dash pepper

To make the sauce: Melt butter. Add remaining ingredients, beating thoroughly, over medium high heat. Leave the sauce over low heat while you poach the eggs.
    Poach the eggs (2 per person) and slip onto toasted and buttered English muffin halves. Top with the sauce. Serve immediately.

EGG SOUFFLÉ
Hersey House (p. 54)

SERVES 6 to 8.

8 slices white bread
4 Tbs. butter
1½ cups grated cheddar cheese
1 cup chopped ham
4 eggs
1 tsp. salt
2 cups milk

Cut crusts from bread; butter 4 slices and place buttered-side down in a greased 9″ × 13″ baking dish. Sprinkle half the cheese over the bread, then cover with half the ham. Butter the remaining 4 slices of bread and place over the ham, buttered-side up. Sprinkle the remaining cheese over this layer, and top with the rest of the ham. In a bowl beat together the eggs, salt and milk; pour over all. *Cover with plastic wrap and refrigerate overnight.* In the morning bake uncovered at 350° for approximately 1 hour. Serve immediately.

QUICHE LORRAINE
Hersey House (p. 54)

SERVES 6 to 8.

Not at all soggy, this quiche has a distinctive Swiss cheese flavor.

1 small onion
1 Tbs. bacon fat
2 eggs
¼ cup sour cream
½ tsp. salt
    dash of pepper
2½ cups Swiss cheese, grated
6 slices bacon, cooked crisp,
    drained and crumbled
    unbaked 9″ pie shell

Preheat oven to 375°F.
    Chop the onion and cook in bacon fat until just tender. Set aside. Beat together the eggs, sour cream, salt and pepper. Stir in the onion, grated cheese and bacon. Pour into the unbaked pie shell. Bake at 375° for 30 minutes or until done. Cool briefly on a rack before slicing to serve. Serve hot.

SAUSAGE MUSHROOM QUICHE
Lafayette House (p. 100)

SERVES 8.

As with all quiches, parts of this may be prepared in advance.

Crust
1½ cups flour
1 tsp. salt
6 Tbs. butter or shortening
3 to 5 Tbs. ice water

Mix together the flour and salt. Using a pastry fork or food processor, cut in the shortening until the mixture resembles coarse sand. Mix in just enough ice water to form a ball. Wrap in plastic wrap and refrigerate for one hour. Roll out the chilled dough on a lightly floured board to about ⅛″ to ¼″ thickness. Line a 9″ quiche pan with the pastry, cover with plastic wrap, and refrigerate until ready to use.

Filling
6 breakfast sausage links
1 cup chopped mushrooms
4 eggs
1½ cups half-and-half
1½ cups grated cheddar cheese

Preheat oven to 350°F.
    Cook the sausage until well browned; drain, cut in half lengthwise and arrange evenly over the bottom of the quiche crust, positioning the sausage like the spokes of a wheel. Sauté the mushrooms; distribute evenly over the sausage. Beat the eggs well; add the half-and-half and beat again. Stir in the cheese. Pour over the sausage and mushrooms and bake at 350° for 35 to 45 minutes. Let cool for a few minutes before slicing to serve.

Hazlewood House

Galveston Island, Texas

HAZLEWOOD HOUSE was built as a wedding gift in 1877. Located on Galveston Island, it is just ten blocks from the sparkling Gulf of Mexico. Galveston is known for its long, sandy beaches and excellent sports-fishing. Also nearby are the world-renowned University of Texas Medical Branch, the Grand Opera House and the Historical Strand.

The interior of Hazlewood House contains cypress woodwork, stained glass doors, antique baths and an eclectic collection of furnishings. The shaded porch is a popular spot for guests to relax and enjoy the quiet privacy of the yard.

Coffee or tea is brought to the guestrooms in the morning, and a hearty continental-plus breakfast is served in the dining room or on the porch.

Hazlewood House
1127 Church Street
Galveston Island, Texas 77550
(409) 762–1668

Pat Hazlewood

Hazlewood House, seen in this vintage photograph, is a lacy, almost gossamer, example of carpenter gothic at its most charming. The style is enhanced by a color scheme of white, light blue and topaz.

TEXAS HAZLEWOOD QUICHE

SERVES 8.

A southwestern twist on a classic French dish.

Crust
Use the recipe for quiche crust given on page 109.

Filling
- 3 eggs
- 1½ cups milk or cream
- ¾ cup grated Monterey jack cheese
- ¾ cup grated cheddar cheese
- 2 Tbs. picante sauce
- 1 tsp. chili powder
- ½ cup chopped onion
- ½ cup chopped green pepper
- 1 clove garlic
- ½ cup chopped black olives
- ½ cup chopped stewed tomatoes, drained

Garnish
- 2 ripe avocados
- ½ cup picante sauce

Preheat oven to 350°F.

In a large bowl beat the eggs well. Add the milk or cream and beat again. Stir in the cheeses, picante sauce and chili powder. In a skillet sauté the onion and peppers. Just before removing from the heat, crush the clove of garlic into the onion and pepper mix. Stir briefly over heat, then remove and set aside to cool slightly. When cooled, add the sautéed vegetables to the egg-cheese mix, along with the olives and stewed tomatoes. Stir well and pour into the unbaked quiche pastry. Bake at 350° for 40 to 45 minutes. Serve with slices of ripe avocado and a little picante sauce.

Aldrich Guest House
Galena, Illinois

LIKE MANY OTHER nineteenth-century houses, Aldrich House was built in several stages by several owners, the oldest part dating to 1845. The house today is a handsome combination of Greek revival and the Italianate style. The interior is a comfortable mix of the nineteenth and twentieth centuries.

An historic town, Galena was home to Ulysses S. Grant, whose residence is open to the public, as are many other historic buildings. Most of the town property is on the Galena Historic Register or the National Historic Register. Antiques lovers will find shops galore; and for the outdoor enthusiast there are boating, golfing and skiing.

Guests are served a full breakfast in the dining room or on the screened porch, which overlooks the side yard where General Grant drilled his troops. A sample breakfast might include cherry coffee-cake, canteloupe and blueberry fruit salad, sausage casserole, juice and coffee.

Aldrich Guest House
900 Third Street
Galena, Illinois 61036
(815) 777-3323

Judy Green

SAUSAGE BREAKFAST CASSEROLE

SERVES 6 to 8.

```
1   lb. bulk sausage
6   slices white bread, crusts removed
1½  cups grated mild cheddar cheese
8   eggs
2   cups half-and-half
1   tsp. salt
1   tsp. basil
1   tsp. dry mustard
    pepper to taste
```

Brown the sausage, stirring to crumble. When done, remove from pan with a slotted spoon and drain well on paper toweling. Cut bread into cubes and distributed evenly over the bottom of a greased 9″ × 13″ pan. Sprinkle sausage over the bread and top with the cheese. In a large mixing bowl combine the remaining ingredients and beat well. Pour over the casserole, *cover and refrigerate overnight.*

Bake at 350° for 30 minutes. Remove from oven, cut into squares and serve hot.

LEFT: *The dining room at the Aldrich Guest House reflects a special ambience, with the emphasis on comfort and color.*

OPPOSITE: *Among its amenities the Catlin–Abbott House numbers antiques, family heirlooms, fresh flowers, working fireplaces, goosedown pillows and triple-sheeted beds.*

The Catlin–Abbott House
Richmond, Virginia

A HANDSOME BRICK structure located in the historic Church Hill district of Richmond, the Catlin–Abbott House was built in 1845 for William Catlin by one of the finest masons in the country. The building is a striking example of the Greek Revival architectural style. The Abbotts, the present owners, combined their name with the original owner's to name their B&B. The house is elegantly furnished with period antiques, oriental rugs, canopied four-poster beds and crystal chandeliers.

Richmond is a lively and stately city, offering much for the visitor to see and do. St. John's Church, scene of Patrick Henry's famous "liberty or death" speech, is only one block away from the Catlin–Abbott House. Many of Richmond's battlefields and parks, as well as famous plantations of the James River, are close by too. The Edgar Allen Poe Museum, the Virginia State Capitol (designed by Thomas Jefferson) as well as the Valentine Museum, the White House of the Confederacy and other historic attractions make Richmond a fascinating place to explore. The city offers a variety of interesting shops, boutiques and fine restaurants.

Guests at the Catlin–Abbott House are served a full breakfast in the elegant dining room. Breakfast includes juice, fresh fruit in season, choices of sausage and pancakes or bacon and eggs, hot breads and coffee and tea. Breakfast can also be served in the guest's bedroom.

The Catlin–Abbott House
2304 East Broad Street
Richmond, Virginia 23223
(804) 780–3746

Dr. and Mrs. William Abbott

CATLIN–ABBOTT BREAKFAST BAKE

SERVES 8 to 10.

A meal in one dish, this must be prepared the day before and refrigerated overnight before baking. The shredded wheat "dissolves," and the casserole comes out of the oven puffy and golden.

```
  3 cups spoon-size shredded wheat
      cereal
1 ½ lbs. bulk sausage, cooked, drained
      and crumbled
  1 cup grated Swiss cheese
  1 cup grated Monterey jack cheese
 12 eggs
1 ½ cups milk
  ¼ cup white wine
  1 cup sour cream
  ¼ cup chicken stock
  ½ cup sautéed mushrooms
  1 onion, minced
  1 Tbs. grainy mustard
  1 Tbs. chopped fresh parsley
      dash black pepper
```

Lightly butter a 9" × 13" baking dish. Distribute cereal over the bottom of the baking dish. Cover this with the sausage, and then the grated cheeses.

In a bowl, beat together the eggs, milk, wine, sour cream and chicken stock. Stir in the mushrooms, onion, mustard, parsley and pepper. Pour evenly into the baking dish, to cover the layer of grated cheeses. *Cover and refrigerate overnight.*

Let casserole come to room temperature (approximately 30 minutes) before baking. Uncover and bake at 325° for approximately 60 minutes. Cool 10 minutes, cut into squares and serve.

Lafayette House
St. Louis, Missouri

A VICTORIAN MANSION built in 1876, Lafayette House is located in a lovely section of the historic city of St. Louis. Visitors to this handsome city along the Mississippi River find much to see and do. Touring the river by paddle boat is a delightful way to spend a day. Another day can be devoted to touring historic houses and visiting the famous Union Station. Excellent dining and shopping are available in this cosmopolitan yet gracious city. St. Louis is also the home of Anheuser-Busch, and many visitors want to tour the facility — including the farm, the brewery and the stables of the famous Clydesdales.

Breakfast at Lafayette House is served at a large mahogany table in the dining room, where the menu includes selections of juice, coffee or tea, chunky applesauce, quiche, casseroles, butter pecan bread, marmalade bread, cream cheese and assorted jams and jellies. The Milligans' prefer to list their B&B with a reservation service, Bed & Breakfast of St. Louis.

Lafayette House
St. Louis, Missouri

Sarah and Jack Milligan

c/o Bed & Breakfast of St. Louis
1900 Wyoming Street
St. Louis, Missouri 63118
(314) 965–4328

Mike Warner

SAUSAGE AND EGG BRUNCH CASSEROLE

SERVES 8 to 10.

This tasty casserole, which comes out of the oven puffy and golden, is ideal for serving a large crowd. This is another dish to assemble the day before.

    2 cups herbed croutons
    1 lb. bulk sausage
    1 cup chopped mushrooms
    2 Tbs. butter
    3 Tbs. flour
 2 ½ cups half and half
    1 tsp. dry mustard
      salt and pepper to taste
 1 ½ cups grated cheddar cheese
    6 eggs

Sprinkle the croutons over the bottom of a greased 10″ × 14″ baking dish. In a large skillet cook the sausage until well browned; drain and distribute over the croutons.

Sauté the mushrooms and set aside.

In a saucepan melt the butter and stir in the flour. Slowly add the half-and-half, whisking constantly, until a sauce is formed. Remove from heat. Add the dry mustard, and salt and pepper to taste. Stir in the mushrooms and cheese. Set aside to cool. Beat the eggs. Mix the eggs into the cooled sauce and pour over the sausage and croutons. *Cover and refrigerate overnight.*

Bring the casserole to room temperature and bake, uncovered, at 350° for 45 minutes. Let stand for 5 minutes before cutting into squares for serve.

The Inn on Kelleys Island
Kelleys Island, Ohio

AN ELABORATELY ITALIANATE villa built entirely of wood, except for its marble fireplaces, the Inn on Kelleys Island was built in 1876. It is furnished with antiques (many original to the home) and a piano in the parlor for sing-alongs. Day and evening, guests enjoy the porch with its clear view of Lake Erie. The inn has its own dock on the lake where guests can sunbathe or fish. The beach is also popular for shell collecting.

In addition to a variety of water sports, Kelleys Island has many historical sites to explore, unique shops and fine restaurants. The island has the world's finest example of Indian hieroglyphics, miles of hiking trails, beautiful beaches and the best walleye and small-mouth bass fishing anywhere from mid-April through November. The Kelleys Island Wine Company, which produces prize-winning wines, offers tours. The island can comfortably be explored on foot, by bicycle or by golf cart. There are boat excursions from the island to neighboring South Bass Island. Kelleys Island is reached by ferry, plane or private boat.

Guests at the inn are served a full breakfast in the dining room or at tables on the lawn.

The Inn on Kelleys Island
Box 11
Kelleys Island, Ohio 43438
(419) 746–2258

REUBEN BRUNCH CASSEROLE

SERVES 8 to 12.

This casserole must be assembled ahead of time and refrigerated overnight. Well suited for a buffet style breakfast or brunch.

    10 slices rye bread, shredded
  1½ lbs. cooked corned beef
  2½ cups grated Swiss cheese
    6 eggs
    3 cups milk
  ¼ tsp. pepper

Sprinkle the bread on the bottom of a greased 9″ × 13″ baking dish. Coarsely shred the corned beef and distribute evenly over the bread. Sprinkle the grated cheese over the top.

Beat together the eggs, milk and pepper. Pour over corned beef mixture. *Cover with foil and refrigerate overnight.*

In the morning bake, covered, at 350° for 45 minutes, then bake uncovered for 10 minutes or until bubbly and puffed.

Cut into squares and serve hot.

This photo of the Inn on Kelleys Island was taken about a century ago. Although the canvas awnings are now gone, the villa looks as welcoming today as it did then.

Holden House
Colorado Springs, Colorado

BUILT IN 1902, Holden House is a big frame house lovingly restored by Sallie and Welling Clark. It is furnished with antiques and with quilts, from Sallie's grandmother and great-grandmother. During the Christmas season, guests see the house decorated with garlands, bows and tiny white lights. Two Christmas trees, handmade decorations and a blazing fire make a cozy setting to enjoy hot mulled cider and cookies at the end of the day.

Situated in the Old Colorado City district, Holden House is convenient to fine restaurants, unique gift shops and many other attractions of Colorado Springs. Two of Colorado's gold rush towns are within easy driving distance. And, of course, the area offers excellent skiing.

In the summer a full breakfast is served on the verandah with a view of Pike's Peak; during cooler weather breakfast is served in the dining room with formal table settings. Occasionally, Sallie Clark sets out her grandmother's Swansea china, more than 250 years old. A full breakfast begins with fresh fruit cup topped with a fruit yogurt sauce. Freshly ground coffee is served daily along with juice and an assortment of teas. Sallie says, "Don't be surprised if you taste a hint of Amaretto or cinnamon in your coffee." Fresh-baked muffins are offered daily, and Sallie varies the menu so guests have something different each morning. On Sundays, champagne is added to the menu. Most of the herbs used in the breakfast dishes are fresh from Sallie's garden.

Holden House
1102 W. Pike's Peak Avenue
Colorado Springs, Colorado 80904
(303) 471-3980

Sallie and Welling Clark

CREPE CUPS

MAKES 12.

You can make the crepes the day before to save time, fill and bake in the morning.

Crepes
1¼ cups flour
2 Tbs. sugar
    pinch salt
3 eggs, beaten
1¼ cups milk
2 Tbs. butter, melted
1 tsp. lemon extract (optional)

Mix all crepe ingredients together, beating well. Make 5" crepes, using either a well-greased skillet or a crepe-maker. Set aside.

Press cooled crepes into 12 well-greased muffin tins, lightly ruffling edges but being careful not to tear the crepes.

Filling
6 slices cooked bacon, crisp and
    crumbled or
½ lb. bulk sausage, cooked and drained
7 eggs
1 cup milk
½ tsp. salt
¼ tsp. pepper

Preheat oven to 350°F.
Distribute the bacon or sausage into the bottoms of the 12 crepe cups.
Mix the other ingredients, beating well, and pour over the bacon or sausage, filling to just below the rims of the muffin cups. Bake for 15 to 20 minutes. Carefully remove the crepe cups from the muffin tins. Top with a dab of sour cream and fresh chopped parsley or dill if desired.
Variation: Substitute a tablespoon of grated cheddar cheese for the bacon or sausage.

The Frederick Fitting House
Belleville, Ohio

FINANCIER, FARMER and contractor, Frederick Fitting brought prosperity to himself and his home town when he brought the railroad to Belleville. His house, built in 1863, is a quintessential midwestern Victorian—an ornately Italianate villa built of wood. The interior is furnished with Ohio antiques, many of them family heirlooms with interesting stories. The magnificent freestanding spiral staircase of walnut, butternut and oak is the centerpiece of the first floor.

Breakfast, served in the stenciled dining room, features home-baked goods, fresh fruit, juice, specially blended coffee and herbal teas served with Richland County honey.

The Frederick Fitting House
72 Fitting Avenue
Belleville, Ohio 33813
(419) 886–4283

Jo and Rick Sowash

SAUSAGE-FILLED CREPES

SERVES 6.

Unless you are a very early riser, these should be assembled the day before and refrigerated overnight to be baked in the morning.

12 crepes
 1 lb. bulk sausage
 ¼ cup chopped onion
 3 oz. pkg. cream cheese
 ½ cup grated cheddar cheese
 ¼ tsp. marjoram

Topping
 ½ cup sour cream
 ¼ cup butter, melted

Make a dozen crepes using your favorite recipe (see page 104). Let the crepes cool while you make the filling.

In a skillet cook sausage and onion together until the sausage is brown and thoroughly cooked. Drain; add the cream cheese, cheddar cheese and marjoram. Stir until well blended. Remove from heat. Place approximately 2 Tbs. of the sausage mixture in each crepe and roll up. Place filled crepes in a greased baking dish, cover with foil, and chill for at least one hour (or overnight).

Bake, covered, at 375° for 40 minutes.

While the crepes are baking, make the topping by combining the sour cream and melted butter; spoon over top of crepes. Bake uncovered for 5 minutes more. Serve hot.

LEFT: *When Frederick Fitting built this house in 1863, he was Belleville's most prominent citizen.*

OPPOSITE: *The formal dining room of Holden House is furnished with period antiques.*

HOT CHICKEN SALAD CREPES

Robin's Nest Inn (p. 79)

MAKES 12 crepes.

If you serve this buffet style, leave the sauce in a dish on the side. You may make the crepes a day ahead to help reduce the preparation time.

Crepes
1½ cups flour
2 Tbs. oil
3 eggs
1½ cups milk

Combine ingredients in blender and process on high for 1 minute. Pour a small amount of batter into small (5″), hot, lightly oiled skillet, tilting to cover bottom. Cook until lightly browned on both sides. Stack between sheets of waxed paper. Cool completely before filling.

Chicken Salad
2 cups chopped chicken (cooked)
2 cups chopped celery
3 Tbs. chopped onion
½ cup sliced mushrooms
¾ cup mayonnaise
1 cup chicken stock
1 Tbs. cornstarch
½ cup sour cream
1 tsp. salt
½ tsp. pepper

Oven temperature: 300°F.
   Combine chicken, celery, onion, mushrooms and mayonnaise in a bowl; mix well. In a cup mix ¼ cup of the chicken stock with the cornstarch. Add to the rest of the chicken stock, pour into a saucepan and heat until it starts to thicken. Remove from heat and cool slightly. Then add the thickened chicken stock and the sour cream to the chicken salad mixture and combine well. Season with salt and pepper. Spoon filling into cooled crepes; roll to enclose filling. Arrange in large greased baking dish. *At this point the dish may be covered with plastic wrap and refrigerated overnight.*
   Bake uncovered at 300° for 30 minutes. Serve topped with sauce.

Sauce
2 Tbs. butter
2 Tbs. flour
½ cup chicken broth
1 cup evaporated milk
   salt and pepper

Melt butter in small saucepan; blend in flour until smooth. Add chicken broth and milk gradually. Cook, stirring, over medium heat until thickened. Season with salt and pepper. Spoon over individual servings of the chicken salad crepes, hot from the oven.

ZUCCHINI CRESCENT PIE

Bridgeford Cottage (p. 58)

SERVES 8.

If you're a gardener, you'll find this is a good way to use overabundant summer zucchini. My guests love it for breakfast, but it is perfectly appropriate for lunch or dinner.

1 10″ unbaked pie crust
   (see page 109)
4 cups thinly sliced zucchini
   (not peeled)
1 cup coarsely chopped onion
½ cup chopped fresh parsley
   (or 2 Tbs. dried parsley)
½ tsp. salt
½ tsp. black pepper
1 clove garlic, crushed
¼ tsp. basil
½ tsp. oregano
2 tsp. Dijon mustard
2 eggs
8 oz. Monterey jack cheese,
   grated

Preheat oven to 375°F.
   Line a pie plate or quiche pan with an unbaked pie crust. Cover and refrigerate. Sauté zucchini and onion until tender. Stir in parsley and seasonings. In a large bowl beat the eggs, and stir in the cheese. Pour in the vegetable mixture and combine well. Spread the Dijon mustard on the bottom of the pie crust. Pour vegetable mixture into the crust. Bake at 375° for 20 minutes. Remove from oven and place on a cooling rack. Let stand 10 minutes before serving.

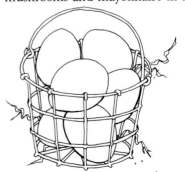

The River Street Inn
Ketchum, Idaho

LOCATED ON A quiet street a few blocks from the heart of Ketchum, the River Street Inn offers breathtaking views of Bald Mountain. Its unconventional architecture is a remarkable blend of arts-and-crafts charm with the light and airy spaces of contemporary western design. Palladian windows, polished brass and whitewashed oak combine to make a pleasant setting. A massive brick fireplace dominates the living room, from which French doors open onto an expansive deck with a view of Trail Creek and a copse of cottonwood and aspen trees.

After a full breakfast, guests find many activities to fill the day — skiing in winter; hiking, horseback riding and hot-air ballooning in summer. Ernest Hemingway died in Ketchum and is buried in a local cemetery. Farther out on Trail Creek in the heart of the country he called home is the Hemingway Memorial. On it is written, "Best of all he loved the fall . . . the leaves yellow on the cottonwoods, leaves floating on the trout streams, and above the hills the high blue windless skies."

River Street Inn
100 River Street West
Ketchum, Idaho 83740

Mailing address:
P.O. Box 182
Sun Valley, Idaho 83353
(208) 726–3611

Ginny Van Doren

ITALIAN SPINACH PIE

SERVES 8.

The Italian sausage gives this handsome dish a special kick.

   8 oz. mild Italian sausage (bulk)
   6 eggs, separated
   2 packages frozen spinach, thawed
     and drained
1 ½ cups cheese, grated (cheddar
     or Swiss)
   3 Tbs. chopped onion
   2 tsp. Worcestershire sauce
     dash Tabasco
   2 unbaked pie crusts (see page 109)
     egg wash: 1 egg beaten with 1
     Tbs. milk
   1 Tbs. sesame seeds

Preheat oven to 350°F.
   Fry sausage until brown and crumbly. Drain thoroughly and set aside. In a large bowl beat the egg yolks well and stir in sausage, spinach, cheese, onions, Worcestershire sauce and Tabasco. In a separate bowl beat egg whites until stiff. Fold whites into spinach mixture. Thoroughly grease a 9″ springform pan, line bottom with pastry so that it overlaps the side. Spoon in spinach mixture. Top with the other crust. Crimp the edges and perforate the top crust with a fork, in a decorative pattern if desired. Brush top crust with egg wash and sprinkle with sesame seeds. (You won't use all the egg wash on this one pie; throw away leftover.)
   Bake at 350° for 30 minutes or until golden brown. Remove from oven and place on cooling rack. Loosen and remove sides of springform pan. Allow to cool 10 minutes before serving.

The River Street Inn is an unusual combination of arts-and-crafts style and modern comfort.

Seafood

KEDGEREE   109
The English House B&B

LOBSTER QUICHE   109
Murphy's B&B

CRAB QUICHE   109
The Carlisle House

MAGIC CANYON QUICHE   110
Magic Canyon Ranch

EGGS PACIFICA   111
The Beech Tree Manor

SHELLFISH CREPE PIE   112
Barnard–Good House

SMOKED SALMON EGG
CREPES   112
Carter House

CAJUN CRABMEAT FILO
PASTRIES   113
Barrow House

LOBSTER NEWBURG   113
Murphy's B&B

FINNAN HADDIE   113
Murphy's B&B

Decked out with yard upon yard of gingerbread and bright with color, the John Palmer House in Portland, Oregon, is a true "painted lady" (see page 71). The horse is named Lady C.J.

_MOGEL ©

S A BREAKFAST DISH, seafood may seem odd to some; but in many parts of the world, it is standard fare. This is not exactly true throughout the United States—the recipes in this section all come from B&Bs in the coastal states. Nevertheless, properly prepared and presented, a seafood dish at breakfast can be an unusual treat. It can be as elaborate as Eggs Pacifica or as simple and old-fashioned as Finnan Haddie.

The ten recipes in this chapter are used for breakfast or brunch at the B&Bs that submitted them, but you'll find that they are also suitable for lunch or dinner. As part of a breakfast or brunch menu, these dishes are well complemented by a fruit course and a bread or pastry to offset their rich and often savory flavor.

Garnish seafood dishes with a sprig of fresh parsley for some color. It's also advisable to offer your breakfast guests an alternative, since many Americans are initially reluctant to try fish for breakfast. For the most part, though, B&B travelers are an adventuresome sort, and I've been pleased to find that many of them—even those who've never heard of it—are happy to try my Finnan Haddie. They usually ask for seconds.

KEDGEREE

*The English House Bed &
Breakfast (p. 94)*

SERVES 6.

This popular English dish is an
example of an adaptation from
England's long association with
India. It makes a rich and savory
breakfast or brunch entrée.

1 cup long grain rice
1 lb. smoked haddock
½ cup milk
½ cup water
½ cup butter
1 tsp. curry powder
  salt and pepper to taste
  pinch of cayenne
2 hard-boiled eggs
1 tsp. chopped parsley
1 Tbs. butter

Cook the rice, drain and set aside
to keep warm. Place the fish in the
milk and water in a covered pan,
and poach for about 4 minutes.
Remove the fish, discarding the liquid. Peel the skin from the fish
and discard. Over a bowl break the
fish into fairly large flakes.

Melt half the butter in a pan.
Stir in the curry powder, and then
add the flaked fish. Season with
the salt, pepper and cayenne. Keep
warm.

Add the other half of the butter
to the rice; heat.

Shell the hard-boiled eggs, remove
the yolks, and coarsely chop the
whites; add the whites to the fish.
Push the yolks through a coarse sieve
and set aside.

Mix the fish with the rice and toss
gently. To serve, sprinkle egg yolks
and a little parsley over the fish-and-
rice combination, dot with butter
and serve immediately.

LOBSTER QUICHE

Murphy's B&B (p. 13)

SERVES 8.

Crust
1½ cups flour
1 tsp. salt
6 Tbs. butter or shortening
3–5 Tbs. ice water

Mix together the flour and salt.
Using a pastry fork or food processor, cut in the shortening until the
mixture resembles coarse sand. Mix
in just enough ice water to form a
ball. Wrap the pastry in plastic wrap
and refrigerate for one hour. Roll
out the chilled dough on a lightly
floured board to ⅛" to ¼" thickness. Line a 9" quiche pan with the
pastry, cover with plastic wrap and
refrigerate until ready to use.

Filling
3 eggs
1½ cups half-and-half
1 Tbs. butter, melted

1½ cups cooked lobster meat,
  chopped coursely
¾ cup grated Swiss cheese
¾ cup grated cheddar cheese
1 small onion
1 clove garlic
¼ tsp. dry mustard
½ tsp. tarragon
1 tsp. parsley
  salt and pepper to taste

Preheat oven to 350°F.

In a large bowl beat the eggs
well. Add the half-and-half and
beat again. Stir in the lobster meat
and cheeses. Set aside. Chop the
onion fine and sauté in a little butter. When the onion is almost done,
crush the garlic and stir in; remove
from heat. Add the onion and garlic, dry mustard, herbs, salt and
pepper to the lobster mixture and
combine well. Pour into the quiche
crust and bake at 350° for 45 minutes. Cool on a rack for 5 minutes
before slicing.

CRAB QUICHE

The Carlisle House (p. 202)

SERVES 8.

1 9" pie crust, unbaked
2 6-oz. cans of crabmeat
2 eggs, beaten
1 cup grated cheddar cheese
1 cup heavy cream
½ cup chopped and sautéed
  scallions
4 slices provolone cheese

Preheat oven to 425°F.

Use your favorite recipe for a
quiche crust (see above) and line
a 9" quiche pan with it. Prick

the bottom with a fork and bake
for 8 minutes at 425°, and then
place on a cooling rack while you
assemble the filling.

Preheat oven to 375°F.

To make the filling: In a large
bowl mix the crabmeat with the
eggs, cheddar cheese, heavy cream
and scallions. Pour into the pie shell.
Place slices of provolone cheese over
top. Bake at 375° for 40 minutes
or until set. After removing from
oven, place on rack to cool for 15
minutes before serving.

Magic Canyon Ranch
Homer, Alaska

MAGIC CANYON RANCH enjoys total seclusion and superb views of mountains and glaciers, although it is only a five-minute drive to downtown Homer. Guests are invited to roam over the ranch property and to enjoy the extensive Alaskan library. An Alaskan historian and anthropologist, the host is eager to share lore about the exciting heritage of Alaska and of Kachemak Bay and to help organize recreational activities.

Homer was a homesteading community, now turned to commercial fishing. Sport fishing for halibut, salmon and trout is popular. The natural beauty of the place has also attracted a community of craftspeople, artisans and artists. A number of architecturally and historically important log buildings built by the early settlers to the area have been preserved and may be viewed on a walking tour.

Situated on Kachemak Bay, important as a habitat for varied marine and other wildlife, Homer is a fascinating destination for the naturalist. The bay is one of the most productive in the world, home to shrimp, salmon, herring, halibut, octopus and other marine fauna. This area is also host to more than a million migrating birds every year. Marine mammals, including beluga, minke and orca whales, sea otters, harbor seals, sea lions and porpoises live in these waters too. The bay is thirty-nine miles long and up to six-hundred feet deep with tidal fluctuations as great as twenty-seven feet.

Guests at Magic Canyon Ranch enjoy a full, home-cooked breakfast in a dining room with a breathtaking view of the bay and mountains. Carrie Reed likes to use local products in cooking—wild berries for jams and sauces, smoked salmon, halibut and local herbs and plants.

Magic Canyon Ranch
40015 Waterman Road
Homer, Alaska 99603
(907) 235–6077

Carrie Reed

OPPOSITE: *Like the drawing room of any English country house worth its salt, the living room of the Beech Tree Manor is intended for comfort.*

MAGIC CANYON QUICHE

SERVES 8.

Pie Crust (makes 3 crusts)
3 cups whole-wheat pastry flour
1 cup wheat germ
1 tsp. salt
1 cup shortening
1 egg
1 Tbs. vinegar
1 Tbs. honey
1 cup water

Mix the flour, wheat germ and salt. Cut in the shortening until the mixture is crumbly. In a separate bowl beat together the egg, vinegar, honey and water. Add to the flour mixture and blend well. Form into three balls, wrap in plastic wrap, and chill for at least 30 minutes. (Extra balls may be frozen.)

Roll out one ball of pastry on a lightly floured board to line a 10" quiche pan. Cover and refrigerate.

Quiche Filling
12 oz. Swiss cheese, grated
½ lb. salmon, cooked
1 Tbs. fresh chives, chopped
1 Tbs. fresh parsley, chopped
½ lb. fresh broccoli, parboiled
      and chopped
3 eggs
2 cups milk
⅛ tsp. salt
  pepper and paprika to taste

Preheat oven to 350°F.

Line crust with half the cheese, layer with the other solid ingredients. Cover with the remaining cheese. Beat together the eggs and milk and pour over the quiche. Sprinkle with a little freshly ground pepper and paprika. Bake at 350° for 1 hour. Cool slightly before serving.

The Beech Tree Manor

Seattle, Washington

NAMED FOR THE MASSIVE copper beech tree on the property, the Beech Tree Manor is a turn of the century mansion situated on historic Queen Ann Hill near downtown Seattle. The house has recently been restored and renovated in a comfortable "English manor house" style.

Electric trolleys link the Beech Tree Manor to downtown Seattle. Considered one of America's most civilized cities, Seattle is proud of all it has to offer the visitor—museums, galleries, parks, fine dining, the performing arts, a bustling waterfront and boating on Puget Sound are just some of the activities available in this clean city.

The ambiance at the Beech Tree Manor is one of quiet charm. Attention to the little details make a stay here special—sherry in the drawing room every evening in front of the fireplace; beds made up with all-cotton, ironed sheets. Virginia Lucero has a small shop specializing in antique linens on the first floor of the house, and special linens are in use throughout the manor.

A full gourmet breakfast is served in the dining room.

The Beech Tree Manor
1405 Queen Ann Avenue North
Seattle, Washington 98109
(206) 281-7037

Virginia Lucero

EGGS PACIFICA

SERVES 8.

Assemble this dish the evening before, and bake in the morning. This is a rich and elegant breakfast or brunch dish.

```
12  hard-boiled eggs
 1  lb. small shrimp
 2  Tbs. butter
 3  Tbs. flour
1⅔  cups half-and-half
 1  tsp. dry mustard
 ½  tsp. salt
    freshly ground pepper to taste
 1  Tbs. parmesan cheese
 2  Tbs. white wine
 2  Tbs. capers
 3  Tbs. chopped fresh parsley
 1  tsp. chopped fresh dill
 ⅓  cup grated Swiss cheese
```

Shell the hard-boiled eggs and run through an egg slicer twice. Set aside in a covered bowl.

Cook, cool and shell the shrimp. Melt the butter in a saucepan. Stir in the flour and whisk. Slowly add the half-and-half, whisking constantly, until a thick sauce is formed. Add the dry mustard, salt, pepper, parmesan cheese, wine, capers, parsley and dill. Stir and remove from heat.

Arrange half the eggs in the bottom of a greased 2-qt. casserole. Layer the shrimp over the eggs. Place the rest of the eggs over the shrimp. Pour the sauce over all and sprinkle with the cheese.

At this point the casserole may be covered and refrigerated overnight.

When ready to bake, bring the casserole to room temperature before baking at 425°, uncovered, for 20 to 25 minutes or until hot and bubbly.

Serve immediately over toast points or puff pastry shells.

SHELLFISH CREPE PIE

Barnard–Good House (p. 14)

SERVES 6.

Although somewhat time-consuming to make, this recipe is worth the effort. It should be assembled the day before and baked in the morning. When I make this, I use lobster meat fresh from my husband's boat. However, frozen lobster meat is fine, as are frozen shrimp or crab if fresh is not available. This is a rich dish, perfect for a special brunch.

Crepes
1 cup water
1 cup flour
4 eggs
  salt

Bechemel Sauce
4 Tbs. butter
6 Tbs. flour
2 cups milk
1 tsp. salt
½ tsp. black pepper
½ tsp. marjoram
¼ tsp. nutmeg
2 Tbs. sherry
1 lb. cooked lobster, crab or
    shrimp or a combination of all
¼ cup fresh grated parmesan cheese

To make the crepes: Beat all ingredients together until smooth. Cook the crepes and set them aside on sheets of waxed paper as they are done. This recipe should make approximately 12 crepes.

To make the sauce: Melt butter in a heavy saucepan. Sprinkle in the flour and cook gently, stirring constantly for 5 minutes. Do not let the flour and butter brown at all. Meanwhile, bring milk to a boil. When milk reaches a boil, pour the butter and flour mixture into the boiling milk all at once. As the mixture boils and bubbles, remove it from heat and beat it vigorously with a wire whisk. When the bubbling stops, return the pan to medium heat and bring the mixture back to a boil, stirring constantly for 5 minutes. Remove from heat. Season to taste with salt, pepper, marjoram, nutmeg and sherry. Mix in the shellfish.

To assemble the pie: Line a large pie plate with 4 crepes overlapping in a circle. Spread one-third of the shellfish mixture evenly over the crepes. Top this with another layer of 4 overlapping crepes. Spread one-third of the shellfish mixture over this layer of crepes. Now add the last layer of 4 overlapping crepes, and top with the remaining shellfish mixture. Sprinkle with the parmesan cheese. *At this point, you may cover the dish with plastic wrap and refrigerate overnight.* If you do, bring the dish to room temperature before baking. Bake at 400° for 20 to 30 minutes, or until the top is bubbly and golden. Cool for 5 to 10 minutes on a rack before cutting into wedges to serve. Serve hot.

SMOKED SALMON EGG CREPES

Carter House (p. 34)

SERVES 4 (makes 8 crepes).

An elegant dish, well suited for a brunch. Since there are a few steps involved in making this recipe, you may want to do some of the preparation, such as making the crepes and the filling, beforehand.

Crepes
3 eggs
1 Tbs. water
⅛ tsp. cream of tartar

Filling
4 ounces smoked salmon
¼ cup sour cream
⅛ cup chopped onion
  salt and pepper
8 blanched chive stems

To make the crepes: Beat the eggs with the water and cream of tartar. Using a crepe pan well-coated with butter, place 1 tablespoon of egg batter in the pan and cook about 1 minute before turning and cooking the other side for about ½ minute. As the crepes are cooked, set them aside on waxed paper. This should give you 8 crepes.

To make the filling: In a food processor, process the smoked salmon, sour cream, onion, salt and pepper until smooth. Place about 1 Tbs. of filling into center of each crepe, pull crepe up around filling and wrap and tie with a chive stem.

Note: The chive stems are blanched by dropping them into boiling water for just a minute. This will soften them just enough to use as ties around the crepes.

Place the filled crepes in a shallow baking dish, cover with foil, and place in a warm oven for 15 minutes before serving.

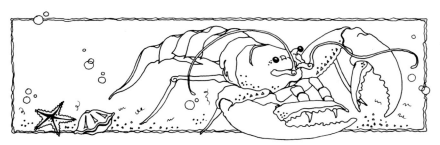

CAJUN CRABMEAT FILO PASTRIES

Barrow House (p. 207)

MAKES 3 to 4 dozen.

These also make excellent hot hors d'oeuvres.

      ¼ cup butter
      ⅓ cup chopped onion
      ⅓ cup chopped celery
      ⅓ cup chopped green bell pepper
      1 clove garlic
      ½ tsp. basil
      ½ tsp. salt
      ¼ tsp. white pepper
      ¼ tsp. black pepper
      ¼ tsp. cayenne pepper
      3 Tbs. flour
      1 lb. crabmeat, cooked and flaked
     20 oz. cream cheese
      3 egg yolks, beaten
      1 box filo dough
    1½ cups butter. melted

Preheat oven to 350°F.

Melt the butter in a large skillet and sauté the chopped vegetables. Lower the heat and stir in the garlic, crushed. Add the spices and stir well. Stir in the flour and cook a couple of minutes more. Now add the crabmeat and cream cheese, stirring until the cheese is smooth and well incorporated. Remove from heat and let cool, then mix in the egg yolks.

Lay out double sheets of filo (cover unused filo with a damp towel to keep it from drying out), and cut into 4 strips, lengthwise. Brush with a little melted butter. Place a spoonful of crabmeat filling on the bottom corner of each strip. Take the corner of the filo and fold over to the other side, repeating this all the way up the strip until you have a little triangular package. Repeat this until filo and filling are all used. Place the triangles on a cookie sheet and brush with a little melted butter. *At this point the pastries may be frozen to be baked later.* Bake at 350° for 20 minutes. Serve hot.

Variation: Shrimp, cooked, shelled and chopped, may be substituted for the crabmeat, or you may use a mixture of both.

FINNAN HADDIE

Murphy's B&B (p. 13)

SERVES 4 to 6.

      2 lbs. smoked haddock
    2½ cups milk
         salt and pepper to taste
      2 Tbs. butter
      3 Tbs. flour
         freshly ground pepper

Preheat oven to 250°F.

Place the haddock in a large cast-iron skillet and cover with the milk. Season with a little salt and pepper. Cover and cook over medium heat (don't let the milk boil) for 15 to 20 minutes, turning the fish over halfway through the process. When done, put fish in a warm oven. Meanwhile, increase the heat under the milk and add the butter, stirring constantly. Whisk in the flour and stir until the sauce thickens slightly. Season with freshly ground pepper. Remove from heat.

Serve the fish on toast or split biscuits, and cover with a generous portion of the sauce. Garnish with a sprig of fresh parsley.

LOBSTER NEWBURG

Murphy's B&B (p. 13)

SERVES 6.

This is more flavorful if prepared a day in advance.

      3 cups cooked lobster meat, chopped
      ½ cup butter
      4 Tbs. flour
    1¼ cups milk
    1¼ cups cream
      ½ cup grated cheddar cheese
      ¼ cup grated parmesan cheese
         salt and pepper
      1 tsp. tarragon
      2 Tbs. sherry
      6 puff pastry shells

Optional
    1 cup fresh peas or
    1 cup chopped celery or
    1 cup sliced mushrooms

Sauté the lobster in the butter for a few minutes. Sprinkle with the flour, stirring until the flour is incorporated into the butter. Slowly add the milk and cream, stirring constantly over medium heat, until the mixture thickens. Lower the heat; stir in the cheeses. Season with salt, pepper, tarragon and sherry. Add the peas, celery or mushrooms. Stir and remove from heat if making a day in advance. Allow to cool before covering and refrigerating. Reheat in a double boiler.

If not making in advance, lower the heat to simmer and allow to sit for at least 30 minutes before serving.

Bake the pastry shells according to the directions on the box.

To serve: Fill hot pastry shells with the sauce and garnish with fresh parsley sprigs.

Breakfast Meats_____

WALNUT SAUSAGE ROLLS   117
The Pullman Inn B&B

SAUSAGE & WILD RICE   117
The Bells B&B

PEARL'S HOMEMADE SAUSAGE   117
Bed 'n' Breakfast—Still Country

SAUSAGE & GRITS CASSEROLE   118
Lowenstein-Long House

SAUSAGE BAKE   120
Marlow House

OKTOBERFEST SAUSAGE   121
Mentone B&B

HERBED SAUSAGE CHEESE
BALLS   122
*The Fleming Jones
Homestead*

HAM LOAF WITH MUSTARD
SAUCE   123
Hidden Pond Farm

BAKED COUNTRY HAM
WITH MUSTARD GLAZE   124
Meramec Farm

CORNED BEEF HASH   125
Murphy's B&B

TENNESSEE GRAVY AND
BISCUITS   125
The Bells B&B

*The Madewood Plantation House (see
page 11), is one of Louisiana's great
antebellum mansions.*

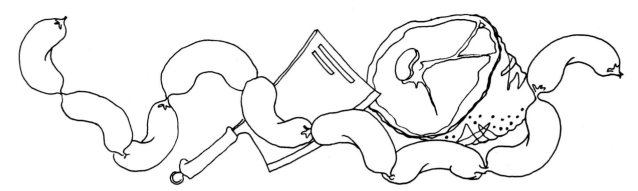

*T*HE AROMA OF sizzling bacon, mingling with those of freshly brewed coffee and bread hot from the oven, is an enticement to come to breakfast that few can resist. With so many Americans in the habit of downing a quick bowl of cereal before dashing off to work, a home-cooked breakfast that includes crisp bacon, sizzling ham or savory sausage is a treat indeed. This chapter includes directions for preparing these simple accompaniments in the best manner, as well as eleven recipes for a variety of interesting meat dishes suitable for breakfast or brunch. This section contains only two recipes that can be served as main dishes. All the rest are meant to be served as side dishes.

The method for cooking bacon I learned as a child—familiar to most people—is to fry it in a cast-iron skillet, turning it with a fork to brown evenly on both sides, removing when cooked to drain on a piece of brown paper or paper toweling. The bacon fat (drippings) is poured off into a can or jar to save for cooking. Now that I have a microwave, I have discovered an even better way to cook bacon, especially for a busy B&B hostess. I assumed that this simple method would be familiar to anyone with a microwave, but I learned from another B&B hostess that she never knew she could cook bacon in this way.

Using a tray made specifically for cooking bacon in a microwave (available at any department store), lay out the strips of bacon so that the edges just touch but don't overlap (most trays will hold from 8 to 10 pieces). Place in the middle of the microwave and cook on full power for 30 seconds per slice of bacon (4 minutes for 8 slices). The well of the tray will collect the bacon fat; save if desired. Remove the slices of bacon and place on a plate lined with a paper towel, turning each piece of bacon so that the opposite side faces up. Cook on full power for an additional 20 to 30 seconds per slice of bacon (approximately 3 minutes for 8 slices of bacon). The bacon will be crisp and flat, and it will not shrink and curl the way it does when cooked in a skillet. Because the final cooking is done on paper toweling, the bacon emerges from the microwave drained and ready to serve. This method frees a burner on the stove, eliminates bacon fat being splattered all over the stove (and the cook) and has no effect on the temperature of the kitchen—especially pleasant in the summer.

The best utensil for cooking sausage (links or patties) or to grill ham is a well-seasoned cast-iron skillet. The sausage should be evenly browned on the outside and thoroughly cooked on the inside. Drain on paper toweling before serving.

If bacon, sausage or ham is cooked before the rest of the breakfast is ready, it may be kept in a warm oven; but it should not be kept this way for more than 15 minutes. A few of the recipes in this section are suitable for dinner as well as breakfast: Sausage and Wild Rice, Oktoberfest Sausage, Ham Loaf with Mustard Sauce. Glazed Ham would probably be cooked for a dinner, with the leftovers showing up at breakfast.

At breakfast, these meat dishes are usually served right on the plate with pancakes or eggs. At a buffet brunch, they are best served on their own plates with the appropriate utensil. Some B&B hostesses serve breakfast meat on a separate platter and let guests help themselves to much, little or none, depending on their personal preferences.

WALNUT SAUSAGE ROLLS

The Pullman Inn Bed & Breakfast (p. 17)

SERVES 6.

"At the Pullman Inn we often serve these for breakfast with coffee, juice, fruit, creamy scrambled eggs, sliced tomatoes and whole wheat toast," says Dennis Morganson.

This is a delicious and elegant way to serve sausage. The puff pastry is buttery and golden, making this simple-to-prepare dish appear quite impressive.

1 box Pepperidge Farm Puff
    Pastry (1 sheet of pastry)
1 lb. seasoned ground pork
1 cup fine bread crumbs
1 cup walnuts, coarsely broken
½ cup chopped scallions

Preheat oven to 400°F.

Using one sheet of puff pastry (each box has 2 sheets), roll out on a lightly floured board to approximately 10″ × 15″. Cut into 3 long strips, about 5″ wide.

In a bowl combine the sausage, bread crumbs, walnuts and scallions. Divide the sausage mixture into 3 equal portions and form into balls. Flatten the balls slightly so that they are cylindrical. Place the sausage at one end of the pastry strip and roll up. Place on an ungreased cookie sheet and bake at 400° for 30 minutes or until golden brown. Cut each roll in half, and serve immediately.

SAUSAGE AND WILD RICE

The Bells Bed & Breakfast (p. 9)

SERVES 10.

This savory dish has been a hit at breakfast, but I've also enjoyed it for a light dinner with salad. Louise Sims says this is one of her most frequently requested recipes. She likes to serve it with scrambled eggs, baked apples and scones.

1 6-oz. pkg. Uncle Ben's Long
    Grain & Wild Rice
1 lb. bulk breakfast sausage
1 medium-sized onion, chopped
½ cup sliced mushrooms
¼ cup butter
¼ cup flour
1½ cups chicken stock
1 tsp. ground black pepper
¼ cup heavy cream

Preheat oven to 350°F.

Cook the rice according to the directions on the package. Set aside. Cook the sausage, breaking into small pieces as it cooks. Drain off all fat and add the onion, mushrooms and butter to the sausage. Sauté just until the onion is tender. Sprinkle with the flour and mix well. Add the chicken stock and pepper. Stir and cook until thickened. Mix in the cream and remove from heat. *At this point you may refrigerate the cooked rice and the sausage mixture (separately) until the next day.* If you do this, bring the ingredients to room temperature before baking.

When you are ready to complete the casserole, combine the rice with the sausage mixture and pour into a 2-quart casserole. Bake at 350° for 30 to 45 minutes, until the casserole is hot and bubbly.

PEARL'S HOMEMADE SAUSAGE

Bed 'n' Breakfast–Still Country (p. 47)

SERVES 4 to 6.

Pearl Thurlow and her husband once raised hogs, along with other live-stock. Here's her simple but tasty recipe for sausage. As she points out, you don't need to live on a farm to make this — just ask your butcher for the best cut of pork for sausage and grind it at home. The results are worth the effort.

2 lbs. pork
2 Tbs. dried sage
3 tsp. salt
2 tsp. pepper

Run the pork through a grinder twice. Place in a large bowl, add the sage, salt and pepper and blend thoroughly. Cover and refrigerate overnight.

Form the sausage into patties and cook in a lightly oiled hot skillet, browning on both sides. Drain on paper toweling and serve immediately.

This sausage may also be used in any recipe that calls for bulk sausage.

Note: Pearl Thurlow suggests that those interested in making different varieties of sausage write to the Morton Salt Company for more recipes and packaged sausage seasonings. Their address: Dept. CGS, 110 North Wacker Drive, Chicago, IL 60606.

The Lowenstein–Long House
Memphis, Tennessee

A LANDMARK OF midtown Memphis, the Lowenstein–Long House is a turn-of-the-century Victorian, which the Longs have restored to its original elegance. The house was built by department-store owner Abraham Lowenstein, whose name the Longs have added to their own for the house.

Situated on almost an acre of lawn, the old mansion is a striking stone structure listed on the National Register of Historic Places. To enter the house is to step back in time. The interior blends art nouveau and beaux arts traditions in its elegant chandeliers, fireplaces, hand-carved woodwork, etched glass and stunning staircase.

The Lowenstein–Long House is located five minutes from downtown Memphis; some of the highlights for visitors are the Orpheum Theatre, Mud Island, Victorian Village and Overton Square. Graceland, Elvis Presley's home, is fifteen minutes away.

The Longs offer their guests a buffet breakfast in the formal dining room. Breakfast includes fresh fruit, juice, rolls, pastry, coffee and tea, all served with Southern hospitality.

The Lowenstein–Long House
217 N. Waldran
Memphis, Tennessee 38105
(901) 274-0509

Martha W. Long

SAUSAGE AND GRITS CASSEROLE

SERVES 4 to 6.

1 cup grits (quick-cooking type)
3 cups beef bouillon
1 lb. spicy sausage, bulk
½ cup butter, melted
4 eggs, beaten
1 cup milk
½ cup sharp cheddar cheese, grated

Preheat oven to 350°F.

Cook the grits in the bouillon until thick, 3 to 4 minutes. Cook sausage until well done; drain on paper towels. Add sausage to grits. Stir in the butter, eggs, milk and half the grated cheese. Mix well and pour into a greased casserole dish or long baking pan. Top with remaining grated cheese.

Bake at 350° for 30 to 40 minutes or until set. Serve hot.

Zinnias, marigolds, snapdragons, impatiens and verbenas from Martha Murphy's cutting garden (see page 13).

The opulence of the Lowenstein-Long House is everywhere apparent—in the tiled fireplace and its immense mahogany surround, the leaded glass, the molded plaster and the hardwood floors. ABOVE: *The sitting room.* LEFT: *One of the bedrooms.*

Marlow House
Marietta, Georgia

BUILT IN 1887 as a boarding house by Idell Marlow, this capacious old Queen Anne house has been carefully restored, and opened in 1983 as the first Victorian B&B in greater Atlanta. Downtown Atlanta is thirty minutes away, but just outside the front door is the newly restored historic Marietta Square, with theatre, art galleries and fine restaurants.

Breakfast is served in the elegant dining room. The high ceiling, large windows, fireplace and mirrored-top table set with china, silver and crystal make this room a lovely setting for a lively meal. A sample breakfast menu includes Sausage Bake, baked tomatoes, fresh fruit tray, hot biscuits with jam and butter, hot bran muffins, orange juice and coffee or tea.

Marlow House
192 Church Street
Marietta, Georgia 30060
(404) 462–1887

Kathleen McDaniel

SAUSAGE BAKE

SERVES 8 to 10.

This is tasty, easy to prepare, and excellent to feed a crowd. It works well for a buffet-style breakfast or brunch.

    2 lbs. bulk sausage (1 lb. spicy,
        1 lb. mild)
    1 cup raw grits
    2 Tbs. butter
    5 eggs
    1½ cups milk
    1½ cups grated cheddar cheese
        salt and pepper

Preheat oven to 350°F.

Cook and drain sausage. Set aside. Cook grits according to directions. Add butter to grits and cool. In a separate bowl beat the eggs. Add milk and beat again. Add egg mixture to grits, stir in cheese and season with salt and pepper. Put sausage in bottom of 9″ × 13″ baking dish, and cover with the grits mixture. Bake at 350° for 45 minutes.

Cool for a few minutes before cutting into squares to serve.

LEFT: *Idell Marlow married the dashing Captain Heggie here in 1890. Scarlett O'Hara and Rhett Butler would have felt quite at home if they had been among the guests.*

OPPOSITE: *High in the mountains of northern Alabama, the Mentone Inn is one of those rambling old buildings that make visitors feel completely at home ten minutes after arriving.*

Mentone Bed & Breakfast
Mentone, Alabama

A LARGE, RAMBLING, comfortable house, Mentone Bed & Breakfast sits atop beautiful Lookout Mountain, site of the Civil War's "battle above the clouds." Guests find that the B&B offers copious amounts of two increasingly scarce commodities—*peace* and *quiet*. The more active among them can set off to explore nearby Sequoyah Caverns, Little River Canyon, DeSoto Falls and Park (with twenty miles of hiking trails), Cloudland Canyon or Cloudmont Golf and Ski Resort.

Guests start off their day with a full breakfast prepared by an excellent cook, Amelia Brooks, who is also a caterer.

Mentone Bed & Breakfast
P.O. Box 284
Mentone, Alabama 35984
(205) 634-4836

Amelia Brooks

OKTOBERFEST SAUSAGE

SERVES 6.

This hearty, savory dish is well suited for fall or winter. This can be served as a breakfast or supper dish.

2 lbs. bulk breakfast sausage
2 apples
1 large onion
2 16-oz. cans sauerkraut
6 potatoes
1 cup apple juice
    salt and pepper to taste

Brown the sausage in a well-seasoned Dutch oven. Remove the oven from heat and drain off any excess grease. Core the apples and cut into wedges; arrange over the sausage. Quarter the onion and slice into thin wedges; arrange over the apples. Layer the sauerkraut over the onion. Wash the potatoes and cut into large chunks. Arrange over the sauerkraut. Pour the apple juice over all and sprinkle with a little salt and pepper. Cover tightly and simmer over low heat, stirring once, for 30 to 40 minutes or until the potatoes test done. Serve hot with a crusty loaf of rye, pumpernickel or sourdough bread.

Variation: Sweet Italian sausage may be substituted for the breakfast sausage.

Fleming Jones Homestead
Placerville, California

HALFWAY BETWEEN Lake Tahoe and Sacramento, the Fleming Jones Homestead is an old farmhouse built in 1883 and nestled on eleven acres in the Sierra Foothills of the Mother Lode. Its setting offers meadows and woods to wander through and groomed gardens to sit and relax in. Animals on the homestead include ponies, burros, ducks, chickens and Rocky, the tireless "fetching dog." Nearby there are Gold Rush mining towns, museums and renowned wineries to explore. During the winter months cross-country skiing is popular, and at other times of the year, white-water rafting, swimming, boating and fishing are available on the rivers and lakes of the region.

Guests are invited to enjoy their first cup of morning coffee on the balcony, deck or porch swing before joining everyone in the dining room for a full, farm-fresh breakfast of hot muffins, baked apples, farmhouse preserves, blue-ribbon fruit breads, rich farm eggs, juice and more freshly ground coffee or a selection of teas.

The Fleming Jones Homestead
3170 Newtown Road
Placerville, California 95667
(916) 626–5840

Janice Condit

OPPOSITE: *Fresh flowers add color to a sunny corner at Murphy's B&B (see page 13).*

BELOW: *Although the Fleming Jones Homestead has gardens, trails and its own menagerie, it also offers proximity to Gold Rush sites and winery tours.*

HERBED SAUSAGE CHEESE BALLS
The Fleming Jones Homestead

MAKES 40 balls.

A very good item at brunch, these also make tasty hot hors d'oeuvres.

2½	lbs. fresh ground pork sausage
2	lbs. sharp cheddar cheese, grated
3	cups flour
3	tsp. baking powder
2	tsp. salt
10	Tbs. mixed Italian herbs
3–5	Tbs. curry

Preheat oven to 350°F.

With sausage and cheese at room temperature, mix together well. In a separate bowl sift together the flour, baking powder, salt, herbs and curry; add to the sausage mixture and mix thoroughly. Shape into 1″ balls. Place on an ungreased cookie sheet and bake at 350° for 15 to 20 minutes. Serve hot.

Storage note: Uncooked balls may be stored in plastic bags indefinitely in your freezer.

Hidden Pond Farm
Fennville, Michigan

SURROUNDED BY TWENTY-EIGHT acres of landscaped woodland, Hidden Pond Farm is an elegant residence where visitors enjoy a stay of peaceful relaxation. Deer can often be seen gathered around the pond from which the B&B takes its name. The surrounding woods are ideal for bird-watching, and for cross-country skiing in winter. The grounds are planted with hundreds of rhododendrons and azaleas, along with pink and white dogwoods, flowering almonds, lilacs, blue spruces and about a thousand irises, making them especially lovely in the spring and early summer. But as Edward Kennedy says, "It is lovely here year-round, with four beautifully distinct seasons."

The house is tastefully decorated and furnished with antiques and art that Edward Kennedy has collected over the years. Mr. Kennedy has also placed a strong emphasis on privacy in designing the layout of guest quarters: "I'll be in your way or out of your way as much as you want."

Guests enjoy a full breakfast, prepared by a gourmet cook. "I hope that every stranger who comes here leaves as a friend," says Edward X. Kennedy.

Hidden Pond Farm
P.O. Box 461
Fennville, Michigan 49408
(616) 561–2491

Edward X. Kennedy

HAM LOAF WITH MUSTARD SAUCE

SERVES 6 to 8.

Ham Loaf
1 cup bread crumbs
1 cup milk
2 eggs, slightly beaten
1 lb. ground ham
1 lb. ground pork
1 tsp. dry mustard
½ cup vinegar
½ cup brown sugar
1½ cups water

Preheat oven to 325°F.

In a large bowl cover the bread crumbs with the milk. Add the slightly beaten eggs and the ground meat. Mix well. Form into a loaf and place in a roasting pan lined with foil (for ease of clean-up).

Combine the dry mustard, vinegar, brown sugar and water in a saucepan; stir and bring to a boil. Pour over the loaf, and bake at 325° for 2 to 2½ hours. Baste frequently.

Mustard Sauce
2½ Tbs. dry mustard
½ cup sugar
   pinch salt
2 eggs
½ cup half-and-half
½ cup vinegar

Combine the dry ingredients. In a separate bowl beat the eggs; add the half-and-half and vinegar and beat well. Stir in the dry ingredients. Heat, stirring constantly, until the mixture boils. Serve cold.

To serve: Remove the loaf from the oven and let it cool for 10 minutes before slicing. Spoon a little sauce on each serving, or if serving buffet-style have the sauce in a dish for guests to serve themselves with the ham loaf.

Meramec Farm Stay B&B

Bourbon, Missouri

A WORKING FARM situated along the Meramec River, Meramec Farm Stay B&B is a comfortable and charming old farmhouse more than a century old "without fancy frills," according to Carol Springer and David Curtis. Guests here find a perfect setting for enjoying the peace and natural beauty of the surrounding countryside. Carol Springer recommends a sunny afternoon spent floating down the river in an inner tube as a good remedy for whatever ails you. But the highlight of a stay here is undoubtedly the good home cooking, using fresh, home-grown ingredients. A full breakfast includes fruit salad, ham, omelets, grits, biscuits, homemade jellies and apple butter, juice and coffee.

Carol and David prefer to list themselves with a reservation service, Bed & Breakfast of St. Louis. Their address and phone number are given below.

Meramec Farm Stay B&B
Bourbon, Missouri
Carol Springer and David Curtis

c/o Bed & Breakfast of St. Louis
1900 Wyoming Street
St. Louis, Missouri 63118
(314) 965–4328

Mike Warner

BAKED COUNTRY HAM WITH MUSTARD GLAZE
Maramec Farm Stay

SERVES 6 to 12.

If you have a real country ham, you should cook it first in an apple juice mixture to reduce its saltiness. This step may be unnecessary for a commercially prepared ham, but even so, it makes the ham more juicy and tender.

1 6-lb. country ham
1 qt. apple juice
1 qt. water
 handful whole cloves
1 cup Carol's Homemade Mustard
  (page 221)
1 cup brown sugar

Place the ham in a large pot and pour in the apple juice and water. Bring to a boil, cover and reduce the heat to simmer for about 1 hour. Remove the ham from the liquid and place in a deep baking pan. Pour enough of the liquid into the baking pan to form a deep puddle for the ham to sit in; if necessary, add more apple juice.

When the ham is cool enough to handle, score the top and stud with cloves. Mix the mustard and brown sugar together and spread over the top of the ham.

Cover with a loose foil tent and bake in a preheated 325°F. oven for 1½ hours. Remove the foil and bake for an additional half hour.

Allow to cool on a rack for 15 minutes before slicing.

Note: If desired, you may add pineapple slices to the top of the ham after applying the glaze.

CORNED BEEF HASH
Murphy's B&B (p. 13)

SERVES 6.

A crisp, fried patty of corned beef hash topped with a poached egg is a breakfast favorite. It's a great way to use leftover corned beef, and even if you don't cook corned beef for a meal, you can buy it at your grocery store for this recipe.

1½ cups finely ground corned beef
 3 cups finely chopped potatoes, pre-boiled and cooled
 1 small onion, minced
 ⅓ cup beef stock
   salt and pepper to taste

In a large bowl mix together all the ingredients. Make 6 patties, and place them in a large, well-oiled, hot skillet. Add a little butter, and cook until the bottoms are crisp and brown. Lower the heat to medium and flip the patties. Cook slowly until crisp and brown on both sides. Serve hot, topped with a poached egg.

Variation: Substitute roast beef for corned beef.

Note: The trick to making good hash is to have all the ingredients finely ground and chopped, so that the hash mix is almost a mush. If the pieces of meat and/or potato are too large the hash will not stay together in a patty. If you prefer, ask your butcher to grind the beef for you.

TENNESSEE GRAVY AND BISCUITS
The Bells Bed & Breakfast (p. 9)

SERVES 6.

There is something very satisfying about this simple dish. The gravy may be made ahead and reheated while the biscuits are baking. This is served with Orange Julius (page 9) and cherry cobbler (page 247) at The Bells.

Biscuits
 2 cups flour
 2 tsp. baking powder
 ¼ cup shortening
 ⅔–¾ cup milk

Preheat oven to 500°F.

Combine the flour and baking powder in a large bowl. Cut in the shortening until the mixture resembles coarse meal. Add milk until the dough pulls away from the side of the bowl. On a lightly floured board knead the dough briefly. Roll out to about ½" thickness and cut with a biscuit cutter. (Do not twist the cutter; this will seal the edges and reduce rise.) Place on an ungreased cookie sheet, just touching, and bake at 500° for 8 minutes.

When done, place on a cooling rack.

Sausage Gravy
 1 lb. breakfast sausage patties
 ¼ cup flour
 1 cup milk
 1 cup water
   pepper

Cook the sausage in a large skillet until browned and crisp on the outside. Place on paper toweling to drain. Reserve ¼ cup of the drippings. When cool enough to handle, break the sausage patties into pieces.

Return ¼ cup of the sausage drippings to the skillet and heat over medium heat. Add the flour, stir and heat until the flour has absorbed the fat, is smoking, and has burned. **Do not leave unattended.** Pour milk and water into the hot fat all at once. Cook, stirring, until thickened. Add a generous amount of pepper and add the sausage. Stir and heat thoroughly.

Split the hot biscuits and top with the sausage gravy.

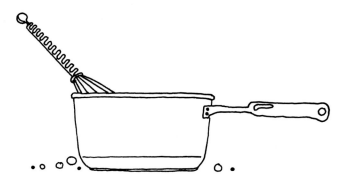

Vegetables & Side Dishes

MORNING POTATOES   129
Carter House

PARMESAN POTATOES   129
Palmer's Chart House

SWEET POTATO PANCAKES   129
Barnard–Good House

DOVER POTATOES   130
The Inn at Mitchell House

POTATO PANCAKES   131
Old Pioneer Garden

LIMA BEAN CASSEROLE   132
Cedar Knoll Farm

BACON-AND-CREAM-
TOPPED TOMATOES   132
Dunbar House, 1880

BRITISH BROILED TOMATOES   132
The Heartstone Inn

CORN FRITTERS   133
Spring House

RELLENOS DIERKER HOUSE   134
Dierker House

BAKED MUSHROOMS   135
The Green Gables Inn

MORNING CARROTS   136
Carter House

BLEU CHEESE MUSHROOMS   136
Palmer's Chart House

ARTICHOKE SQUARES   136
Mentone Bed & Breakfast

AUNT MARTE'S CHEESE
STRAWS   137
The Capers–Motte House

BAKED GARLIC CHEESE GRITS   137
Meramec Farm Stay B&B

CHEESE GRITS   137
Oak Square

*The Manor House is a landmark in
Norfolk, Connecticut (see page 171).*

*A*DDING VEGETABLES to the breakfast menu is healthy and inexpensive. The seventeen recipes in this section make excellent accompaniments to a variety of egg dishes. There are five different ways to prepare potatoes, probably the most popular breakfast vegetable. Tomatoes are also a marvelous complement to eggs, adding a lovely splash of color to the breakfast table. Other vegetables served for breakfast at B&Bs across the country include corn, carrots, lima beans, green peppers, artichokes and mushrooms. Grits are traditionally popular for breakfast at Southern B&Bs, and this section contains two different recipes for grits.

If you grow any of your own vegetables, like the hosts of many of the B&Bs listed in this book, you'll find these recipes offer excellent ways to showcase your fresh produce at breakfast. Most of these recipes are fairly quick to make, but they add tremendously to the appeal of an otherwise plain breakfast. A dish as simple as a fried egg can be transformed into something special when it is accompanied by Parmesan Potatoes and Bacon-and-Cream-Topped Tomatoes. Lightly steamed asparagus goes especially well with eggs Benedict and with many other egg dishes at a spring brunch. I like to add snow peas to my lobster Newburg during the brief time that those delicacies are available. If you are in the habit of shopping at a good produce market and following the seasons, it is likely that you have automatically started to add the freshest, ripest vegetables to your menus. Vegetables can serve as a garnish, a side dish or one of the main items at a brunch buffet.

Use the best produce available, and follow the seasons in determining your menu. Potatoes are always available in excellent condition year-round, as are carrots and mushrooms. Corn fritters can be made with fresh or canned corn, but they are a special treat when made with fresh sweet summer corn. In using these vegetable recipes, you may find that you come up with a new use for one of the vegetables in your own garden. Be creative—well-prepared vegetables are always welcome at breakfast.

MORNING POTATOES
Carter House (p. 34)

SERVES 4.

An excellent complement to breakfast eggs.

2 large potatoes
1 garlic clove
1 onion
1 green bell pepper
1 red bell pepper
4 Tbs. butter
   salt and pepper
1 tsp. fresh parsley, finely
   chopped
½ tsp. fresh rosemary, finely
   chopped

Peel the potatoes and cut into chunks. Place the potatoes in a pot of boiling water along with the garlic and blanch just until tender.

Chop the onion and bell peppers coarsely. Melt the butter in a large skillet and sauté the onion until soft. Toss in the bell peppers and cook for 1 minute.

Add the blanched, drained potatoes to the skillet with the onions and peppers. Toss the vegetables together over medium-high heat until the potatoes are thoroughly cooked and hot. The potatoes will be golden brown. Sprinkle with the fresh herbs and serve immediately.

PARMESAN POTATOES
Palmer's Chart House (p. 220)

SERVES 8.

These tasty potatoes fill the kitchen with a wonderful aroma as they bake. At Palmer's Chart House they are served for breakfast with Canadian bacon, eggs and hot applesauce sprinkled with nutmeg.

6 medium size potatoes
½ cup grated parmesan cheese
¼ cup flour
1 tsp. salt
1 tsp. pepper
4 Tbs. butter

Preheat oven to 350°F.

Peel the potatoes and cut each into eight pieces. Put the parmesan cheese, flour, salt and pepper into a paper bag. Place the potatoes in the bag, hold the top shut and shake. Put the butter into a 9″ × 13″ pan; place in the heated oven until butter melts, remove and add the coated potatoes. Bake at 350° for 30 minutes. Use a spatula to turn the potatoes over, then bake for an additional 30 minutes. Serve hot.

SWEET POTATO PANCAKES
Barnard–Good House (p. 14)

MAKES 12 to 16 small pancakes.

An interesting variation on a potato pancake, these are a flavorful accompaniment to a variety of egg dishes. Since they also complement meat well, they are good for dinner, too.

1 large sweet potato
1 small onion
2 eggs
2 Tbs. flour
⅛ tsp. ground cardamom
   salt and pepper to taste
3 Tbs. oil

Peel the sweet potato and grate (by hand or with a food processor). Grate the onion in the same manner. Wrap the grated potato and onion in a kitchen towel and squeeze out as much moisture as possible. Transfer to a mixing bowl and stir so that the onion is evenly distributed. Beat together the eggs, flour, cardamom, salt and pepper. Stir the egg mixture into the sweet potato mixture and blend well.

Heat the oil in a skillet over moderate heat. Drop the mixture into the skillet by the tablespoon. Cook the pancakes about 1 minute on each side or until crisp and lightly browned. Serve warm with butter.

OPPOSITE: *The Casa de Solana lies in the heart of St. Augustine's historic district, among other survivors of the Spanish colonial past.*

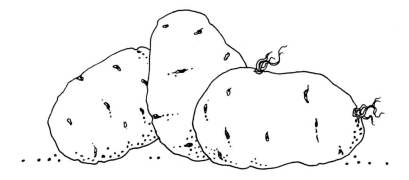

The Inn at Mitchell House
Chestertown, Maryland

A FINE OLD Georgian manor, Mitchell House was built in 1743 just outside Chestertown. This handsome stone house is set on ten rolling acres, where guests are welcome to roam. The gracious interior is comfortably furnished with period pieces. Many fireplaces add a cozy ambiance, and every window offers a tranquil view.

Established in colonial times, Chestertown is filled with landmarks. The historic buildings and quaint shops make this a delightful town to explore on foot. Other points of interest nearby include the Eastern Neck Island National Wildlife Refuge, the Chesapeake Bay Maritime Museum, St. Michael's and Annapolis—home of the United States Naval Academy. For those travelling by boat, Tolchester Marina is just a half-mile away.

After being awakened by birdsong or migrating geese, guests look forward to a hearty, homecooked breakfast in the dining room.

The Inn at Mitchell House
Box 329, R.D. 2, Tolchester Estates
Chestertown, Maryland 21620
(301) 778-6500

Jim and Tracy Stone

DOVER POTATOES

SERVES 12.

These potatoes have a beautiful, crisp, golden skin while being hot and fluffy on the inside. A perfect accompaniment for eggs at breakfast or brunch.

12 medium potatoes
 1 large can of Crisco
    salt

Preheat oven to 450°F.

Clean and peel potatoes. Boil for 20 minutes. Drain and set on paper towelling to dry. Place the Crisco in roasting pan and put in preheated oven. Let this get very hot. Carefully place the potatoes in the hot fat. Roast for 45 minutes, turning every 15 minutes, until brown. Remove from the fat with a slotted spoon and place on brown paper to drain. Salt to taste. Serve immediately.

LEFT: *A minor engagement of the War of 1812, the Battle of Caulk's Field took place near Mitchell House. According to legend, the British commander, Sir Peter Parker, was taken there mortally wounded. Upon his death, his body was immersed in a barrel of rum to preserve it for the trip to his homeland.*

OPPOSITE: *The hot afternoon sun splashes the windows of the parlor with bright light at Old Pioneer Garden. The interior remains restful and shadowed.*

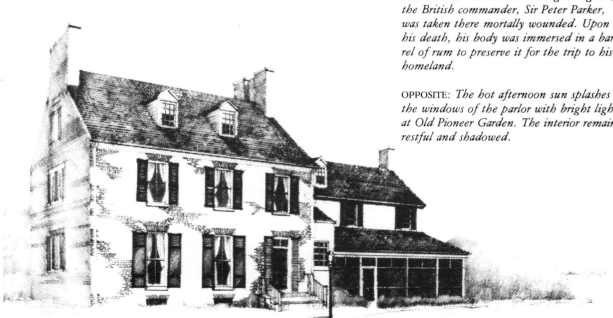

Old Pioneer Garden

Unionville, Nevada

WHEN MARK TWAIN visited Unionville in the 1860s, it was a raucous Nevada mining camp. Today, this quiet, tree-shaded canyon is home to about twenty people.

The remoteness of the area makes Old Pioneer Garden an ideal spot for rest and relaxation. The canyons of the Humboldt Mountain Range offer miles of hiking; excellent fishing and swimming are available in the nearby Humboldt River and in Rye Patch State Park.

Old Pioneer Garden consists of three buildings erected between 1861 and 1868. Tastefully maintained and furnished, they retain the rustic charm of a bygone era. A full, hearty breakfast consisting mostly of home-grown ingredients is the order of the day. During warm weather, it is served in the gazebo; during the cooler months, the large kitchen, warmed by an old fashioned wood stove, makes a cozier setting.

Old Pioneer Garden
Unionville No. 79, Nevada 89418
(702) 538–7585

Mitzi Jones

POTATO PANCAKES

SERVES 4.

Crisp and golden brown outside, steaming hot inside, these tasty "pancakes" are a perfect accompaniment to eggs.

 4 medium-large potatoes
 1 small onion
 1 egg
 ¾ tsp. salt

Peel the potatoes and grate them into a bowl. Peel the onion and grate into the bowl with the potatoes. Beat the egg; add to the potatoes and onion; add the salt. Mix well. Drop by large spoonfuls onto a hot, well-oiled griddle. Cook until crisp and golden brown on both sides. Serve hot.

LIMA BEAN CASSEROLE

Cedar Knoll Farm (p. 24)

SERVES 8.

This is an old Midwestern farm recipe handed down to Mavis Christensen by her grandmother. It makes a good accompaniment to almost any egg dish for breakfast or brunch.

3 10-oz. packages of frozen lima beans
8 slices bacon
¾ cup chopped onion
½ cup stewed tomatoes
1 tsp. salt
½ tsp. pepper
1 cup grated cheddar cheese
6 Tbs. bread crumbs

Preheat oven to 375°F.

Remove the lima beans from their boxes and set aside in a colander to thaw. Cook the bacon until crisp, drain on paper towels, crumble and set aside. Sauté the chopped onion until tender, set aside. Chop the stewed tomatoes. In a large bowl mix together the lima beans, bacon, onion, salt, pepper, tomatoes and cheese. Spoon into a well-buttered 2-quart casserole. Sprinkle with the bread crumbs. Bake at 375° for 45 minutes. Serve hot.

BACON-AND-CREAM-TOPPED TOMATOES

Dunbar House, 1880 (p. 10)

SERVES 4 or 8 (½ or 1 tomato each).

These not only make a tasty accompaniment to egg dishes, but also add color to the breakfast plate.

4 slices bacon
½ cup sour cream
4 medium-sized tomatoes
   salt
   freshly ground pepper

Cook the bacon until crisp; drain on paper toweling. Reserve the drippings. Crumble the bacon into a small bowl and mix in the sour cream; set aside.

Cut the tomatoes in half and cut off the ends so that each half will sit flat. Sauté the tomatoes in the bacon drippings. When one side is golden, turn over, sprinkle with a little salt and pepper, and top with the sour cream/bacon mixture. Cover the skillet, lower the heat slightly and cook another 2 minutes. Serve immediately.

BRITISH BROILED TOMATOES

The Heartstone Inn (p. 160)

SERVES 8.

These delicious tomatoes add a pretty splash of color to a breakfast plate. An excellent complement to any egg dish, they especially enhance eggs Benedict. They are also a great way to use up those overabundant tomatoes in August. This recipe is perfectly suitable for lunch or dinner too.

4 large ripe tomatoes
2 Tbs. olive oil
   salt and pepper to taste
1 clove garlic, crushed
½ cup grated parmesan cheese
4 Tbs. cubed butter
¼ cup fresh chopped parsley
   parsley sprigs for garnish

Wash the tomatoes and cut into halves. Drain on paper towels, cut side down, for about 20 minutes. Place the tomatoes, cut side up, in a baking dish. Brush the tops with olive oil. Season with salt and pepper, and the crushed garlic. Sprinkle with cheese and dot with the butter. Sprinkle with chopped parsley.

Place under the broiler until the cheese is bubbly and browned, approximately 3 minutes. Watch closely so as not to burn. Serve immediately, with a parsley sprig garnish.

Spring House
Airville, Pennsylvania

SPRING HOUSE is a handsome stone structure dating from 1798. Built of honey-colored local fieldstone, this lovely house sits at the hub of historic Muddy Creek Forks, right over the village's main source of water, an abundant spring. The surrounding countryside consists of rolling meadows and woods, where hikers can walk for miles—birdwatching, identifying the multitude of wildflowers or just enjoying the natural beauty of the place. Muddy Creek is used for canoeing, swimming, trout fishing and, in the winter, ice-skating. Three wineries in the vicinity are open for tours and wine-tasting, and the area is also well known for its antiques shops and Amish crafts.

A full breakfast, which includes local fresh eggs, locally produced sausage and honey from Ray Hearne's beehives, is served on the porch overlooking Muddy Creek Valley. Part of the view includes rosebushes and honeysuckles. In the summer hummingbirds can be watched feeding at the fuchsias. When strawberries are in season, there is fresh strawberry shortcake for breakfast. "Breakfast is always fresh, wholesome and plentiful," says Ray Hearne.

Spring House
Muddy Creek Forks
Airville, Pennsylvania 17302
(717) 927–6906

Ray Hearne

CORN FRITTERS

SERVES 4 to 6.

An especially wonderful treat when fresh corn is available.

2 cups fresh, uncooked corn
    (about 3 ears)
4 eggs, separated
4 Tbs. flour
    dash of nutmeg

Cut the corn off the cob with a sharp knife. Do this over a bowl to catch any liquid. Set aside.

Beat the egg yolks until lemon colored. Add the corn, flour and nutmeg and mix well. In a separate bowl beat the egg whites until stiff. Fold into the corn mixture.

Drop the fritter batter by large spoonfuls into a hot skillet with a little butter in the bottom. When the bottoms of the fritters are golden, turn them and cook until both sides are golden. Serve hot, either plain or with dark maple syrup or wildberry syrups and butter.

Variation: These are best when the corn is freshly picked, but in the winter canned creamed corn may be substituted.

Spring House is typical of the fieldstone houses that dot southern Pennsylvania and Maryland.

Dierker House Bed & Breakfast
Flagstaff, Arizona

A CHARMING OLD house in the arts and crafts style, Dierker House is decorated with antiques that Dorothea Dierker has collected over the years. Conveniently close to downtown Flagstaff with parks, tennis courts and restaurants, as well as Northern Arizona University and Lowell Observatory, the location provides guests with much to do. Flagstaff is situated at the base of the San Francisco Peaks, which at twelve-thousand feet are the state's tallest mountains. This picturesque setting also offers excellent skiing during the winter months. Guests may also make day trips to nearby Indian country, Sedona and Oak Creek, the Grand Canyon and the Colorado River. River trips, including white-water rafting, are available.

Dorothea Dierker serves a full and beautifully presented breakfast in the dining room, for she believes that a pretty table is as important as good food. Breakfast includes a special mix of freshly ground coffees, fresh fruit, juice, breakfast meats, eggs, potatoes and coffeecakes, prepared in a variety of ways. Sometimes in the summer (short and cool as it is at seven thousand feet), Dorothea serves breakfast on the garden patio.

Dierker Hosue
423 West Cherry
Flagstaff, Arizona 86002
(602) 774-3249

Dorothea Dierker

RELLENOS DIERKER HOUSE

SERVES 6 to 8.

A typical Southwestern dish, this is perfect at brunch, lunch or dinner. This casserole comes out of the oven puffy and golden; the flavor is delicious. Dorothea Dierker likes to serve this with fresh melon, sausage and warm coffeecake.

 6 large green bell peppers
¾ lb. Monterey jack cheese, grated
¾ lb. medium-sharp cheddar cheese, grated
12 eggs
 1 qt. sour cream

Preheat oven to 350°F.

Wash, seed and slice the peppers into ½" slices. In a large greased casserole layer the peppers with the cheeses, repeating the layers 2 or 3 times. In a large bowl beat the eggs with the sour cream. Season with a little salt and pepper. Pour this over the layers in the casserole. Bake at 350° for about 45 minutes; it should be golden brown and puffed on top. Remove from oven and let cool 10 minutes before serving.

From Dierker House a visitor to Arizona can easily reach the state's highest mountains or the deep valley of the Grand Canyon.

The Green Gables Inn

Pacific Grove, California

BUILT IN 1888, this elaborate Queen Anne mansion, with Tudor half-timbering and California fantasy, is a gem among Pacific Grove's many Victorian houses. Located on the Monterey Peninsula near the more famous towns of Monterey, Carmel and Pebble Beach, Pacific Grove offers a shoreline trail for jogging and strolling, and a public beach perfect for swimming, picnicking and scuba-diving. A short walk will bring you to Monterey's famous Cannery Row with its myriad shops and restaurants, as well as the Monterey Bay Aquarium. Carmel and Monterey with their many attractions, including famous golf and tennis facilities, are only minutes away by car.

In the afternoon, tea, sherry and wine are available in front of a cheery fire as guests gather for hors d'oeuvres before dining at one of the excellent Peninsula restaurants. In the morning, breakfast is served in the dining room, with a panoramic view of Monterey Bay and the sea.

The Green Gables Inn
104 Fifth Street
Pacific Grove, California 93950
(408) 375-2095

Claudia Long

BAKED MUSHROOMS

SERVES 6.

These, along with a vegetable tray and dip, sliced baguettes and a selection of sweet breads, are served as an hors d'oeuvre with a choice of sherry, wine or tea at the Green Gables Inn afternoon tea.

  1 lb. mushrooms, cleaned and sliced
  3 Tbs. butter
    salt and pepper to taste
  1 tsp. flour
  1 cup sour cream
  ⅓ cup Swiss cheese, grated
  ⅓ cup parmesan cheese

Preheat oven to 400°F.
  Sauté the mushrooms in 2 Tbs. butter until they render liquid. Season with salt and pepper. Sprinkle with flour, and continue to cook, gradually stirring in the sour cream. Bring to a boil; pour into an ungreased gratin dish. Melt remaining butter and pour over top. Sprinkle with cheeses. Bake at 400° for 12 to 15 minutes or until bubbly and lightly golden. Serve hot.

Since its days as the Spanish capital of California, the Monterey peninsula has seemed both remote and serenely different. Surely the elaborate bays and gables of the Green Gables Inn belong to this world where fantasy can become reality.

MORNING CARROTS
Carter House (p. 34)

SERVES 8.

An elegant side dish for brunch. These go very well with Ham Loaf with Mustard Sauce (page 123).

4 carrots
1 Tbs. Grand Marnier
1 Tbs. butter
1 tsp. sugar

Peel the carrots and cut into strips about 3 inches long. Put the carrots into a small pot of boiling water and cook for just 3 minutes. Drain and place in a saucepan with the other ingredients. Cook over medium heat, stirring occasionally, until the carrots are tender. Serve hot.

BLEU CHEESE MUSHROOMS
Palmer's Chart House (p. 220)

SERVES 4 to 6.

A savory side dish at brunch, these also make excellent hot hors d'oeuvres.

12–14 extra-large fresh mushrooms
¼ cup butter
¼ cup blue cheese, crumbled
5 Tbs. fine bread crumbs
salt and pepper to taste

Preheat oven to 350°F.
Remove stems from the mushrooms; clean the caps and set aside. Clean the stems, chop, and sauté in the butter. Stir in the blue cheese and 2 Tbs. of the bread crumbs. Add salt and pepper to taste. Remove from heat.
Fill the mushroom caps with the mushroom/cheese mixture. Place on an ungreased baking sheet and sprinkle with the remaining bread crumbs. Bake at 350° for 12 minutes. Serve hot.

ARTICHOKE SQUARES
Mentone Bed & Breakfast (p. 121)

SERVES 12.

A tasty, savory treat, this is an excellent side dish for a brunch, lunch or dinner. Also good as hot hors d'oeuvres.

6 scallions
1 clove garlic
4 eggs
½ lb. sharp cheddar cheese, grated
6 soda crackers, crumbled
2 6-oz. jars marinated artichokes, drained and chopped
dash of Tabasco
1 Tbs. chopped fresh parsley

Preheat oven to 325°F.
Chop the scallions, including the green stems, and sauté in a skillet, using a little of the oil from the artichokes. When the scallions are just tender, press the garlic through a garlic mincer, add to the skillet and stir. Remove from heat and set aside. In a large bowl, beat the eggs. Stir in the grated cheese, crushed crackers, chopped artichokes, Tabasco and parsley. Last, add the sautéed scallion and garlic. Combine well.
Pour into a well oiled 9″ × 13″ × 2″ pan, and bake at 325° for 35 to 40 minutes. Cut into squares, serve hot.

AUNT MARTE'S CHEESE STRAWS

The Capers–Motte House (p. 21)

MAKES about 100.

These are buttery and light with a delicate cheese flavor. The Capers–Motte House serves them at breakfast or at afternoon tea. We've enjoyed them with a sweet, spicy iced tea in the summer as an afternoon tea item, or as an hors d'oeuvre with cocktails.

1 lb. sharp or extra-sharp cheddar cheese, grated
2 cups flour
½ tsp. salt
    dash red cayenne pepper
1 cup butter

In a large bowl mix the grated cheese with the flour, salt and pepper. Work the butter, softened to room temperature, into the cheese/flour mixture until there are no lumps and it resembles coarse meal. Form into a ball and refrigerate, tightly wrapped in plastic wrap, until well chilled. When chilled and stiff, roll out and cut into strips resembling French fries, approximately 5″ × ¼″.

Place the "straws" on an ungreased cookie sheet and bake at 375° on the lower rack of the oven for a few minutes. Then move to the middle rack and continue baking for about 10 to 12 minutes overall. Don't let them get very brown.

Remove cookie sheet from oven, place on rack and cool completely.

These can be stored well in an airtight container. The dough can also be frozen until ready to use.

BAKED GARLIC CHEESE GRITS

Meramec Farm Stay (p. 124)

SERVES 4 to 6.

Carol Springer says this casserole is always popular with guests. "Since there's some prejudice against grits, I don't always declare their presence until they've been sampled and enjoyed," she notes.

1 cup grits
4 cups boiling water
¼ cup butter
3 eggs, beaten
1 clove garlic, crushed
½ tsp. salt
½ cup finely chopped bell pepper
1 Tbs. chopped fresh chives
¾ cup grated cheddar cheese

Preheat oven to 350°F.

In a large bowl stir the grits into the boiling water until slightly thickened. Add the rest of the ingredients and stir until the cheese melts. Pour into a greased casserole dish and bake at 350° for 40 minutes or until firm. Cool slightly before serving. Serve hot.

CHEESE GRITS

Oak Square (p. 158)

SERVES 6.

Creamy and flavorful, these are good with ham and eggs.

1 cup quick-cooking grits
4 cups water
1 tsp. salt
½ lb. cheddar cheese, grated
4 Tbs. butter
2 eggs
    milk

Preheat oven to 350°F.

Cook grits in the water with salt as directed on package. When done, add cheese and butter and mix thoroughly until well blended. Put 2 eggs in a measuring cup; beat, then add enough milk to make 1 cup. Add gradually to grits and mix well. Spoon into a greased casserole or baking pan and bake at 350° for 50 to 60 minutes. Serve hot.

Muffins, Biscuits & Scones

BANANA-PRALINE MUFFINS 141
Milburn House B&B

BANANA MUFFINS 141
The Inn on Cove Hill

MAINE BLUEBERRY MUFFINS
WITH TOPPING 141
The 1859 Guest House

BANANA BRAN MUFFINS 142
Crondahl's B&B

BLUEBERRY MUFFINS 143
High Meadows B&B

OAK TREE GRANOLA
MUFFINS 144
The Oak Tree Inn

RAISIN BRAN MUFFINS 144
Wal–Mec Farm

MOIST BRAN MUFFINS 144
The Inn on Cove Hill

BLUEBERRY MUFFINS 145
Chaffin Farms B&B

FELSHAW TAVERN
BRAN MUFFINS 146
Felshaw Tavern

BRAN MUFFINS 147
Green Meadow Ranch

BRAN PINEAPPLE MUFFINS 148
Heart of the Hills Inn

MORNING GLORY MUFFINS 148
Carter House

DR. FOWLER'S MUFFINS 148
The Fowler House

BRAN MUFFINS 149
Brigham Street Inn

CRANBERRY-APPLE MUFFINS 150
Gardner House

ORANGE BUTTERMILK
MUFFINS 151
The Inn on Cove Hill

APPLESAUCE OATMEAL
MUFFINS WITH MAPLE GLAZE 152
Murphy's B&B

SWEET POTATO MUFFINS 152
The Frederick Fitting House

PUMPKIN MUFFINS 153
Edith Palmer's Country Inn

JALAPEÑO CHEESE MUFFINS 154
Grant Corner Inn

POPOVERS 155
The Beal House Inn

CREAM CHEESE BISCUITS 156
The Capers-Motte House

BUTTERMILK BISCUITS 156
Hillcrest House

BRIDGEFORD BISCUIT MIX 156
Bridgeford Cottage

BETSY'S BISCUITS 157
Betsy's Bed & Breakfast

SOUTHERN BUTTERMILK
BISCUITS 158
Oak Square

SCONES 159
Fool's Gold

WELSH COUNTRY SCONES 160
The Heartstone Inn

DAD'S SCOTCH SCONES 161
Gardner House

ENGLISH CURRANT BUNS 161
The Heartstone Inn

*The table settings at Barnard–Good House
(see page 14) are as thoroughly Victorian as
the house itself, with a footed pie server
and a footed coffee pot, a lace tablecloth
and damask napkins in silver rings.*

MUFFINS ARE a perennial breakfast favorite. Some B&Bs offering a continental breakfast simply serve coffee, juice and a basket full of fresh, hot muffins. For many travelers this is more than satisfactory. Quick and easy to prepare, muffins should always be served fresh out of the oven. Do not bake more muffins than you need in order to stretch the batch over a few days. A day-old muffin is quite disappointingly different from a fresh baked one. Set out your stale muffins on a bird feeder and enjoy watching the birds as you have your morning coffee and wait for fresh muffins from the oven.

When making muffins, always use high-quality ingredients: a very good unbleached white flour, fresh eggs—local if possible. When I tested the recipes in this section, I used extra-large grade-A eggs, which I find most satisfactory for all my cooking. Many of these recipes call for buttermilk. If you discover at the last minute that you do not have buttermilk, you can make a substitution as follows: Place one tablespoon of white vinegar in the bottom of a glass measuring cup and add enough milk to yield 1 cup. Let it sit for five minutes before using. Blueberries can be frozen beautifully, making it possible to serve blueberry muffins in the dead of winter.

In general, when making muffins, you will sift together the dry ingredients in one bowl, beat together the wet ingredients in a separate bowl and then combine the two, blending until the dry ingredients are just moistened. *Do not overbeat.* Overbeating makes muffins tough and reluctant to rise.

A little trick I discovered that makes it easier to remove muffins from the tin is to line the muffin tin with paper muffin cups and then brush or spritz the inside of cups with a little vegetable oil before spooning in the batter. The muffins slip right out of the tin, and the paper peels easily off the muffins without tearing them.

These muffin recipes are given with yields based on standard-size muffin tins. If you use larger muffin tins (there is a wide range of sizes available), you will need to allow a slightly longer baking time. If you experiment with larger tins, note the baking time and yield next to the recipe.

When muffins are baked, they should be removed from the tin immediately to a cooling rack. Muffins should not sit in the tin before turning out as is often done with bread. Letting muffins sit in the tin causes them to compress; they may fall somewhat and become soggy. After the muffins sit on a cooling rack a few minutes, place them in a basket lined with a linen towel to serve. Have butter on the table and a selection of jams and jellies.

Like muffins, biscuits are quickly and easily prepared and should always be baked just before serving. When you make biscuits, work quickly and sparingly with the dough. Don't overwork it or the biscuits will come out tough and flat. Roll or pat the dough out quickly, lightly and not too thin. A generous three-quarter inch to one inch is the ideal thickness. When you cut the dough, don't twist the biscuit cutter. Twisting seals the edges and decreases the rise. When biscuits have finished baking, immediately remove them from the baking sheet to a cooling rack. Serve them hot in the same manner as muffins. Besides butter, jams and jellies, honey makes a good accompaniment for biscuits.

The rules for making biscuits apply to scones, except for the way they are shaped. Scones may be cut with a biscuit cutter, cut into diamond shapes or dropped from a spoon. They are just as quickly made and should be served the day they are made. Serve them with butter and a selection of jams. Scones are good at breakfast, but they are especially appropriate for afternoon tea. The four scone recipes here offer the cook a well-rounded repertoire.

BANANA-PRALINE MUFFINS

Milburn House (p. 50)

MAKES 12 muffins.

A wonderful taste combination, these have become a favorite in my house.

3 Tbs. brown sugar
1 Tbs. sour cream
½ cup broken pecans
3 bananas, ripe
1 egg
½ cup sugar
¼ cup oil
1¼ cups flour
2 tsp. baking powder
¼ tsp. salt

Preheat oven to 400°F.
   In a small bowl mix together the brown sugar and sour cream; stir in the pecans and set aside.
   In a large bowl mash the bananas; add the egg, sugar and oil and beat well. In a separate bowl combine the flour, baking powder and salt. Add the dry ingredients to the banana mixture and stir just until moistened.
   Spoon the batter into greased muffin tins and top each with a spoonful of the pecan mixture. Bake at 400° for 15 minutes or until golden brown. Serve warm.

BANANA MUFFINS
The Inn on Cove Hill (p. 151)

MAKES 12 muffins.

After blueberry muffins, banana muffins seem to be everyone's favorite. These are light and tasty.

6 Tbs. butter
½ cup sugar
2 eggs
3 Tbs. milk
2 ripe bananas, mashed
2 cups flour
2 tsp. baking powder
1 tsp. baking soda
   dash salt

Preheat oven to 400°F.
   Cream together the butter and sugar until light and fluffy. Add the eggs and beat well. Add milk and banana and combine thoroughly. In a large separate bowl combine all the dry ingredients. Stir the wet ingredients into the dry, just until moistened. Do not overbeat.
   Spoon into greased muffin tins and bake at 400° for 20 minutes. When done, remove from muffin tin immediately and place on cooling rack until ready to serve. Best if served hot.

MAINE BLUEBERRY MUFFINS WITH TOPPING
The 1859 Guest House (p. 217)

MAKES 12 muffins.

The topping makes these muffins flavorful enough to serve as dessert.

Muffins
¾ cup sugar
¼ cup shortening
1 egg
½ cup milk
2 cups flour
½ tsp. salt
2 tsp. baking powder
2 cups blueberries

Topping
½ cup sugar
½ cup flour
¼ tsp. cinnamon
¼ cup soft butter

Preheat oven to 350°F.
   Cream together the sugar and shortening. Beat in egg and milk. In a separate bowl sift together the flour, salt and baking powder. Stir dry ingredients into wet. Add blueberries and combine well.
   Spoon into greased muffin tins and bake at 350° for 5 minutes. While the muffins are baking, combine the ingredients for topping; mix until crumbly. After the muffins have baked for 5 minutes, sprinkle topping over muffins and return to oven to bake for an additional 15 minutes.

Crondahl's Bed & Breakfast

Juneau, Alaska

SET ON GASTINEAU CHANNEL, Juneau is backed by snowcapped mountains and evergreen forests. Judy Crondahl thinks it is the most beautiful city in the world, whether glistening in sunlight or rising up out of the mist on a rainy day. In the summer, the sight of the cruise ships of the Holland America and Princess lines steaming up Gastineau Channel—with the mountains rising three thousand feet on each side—is a breathtaking spectacle. Another perennial attraction for visitors is Mendenhall Glacier. Judy nevertheless believes it is the people of Juneau as much as its scenery that make a visit memorable.

Crondahl's B&B has views of downtown and of the harbor with the Douglas Island Mountains rising on the opposite side. Guests are served a full breakfast in the large kitchen or, during the warm weather, on the deck, with its view of the city and the harbor. The coffee the Crondahls serve is not only ground fresh in their kitchen, it is roasted in Juneau, one of the few places in the country with its own coffee-roasting plant.

Crondahl's Bed & Breakfast
626 Fifth Street
Juneau, Alaska 99801
(907) 586–1464

Jay and Judy Crondahl

BANANA BRAN MUFFINS

MAKES 12 muffins.

Judy Crondahl developed this recipe when she and her husband realized they had to watch their cholesterol and increase their fiber intake. Besides being healthful, these muffins are delicious.

1½ cups oat bran
  1 tsp. baking soda
  1 cup bran flakes
  ¼ cup brown sugar
  ¼ cup vegetable oil
  2 eggs
  3 bananas, very ripe
  1 tsp. lemon juice
  1 Tbs. milk
  ¼ cup chopped nuts
  ¼ cup raisins or chopped dates

Preheat oven to 375°F.
  Combine the oat bran and baking soda. Stir in the bran flakes, set aside. In a separate bowl beat together the brown sugar, oil and eggs. Mash the bananas and add to the sugar mixture. Beat in the lemon juice and milk. Stir the banana mixture into the bran mixture. Add the nuts and fruit and blend well. Spoon into greased muffin tins and bake at 375° for 15 minutes, or until done.

High Meadows Bed & Breakfast
Eliot, Maine

SITUATED ON the side of a hill, High Meadows is surrounded by meadows and woods. This colonial house was built in 1736 by Elliott Frost, a merchant shipbuilder and captain. Today it is the home of the Raymonds and a hospitable B&B offering the traveler a "quiet atmosphere in a relaxed country setting."

High Meadows is just a short drive from historic Portsmouth, New Hampshire, and from both Kittery and York, Maine. The scenic coastal villages of this area are known for their art galleries and fine restaurants. Sightseeing and whale-watching cruises leave from these ports. High Meadows is an area favored for enjoying fall foliage; and in the winter, cross-country skiing is popular.

A continental breakfast is served in the country kitchen, or on the terrace in warmer weather.

High Meadows Bed and Breakfast
Route 101
Eliot, Maine 03903
(207) 439–0590

Elaine Raymond

BLUEBERRY MUFFINS

MAKES 12 muffins.

These muffins are chock full of berries.

½ cup butter
1¼ cups sugar
2 eggs
½ cup milk
2 cups flour
2 tsp. baking powder
2 cups fresh blueberries

Preheat oven to 375°F.

Cream together the butter and sugar. Add eggs, one at a time, and beat well. In a separate bowl sift together the flour and baking powder; add alternately to the batter with the milk, beating well. In a small bowl, mash 1 cup of the blueberries, and stir into batter. Add the rest of the blueberries whole and stir in well.

Spoon into greased muffin tins and bake at 375° for 20 minutes or until done. Remove from oven and immediately turn out of tins onto a cooling rack. Serve hot.

OPPOSITE: *From the shaded terrace, visitors to Crondahl's B&B can survey mountains rising three thousand feet on either side of the Gastineau Channel.*

LEFT: *Flowers from the cutting garden at Murphy's B&B (see page 13).*

OAK TREE GRANOLA MUFFINS

The Oak Tree Inn (p. 175)

MAKES 24 muffins.

Good flavor and texture and quick to make.

2 cups flour
1 cup oats
1½ cups granola (homemade or Quaker 100% Natural)
2 Tbs. baking powder
2 tsp. salt
1 cup sugar
3 tsp. cinnamon
2 eggs
2 cups water
½ cup vegetable oil
1 cup raisins

Preheat oven to 350°F.
Mix all dry ingredients together. In a separate bowl combine water, eggs and oil. Add wet ingredients to dry ingredients and blend just until moistened. Stir in raisins. Spoon into greased muffin tins. Bake at 350° for 20 minutes. Serve hot.

RAISIN BRAN MUFFINS

Wal-Mec Farm (p. 166)

MAKES 50 to 60 muffins.

These are tasty muffins, and the unused batter stores very well in the refrigerator.

5 cups flour
2 tsp. salt
5 tsp. baking soda
1 15-oz. box Raisin Bran cereal
2½ cups sugar
4 eggs
4 cups buttermilk
1 cup oil

In a very large bowl sift together flour, salt and baking soda. Add Raisin Bran and sugar; mix well. In a separate bowl beat the eggs; beat in the buttermilk and oil. Add this to the dry ingredients and stir well. *Refrigerate the batter at least 6 hours before using.*
When ready to use, spoon the batter into greased muffin tins, and bake at 375° for 15 to 20 minutes. Serve hot.
Note: Unused batter can be stored in the refrigerator for weeks. Make only as many muffins as you want to serve at one time.

MOIST BRAN MUFFINS

The Inn on Cove Hill (p. 151)

MAKES 12 muffins.

1 cup buttermilk
¼ peel of fresh lemon
⅓ cup oil
½ tsp. vanilla
⅔ cup brown sugar
1 cup bran
½ cup oatmeal
1 cup flour
1 tsp. baking soda
1 tsp. baking powder
dash salt
½ cup raisins or dates

Preheat oven to 400°F.
Place buttermilk and lemon peel in blender and purée. Add oil, vanilla and brown sugar and mix well. In a separate large bowl mix together all dry ingredients. Add the wet ingredients and mix until just moistened. Stir in the raisins or dates.
Spoon into greased muffin tins and bake at 400° for 20 minutes. When done, remove from muffin tin immediately and place on cooling rack until ready to serve. Best if served hot.

Chaffin Farms Bed & Breakfast
Ithaca, Michigan

CHAFFIN FARMS Bed & Breakfast is a turn-of-the-century farm house located on a six-hundred-acre working farm. After a restful night of peace and quiet, guests may tour the farm or venture out for some good antiques shopping available in three neighboring towns.

The house is furnished with antiques, and guests enjoy a full country breakfast in the keeping room—with a fire in the fireplace on nippy mornings. The breakfast table is set with Desert Rose china and antique pitchers and accessories. The jams and jellies are home-made from the farm's produce.

Chaffin Farms Bed & Breakfast
3239 West St. Charles Road
Ithaca, Michigan 48847
(517) 463–4081

Sue Chaffin

BLUEBERRY MUFFINS

MAKES 12 muffins.

My personal favorite.

2½ cups flour
2½ tsp. baking powder
 1 cup sugar
 1 cup buttermilk
 2 eggs
½ cup melted butter
1½ cups blueberries

Preheat oven to 400°F.

Sift together the flour, baking powder and sugar. In a separate bowl mix the buttermilk, eggs and melted butter; beat well. Add the wet ingredients to the dry and mix until just moistened. Stir in the blueberries. Spoon into greased muffin tins and bake at 400° for about 20 minutes. Turn out of muffin tins immediately and serve hot.

Charming both within and without, Chaffin Farms' clapboard house makes a fine base for exploring the farm and neighboring towns.

The Felshaw Tavern
Putnam, Connecticut

SOMETIME AROUND 1742, John Felshaw built this handsome tavern in the green hills of northeastern Connecticut near the crossroads of two major colonial highways. The building is full of history, as is the surrounding area, for it once served as an inn to colonial militia men, including General Israel Putnam. During the nineteenth century, the tavern became first a post office and then a private home. In 1980, the Kinsmans moved from California and began restoring it to its former dignity and in 1982 they opened it as a Bed and Breakfast. The guest rooms, furnished with antiques, have working fireplaces that feed the massive central chimney.

A hearty English-style breakfast is served either in the dining room or in the more casual and sunny breakfast room. Guests are served "whatever they like," such as eggs (fresh from Cady Brook Farms three miles down the road), orange juice, beef sausage, cereal if desired, coffee or tea and of course freshly baked muffins.

The Felshaw Tavern
Five Mile River Road
Putnam, Connecticut 06260
(203) 928–3467

Herb and Terry Kinsman

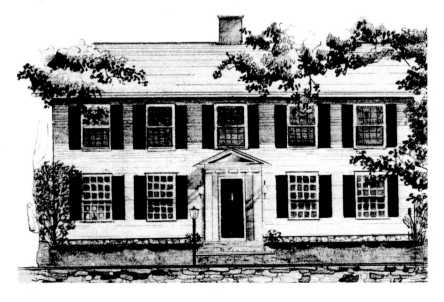

FELSHAW TAVERN BRAN MUFFINS

MAKES about 36 muffins.

"The best thing about this recipe (aside from excellent flavor and healthfulness) is its keeping ability. Make only as many muffins as you wish for one meal, then cover and refrigerate remaining batter. It will keep for weeks. Be prepared to share this recipe, because you will be asked for it often." —TERRY KINSMAN

1½ cups oat bran
1½ cups wheat bran
1 cup granola
1 cup boiling water
2½ cups whole wheat flour
1 Tbs. baking soda
½ cup vegetable oil
1 cup molasses
3 eggs, beaten
2 cups buttermilk
2 cups raisins

Preheat oven to 400°F.
In a large mixing bowl combine the oat bran, wheat bran and granola. Pour the boiling water over this, mix and let stand. In a separate bowl sift together the flour and baking soda; set aside. In another bowl mix together the oil, molasses, eggs and buttermilk, and add this with the flour mixture to the bran and granola mixture. Mix until just moistened. Stir in the raisins. Spoon into greased muffin tins, filling about three-quarters full. Bake at 400° for about 20 minutes or until done. Turn out of muffins tins immediately and serve warm.

Green Meadow Ranch
Shipshewana, Indiana

SCENIC ELKHART COUNTY lies at the heart of Indiana's Amish country and Green Meadow Ranch offers the traveler a charming farm setting in which to enjoy its beauty. The house is furnished with antiques, including Ruth Miller's collection of antique toys, which are displayed throughout.

Guests are invited to walk the well-planted grounds, home to miniature ponies, tiny goats and laying hens. After a day of exploring crafts and antiques shops and beautiful rolling farmland, guests at Green Meadow Ranch relax in a "quiet broken only by the sounds of Nature and the clip-clop of horses as they draw buggies past on the road nearby."

In the morning, guests enjoy a breakfast served in the sunny porch-room, decorated with ferns and white wicker, where Ruth Miller's homemade muffins are always a hit. "You are a stranger only once at Green Meadow Ranch," say Ruth and Paul Miller.

Green Meadow Ranch
Rt. 2, Box 592
Shipshewana, Indiana 46565
(219) 768–4221

Paul and Ruth Miller

BRAN MUFFINS

MAKES 60 muffins.

A tasty, high-fiber muffin. This batter keeps well in the refrigerator; good to keep on hand for those unexpected guests.

2 cups bran
2 cups boiling water
2 cups sugar
1 cup shortening (Crisco is best)
4 eggs
4 cups buttermilk
5 cups flour
1 tsp. salt
5 tsp. baking soda
4 cups All-Bran breakfast cereal
3 cups raisins (optional)

Preheat oven to 400°F.

Mix together the bran and boiling water; set aside to cool.

In a large bowl beat together the sugar, shortening, eggs and buttermilk; beat in the cooled bran mixture; set aside. In a separate bowl combine the flour, salt, baking soda and All-Bran. Add the dry ingredients to the wet and stir just until all dry ingredients are moistened. If desired, add raisins.

Spoon into greased muffin tins and bake at 400° for 20 minutes. Serve hot.

Note: Cover and refrigerate unused batter and make only as many muffins as you want each morning. Batter will keep well for weeks (supposedly up to 6 weeks, although I've always used it up sooner than that).

OPPOSITE: *Like other colonial Connecticut buildings, the Felshaw Tavern has a massive central chimney serving fireplaces in all the principal rooms.*

LEFT: *Craft objects enliven the breakfast room at Green Meadow Ranch.*

BRAN PINEAPPLE MUFFINS

Heart of the Hills Inn (p. 195)

MAKES 24 to 36 muffins.

These muffins are moist, delicious and wholesome.

    2 cups bran cereal
        (such as All-Bran)
    2 cups buttermilk
    2 eggs
    1 20-oz. can crushed pineapple
        & juice
    ½ cup vegetable oil
    2½ cups flour
    ¾ cup brown sugar
        (firmly packed)
        dash of salt
    2 Tbs. baking soda
    1 cup chopped walnuts

Preheat oven to 375°F.
    In a large bowl combine the bran cereal and the buttermilk. Let stand 5 minutes. Then add eggs, pineapple and juice along with the oil. Mix well.
    In a separate bowl combine flour, brown sugar, salt, baking soda and nuts. Turn into the bran mixture all at once. Stir just until mixed. Batter will not be smooth. At this point the batter may be used or refrigerated in a tight container for later use. Batter will keep up to 3 weeks.
    When ready to bake, spoon batter into greased muffin tins, about three-quarters full. Bake at 375° for 20 minutes.

MORNING GLORY MUFFINS

Carter House (p. 34)

MAKES 18 muffins.

Dense, moist and spicy.

    2 cups flour
    1 cup sugar
    2 tsp. baking soda
    1 tsp. cinnamon
    1 tsp. nutmeg
    1 apple, peeled, cored and grated
    ½ cup raisins
    ½ cup shredded coconut
    ½ cup pecans, chopped
    1 cup grated carrot
    3 eggs
    1 cup vegetable oil
    2 tsp. vanilla extract

Preheat oven to 350°F.
    Combine the flour, sugar, baking soda, cinnamon and nutmeg in a large mixing bowl. Add the grated apple, raisins, coconut, chopped pecans and grated carrots. Mix together thoroughly until mixture resembles a coarse meal.
    In a separate bowl, beat the eggs slightly. Add the vegetable oil and vanilla extract and beat well. Pour into the dry ingredients and quickly combine. Do not overbeat. Spoon into greased muffin tins. Bake at 350° for 20 to 25 minutes or until golden brown.

DR. FOWLER'S MUFFINS

The Fowler House (p. 64)

MAKES 12 muffins.

The filling is a nice surprise in these moist, tasty muffins.

    2¾ cups flour
    4 tsp. baking powder
    ¼ tsp. salt
    ½ cup sugar
    3 eggs
    ⅓ cup butter, melted and cooled
    1 cup milk
    ¼ cup honey
    1 tsp. almond extract
    1 cup marmalade (approximately)
    ½ cup ricotta cheese
        (approximately)
    ¼ cup sugar
    ⅛ cup cinnamon

Preheat oven to 400°F.
    In a large bowl sift together flour, baking powder, salt and sugar. In a separate bowl beat the eggs. Add butter, milk, honey and almond extract to the beaten eggs, mixing well. Add liquid ingredients to the flour mixture and combine quickly; stir as little as possible. Swirl ½ cup of the marmalade into batter.
    Spoon the batter into well greased muffin tins, filling just half full; then spoon ½ teaspoon each of ricotta cheese and marmalade into center of muffin cups. Fill muffin tins with the remaining batter. Mix the sugar and cinnamon together and sprinkle it over the tops of the muffins.
    Bake at 400° for 10 minutes, then lower temperature to 350° and bake 10 minutes more. Remove from muffin tins immediately and serve hot.

Brigham Street Inn
Salt Lake City, Utah

ABANDONED BY his family at the age of twelve, Walter C. Lynn nonetheless went on to become very successful in the wool business. In 1898, when he was thirty-nine, he built the handsome mansion that has become the Brigham Street Inn.

The building combines the Queen Anne and classical revival styles popular at the time. The foundation, retaining wall and exterior stairs and walks of this red brick house are constructed of red sandstone quarried in Emigration Canyon. The interior is spacious, with high ceilings and endless examples of superb craftsmanship. There are coffered wainscoting, birdseye maple mantels, golden-oak moldings and woodwork, and imported Dutch tiles around the fireplaces. John and Nancy Pace bought the building in 1981 and a year later opened it as one of Salt Lake City's first (and most exclusive) B&Bs.

Located in the South Temple Historic District, the Brigham Street Inn is close to many points of interest, including Mormon Square, site of the famed Mormon Tabernacle and the Mormon Temple. Brigham Young University is nearby, as is Beehive House, Young's home. The area offers excellent skiing during the winter months; and the Great Salt Lake, for which the city is named, is a geographic peculiarity always of interest to visitors.

Guests at the Brigham Street Inn help themselves to a continental breakfast in the elegant formal dining room.

Brigham Street Inn
1135 East South Temple
Salt Lake City, Utah 84102
(801) 364-4461

John and Nancy Pace

BRAN MUFFINS

MAKES 50 to 60 muffins.

Another tasty recipe for moist bran muffins. This recipe makes a large batch that can be refrigerated for weeks. Use the amount you want for fresh muffins each morning.

  2 cups All-Bran cereal
  1 cup boiling water
2½ cups flour
  1 cup 100% Bran cereal
2½ tsp. baking soda
  ½ tsp. salt
  ½ cup butter
1¼ cups sugar
  2 eggs
  2 cups buttermilk

Preheat oven to 350°F.

In a medium size bowl, pour boiling water over the All-Bran; stir and set aside. In a separate bowl combine the flour, 100% Bran, baking soda and salt; set aside. In a large bowl cream together the butter and sugar. Beat in the eggs and buttermilk. Now add the flour mixture, blending thoroughly. Add the soaked All Bran; mix thoroughly.

Spoon into greased muffin tins and bake at 350° for 20 minutes.

The interior of the Brigham Street Inn is an excellent example of the superb craftsmanship displayed in turn-of-the-century mansions.

Gardner House
Wakefield, Rhode Island

BUILT IN 1818, Gardner House is a charming federal-style house, situated on Main Street in the old part of Wakefield. Originally part of a working farm, the house is now surrounded by lawns and gardens (with an in-ground pool), and backed by woods. The flower and herb gardens are lovely, and Nan Gardner brings their beauty into the house with fresh or dried arrangements.

The house is furnished with the excellent American antiques the Gardners accumulated during their years as antiques dealers. Fireplaces, wide-plank floors and horsehair-plaster walls add to the charm. The rugs were all braided by Nan Gardner herself, who teaches rug-braiding locally and makes rugs to order. Gardner House is about four miles from the University of Rhode Island and just two miles from the ocean with its beautiful swimming beaches.

Guests are served a full breakfast in the dining room at two artfully set tables. Will Gardner does the cooking (he says, "The kitchen is my second love, Nan is of course my first"), while Nan helps serve. Breakfast consists of fresh fruit in season, juice, coffee or tea, an egg dish, or perhaps pancakes, sausage, scones, jam and "plenty of good conversation."

Gardner House
629 Main Street
Wakefield, Rhode Island 02879
(401) 789–1250

Nan and Will Gardner

CRANBERRY–APPLE MUFFINS

MAKES 12 muffins.

These fruity, moist muffins have a delicious filling.

½ cup whole cranberry sauce
½ tsp. grated orange peel
1½ cups flour
½ cup sugar
1 tsp. cinnamon
½ tsp. baking soda
¼ tsp. baking powder
¼ tsp. salt
1 egg
⅓ cup milk
½ cup oil
1 cup finely chopped apples, cored and peeled

Preheat oven to 350°F.

In a small bowl mix together the whole cranberry sauce and orange peel; set aside. Sift together flour, sugar, cinnamon, baking soda, baking powder and salt. In a separate bowl beat the egg with milk and oil; stir in apples. Add flour mixture to egg mixture. Combine well.

Spoon the muffin batter into greased tins. Make a well in the center of the batter and spoon in a teaspoon of the cranberry-orange mixture. Bake at 350° for 15 to 20 minutes. Serve warm.

LEFT: *The table settings and interior decoration of Gardner House are carefully selected to complement the old building.*

OPPOSITE: *The Inn on Cove Hill was built in 1791 from the proceeds of pirate gold found a short distance away at Gully Point.*

The Inn on Cove Hill

Rockport, Massachusetts

A SMALL SEAPORT TOWN with cobblestone streets, colonial houses and roses climbing its picket fences every summer, Rockport lies at the northern end of the North Shore of Massachusetts. The Inn on Cove Hill is located in the heart of town. Two hundred years old, this federal-style house has been carefully restored, including the original wide-pine floors, and furnished with comfortable antiques.

Rockport is well known for its art galleries, fine restaurants, antiques shops and, in summer, its harbor afloat with sailboats. The waters offshore are known for boating and fishing, and there are good swimming beaches nearby. This town is so picturesque that it's not uncommon to see artists with their easels set up throughout the narrow streets and along the waterfront. It is said that Rockport's waterfront has been rendered by artists more than any other New England scene.

Guests at the Inn on Cove Hill enjoy a continental breakfast served at umbrella tables in the garden or in their rooms on chilly mornings. Including fresh baked muffins and breads, coffee and juice, breakfast is beautifully served on Wedgwood or Royal Doulton china.

The Inn on Cove Hill
37 Mount Pleasant Street
Rockport, Massachusetts 01966
(617) 546–2701

John and Marjorie Pratt

ORANGE BUTTER-MILK MUFFINS

MAKES 12 muffins.

This is one of three muffin recipes sent by the Inn on Cove Hill. "If you find that your muffins are failing, we have conspired to leave out one essential ingredient from each recipe: that is umbrella tables in the summer and breakfast in bed in the winter. For access to both, come see us. While you relax with your freshly baked muffins, page through your calendar and make plans for a visit to the Inn on Cove Hill."—MARJORIE PRATT

6 Tbs. butter
1 cup buttermilk
½ orange
1 egg
½ cup sugar
2 cups flour
1 tsp. baking powder
1 tsp. baking soda
   dash salt

Preheat oven to 400°F.
   Melt the butter, set aside to cool. Put the buttermilk and half a sweet orange, seeds removed, in a blender and purée. Add the egg and butter and blend well. In a separate bowl combine all the dry ingredients. Mix the liquid ingredients into the dry ingredients until just mixed. Do not overbeat.
   Spoon into greased muffin tins and bake at 400° for 20 minutes. When done, turn out of muffin tin immediately and place on cooling rack until ready to serve. Best if served hot.

APPLESAUCE MUFFINS WITH MAPLE GLAZE

Murphy's B&B (p. 13)

MAKES 12 muffins.

Wholesome and tasty muffins, the glaze makes them extra special.

Muffins
1½ cups rolled oats
1¼ cups flour
½ tsp. cinnamon
1 tsp. baking powder
¾ tsp. baking soda
1 cup applesauce
½ cup milk
½ cup brown sugar
3 Tbs. oil
1 egg white

Preheat oven to 400°F.

In a large bowl combine the oats, flour, cinnamon, baking powder and baking soda. In separate bowl beat together the applesauce, milk, brown sugar, oil and egg white.

Add the wet ingredients to the flour and oats mixture and blend until the dry ingredients are just moistened.

Spoon into greased muffin tins and bake at 400° for 20 minutes.

Remove from muffin tin and place on a cooling rack. Make the glaze.

Glaze
1 Tbs. butter, melted
½ cup confectioners' sugar
2 Tbs. maple syrup

Place all ingredients in a blender and process until smooth. Spread the glaze over the tops of the muffins while they are still warm. Allow the glazed muffins to cool slightly before serving, so that the glaze has time to set.

SWEET POTATO MUFFINS

The Frederick Fitting House (p. 103)

MAKES 24 muffins.

These moist, spicy muffins could pass for pumpkin muffins, but there is a subtle difference.

½ cup butter, soft
1¼ cups sugar
1¼ cups sweet potatoes, peeled, boiled and mashed
2 eggs
1½ cups flour
2 tsp. baking powder
1 tsp. salt
2 tsp. nutmeg
1 tsp. cinnamon
1 cup milk
½ cup raisins
¼ cup chopped walnuts or pecans
cinnamon-sugar, as topping

Preheat oven to 400°F.

In a large bowl cream together the butter, sugar and sweet potatoes until smooth; add eggs; blend well. In a separate bowl sift together the flour, baking powder, salt and spices; add alternately to the sweet potato batter with the milk. Do not overmix. Fold in raisins and nuts last.

Spoon into greased muffin tins. Sprinkle with a little cinnamon-sugar. Bake at 400° for 25 minutes. Turn out of muffin tins onto a cooling rack when done. Serve hot.

Note: Two large or three medium sweet potatoes will yield 1¼ cups mashed sweet potato.

Edith Palmer's Country Inn
Virginia City, Nevada

BUILT IN 1862 as a private home for a wine merchant, this historic house is now a Bed & Breakfast. In the stone wine cellar, Edith Palmer once operated a four-star gourmet restaurant that was internationally renowned. The Inn has entertained both Hollywood stars and world leaders; Marilyn Monroe called Edith Palmer's Inn her "oasis in the desert." Norm and Erlene Brown, who now own and operate the inn, carry on the tradition of Edith Palmer's famous hospitality.

Nestled in the Sun Mountain, this country house is within walking distance of Virginia City. Now a historic landmark, Virginia City was once the richest town in the world, home of the Comstock Lode, the largest silver mine of the nineteenth century. The resulting wealth made this into a beautiful town, replete with opulent mansions, opera house, Victorian hotels and grand public buildings. Today many of these buildings are restored and open for touring. Besides historic buildings and museums, there are antiques shops and fine restaurants. Virginia City is a thirty-minute drive from Reno and forty-five minutes from Lake Tahoe.

Breakfast at Edith Palmer's Country Inn is always plentiful, served in the sunny breakfast room with its view of the gardens. In the warmer months, guests may have their coffee on the patio overlooking gardens and fruit trees. The shade of huge trees and the cooling breeze off the mountain make the gardens a welcome spot.

Edith Palmer's Country Inn
P.O. Box 756
Virginia City, Nevada 89440
(702) 847–0707

Norm and Erlene Brown

PUMPKIN MUFFINS

MAKES 18 muffins.

These moist, spicy muffins are especially well suited for a fall breakfast.

    3 cups flour
1 ½ tsp. baking powder
    1 tsp. baking soda
    1 tsp. cinnamon
    1 tsp. nutmeg
    1 1-lb. can pumpkin
    2 cups sugar
    3 eggs
    ¼ cup oil
    ½ cup water
    1 cup raisins

Preheat oven to 375°F.

In a large bowl, combine the flour, baking powder, baking soda, cinnamon and nutmeg. In a separate bowl beat together the pumpkin, sugar, eggs, oil and water. Add the pumpkin mixture to the flour and blend quickly. Stir in the raisins. Spoon into greased muffin tins and bake at 375° for 15 to 20 minutes.

Virginia City, a glorious relic of the frontier, was once a place of fabulous riches. Today it remains a treasured reminder of the opulence that survived the end of the Comstock Lode. Edith Palmer herself was a restaurateur of international reputation, and the Country Inn carries on her traditions.

Grant Corner Inn
Santa Fe, New Mexico

A STUCCO MANOR in the Spanish colonial style, with a red tile roof, the Grant Corner Inn was built at the turn of the century for the Windsors—a wealthy New Mexican ranching family. Located in downtown Santa Fe just two blocks from the historic Plaza, the old house—with its columned verandah and well planted lawns and gardens surrounded by a low fence—creates a peaceful oasis in the heart of the old city. The antiques that Pat and Louise Walter purchased while traveling the world over furnish the house and reflect the old world hospitality the Walters take pride in extending to guests.

Shops, restaurants, galleries and museums are all within walking distance. The Walters will both help guests plan day excursions and make arrangements for gourmet picnics, dinner reservations and special catered meals.

Breakfast at Grant Corner Inn is served in one of two places—before a crackling fire in the dining room or on the verandah in the summer months. The varied menu includes such treats as banana waffles, New Mexican soufflé or homemade rolls and muffins, along with freshly ground coffee and a selection of juices.

Grant Corner Inn
122 Grant Avenue
Santa Fe, New Mexico 87501
(505) 983-6678

Pat and Louise Walter

JALAPEÑO CHEESE MUFFINS

MAKES 16 muffins.

An unusual muffin with a Southwestern accent, these are a good accompaniment to almost any egg dish.

2 ½ cups yellow cornmeal (preferably stone ground)
½ cup flour
2 tsp. baking powder
½ tsp. baking soda
1 tsp. salt
2 eggs
2 cups buttermilk
½ cup vegetable oil
2 fresh jalapeños, seeded and finely chopped
1 cup grated sharp cheddar cheese
1 cup fresh or frozen corn

Preheat oven to 425°F.
In a large bowl, combine cornmeal, flour, baking powder, soda and salt, stirring well. Set aside.
In a separate bowl beat eggs with buttermilk and oil. Pour into dry ingredients, stirring just to moisten. Stir in jalapeños, cheese and corn. Spoon into well-greased muffin tins, filling three-quarters full.
Bake at 425° for 15 to 18 minutes or until lightly browned. Serve hot.

Breakfast at the Grant Corner Inn is always plentiful. In summer months, the dining room yields to the columned verandah.

The Beal House Inn
Littleton, New Hampshire

BUILT IN 1833, the Beal House Inn began as a Greek Revival farm-house, originally at the edge of the town of Littleton in New Hampshire's White Mountains. Over the years, the house and barn gradually grew together, connecting through the carriage house. The Beal family turned the house into a comfortable inn and the five-stall horse barn into an antiques shop. Now the Carvers carry on the tradition.

With its location in the White Mountains, the Beal House Inn offers guests downhill and cross-country skiing, canoeing, hiking and golf. Fall foliage is breathtaking in this area, and in the winter horse-drawn sleigh rides are available.

A full breakfast is served at long tables in an antique-filled room with a big fireplace. Hot popovers, a specialty, are served with creamy scrambled eggs. Other choices might include fresh fruit, juice, homemade waffles, breads, ham, bacon or country sausage and fresh coffee.

The Beal House Inn
247 West Main Street
Littleton, New Hampshire 03561
(603) 444–2661

Jim and Ann Carver

POPOVERS

MAKES 6 popovers.

A New England tradition, popovers rise very high while baking to become crusty shells that are hollow inside. They are spectacular served at breakfast directly from the oven, complemented by butter, honey, jams and creamy scrambled eggs.

1 cup flour
  dash salt
1 cup milk
2 eggs

Preheat oven to 400°F.
Combine all ingredients and stir until mixed. Overbeating will reduce volume. Fill greased popover cups almost to top. Bake at 400° for 30 to 45 minutes. Serve immediately.

The Beal House Inn offers buffet-style break-fasts at long tables, while the parlor offers a quiet retreat.

CREAM CHEESE BISCUITS

The Capers–Motte House
(p. 21)

MAKES 12 biscuits.

A buttery, flaky biscuit. Delicious with jams and jellies or filled with thinly sliced ham.

6 oz. cream cheese
1 cup butter
2 cups flour

Soften cream cheese and butter to room temperature. Cream together. Blend in flour. Shape into long rolls with a 3″ diameter and wrap in wax paper. *Chill several hours, or overnight in the refrigerator.*

When ready to bake, slice into ¾″ sections and place on ungreased cookie sheets. Bake at 400° for 20 minutes or until done. Watch carefully so that bottoms don't burn. Serve hot.

BUTTERMILK BISCUITS

Hillcrest House (p. 60)

MAKES 12 biscuits.

A melt-in-your-mouth delicious biscuit recipe.

2 cups flour
1 tsp. salt
½ tsp. baking powder
¼ tsp. baking soda
8 heaping Tbs. shortening
¾ cup buttermilk

Preheat oven to 425°F.

In a large bowl sift together the flour, salt, baking powder and baking soda. Cut in shortening until the mixture resembles a coarse meal; add buttermilk and stir only until dough leaves sides of bowl. Turn the dough onto floured board. Gently pat into ¾″ thickness. Cut with biscuit cutter and place on an ungreased cookie sheet. Bake at 425° for 10 to 12 minutes. Serve with butter, preserves and honey.

BRIDGEFORD BISCUIT MIX

Bridgeford Cottage (p. 58)

MASTER MIX yields 10 batches; batch makes 18 biscuits.

A flaky, buttery biscuit, this is a good recipe for anyone who likes to serve biscuits in the morning, especially to a large crowd, because the master mix permits fresh, hot biscuits to be ready in minutes. Also handy for those unexpected guests.

Master Mix
5 lbs. flour
¾ cup baking powder
2 Tbs. salt
2 Tbs. cream of tartar
½ cup sugar
2 lbs. shortening

Mix all ingredients well, with a pastry blender or by-hand. Store in refrigerator in a tightly covered container. Will keep for weeks.

Batch
3 cups of the above mix
⅔ cup milk

Preheat oven to 325°F.

Mix together well in a large bowl. Drop by spoonfuls onto an ungreased baking sheet, or roll out on a floured board to ½″ to ¾″ thickness and cut with a biscuit cutter. Bake at 350° for 8 to 10 minutes or until golden brown. Serve hot or cold with honey, butter, jams and jelly.

Betsy's Bed & Breakfast
Baltimore, Maryland

THIS TURN-OF-THE-CENTURY townhouse is located in the historic Bolton Hill district of Baltimore. The centerpiece of the interior is a central hall and stairwell that opens all the way up to the fourth-story skylight. The house is decorated with antiques, family-heirloom quilts and original brass rubbings made in England by Betsy Grater. Adding to the graciousness are six marble fireplaces and gleaming hardwood floors.

The Bolton Hill district, listed in the National Register of Historic Places, is a lovely section for a walking tour. Betsy's B&B is just seven minutes by car from the Inner Harbor, with its fine shopping and dining, and other waterfront attractions such as the Aquarium and the Science Center.

A full, home-cooked breakfast, served in the dining room, might include juice, fresh fruit in season, scrambled eggs, ham or sausage, fried apples and biscuits, with coffee, tea or milk.

Betsy's Bed & Breakfast
1428 Park Avenue
Baltimore, Maryland 21217
(301) 383-1274

Betsy Grater

BETSY'S BISCUITS

MAKES 12 biscuits.

Easy to make, these can be baking while you have your second cup of coffee.

2 cups flour
2 tsp. baking powder
1 tsp. salt
2 Tbs. shortening
1 cup milk

Preheat oven to 450°F.

Place the flour, baking powder and salt in a bowl and mix together lightly. Cut in shortening until the mixture resembles a coarse meal; add milk and stir to make stiff dough. Roll out on a lightly floured board and cut with a round biscuit cutter. Place on an ungreased baking sheet and bake at 450° for 10 minutes. Serve warm with butter and homemade jam.

Note: If biscuits are made a little larger than usual, using a 3″ biscuit cutter, they are delicious split and topped with chicken à la king or lobster Newburg for dinner.

Like other townhouses, Betsy's Bed & Breakfast presents a façade to the world that only hints at the amenities waiting on the other side—marble mantelpieces, hardwood floors and a lofty spiral staircase.

Oak Square

Port Gibson, Mississippi

PORT GIBSON IS one of the oldest towns in Mississippi; and conquering General U.S. Grant said it was "too beautiful to burn." Built in 1850, Oak Square—the largest and most palatial of Port Gibson's antebellum mansions—is listed in the National Register of Historic Places. Named Oak Square because of the massive oak trees that surround it, the plantation includes a courtyard, a fountain and a gazebo.

Six fluted columns, twenty-two feet tall with terra cotta Corinthian capitals, support the front pediment. Inside, the large, gracious rooms are furnished with period antiques. A rare collection of Civil War memorabilia, including many original family documents and a Confederate sword belonging to Major R. C. McCay, Mr. Lum's great-grandfather, are also on display. Martha and William Lum, whose families have lived in Mississippi for more than two centuries, restored Oak Square to its original splendor, and enthusiastically share local history with guests.

Guests at Oak Square enjoy a full breakfast in the dining room or on the patio, where they are pampered with true "Southern style hospitality."

Oak Square
1207 Church Street
Port Gibson, Mississippi 39150
(601) 437–4350

Martha and William Lum

SOUTHERN BUTTERMILK BISCUITS

MAKES 12 biscuits.

2 cups flour
3 tsp. baking powder
½ tsp. salt
4 Tbs. shortening
½ tsp. baking soda
1 cup buttermilk

Preheat oven to 450°F.

Sift together flour, baking powder and salt. Cut in the shortening until it resembles a coarse meal. Mix baking soda in buttermilk. Add slowly to the flour mixture and mix to a soft dough. *(At this point the dough may be stored in a covered dish in the refrigerator for several days.)* When ready to use, roll out on a lightly floured board to ½" to ¾" thickness and cut with a biscuit cutter. Place on an ungreased cookie sheet and bake at 450° for 10 to 15 minutes. Serve hot.

LEFT: *It is easy to understand why General Grant spared Oak Square, saying it was "too beautiful to burn."*

OPPOSITE: *Like other rooms, the parlor of Oak Square is furnished with period antiques, many of them original with the house.*

Fool's Gold

Silverton, Colorado

SENATOR ARTHUR W. HUDSON built this house for Olive Kellog, his bride, in 1883. It stands on Quality Hill, overlooking the rustic town of Silverton, a mountain community that still has working silver mines nestled in the San Juan Mountains. The house affords spectacular views of these mountains, which guests can enjoy while sipping an afternoon glass of sherry.

Tennis courts, museums, shops, restaurants, visits to abandoned mines, tours on a narrow-gauge railroad and interesting hiking are all within a short walk of Fool's Gold. The exceptional cross-country skiing, as well as the Purgatory ski area twenty miles to the south, make Silverton an ideal winter vacation spot, and "a great place for the whole family to celebrate a Victorian Christmas," according to Ann Marie Wallace.

Buffet brunch-style breakfasts feature a variety of home-baked goodies, such as the scones in the accompanying recipe.

Fool's Gold
1069 Snowden
Silverton, Colorado 81433
(303) 387–5879

Ann Marie Wallace

SCONES

MAKES 12 scones.

The vanilla flavor in the currants makes these special. Don't roll the dough too thin; if you get more than a dozen scones, they aren't as thick as they should be.

    1 cup currants or raisins
    1 tsp. vanilla
    2 cups flour
    1 Tbs. baking powder
    1 tsp. salt
    ½ cup sugar
    ½ cup chilled shortening
    1 egg, beaten
    ¾ cup milk

Preheat oven to 450°F.

Place currants or raisins in a bowl; stir in vanilla and add very hot water until the fruit is just covered. This "plumps" the fruit. Stir and set aside.

In a large bowl sift together the flour, baking powder, salt and sugar. Cut in shortening only until mixture is crumbly. Stir in the egg and milk. Drain the currants or raisins and add to the dough, mixing well. Add more milk if the dough is not moist enough to hold together.

Knead gently on a floured surface about 18 times. Pat or roll dough into a rectangle, a generous ½" to ¾" thick. Cut into 12 diamond shapes. Place on an ungreased cookie sheet.

Bake at 450° for 12 to 15 minutes. Don't overbake! Remove from cookie sheet immediately and serve warm.

The Heartstone Inn
Eureka Springs, Arkansas

THE HEARTSTONE INN is a pretty clapboard house with first and second floor porches and a front lawn and garden surrounded by a neat picket fence. Visitors to this restored turn-of-the-century spa (where it was once popular to "take the waters"—to drink and bathe in hot mineral water for the sake of one's health) can enjoy either a walking tour or a tour by a horse-drawn buggy. The quaint streets are lined with interesting shops and cafes, as well as a number of museums.

The hostess is originally from England, and the Heartstone Inn flies both the Union Jack and the American flag. In true English fashion, the Heartstone Inn serves a full breakfast. The recipes Iris Simantel sent are favorites from England.

The Heartstone Inn
35 Kings Highway
Eureka Springs, Arkansas 72632
(501) 253–8916

Bill and Iris Simantel

WELSH COUNTRY SCONES

MAKES about 16 scones.

½ cup dried currants
2 cups all-purpose flour
3 Tbs. sugar
2 tsp. baking powder
¾ tsp. salt
½ tsp. baking soda
5 Tbs. butter
1 cup sour cream
1 egg yolk
1 egg white, slightly beaten
1 tsp. sugar
⅛ tsp. ground cinnamon

Preheat oven to 425°F.

In a small bowl pour enough hot water over the currants to just cover them; let stand for 5 minutes. Drain well and set aside. In a large bowl combine flour, sugar, baking powder, salt and baking soda. Cut in the butter until the mixture resembles coarse crumbs. Stir in the currants. In a small bowl blend the sour cream and the egg yolk. Add all at once to the crumb mixture, stirring just until dough clings together.

On a lightly floured surface, knead gently for 10 to 12 strokes. Pat or roll the dough into a 9" circle about ½" thick. Using a 2½" cookie or biscuit cutter, cut into circles. Place on ungreased baking sheet. Brush with the egg white. Sprinkle with sugar and cinnamon. Bake at 425° for 15 to 18 minutes. Serve hot with butter and jam.

With its white picket fence, its upstairs porch and its garden, the Heartstone Inn is an ideal place to spend a leisurely sojourn in the old spa town of Eureka Springs.

ENGLISH CURRANT BUNS

MAKES 24 buns.

The frosting turns these delicious buns into a special treat. Great for breakfast, but especially well suited for afternoon tea.

Buns
½ cup dried currants
1 cup water
½ cup butter
1 tsp. sugar
¼ tsp. salt
1 cup flour
4 eggs

Preheat oven to 375°F.

Place currants in a bowl and add 1½ cups boiling water to plump. Set aside. Combine water, butter, sugar and salt in a saucepan. Bring to a boil. Add flour all at once, lower the heat and beat until the mixture leaves the sides of the pan. Remove from heat and stir until slightly cooled. Add the eggs, one at a time, beating well after each addition. Drain the currants, and add them to the batter, stirring well.

Drop batter by tablespoonfuls about 1 inch apart onto a greased baking sheet. Bake at 375° for 30 minutes. Remove from oven and cool on a rack.

Frosting
1 Tbs. butter
1½ Tbs. heavy cream
¾ cup confectioners' sugar
1 tsp. vanilla

Melt butter in a small pan, stir in the cream and remove from the heat. Stir in the powdered sugar and vanilla and beat well. Chill until stiff enough to use as frosting. The buns must be completely cooled before frosting.

DAD'S SCOTCH SCONES
Gardner House (p. 150)

MAKES 8 scones.

These scones are light and floury with a good flavor.

2 cups flour
2½ tsp. baking powder
1 tsp. salt
2 Tbs. sugar
¼ cup shortening
½ cup milk
1 egg, slightly beaten

Preheat oven to 450°F.

In a large bowl sift together flour, baking powder, salt and sugar. Cut in the shortening until the mixture resembles coarse meal; stir in the milk, then the egg. Roll the dough into a ball and knead on a lightly floured board. Cut the dough in half; form each half into a slightly flattened ball. Cut the balls into four equal wedges. Place on greased cookie sheet and bake at 450° for 10 to 12 minutes. Serve hot or cold.

Coffeecakes, Quickbreads & Unyeasted Pastries

SWEDISH BUTTERMILK
COFFEECAKE — 165
Teton Tree House

SOUR CREAM COFFEECAKE — 166
Wal-Mec Farm

BLUEBERRY COFFEECAKE — 167
Pat Wilson's Bed &
Breakfast-Valdez

SOUR CREAM VANILLA
COFFEECAKE — 168
Pat Wilson's Bed &
Breakfast-Valdez

COFFEECAKE GLENDEVEN — 168
Glendeven

CINNAMON COFFEECAKE — 169
Maple Crest Farm

BUTTERMILK POPPYSEED
CAKE — 169
Dunbar House, 1880

CHRISTEL'S APPLE CAKE — 169
The Inn at Mitchell House

MORNING CAKE DELIGHT
WITH TOPPING — 170
Hawthorne Inn

RHUBARB COFFEECAKE — 171
Manor House

APPLE RAISIN COFFEECAKE — 172
The River Street Inn

FRESH APPLE WALNUT CAKE — 172
The Frederick Fitting House

PUMPKIN APPLE CAKE — 173
Dunbar House, 1880

RAISIN-FILLED COFFEECAKE — 173
The Frederick Fitting House

SPECIAL DRIED APRICOT
FRUIT CAKE — 174
Adams Inn

OAK TREE COFFEECAKE — 175
The Oak Tree Inn

OATMEAL CAKE — 176
Purple Mountain Lodge

ENGLISH MORNING CAKE — 177
Ferris Mansion

COUS COUS CAKE — 178
Singleton House

STRAWBERRY BREAD — 179
The Strawberry Inn

PEAR BREAKFAST CAKE — 180
Hawthorne Inn

IRISH SODA BREAD — 180
Britt House

PEACH BREAD — 180
Barley Sheaf Farm

SOUR CREAM CINNAMON
LOAVES — 181
The 1735 House

BANANA BREAD — 182
The Bailey House

VALERIE'S SOUR CREAM
BANANA BREAD — 183
The Gingerbread Mansion

MARMALADE BREAD — 184
Lafayette House

LEMON YOGURT BREAD — 184
The Fowler House

VERY LEMONY LEMON BREAD — 184
The Gingerbread Mansion

LEMON LAYER LOAF — 185
Eastover Farm B&B

MANGO BREAD — 186
Hilo B&B

COUNTRYSIDE'S APPLE BREAD — 187
Countryside B&B

HARVEST APPLE CAKE — 188
The Gingerbread Mansion

APPLE NUT BREAD — 188
1837 Bed and Breakfast

PUMPKIN BREAD — 188
The Bailey House

PUMPKIN CRANBERRY
NUT BREAD — 189
Adams Inn

CRANBERRY NUT BREAD — 189
The Frederick Fitting House

PUMPKIN GINGERBREAD — 189
The Gingerbread Mansion

CARROT-PINEAPPLE BREAD — 190
O'Connors Guest House B&B

ZUCCHINI PINEAPPLE LOAF — 191
Adams Inn

ZUCCHINI BREAD — 191
Teton Tree House

ZUCCHINI BREAD — 191
Wal-Mec Farm

ALMOND TEA BREAD — 192
The Frederick Fitting House

BUTTER PECAN BREAD — 192
Lafayette House

CHOCOLATE TEA BREAD — 192
Murphy's B&B

DATE NUT BREAD — 193
The Bailey House

GRAPE NUT BREAD — 193
Ferris Mansion

BROWN BREAKFAST BREAD — 193
Hawthorne Inn

ONION-CHEESE BREAD — 194
General Hooker's House

POPPYSEED BREAD — 195
Heart of the Hills Inn

SOLDIERS BREAD — 196
The Strawberry Inn

CORNBREAD — 196
Murphy's B&B

COFFEE STRUDEL — 196
Purple Mountain Lodge

L'ORANGE FROMAGE
COFFEE PASTRY — 197
The Heirloom

ICE CREAM STRUDEL — 197
The Bells B&B

An elaborate buffet at Carter House,
Eureka Springs, California (see page 34).

FRESH BAKED GOODS have a timeless appeal. A warm, fragrant coffeecake, baked in a large bundt pan, is a handsome and inviting addition to the breakfast table. Quickbreads, whether on bread boards or in baskets, make an equally attractive presentation. Breakfast pastries brought out after the main course often cause those who say they've had their fill to try "just a small piece."

Coffeecakes, quick and easy to assemble, should be baked and served the same morning. The shapes vary; coffeecakes are baked in bundt, tube or angelfood cake pans; springform pans or rectangular baking pans. Each recipe specifies the pan required.

Quickbreads are generally shaped like loaves but are leavened with baking soda or baking powder rather than yeast, making them very quick to prepare and bake — hence the name. Unlike coffeecakes, quickbreads — especially those made with puréed fruit — may be served a day old and are often the better for it. I have made note of which quickbreads actually improve with a day's age and which are good toasted if they are not completely eaten the day they are baked.

There are also three recipes for unyeasted breakfast pastries in this section. They require more time to assemble, but they make a fancy and impressive addition to the table. Two of the pastries are to be partly assembled and refrigerated overnight.

Whenever possible, use real extracts for flavoring. For some baking, you may want to use vanilla sugar made by placing three vanilla beans into a canister with five pounds of sugar to give it a subtle and delicious vanilla aroma and flavor. When a recipe calls for brown sugar, use light or dark brown sugar depending on your preference. Dark brown sugar produces a slightly darker color and stronger flavor. When a recipe specifies light or dark brown sugar, you should follow the instructions. Many of these recipes call for buttermilk, which makes baked goods dense and moist. If you find at the last minute that you're out of buttermilk, you will find instructions for an easy substitution on p. 140.

Be sure that coffeecakes and quickbreads are baked thoroughly. If you are unsure, test for doneness by inserting a metal cake tester, broom straw or toothpick into the center of the cake or loaf. If it comes out clean, the baking is completed; if not, more baking time is needed. This is especially important in preparing recipes that call for puréed pumpkin. Since these dishes are very moist, they must be baked completely or they come out soggy and inedible.

Each recipe indicates how the cake or loaf should be cooled. Follow the directions; this is an important part of successful execution of the recipe. Most coffeecakes and quickbreads must be cooled *at least fifteen minutes,* if not completely, before they can be sliced and served. This step prevents sogginess and permits neater slicing. You should use a good serrated-edge knife for coffeecakes and quickbreads, otherwise you run the risk of crushing them.

Teton Tree House
Wilson, Wyoming

TETON TREE HOUSE is a rustic, open-beam house set on a private, forested spot on the side of a mountain. The house is situated at the base of Teton Pass, less than a mile from the village of Wilson, and eight miles from Jackson Hole. The large windows and decks of this striking house take advantage of the spectacular setting.

Excellent winter skiing, white-water rafting, canoeing and hiking are just some of the attractions for visitors. Chris and Danny Becker, enthusiasts of the outdoor life, are happy to help guests make arrangements for any of these activities.

Guests are served a hearty continental-plus breakfast that includes homemade granola, choice of hot cereals, fresh fruit in season, homemade coffeecakes, muffins, biscuits, juices, coffee, tea or hot chocolate.

> *Teton Tree House*
> *Box 550*
> *Wilson, Wyoming 83014*
> *(307) 733–3233*
>
> *Chris and Danny Becker*

SWEDISH BUTTERMILK COFFEECAKE

SERVES 8 to 12.

The aroma of this cake baking will bring guests down for breakfast early. It's delicious, and not too sweet.

1½ cups whole wheat flour
1 cup sugar
1 tsp. cinnamon
1 tsp. nutmeg
½ cup butter
1 cup buttermilk
1 tsp. baking soda
¼ tsp. salt
1 egg
½ cup chopped walnuts

Preheat oven to 350°F.

Mix together flour, sugar and spices. Cut in the butter. Save ¼ cup of this mixture and set aside to be used later. Add buttermilk, baking soda and salt to remainder and blend well. Beat the egg and stir into batter. Mix well. Pour into a greased and floured 8-inch spring-form pan. Now mix the chopped nuts with the reserved mixture. Sprinkle on top of batter. Bake at 350° for 35 minutes. Remove from oven and place on cooling rack. Loosen and remove the sides of the springform pan. Let cool for at least 15 minutes before serving.

OPPOSITE: *The Beal House began as a farmhouse* (left) *and a barn* (right) *which gradually grew together.*

LEFT: *With its large windows and many decks, the Teton Tree House looks right into the forest near Jackson Hole.*

Wal–Mec Farm

Thornville, Ohio

A STATELY VICTORIAN house surrounded by lush trees and lawns, the Wal–Mec Farm was built around 1860. It is located near the historic "Zane's Trace," a highway built by Ebenezer Zane in 1797 which ran from Wheeling, West Virginia, through present day Zanesville, Lancaster and Chillicothe, Ohio, to Maysville, Kentucky.

The colorful countryside around Wal–Mec Farm is dotted with day lillies and hollyhocks, wheat fields, grazing cattle and tidy Amish farms. It's not unusual to glimpse fox, deer and quail.

Guests at Wal–Mec Farm B&B enjoy a full breakfast in either the dining room—part of the original old house with its wide-plank floors and stenciled walls—or in the casual eating area that is part of a newer addition.

Wal–Mec Farm
5663 State Route 204 NW
Thornville, Ohio 43076
(614) 246–5450

Anne and Paul Mechling

SOUR CREAM COFFEECAKE

MAKES 1 coffeecake.

This simple coffeecake is always popular at breakfast.

1½ cups sugar
 1 cup shortening
 4 eggs
 2 tsp. vanilla
 1 cup sour cream
2½ cups flour
1½ tsp. baking soda
 ½ tsp. salt
 ½ cup chopped walnuts
 2 tsp. cinnamon
 ½ cup brown sugar

Preheat oven to 350°F.

In a large bowl cream together the shortening and sugar until light and fluffy. Beat in the eggs, one at a time. Next beat in vanilla and sour cream. In a separate bowl sift together the flour, baking soda and salt. Add the flour mixture to the creamed mixture and blend thoroughly.

In a small bowl combine the walnuts, cinnamon and brown sugar. Set aside.

Pour half the batter into a greased and floured angel food cake pan. Sprinkle with half the nut mixture. Pour the remaining batter over this, and top with remaining nut mixture.

Bake at 350° for 45 minutes or until done. Cool thoroughly on rack before removing from pan.

LEFT: *The Wal–Mec Farm is located in the quiet quadrant of Ohio that lies west of West Virginia.*

OPPOSITE: *The dining room of the old farm has wide plank floors and stencilled walls.*

Pat Wilson's Bed & Breakfast–Valdez
Valdez, Alaska

VALDEZ, KNOWN AS the "Little Switzerland of the North," is the home of this B&B. Snowcapped mountains, waterfalls, glaciers and a harbor full of fishing and pleasure boats make up the setting. In the summer sports-fishing is popular, but according to Pat Wilson, winter is the most beautiful season—the snow turns Valdez into a winter wonderland.

Bed & Breakfast–Valdez is furnished with Victorian oak furniture and decorated in a light and airy country style. Pat Wilson keeps a cookie jar full of homemade chocolate-chip cookies on hand at all times and tells guests to help themselves. In the morning, guests are served a full breakfast. Pat Wilson invites travelers to come visit and experience Alaskan hospitality.

Bed & Breakfast–Valdez
Box 442
Valdez, Alaska 99686
(907) 835–4211

Pat Wilson

BLUEBERRY COFFEECAKE

SERVES 10 to 12.

Cake
2 cups flour
⅔ cup sugar
3 tsp. baking powder
½ tsp. baking soda
1 tsp. salt
1 cup milk
2 Tbs. lemon juice
2 eggs
½ cup melted butter
2 cups fresh or frozen whole
    (unthawed) blueberries

Crumb Topping
⅔ cup sugar
½ tsp. cinnamon
½ cup flour
4 Tbs. butter
1 cup chopped nuts

Preheat oven to 350°F.

To make topping: Combine the sugar, cinnamon and flour. Cut in the butter. Mix in the nuts until the mixture is evenly blended. Set aside.

In a large bowl combine the flour, sugar, baking powder, baking soda and salt. In a separate bowl mix together the milk, lemon juice, eggs and butter. Stir the liquid ingredients into dry ingredients until blended.

Spoon the batter into a buttered 9″ × 13″ baking dish. Sprinkle blueberries evenly over batter. Top with crumb topping and bake at 350° for 40 to 45 minutes. Cool briefly on a rack before serving.

SOUR CREAM VANILLA COFFEECAKE

Pat Wilson's Bed & Breakfast Valdez (p. 167)

SERVES 10 to 12.

This is one of my favorite coffeecake recipes. The vanilla aroma while it's baking is heavenly. A large, heavy cake with a great flavor, it may be baked a day before serving; it is excellent the next day.

Cake
3 cups flour
1½ tsp. baking powder
1½ tsp. baking soda
¼ tsp. salt
1½ cups butter at room temperature
1½ cups sugar
3 eggs
1½ cups sour cream
1 tsp. vanilla

Filling
1 cup firmly packed brown sugar
1 cup chopped walnuts
1½ tsp. cinnamon

Topping
2 Tbs. milk
2 Tbs. vanilla
⅛ cup confectioners' sugar for dusting

Preheat oven to 325°F.

To make the cake: Sift together the flour, baking powder, baking soda and salt. In a separate bowl combine butter and sugar; beat until soft and fluffy. Add eggs, one at a time, beating well after each addition. Mix together the sour cream and vanilla and blend into the creamed mixture alternately with the dry ingredients. Beat well. Set aside.

To make the filling: Combine the brown sugar, nuts and cinnamon. Set aside.

Pour ⅓ of the batter into a greased and floured 10- to 12-inch tube pan, sprinkle with half the brown sugar mixture; repeat with another ⅓ of the batter and the rest of the brown sugar mixture; then cover with the remaining batter.

To make the topping: Combine the milk and vanilla and pour evenly over the top of the batter.

Bake at 325° for 50 to 60 minutes (until done). Cool 10 minutes before removing from pan, then dust generously with confectioners' sugar. Cool slightly before serving.

COFFEECAKE GLENDEVEN

Glendeven (p. 31)

MAKES one 10-inch cake.

The quintessential coffeecake. This fragrant and flavorful cake is always a hit at breakfast.

2¼ cups flour
1½ tsp. salt
2 tsp. cinnamon
¼ tsp. ginger
1 cup brown sugar
¾ cup white sugar
¾ cup salad oil
1 cup chopped walnuts
1 tsp. baking soda
1 tsp. baking powder
1 egg
1 cup buttermilk

Preheat oven to 350°F.

Mix together flour, salt, 1 tsp. cinnamon, ginger, brown sugar, white sugar and salad oil. Reserve ¾ cup of the mixture; add the chopped walnuts and 1 tsp. cinnamon, mix and set this aside to be used as the topping.

To the remaining mixture, add the baking soda, baking powder, egg and buttermilk. Beat until smooth. Spread the batter in a greased and floured 10-inch springform pan. Sprinkle the topping evenly over the batter and bake at 350° for 40 to 45 minutes. Place the pan on a cooling rack, and loosen and remove the sides of the pan. Let the cake cool for at least 15 minutes before serving.

CINNAMON COFFEECAKE
Maple Crest Farm (p. 46)

SERVES 8.

This is quick and easy to make. The aroma of this cake baking in the morning is delightful to wake up to.

Cake
¼ cup shortening
¾ cup sugar
2 eggs
2 cups flour
¾ tsp. salt
3 tsp. baking powder
1½ tsp. cinnamon
1 cup milk

Topping
1½ tsp. cinnamon
½ cup sugar
2 tsp. melted butter

Preheat oven to 375°F.
Cream together shortening and sugar. Add eggs. Beat until light and fluffy. In a separate bowl sift together flour, salt, baking powder and cinnamon. Add alternately to creamed mixture with milk, continuing to beat.
Pour into greased 9-inch springform pan. In a small bowl combine the ingredients for the topping. Sprinkle topping mixture over batter. Bake at 375° for 45 minutes. Cool on a rack 10 minutes before serving.

BUTTERMILK POPPYSEED CAKE
Dunbar House, 1880 (p. 10)

MAKES 1 cake.

This is one of the best poppyseed cake recipes I've ever had.

1 cup butter, softened
1½ cups sugar
3 eggs
½ tsp. vanilla extract
2½ cups flour
3 tsp. baking powder
1 tsp. cinnamon
½ tsp. salt
1 cup buttermilk
⅓ cup poppy seeds
1½ tsp. grated lemon peel
confectioners' sugar for dusting

Preheat oven to 350°F.
In a large bowl cream together the butter and sugar. Beat in eggs and vanilla. In a separate bowl sift together the flour, baking powder, cinnamon and salt. Blend flour mixture into creamed mixture alternately with the buttermilk. Stir in poppy seeds and lemon peel.
Pour into greased and floured bundt pan. Bake at 350° for 50 minutes or until cake tests done. Cool in pan for 10 minutes, then release onto a cooling rack. Dust with sifted confectioners' sugar. Serve warm or completely cooled.

CHRISTEL'S APPLE CAKE
The Inn at Mitchell House (p. 130)

MAKES 1 large cake.

This big, beautiful cake with its marvelous flavor and texture is a perennial favorite.

1½ cups oil
2 cups sugar
3 eggs
3 cups flour
1 tsp. salt
1 tsp. cinnamon
1 tsp. baking soda
1 tsp. vanilla
3 cups apples, peeled, cored and coarsely chopped
1 cup walnuts
1 cup raisins

Preheat oven to 350°F.
In a large bowl beat together the oil and sugar. Beat in the eggs. In a separate bowl combine the flour, salt, cinnamon and baking soda. Add to the egg mixture, blend, add the vanilla and beat together well. Then stir in the apples, nuts and raisins. Pour into a greased and floured tube pan. Bake at 350° for 50 to 60 minutes, until it tests done. Cool in the pan for 10 minutes, then turn out onto a cooling rack to continue cooling. Serve slightly warm or thoroughly cooled.

Hawthorne Inn

Concord, Massachusetts

BUILT IN 1870, the Hawthorne Inn stands on land that belonged in turn to Ralph Waldo Emerson, the Alcotts and Nathaniel Hawthorne. Here, through Emerson's largess, Bronson Alcott planted his fruit trees. When Nathaniel Hawthorne purchased the land he flanked a path to his house by planting a row of trees on either side; two of the trees still stand to the west of the inn. Today, the yard surrounding the inn contains a small pond, vegetable gardens, fruit trees, grape vines, berry bushes and flower gardens.

Historic Concord is home to the Antiquarian Society Museum, Emerson's House, the Old North Bridge (where the "shot heard round the world" was fired) and Sleepy Hollow Cemetery where Emerson, the Alcotts, the Thoreaus, Hawthorne and other notable Americans are buried. Walden Pond is nearby.

Guests at the Hawthorne Inn are served a continental breakfast of home-baked goods, fresh fruit, coffee and tea. The raspberries and grapes served are home-grown, and the honey comes from the inn's own beehives.

Hawthorne Inn
462 Lexington Road
Concord, Massachusetts 01742
(617) 369–5610

Gregory Burch and Marilyn Mudry

MORNING CAKE DELIGHT WITH TOPPING

MAKES 1 large cake.

Cake
1 lb. butter
2 cups sugar
6 eggs
½ cup sour cream
½ cup milk
1 banana, mashed
1½ tsp. almond extract
4 cups flour
1 Tbs. baking powder
1 cup berries (raspberries, blueberries or blackberries)

Topping
½ cup whipping cream
½ cup yogurt with fruit
½ cup sour cream

Preheat oven to 350°F.

In a large bowl cream together the butter and sugar. Beat in eggs. Then add sour cream, milk, almond extract and banana. Mix well. In a separate bowl combine flour and baking powder. Add to creamed mixture and blend well but do not overbeat.

Pour *half* the batter into a greased and floured 12" bundt pan, sprinkle with berries, and cover with remaining batter. Bake at 350° for 50 to 60 minutes. This is a big cake, so be sure to test with a toothpick to be certain it's done.

Cool in pan for a few minutes, and then turn out of pan to cool completely on a rack.

To make topping: Whip the cream. Fold in the yogurt and sour cream.

Serve each portion of cake with a generous dollop of the topping.

Manor House
Norfolk, Connecticut

CHARLES SPOFFORD, architect of London's subway system and son of Ainsworth Rand Spofford, Abraham Lincoln's Librarian of Congress, built Manor House in 1898. Set on five acres, this sprawling arts-and-crafts mansion is decorated with carved cherry panelling, stained-glass and leaded-glass windows and a massive six-foot fireplace in the living room. Furnishings throughout are antique. Some of the guest rooms have fireplaces, others have balconies, and all have views of the beautiful grounds.

Host to the Norfolk Early Music Society concerts, Manor House is also within walking distance of the Yale Summer School of Music and Art, which is host to an annual Summer Chamber Music series. The Berkshire Music Festival at Tanglewood and Music Mountain are both within easy driving distance, making Manor House an ideal base for music lovers. Other attractions in the area include the Norfolk Historical Museum, riding stables, antiques and craft shops and some of Connecticut's finest vineyards. The picturesque countryside is ideal for biking and hiking in the spring, summer and fall; the winter provides excellent cross-country and downhill skiing.

To give guests a sense of what life was like in the late Victorian era, the Tremblays offer horse-drawn sleigh or carriage rides.

Breakfast at Manor House is served in one of three locations: in the elegant dining room, on the sunlit porch or, if desired, in bed. These hearty breakfasts include many home-grown ingredients such as fruits, vegetables, herbs, honey (harvested from hives on the grounds) and locally produced maple syrup.

Manor House
P.O. Box 701, Maple Avenue
Norfolk, Connecticut 06058
(203) 542–5690

Diane and Henry Tremblay

OPPOSITE: *The living room of the Manor House exemplifies arts-and-crafts architecture and design—the materials are fine and solid and the workmanship impeccable.*

RHUBARB COFFEECAKE

MAKES 1 bundt cake.

The tangy rhubarb contrasts nicely with the butterscotch flavor of the cake.

Cake
1½ cups packed brown sugar
⅔ cup vegetable oil or melted butter
1 egg
1 tsp. vanilla
2½ cups flour
1 tsp. salt
1 tsp. baking soda
1 cup milk
1½ cups chopped rhubarb
½ cup slivered almonds

Topping
½ cup sugar
1 Tbs. butter
¼ cup slivered almonds

Preheat oven to 350°F.

In a large bowl beat together brown sugar, oil or butter, egg and vanilla. In a separate bowl sift together flour, salt and baking soda. Stir dry ingredients into the batter alternately with the milk. Beat until smooth. Stir in the rhubarb and the almonds.

Spoon into a 10-inch bundt pan, greased and floured. Mix together the ingredients for the topping, and sprinkle on top of batter.

Bake at 350° for 35 to 45 minutes, until done. Cool in pan briefly, then turn out to cool on a rack.

Serve plain, or topped with a little unsweetened whipped cream.

APPLE RAISIN COFFEECAKE

The River Street Inn (p. 105)

MAKES 2 cakes.

A sweet, spicy, fruity cake made more special by the glaze over the topping. Since this recipe makes 2 cakes, you may want to use one at breakfast and one at afternoon tea.

Cake
¾ cup oil
1½ cups sugar
3 eggs
2 tsp. vanilla
3 cups flour
2 tsp. baking soda
2 tsp. cinnamon
1 tsp. allspice
2 cups raisins
2½ cups chunky homemade applesauce

Crumb Topping
1½ cups flour
½ cup brown sugar
½ cup white sugar
½ cup oil
1 tsp. nutmeg
½ cup chopped walnuts

Glaze
1 cup confectioners' sugar
1 Tbs. lemon juice
2 Tbs. hot milk

Preheat oven to 350°F.
Combine oil and sugar, beat well. Beat in the eggs and vanilla. In a separate bowl mix together the flour, baking soda, cinnamon and allspice. Add to wet ingredients and mix well. Stir in raisins and applesauce and mix gently.
Divide batter in half and spoon into 2 greased and floured 8-inch springform pans.
Make topping by combining all ingredients thoroughly; sprinkle over top of cake batter.
Bake at 350° for 40 minutes. Remove from oven and place on cooling rack. Loosen and remove sides of springform pans. Cool slightly. Make the glaze by combining ingredients in a blender. Drizzle glaze over cakes.

FRESH APPLE WALNUT CAKE

The Frederick Fitting House (p. 103)

MAKES 1 bundt cake.

This large, good-looking cake is spicy, moist and chock-full of apples and nuts.

1 cup butter, soft
2 cups sugar
1½ tsp. vanilla
3 eggs
3 cups flour
1½ tsp. baking soda
½ tsp. salt
1 tsp. cinnamon
¼ tsp. mace
3 cups chopped apples
2 cups chopped walnuts

Preheat oven to 325°F.
In a large bowl cream together the butter and sugar until fluffy. Beat in the vanilla. Add eggs, one at a time, beating well after each addition. In a separate bowl sift together the flour, baking soda, salt, cinnamon and mace; add gradually to the creamed mixture, combining well. Stir in the apples and walnuts. Batter will be stiff. Spoon into a greased and floured 10-inch tube pan. Bake at 325° for 60 to 90 minutes, until done. Cool on a rack for 10 minutes before turning cake out of pan to continue cooling. Serve slightly warm, or completely cooled.

PUMPKIN APPLE CAKE

Dunbar House, 1880 (p. 10)

MAKES 1 cake.

A very good coffeecake, especially for fall or winter. The orange rind adds a great flavor. As with all recipes using pumpkin, make sure this is done in the center before removing from oven.

½ cup butter
1½ cups sugar
2 eggs
1 tsp. vanilla extract
2 medium apples, (peeled, cored and diced)
1 cup canned pumpkin
2 cups flour
1 tsp. baking powder
¾ tsp. baking soda
½ tsp. salt
½ tsp. cinnamon
¼ tsp. nutmeg
¼ tsp. cloves
¼ tsp. ginger
2 tsp. grated orange rind

Preheat oven to 350°F.
Cream together butter and sugar. Add eggs, one at a time, beating well. Stir in vanilla, apple and pumpkin. In a separate bowl combine all the dry ingredients. Add to creamed mixture, along with the orange rind, and blend well.

Pour into greased and floured 9-inch bundt or angelcake pan. Bake at 350° for 60 minutes. Cool in pan for 10 minutes, then turn onto rack to cool. When completely cooled, sprinkle with powdered sugar and serve.

RAISIN-FILLED COFFEECAKE

The Frederick Fitting House (p. 103)

MAKES 9-inch cake.

The cake is similar to a pound cake, and the filling is fruity and delicious.

Filling
1 Tbs. cornstarch
½ cup water
½ cup chopped walnuts
½ cup sugar
1 cup raisins
grated peel and juice of one small lemon

Batter
2 cups flour
2 tsp. baking powder
½ tsp. salt
¼ cup sugar
½ cup brown sugar
½ cup butter
½ tsp. vanilla
2 eggs
½ cup milk

Topping
2 Tbs. butter, melted
¼ tsp. cinnamon
2 Tbs. sugar

Preheat oven to 350°F.

To make the filling: In a saucepan, dissolve cornstarch in water. Add walnuts, sugar, raisins, lemon peel and lemon juice. Bring to a boil over medium heat, stirring constantly. Cook for one minute, then remove from heat. Set aside to cool while you prepare the cake batter.

To make the batter: Sift together the flour with the baking powder and salt. In a separate bowl cream together sugar, brown sugar and butter. Add vanilla and eggs; beat until light and fluffy. Mix in the flour and milk alternately, stirring after each addition.

To assemble: Spread half the batter in the bottom of a greased and floured 9-inch springform pan. Cover with raisin filling. Spread remaining batter carefully over the filling. Carefully spread the melted butter over the top, and sprinkle with the cinnamon and sugar.

Bake at 350° for about 30 minutes. When done, remove from oven and place on a cooling rack. Loosen and remove the sides of the pan. Cool completely before serving.

Adams Inn

Washington, District of Columbia

LOCATED TWO MILES north of the White House, Adams Inn is in the middle of the Adams-Morgan district, which many consider to be Washington's most diverse and interesting neighborhood. Excellent restaurants abound, presenting the cuisine of many cultures and nationalities. Boutiques, antiques shops and international shops are equally plentiful. The Thompsons are happy to help select restaurants and give advice about sightseeing.

The Adams Inn lies in a neighborhood of turn-of-the-century houses set on tree-lined streets. Originally the domain of upper-class merchants and professionals, its famous residents included Al Jolson and Woodrow Wilson. Today this section of Washington bustles with the accents of Europe, Asia, Africa and Latin America. It is home to diplomats, media personalities, professors, attorneys and government workers.

A continental-plus breakfast is served in the spacious dining room.

Adams Inn
1744 Lanier Place N.W.
Washington, D.C. 20009
(202) 745–3600

Nancy Thompson

The Adams Inn consists of all three of these turn-of-the-century townhouses.

SPECIAL DRIED APRICOT FRUIT CAKE

MAKES 1 cake.

This makes a large, solid "fruit cake," but not the traditional kind that so many people are not fond of. This cake is delicious; flavorful and wholesome, it makes a spectacular contribution to breakfast or afternoon tea.

½ cup butter
1 cup sugar
3 eggs
¼ cup orange juice
1 cup flour
½ tsp. baking powder
¼ tsp. soda
¼ tsp. salt
½ tsp. nutmeg
¼ cup milk
¼ cup molasses
4 cups dried fruit: apricots, raisins, prunes, apples and the like
2 cups chopped nuts

Preheat oven to 300°F.
Cream together the butter and sugar. Add the eggs and beat well; beat in the orange juice. In a separate bowl combine the flour, baking powder, baking soda, salt and nutmeg. Stir the flour mixture into the creamed mixture. Add the milk and molasses and blend thoroughly. Stir in the fruit and nuts.

Spoon into a greased and floured tube pan. Bake at 300° for 2 hours. (Check at 1½ hours.) When done, remove from oven and let cool in pan for a few minutes. Then turn out of pan onto a cooling rack and cool completely before serving.

The Oak Tree Inn
Heber Springs, Arkansas

BUILT IN 1983 to be both a home and a B&B, Oak Tree Inn looks much older, more like a survivor from pioneer days, with its weathered clapboard siding, twenty paned windows and handsome brick chimneys at either end. The interior is furnished with a tasteful collection of antiques and oriental rugs.

The Oak Tree Inn is located in Heber Springs, Arkansas, beside Greers Ferry Lake—forty-five thousand acres of crystal-clear water. The Little Red River, the source of the lake, abounds with rainbow trout and brown trout. This beautiful part of the Ozarks is spectacular in the spring with dogwood in bloom and brilliant in the fall with bright foliage.

Guests are served a full breakfast at Oak Tree and are also offered a dessert in the evening. Freddie Lou Lodge says that running a B&B "has been a wonderful experience, and many of my guests I count as dear friends."

The Oak Tree Inn
Vinegar Hill, 110 W
Heber Springs, Arkansas 72543
(501) 362–7731

Freddie Lou Lodge

The cedar clapboard of the Oak Tree Inn has weathered to a handsome brown-gray. The tree from which the inn derives its name soars on the left.

OAK TREE COFFEECAKE

SERVES 10 to 12.

Bottom Layer
2 cups flour
1 tsp. salt
2 tsp. baking powder
1 cup sugar
2 tsp. cinnamon
1 cup chopped nuts
2 eggs
½ cup vegetable oil

Preheat oven to 350°F.
Combine dry ingredients in a bowl. Beat the eggs and oil and add to the dry ingredients and mix well. Pat the mixture into a greased 9" × 13" glass baking pan.

Middle Layer
8 oz. cream cheese, softened
⅓ cup sugar
1 egg
dash of salt
1 tsp. vanilla

Combine and beat well. Spread over the batter in pan. Top with fruit topping (see below).

Fruit Topping
1 pint blueberries
⅓ cup sugar
1 Tbs. lemon juice
⅓ cup water
1 Tbs. cornstarch

Combine the blueberries, sugar and lemon juice. Mix the cornstarch with the water. Add to the berries and cook over medium heat until the sugar is dissolved and the juice is getting thick.
Bake at 350° for 1 hour. Cool on a rack before cutting into squares.

Purple Mountain Lodge

Crested Butte, Colorado

PURPLE MOUNTAIN LODGE takes pride in offering a relaxed setting from which to enjoy this area. In the winter there is excellent skiing, and in the warm weather hiking is popular.

Breakfast is served in the dining room with its spectacular view of Crested Butte and the valley beyond, with even higher mountains rising in the distance. In the summer, a continental breakfast is served; in the winter, a full breakfast.

Purple Mountain Lodge
P.O. Box 897
Crested Butte, Colorado 81224
(303) 349-5888

Dorothy Lockwood

OATMEAL CAKE

SERVES 10.

The simplicity of this cake is a large part of its appeal.

- ½ cup butter
- 1 cup quick cooking oatmeal
- 1¼ cups boiling water
- 1 cup sugar
- 1 cup brown sugar
- 2 eggs
- 1⅓ cups flour
- 1 tsp. baking soda
- 1 tsp. cinnamon
- 1 tsp. ground nutmeg
- ½ tsp. salt

Preheat oven to 350°F.

In a large mixing bowl, combine butter, oatmeal and boiling water. Cover and set aside for 20 minutes. Then add sugar, brown sugar and eggs and beat well. In a separate bowl combine flour, baking soda, cinnamon, nutmeg and salt. Add to wet ingredients and beat until smooth.

Pour into an ungreased 9″ × 13″ pan and bake at 350° for 35 minutes. Cool a few minutes; then cut into squares and serve warm with butter and a selection of jams and jellies.

Ferris Mansion
Rawlins, Wyoming

A CLASSIC Queen Anne–style mansion (listed on the National Register of Historic Places), this three-story brick house was built in 1903 by Mrs. Julia Ferris. Two years earlier, her husband had been killed by a runaway team of horses as he was returning from his copper mine in the Grand Encampment Mining District. Mrs. Ferris lived in the mansion until her death in 1931 at the age of 76. The present owners acquired the house in 1979 and have been restoring it ever since.

The house is furnished with Victorian antiques, and the guest rooms have working fireplaces. The parlor (with its grand piano), the sitting room and the library are open to guests. Centrally located in Rawlins, Ferris Mansion is close to many points of interest, including the Carbon County Museum, Pollard Jade Factory, Frontier Prison, Cedar Market Place Antiques and a variety of shops and restaurants.

A continental-plus breakfast is served in the dining room, or in the privacy of a guest's room. Breakfast might include croissants with chokecherry jelly (handpicked and homemade), banana bread, fresh fruits, yogurt, a selection of juices, hot chocolate, tea and coffee.

Ferris Mansion
607 West Maple
Rawlins, Wyoming 82301
(307) 324–3961

Janice Lubbers

ENGLISH MORNING CAKE

SERVES 12.

A treat for children, but adults like it too.

½ cup butter
2 cups flour
1 cup brown sugar
½ cup white sugar
1 cup buttermilk
1 tsp. baking soda
1 egg, beaten
1 tsp. vanilla
4 Heath candy bars, crushed
¼ cup pecan pieces

Preheat oven to 350°F.
Blend butter, flour, brown sugar and white sugar together; reserve half the mixture for later use. With the other half, mix in buttermilk, baking soda, egg and vanilla; beat well. Pour the batter into a greased and floured 9" × 13" pan.
Mix the reserved butter mixture with the crushed Heath bars and pecans. Sprinkle over batter in pan. Bake at 350° for 30 minutes. Cool on a rack for a few minutes before cutting into squares to serve.

The Ferris Mansion was designed by the noted firm of Barber and Klutz of Knoxville, Tennessee. For twenty-eight years, the widow Ferris lived here alone—not counting the servants.

Singleton House
Eureka Springs, Arkansas

THIS LOVELY RESTORED Victorian lies in the historic district of Eureka Springs. The decor is light, airy and eclectic; it includes folk art and comfortable antiques. A full, wholesome breakfast is served on the balcony, overlooking a very special garden where stone paths, a lily-filled fish pond and flower-covered arches are just part of its fantasy and charm. A secret footpath leads to the quaint shops and cafes of the historical district. The old town also features trolleys and an abundance of horse-drawn carriages. Barbara Gavron is happy to take guests on a walking tour of her town.

Singleton House
11 Singleton
Eureka Springs, Arkansas 72632
(501) 253-9111

Barbara Gavron

COUS COUS CAKE

SERVES 10 to 12.

This recipe requires no baking and no sugar. Its sweetness comes from the apple juice, blueberries and honey. The texture is creamy, the flavor delicious—a wonderful breakfast cake.

Cake
5 cups apple juice
  pinch of sea salt
1 lemon (juice & grated zest)
7 Tbs. agar agar flakes (a flavorless seaweed that gels, available in health-food stores and many supermarkets)
2 cups cous cous
1 pint blueberries

Bring apple juice to a boil, add salt, juice of the lemon, and the grated rind. Add agar agar and cook until flakes are dissolved. Add cous cous and reduce to simmer. Cook over medium heat, stirring occasionally, until almost thick. Remove from the heat. Stir in the blueberries.
  Pour into an oiled bundt pan. Cover and refrigerate overnight.
  Unmold onto serving plate, pour glaze over the cake, and sprinkle with toasted slivered almonds.

Glaze
1 Tbs. arrowroot
3 cup apple juice, chilled
2 Tbs. honey
½ cup blueberries
½ cup slivered almonds, toasted

Mix arrowroot in ½ cup cold apple juice. Stir in the rest of the apple juice. Place over medium-high heat and simmer, stirring constantly. Add the honey. Cook until thick in consistency. Remove from heat and stir in blueberries. Allow to cool slightly before spooning over cake. Sprinkle almonds over glaze.

Strawberry Inn
New Market, Maryland

HISTORIC NEW MARKET, founded in 1793, is listed on the National Register of Historic Places. The many well-restored houses serve as homes and antiques shops. With more than forty antiques shops, it is justly called the "antiques capital of Maryland." Cunningham Falls and Catoctin Mountain National Park are eighteen miles away. There is a wealth of trails for cross-country skiing, bicycle riding, hiking, and just enjoying the view. New Market is less than one hour from Washington, Baltimore, Gettysburg, Harpers Ferry and Leesburg — four states and the nation's capital.

The Strawberry Inn is a restored Victorian frame house furnished with antiques and period pieces, and offers each guest a continental breakfast in the morning, either brought to the room on a butler's tray or served on the back porch overlooking a beautiful yard.

The Strawberry Inn
Box 237, 17 Main Street
New Market, Maryland 21774
(301) 865–3318

Jane and Ed Rossig

STRAWBERRY BREAD

MAKES 1 loaf.

A moist and flavorful loaf, perfect for breakfast or afternoon tea.

    1 10-oz. package frozen straw-
          berries, thawed
    2 eggs
    ¾ cup oil
    1 cup sugar
 1 ½ cups flour
    ½ tsp. baking soda
    1 tsp. cinnamon

Preheat oven to 325°F.
Purée strawberries in a food processor or blender; set aside. Beat together the eggs and oil. In a separate bowl combine the sugar, flour, baking soda and cinnamon. Add the egg and oil mixture to the dry ingredients and mix well. Blend in the strawberries. Pour into a greased and floured loaf pan. Bake at 325° for approximately 50 minutes or until done. Cool on a rack in the pan for a few minutes, then turn loaf out of pan to cool completely before slicing.

OPPOSITE: *Singleton House is far enough from the hustle and bustle of downtown Eureka Springs to enjoy peace and quiet, but close enough to reach on foot.*

LEFT: *Strawberry Inn, a fine example of carpenter gothic, is part of New Market, Maryland. The entire town is listed on the National Register of Historic Places as a historic district.*

PEAR BREAKFAST CAKE
Hawthorne Inn (p. 170)

MAKES 1 cake.

½ cup butter
¾ cup honey
1 tsp. vanilla
½ cup milk
2 cups flour
1 tsp. baking soda
1 tsp. cinnamon
½ tsp. ginger
3 pears, peeled, cored and
   finely chopped
¾ cup chopped walnuts

Preheat oven to 350°F.
   In a large bowl cream together
the butter, honey, vanilla and milk.
In a separate bowl combine the
flour, baking soda and spices. Add
the flour to the creamed mixture,
beat well. Stir in the fruit and nuts,
blending well. Pour into a greased
and floured bundt pan and bake at
350° for 40 minutes. Cool in the
pan for a few minutes before turning out onto a cooling rack. Cool
completely before slicing.

IRISH SODA BREAD
Britt House (p. 16)

MAKES 1 loaf.

Always well liked at breakfast, this
bread is also served as an afternoon
tea item at Britt House. Make it a
day ahead.

2 cups flour
½ tsp. baking soda
¾ tsp. salt
1 cup buttermilk
¾ cup raisins

Preheat oven to 350°F.
   Mix together the flour, baking
soda and salt. Beat in the buttermilk. Add the raisins and combine
thoroughly. Turn out the dough
onto a lightly floured board and
knead for a few minutes.
   Shape into slightly flattened ball.
Cut an "x" in the top of the round-
ed dough and place on a greased
cookie sheet. Bake at 350° for 30
minutes. When done, cool on a
rack. *When completely cooled,
wrap in a just slightly damp linen
towel and let sit 6 to 8 hours.* When
ready to serve, rewarm and serve
with butter and jam.

PEACH BREAD
Barley Sheaf Farm (p. 25)

MAKES 2 small loaves.

"This peach bread is a big summer
favorite, when peaches are bountiful
and can be purchased by the bushel
at our many farmers' markets. The
scent of this bread baking is always
heavenly." — AMY DONOHUE

½ cup butter
1 cup sugar
3 eggs
2¾ cups flour
1½ tsp. baking powder
½ tsp. salt
½ tsp. baking soda
1½ tsp. cinnamon
½ cup fresh orange juice
1 tsp. vanilla extract
2 cups peeled, sliced fresh
   peaches

Preheat oven to 350°F.
   Cream together butter and sugar.
Add eggs, one at a time, and beat
well. In a separate bowl sift together
the flour, baking powder, salt,
baking soda and cinnamon. Stir
into creamed mixture alternately
with the orange juice and vanilla
extract. Gently stir in the peaches.
Spoon the batter into 2 greased and
floured loaf pans. Bake at 350° for
45 minutes. When done, cool briefly
in the pans before turning out onto
a cooling rack. Cool completely before slicing.

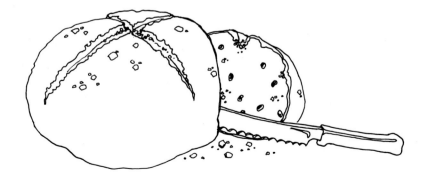

OPPOSITE: *The 1735 House includes a four-
story lighthouse that can house up to six
guests.*

The 1735 House
Amelia Island, Florida

BEAUTIFUL AMELIA ISLAND lies off the east coast of Florida, north of Jacksonville near the Georgia–Florida state line. The 1735 House is close to the historic harbor city of Fernandina Beach. A large portion of the downtown area is listed on the National Register of Historic Places, and a walking tour is a rewarding experience. There are plenty of shops and boutiques, as well as excellent seafood restaurants. Amelia Island is best known for its long, sandy beaches, but the golfer can enjoy a vacation here as well. The lovely seaside location enjoyed by the 1735 House includes a lighthouse with "four floors of memories that sleeps up to six." Delivered to each guest room in a wicker basket along with a morning paper, breakfast includes fresh juice, fruit, coffee, tea, milk and baked goods, such as individual sour-cream cinnamon loaves.

The 1735 House
584 South Fletcher
Fernandina Beach
Amelia Island, Florida 32034
(904) 261-5878

David and Susan Caples

SOUR CREAM CINNAMON LOAVES

MAKES 2 small loaves.

A wonderful aroma fills the kitchen while these are baking. Each slice has a pretty swirl of cinnamon; good fresh out of the oven or toasted.

```
  2 cups flour
1 ½ tsp. baking powder
  1 tsp. baking soda
  ½ tsp. salt
  1 cup sugar
  ½ cup butter
  2 eggs
  1 tsp. vanilla
  1 cup sour cream
  ¼ cup milk
  ¼ cup sugar
  2 tsp. cinnamon
1 ¼ tsp. grated orange peel
```

Preheat oven to 350°F.

Sift together the flour, baking powder, baking soda and salt in a mixing bowl. Set aside. In a separate larger bowl, cream together 1 cup sugar and butter until light and fluffy. Add eggs and vanilla; beat well. Blend in sour cream and milk. Add the flour mixture to the batter and mix well. In a small bowl combine ¼ cup sugar, cinnamon and grated orange peel; set aside.

Spread half the batter into 2 small greased and floured loaf pans. Sprinkle the batter with all but 1 Tbs. of the sugar, cinnamon and orange-peel mixture. Cover carefully with the remaining batter. Using a knife, cut through the batter gently to make a swirling effect with cinnamon. Sprinkle tops of loaves with the remaining mixture.

Bake at 350° for 35 minutes, or until done. Cool in pans for 10 minutes, and then remove from pans and cool on racks. Serve slightly warm or completely cooled.

The Bailey House
Fernandina Beach, Florida

BUILT IN 1895 at the extravagant cost of ten thousand dollars, the Bailey House is a fine example of Queen Anne-style architecture, individually cited in the national register. This exceptional house, which required three years to build, contains turrets, gables, bays, fish-scale shingles, many stained-glass windows and six fireplaces. The interior is appropriately furnished with carved furniture, marble-topped tables, fringed lamps, footed bathtubs, brass beds and a pump organ.

The Bailey House is located in Fernandina Beach, on beautiful Amelia Island, Florida, famous for its long, sandy, unspoiled beaches. Visitors may also enjoy golfing and sportfishing or taking in the local color of the commercial fishing port. A thirty-block section of the downtown area, listed in the National Register of Historic Places, offers much to see for anyone interested in architecture.

A continental breakfast served in the lovely dining room always features a variety of home-baked breads.

The Bailey House
28 7th Street South
Fernandina Beach, Florida 32034
(904) 261-5390

Tom and Diane Hay

BANANA BREAD

MAKES 2 loaves.

This recipe is an excellent way to use bananas that are too ripe to serve but have not gone bad. Keeping pace with ripening bananas is often a challenge for the B&B host.

  2 cups sugar
  1 cup butter
  5 bananas, well ripened
  4 eggs
1 ½ cups flour
  1 tsp. salt
  2 tsp. baking soda

Preheat oven to 350°F.

In a large bowl cream together the sugar and butter until light and fluffy. Mash the bananas and add them to the mix. Beat the eggs well, and then mix well into banana batter. In a separate bowl sift together the flour, salt and baking soda; add to the banana mixture and blend well. Pour into 2 greased and floured 9" × 5" breadloaf pans. Bake at 350° for approximately 45 minutes, or until done. Cool in the pans for 5 minutes and then turn out to cool completely on a rack. Cool completely before slicing. This bread can be frozen well; it is tasty served toasted.

Built in the Queen Anne style popular at the turn of the century, the Bailey House is notable for the excellence of its details. The wealthy builder spared no expense to make his home perfect in every way.

The Gingerbread Mansion
Ferndale, California

WITH INTRICATE WOODEN fretwork running riot from every turret, gable and cornice, the Gingerbread Mansion, built in 1899, is such a beautiful example of Victorian architecture at its most ornate that it has become one of the most photographed buildings in California. Painted in shades of peach and yellow, it is surrounded by English-style flower gardens. The interior, carefully restored to its original elegance, is decorated with appropriate antiques.

The town of Ferndale has been designated a state historical landmark because of its many well-preserved Victorian buildings. The delightfully unusual shops and art galleries, outdoor cafes and interesting eateries make this charming town a delight to visit. If they are so inclined, guests can explore the town on bicycles supplied by the Gingerbread Mansion.

Every afternoon, the Gingerbread Mansion serves tea with cake in the four large parlors. A continental-plus breakfast of homebaked goods, cheeses, fruits and beverages is served in the formal dining room overlooking the garden.

The Gingerbread Mansion
400 Berding Street
Ferndale, California 95536
(707) 786–4000

Wendy Hatfield and Ken Torbert

VALERIE'S SOUR CREAM BANANA BREAD

MAKES 1 loaf.

This dense bread has a delicate banana flavor. Good plain or toasted.

  1 cup sugar
  ½ cup butter
  2 eggs
  1 tsp. vanilla
1 ½ cups flour
  1 tsp. baking soda
  ½ tsp. salt
  1 cup bananas, mashed (1 or
      2 bananas)
  ½ cup sour cream
  ½ cup nuts

Preheat oven to 350°F.
Cream together butter and sugar. Beat in eggs and vanilla. In a separate bowl combine the flour, baking soda and salt. Mix into creamed mixture, blending well. Finally add bananas, sour cream and nuts. Mix well. Spoon into a greased loaf pan and bake at 350° for 1 hour. Make sure center of bread is done by testing with a toothpick before removing from oven. Turn out onto a rack and cool completely before slicing.

The Gingerbread Mansion includes many of the architectural flourishes popular when it was built, including fluted woodwork, picture moldings and transoms.

MARMALADE BREAD

Lafayette House (p. 100)

MAKES 1 loaf.

The orange glaze makes this delicious bread special.

2 cups flour
3 tsp, baking powder
1 tsp. salt
¼ tsp. baking soda
1½ cups orange marmalade
1 egg
¾ cup orange juice
¼ cup oil
1 cup pecan pieces

Preheat oven to 350°F.

In a large bowl combine the flour, baking powder, salt and baking soda. Reserve ¼ cup of the marmalade and set aside; in a separate bowl mix together 1¼ cups marmalade, egg, oil and juice. Add the wet ingredients to the dry and mix well. Stir in the nuts. Pour into a greased loaf pan and bake at 350° for 50 to 60 minutes. When done, cool briefly and then remove the bread from the pan. Place the bread in a baking dish, glaze with the reserved marmalade and return to the oven for 1 minute. Place on a rack and cool completely before slicing. This bread will be easier to slice if you chill it beforehand.

LEMON YOGURT BREAD

The Fowler House (p. 64)

MAKES 2 loaves.

Suitable either for breakfast or for afternoon tea, this bread has a light, delicate lemon flavor and a fine texture.

3 cups flour
1 tsp. salt
1 tsp. baking soda
½ tsp. baking powder
1 cup very finely ground almonds
3 eggs
1 cup oil
1¾ cups sugar
2 cups lemon yogurt
1 Tbs. lemon extract

Preheat oven to 325°F.

Sift together the flour, salt, baking soda and baking powder. Stir in nuts and set aside. In large bowl beat eggs, then add oil and sugar; beat well. Mix the lemon extract into the lemon yogurt. Add the flour mixture to the egg alternately with lemon yogurt, ending with yogurt.

Spoon into 2 greased and floured loaf pans or a 10-inch bundt pan. Bake at 325° for 50 to 60 minutes, or until done. Cool briefly in pans on rack, then turn out of pans and cool thoroughly on rack before slicing.

Note: This bread can be frozen well.

VERY LEMONY LEMON BREAD

The Gingerbread Mansion (p. 183)

MAKES 1 loaf.

The combination of lemon tartness and a sweetened lemon juice glaze makes this a perfect accompaniment to afternoon tea.

Loaf
½ cup butter
1 cup sugar
2 eggs (slightly beaten)
1¼ cups flour (sifted before measuring)
1 tsp. baking powder
½ tsp. salt
½ cup milk
½ cup finely chopped nuts
grated peel of 1 lemon

Topping
⅛ cup sugar
juice of 1 lemon

Preheat oven to 350°F.

Cream butter with sugar. Mix in eggs. In a separate bowl sift flour with baking powder and salt. Alternately add flour mixture and the milk to the butter mixture, beating constantly. Mix in the nuts and the lemon peel.

Pour into a greased 5″ × 9″ loaf pan and bake at 350° for 45 minutes.

Just before the bread is due to come out of the oven, make the topping. To make this glaze, combine the sugar and lemon juice and mix well. As soon as bread comes out of oven, turn out of pan onto a cooling rack. Poke holes in the top with a fork and slowly spoon the topping over the loaf. Let cool completely before slicing.

Note: Mix the topping just before using or it will not be smooth.

Eastover Farm
Bethlehem, Connecticut

BUILT IN 1773, this charming country house has been maintained by the same family for sixty years. Their methodical restoration has enhanced its beauty. One project exposed a large stone fireplace, complete with oven, crane and pothooks for use over an open fire. Eastover Farm B&B—nestled in the foothills of the Berkshires on seventy acres of rolling hills and fields—also offers several acres of manicured lawns and gardens, including a tree-shaded flagstone terrace. Glassed-in porches, upstairs and down, overlook it all.

Guests at Eastover Farm B&B are served a hearty continental breakfast before they begin a day that might include antiquing, skiing, visiting the four-thousand-acre White Memorial Park, or the world-famous White Flower Farm, all nearby. During the fall months, visitors enjoy a breathtaking display of color; and year-round they enjoy the peace and tranquillity of a stay at Eastover Farm.

Eastover Farm B&B
P.O. Box 275
Bethlehem, Connecticut 06751
(203) 266-5740

Erik and Mary Hawvermale

LEMON LAYER LOAF

MAKES 1 loaf.

One of my favorites, this spectacular bread combines lemon and raspberry in a unique flavoring. It is perfect for afternoon tea.

½ cup soft butter
⅔ cup sugar
2 eggs
1½ cups flour
1 tsp. baking powder
1 tsp. salt
½ cup milk
3 Tbs. fresh lemon juice
1½ Tbs. grated lemon rind
½ cup seedless raspberry jam

Preheat oven to 325°F.

In a large bowl cream together butter and sugar. Beat in eggs. In a separate bowl sift together the flour, baking powder and salt; mix into the creamed mixture, along with the milk. Beat well, adding lemon juice and rind.

Pour half the batter into a greased and floured 9″ × 5″ × 3″ loaf pan. Carefully spread jam over the top. Pour remainder of batter over the layer of jam, being careful not to disturb it.

Bake at 325° for 50 minutes, or until a toothpick inserted in center comes out clean. Cool in pan for 10 minutes and then turn out onto rack to cool thoroughly. Cool completely before slicing.

The lawns and gardens adjacent to Eastover Farm cover several acres.

Hilo B&B
Hilo, Hawaii

HIGH ON A BLUFF overlooking the ocean, this B&B has been called the most beautiful house in Hilo. The setting also includes an oceanfront pool with a view of a popular surfing beach. The house has large decks facing the ocean from which guests can enjoy a view of passing cruise ships—and even whales! Although just two miles from downtown Hilo, the house offers an ambiance of quiet privacy.

Hilo is located on the east coast of Hawaii, the "Big Island." The town itself has interesting shops and galleries, including the Hawaiian Handcraft Store, where visitors can watch artisans at work. Every spring, Hilo is the home of the Merry Monarch Festival, which features the world's most accomplished hula dancing and maile chanting. The Lyman Mission House and Museum, built in 1839, was once a gathering place for Hawaiian royalty and their foreign dignitaries. It contains one of the best shell collections in the world. On the third Saturday of each month, the historical society leads a walk through the downtown Hilo area starting at the Lyman Museum. Day trips include visits to the volcano, to Waipio Valley, to Liliuokalani Gardens, to Hilo Tropical Gardens or to one of the abundant beautiful beaches.

Guests at Hilo B&B are served a continental breakfast that includes fresh fruit, coffee, juice, rolls and breads, on the deck with its fabulous view of the ocean.

Hilo B&B
c/o Bed & Breakfast Hawaii
Box 449
Kapaa, Hawaii 96746
(808) 822-7771

Evie Warner

MANGO BREAD

MAKES 2 loaves.

The name alone of this bread conjures up visions of tropical islands. Mangos, with their unique and somewhat delicate flavor, are nevertheless available throughout the country from the produce department of any well-stocked supermarket.

  2 cups flour
  ½ tsp. salt
  2 tsp. baking soda
  2 tsp. cinnamon
  1 cup shortening
1 ½ cups sugar
  1 tsp. vanilla
  3 eggs
  2 cups diced mango (approximately
     3 mangos)
  ¼ cup chopped nuts

Preheat oven to 350°F.
In a large bowl sift together the flour, salt, baking soda and cinnamon. In a separate bowl beat together the shortening, sugar, vanilla and eggs. Make a well in the dry ingredients and pour in the egg mixture; beat together well. Blend in the mango and nuts. Spoon batter into 2 greased and floured bread pans. Bake at 350° for 45 to 60 minutes. Cool in pans briefly; turn out onto a rack to cool completely before slicing.

Fresh, ripe fruit has an appeal few can resist. This simple but elegant presentation is from General Hooker's House (page 194).

Countryside

Summit Point, West Virginia

THE VERY FIRST B&B in West Virginia, Countryside is located in the quaint village of Summit Point, in the Shendoah Valley. The region is rich in both history and natural beauty. Set on the edge of an apple orchard, the house affords lovely views throughout the changing seasons.

A visit to Harper's Ferry, scene of John Brown's famous raid, makes an interesting day trip, with many local craft and antiques shops along the way. This is also an excellent area for hiking and bicycling, particularly in the spring and fall. "Our location is ideal, as it offers the traveler excellent sightseeing opportunities, yet is far enough away from it all to be private and relaxing," says Lisa Hileman.

The Hilemans' guests start the day with a home-cooked breakfast brought to their rooms. There in privacy they can enjoy a picture-postcard view of the orchard and hills beyond.

Countryside
Box 57
Summit Point, West Virginia 25446
(304) 725–2614

Lisa and Daniel Hileman

COUNTRYSIDE'S APPLE BREAD

MAKES 2 loaves.

This is a sweet, chock-full-of-apples bread. With its good solid texture, it is ideal for breakfast or afternoon tea.

  4 cups chopped apples, unpeeled
  3 eggs
  1 cup oil
  2 cups flour
  2 cups sugar
  1 tsp. salt
1½ tsp. baking soda
  1 tsp. cinnamon
⅛ cup cinnamon sugar

Preheat oven to 350°F.

Core the apples but do not peel. Chop into small pieces and set aside. In a large bowl beat together the eggs and oil. Stir in the apples. In a separate bowl combine the flour, sugar, salt, baking soda and cinnamon. Add the flour mixture to the batter, blending well. Grease 2 loaf pans and sprinkle with the cinnamon sugar to coat completely. Spoon the batter into the pans and bake at 350° for 50 to 60 minutes. Cool briefly in pans, then turn out onto a cooling rack to cool completely before slicing.

This charming little Art Deco house in the Shenandoah Valley was West Virginia's first Bed & Breakfast.

HARVEST APPLE CAKE

The Gingerbread Mansion
(p. 183)

MAKES 2 loaves.

This moist, dense, flavorful bread, chock full of apples, is served at afternoon tea at the Gingerbread Mansion. My guests loved it at breakfast, and it was very good toasted the following day.

    2 eggs
    2 cups sugar
    ½ cup salad oil
    2 cups flour
    2 tsp. cinnamon
    2 tsp. baking soda
    ½ tsp. salt
    1 tsp. vanilla or rum flavoring
    4 cups apples (peeled, cored
        and chopped)
    1 cup walnuts, coarsely broken
    ½ cup raisins

Preheat oven to 350°F.
  Beat together eggs, sugar and salad oil. In a separate bowl combine the flour, cinnamon, baking soda and salt. Add to egg mixture and beat well. Add vanilla and apples; then add nuts and raisins. Stir until well combined. Spoon into greased loaf pans and bake at 350° for 45 minutes or until done. Turn out of pans onto cooling rack and cool completely before slicing.

APPLE NUT BREAD

1837 Bed & Breakfast (p. 225)

MAKES 6 small loaves.

A dense, flavorful bread. At 1837 Bed & Breakfast this is served with homemade Lemon Curd (page 225) as a spread.

    6 cups flour
    1 tsp. baking powder
    3 tsp. baking soda
    1 Tbs. and 1 tsp. cinnamon
    2 tsp. allspice
    3 tsp. salt
    2½ cups vegetable oil
    5 cups sugar
    8 eggs
    2 Tbs. and 2 tsp. vanilla
    6 cups chopped apples (cored
        and peeled)
    2 cups chopped walnuts
    1⅓ cups raisins

Preheat oven to 350°F.
  In a large bowl combine the flour, baking powder, baking soda, spices and salt. In a separate bowl beat the oil and sugar together. Add the eggs and continue to beat well. Add the vanilla and combine thoroughly. Add the flour mixture to the creamed mixture and stir until well blended. Stir in apples, nuts and raisins. Spoon into greased and floured loaf pans and bake at 350° for 20 to 30 minutes. Remove from oven and immediately turn out of pans onto cooling rack. Cool thoroughly before slicing.

PUMPKIN BREAD

The Bailey House (p. 182)

MAKES 2 standard-size or 4 small loaves.

    3 cups sugar
    1 cup oil
    4 eggs
    3½ cups flour
    2 tsp. baking soda
    1 tsp. nutmeg
    1 tsp. cinnamon
    1½ tsp. salt
    1 16-oz. can of pumpkin
    1 cup pecans, chopped fine

Preheat oven to 350°F.
  In a large bowl beat together the sugar and oil. Add the eggs, one at a time, and beat until light and fluffy. In a separate bowl sift together the flour, baking soda and spices. Add the dry ingredients to the creamed mixture and blend well. Mix in the pumpkin and beat until batter is smooth. Stir in chopped pecans. Pour into 2 regular size or 4 small greased and floured loaf pans. Bake at 350° for 45 minutes, or until done. Cool on rack for 5 minutes before removing from pans. Cool completely before slicing.
  Note: As with all recipes that call for pumpkin, test the center of the bread to be sure it's done before removing from oven.

PUMPKIN-CRANBERRY NUT BREAD
Adams Inn (p. 174)

MAKES 3 loaves.

A sweet, dense, moist bread. Very good at breakfast, or afternoon tea.

4 cups sugar
1 cup vegetable oil
3 eggs
2 16-oz. cans pumpkin
5 cups flour
1 Tbs. baking soda
2 tsp. cinnamon
2 cups chopped walnuts
2 cups raw cranberries, coarsely chopped

Preheat oven to 350°F.
    In a large bowl beat together the sugar and oil. Add the eggs and beat again. Mix in the pumpkin. In a separate bowl combine the flour, baking soda and cinnamon. Add the flour mixture to the pumpkin mixture and blend well. Stir in the nuts and cranberries.
    Spoon into 3 greased and floured bread pans and bake at 350° for approximately 1 hour. As with any recipe using pumpkin, check to be sure the center of the bread is done before removing from the oven. When done, turn out of the pans onto cooling racks and cool completely before slicing.

CRANBERRY NUT BREAD
The Frederick Fitting House (p. 103)

MAKES 1 large or 2 small loaves.

The orange rind and juice, raw cranberries and the walnuts give this bread a wonderful flavor and texture. It's good for breakfast or afternoon tea bread.

1 cup whole raw cranberries
1 cup chopped walnuts
2 cups flour
1 cup sugar
½ tsp. salt
1½ tsp. baking powder
½ tsp. baking soda
2 eggs
2 Tbs. butter, melted
    juice of 1 orange
    grated rind of 1 orange
    boiling water

Preheat oven to 350°F.
    Cut the cranberries in half, place in a bowl with the walnuts, and dredge with 1 tablespoon of the flour. Set aside. In a separate bowl sift together the remaining flour, sugar, salt, baking powder and baking soda. In a 2-cup measuring cup, combine eggs, melted butter, orange juice and rind. Add enough boiling water to make 1 cup liquid. Stir into dry ingredients until well mixed. Fold in cranberries and nuts.
    Spoon into 1 large or 2 small greased and floured loaf pans. Bake at 350° for 45 to 60 minutes. Cool thoroughly on a rack before slicing.

PUMPKIN GINGERBREAD
The Gingerbread Mansion (p. 183)

MAKES 2 loaves.

A spicy, delicious bread. This can be served warm with butter or cold with whipped cream as a dessert.

3 cups sugar
1 cup vegetable oil
4 eggs
3½ cups flour
2 tsp. baking soda
1½ tsp. salt
½ tsp. baking powder
2 tsp. ginger
1 tsp. each: cinnamon, nutmeg, cloves and allspice
⅔ cup water
1 1-lb. can pumpkin

Preheat oven to 350°F.
    Cream together sugar, oil and eggs. Sift together flour, baking soda, salt, baking powder, ginger, cinnamon, nutmeg, cloves and allspice. Add sifted ingredients and water alternately to creamed mixture. Beat in pumpkin. Pour into two greased 5″ × 9″ loaf pans; bake at 350° for 1 hour, testing to be sure it is thoroughly cooked. Cool on a rack.

O'Connor's Guest House Bed & Breakfast
Rehoboth Beach, Delaware

A COUNTRY QUEEN ANNE house from the turn of the century, O'Connor's Guest House B&B is located a half-block from the ocean. Visitors to Rehoboth Beach come primarily to enjoy the miles of white sandy beaches, the quiet atmosphere of the town, the gracious Victorian architecture and the excellent restaurants.

Guests at O'Connor's are served a continental-plus breakfast on the big screened-in porch, which is furnished with wicker and cooled by sea breezes.

O'Connor's Guest House B&B
20 Delaware Avenue
Rehoboth Beach, Delaware 19971
(302) 227-2419

Pat O'Connor

CARROT-PINEAPPLE BREAD

MAKES 2 loaves.

A tasty, moist bread, well complemented by cream cheese. This bread keeps well and is very good toasted.

        3 eggs
        2 cups sugar
        1 cup oil
        2 tsp. vanilla
        1 cup grated carrots
        1 20-oz. can crushed pineapple,
             not drained
        1 cup chopped walnuts
        3 cups flour
    1 ½ tsp. cinnamon
        1 tsp. salt
        1 tsp. baking soda

Preheat oven to 325°F.

In a large bowl beat together the eggs, sugar, oil and vanilla. Stir in the grated carrots, pineapple and walnuts. In a separate bowl sift together the flour, cinnamon, salt and baking soda. Add the dry ingredients to the carrot-pineapple mixture and combine well. Pour into 2 greased and floured loaf pans.

Bake at 325° for 50 minutes. Cool in pans for 10 minutes, then turn out onto a rack and cool thoroughly before slicing.

A big, screened-in porch like the one at O'Connor's Guest House is an invitation to a quiet afternoon of reading or a cook-out without threat of mosquitoes.

ZUCCHINI PINEAPPLE LOAF
Adams Inn (p. 174)

MAKES 2 loaves.

Our neighbor John Morris, 8 years old at the time, helped with this book by taste-testing samples during its preparation. He was always honest in his assessments. When he tried this bread, he said quite sincerely, "Best cake I ever had."

2 cups sugar
1 cup vegetable oil
3 eggs
3 tsp. vanilla
2 cups peeled and grated zucchini, well-drained
3 cups flour
1 tsp. baking powder
1 tsp. baking soda
1 tsp. salt
1 8-oz. can crushed pineapple, undrained
1 cup chopped pecans or walnuts

Preheat oven to 350°F.
In a large bowl beat together the sugar and oil. Beat in the eggs and vanilla. Stir in the zucchini. In a separate bowl combine the flour, baking powder, baking soda and salt. Add the flour mixture to the zucchini mixture and blend well. Add the pineapple and blend in thoroughly. Stir in the nuts. Spoon the batter into 2 greased and floured loaf pans and bake at 350° for 45 to 60 minutes. When done, turn out of pans onto cooling racks and cool completely before slicing.

ZUCCHINI BREAD
Teton Tree House (p. 165)

MAKES 2 loaves.

Unlike some other zucchini bread, this variation is not particularly sweet. It has a good grainy texture and wholesome flavor.

3 eggs
1 cup vegetable oil
2 cups brown sugar
1 tsp. vanilla
2 cups grated zucchini, with juice
1 cup chopped walnuts
3 cups whole wheat flour
1 tsp. salt
1 tsp. baking soda
1¼ tsp. baking powder
1 tsp. ginger
1 tsp. cinnamon
1 tsp. cloves

Preheat oven to 350°F.
In a large bowl, beat together the eggs, oil, sugar and vanilla. Stir in the zucchini and walnuts. In a separate bowl combine the flour with the other dry ingredients. Add to the zucchini batter and stir well, until completely blended. Spoon into greased and floured 5″ × 7″ loaf pans. Bake at 350° for about 40 minutes or until done in center (test with a toothpick). When done, remove from oven, turn out of pans onto a cooling rack and cool thoroughly before slicing.
Variation: This batter may be used for muffins. Spoon into greased muffin tins and bake at 350° for 20 minutes.

ZUCCHINI BREAD
Wal–Mec Farm (p. 166)

MAKES 2 loaves.

A moist and delicious bread, suitable for breakfast or afternoon tea. Another good way to use overabundant summer zucchini.

2 cups flour
2 tsp. baking soda
1 tsp. salt
¼ tsp. baking powder
3 tsp. ground cinnamon
3 eggs
1 cup vegetable oil
1½ cups sugar
2 tsp. vanilla
2 cups grated zucchini
1 cup raisins
1 cup chopped walnuts

Preheat oven to 350°F.
Sift together flour, baking soda, salt, baking powder and cinnamon; set aside. In a large bowl beat together the eggs, oil, sugar and vanilla. Stir in the zucchini. Gradually add the flour mixture, blending well. Stir in the raisins and nuts.

Spoon the batter into 2 greased and floured loaf pans. Bake at 350° for 30 minutes. Cool in pans for a few minutes before turning out onto a cooling rack. Cool completely before serving.

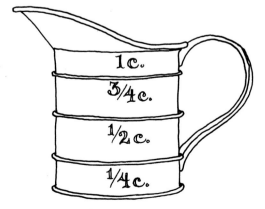

ALMOND TEA BREAD

The Frederick Fitting House (p. 103)

MAKES 1 loaf.

The toasted almonds make this bread special. Very good toasted when it's a day old.

½ cup butter
1 cup sugar
1 egg
2 cups flour
¼ tsp. baking powder
¼ tsp. baking soda
¼ tsp. salt
½ cup light cream
¼ tsp. almond extract
½ cup slivered almonds, toasted

Preheat oven to 325°F.
  In a large bowl cream together the butter and sugar until light and fluffy. Mix in the egg until well blended. In a separate bowl sift together the flour, baking powder, baking soda and salt. Add the flour mixture alternately with the cream to the creamed mixture, mixing until well blended. Stir in the almond extract and the almonds. Pour into a greased and floured 5″ × 9″ loaf pan. Bake at 325° for 50 to 60 minutes. Cool thoroughly before slicing.

BUTTER PECAN BREAD

Lafayette House (p. 100)

MAKES 1 loaf.

This bread is as rich as it sounds. Easy to make, it has a wonderful texture and flavor. It is especially good toasted the following day.

2½ cups flour
2 tsp. baking powder
½ tsp. baking soda
½ tsp. salt
½ tsp. cinnamon
¼ tsp. nutmeg
1 cup brown sugar
1 cup chopped pecans
1 egg, slightly beaten
1 cup buttermilk
2 Tbs. butter, melted

Preheat oven to 350°F.
  Sift together the flour, baking powder, baking soda, salt, spices and sugar. Stir in the nuts. In a separate bowl combine the egg, buttermilk and butter, beating together well. Add to the flour mixture, stirring until just moistened.
  Spoon into a greased loaf pan, and bake at 350° for 45 minutes, or until done. Cool slightly before removing from pan and cool completely on a rack before slicing.

CHOCOLATE TEA BREAD

Murphy's B&B (p. 13)

MAKES 1 loaf.

When my friend Lisa Wilkinson du Hamel presented me with a loaf of this bread at Christmas a few years ago, I immediately asked for the recipe. It is unusual and delicious. I serve it to guests at afternoon tea (it's wonderful with iced Earl Gray tea), but it's very good toasted for breakfast too.

3 cups flour
1½ tsp. baking soda
½ cup cocoa
1 cup sugar
1 egg
1½ cups buttermilk
⅓ cup melted butter or oil
½ cup chopped walnuts
¼ cup raisins
¼ cup chopped dates

Preheat oven to 350°F.
  In a large bowl sift together the flour, baking soda, cocoa and sugar. In a separate bowl beat the egg, buttermilk and melted butter or oil. Add the wet ingredients to the dry and stir well. Stir in the nuts, raisins and dates. The batter will be stiff. Spoon into a greased and floured loaf pan and bake at 350° for 45 to 55 minutes. Cool briefly in pan, then turn out onto cooling rack to cool completely before slicing.
  Serve this bread well chilled, plain or with a little unsalted butter if desired.

DATE NUT BREAD
The Bailey House (p. 182)

MAKES 6 loaves.

The cylindrical shape of this moist, delicious bread makes it fun to serve. Serve plain or toasted, with cream cheese as a spread.

1 cup chopped dates
2 tsp. baking soda
2 cups boiling water
2 cups sugar
4 Tbs. butter
2 eggs
2 tsp. vanilla
4 cups flour
1 tsp. salt
2 tsp. baking powder
1 cup chopped nuts, pecans or
    walnuts

Preheat oven to 300°F.
   Sprinkle the dates with the baking soda and cover with the boiling water. Stir, and set aside to cool. In a large bowl cream together the sugar and butter. Beat in the eggs, and mix in the cooled date mixture. Add vanilla and blend well. In a separate bowl sift the flour, salt and baking powder. Stir into the date batter, mixing well. Mix in the nuts.
   Thoroughly grease 6 No. 303 cans (16-oz.). Fill each can about half full of batter. Bake at 300° for approximately 80 minutes, or until done. Begin to check after 40 minutes. When done, remove the cans from oven and let cool briefly on a rack. Loosen the edge of the loaves from the cans with a knife and remove from cans. Let cool completely before slicing.

GRAPE NUT BREAD
Ferris Mansion (p. 177)

MAKES 2 loaves.

This bread has a chewy texture that my guests and I love. The flavor is somewhat plain—the taste of the buttermilk comes through subtly— and therefore it makes a good backdrop for homemade jams and jellies, honey and butter. Very good toasted.

1 cup Grape Nuts cereal
2 cups buttermilk
2 cups sugar
2 eggs
3½ cups flour
½ tsp. salt
1 tsp. baking soda
2 tsp. baking powder

Preheat oven to 350°F.
   Soak Grape Nuts in buttermilk in a large bowl for 10 minutes. In a separate bowl cream together sugar and eggs; add to Grape Nuts mixture. In a separate bowl combine flour, salt, baking soda and baking powder. Add dry ingredients to wet and mix well. Pour into 2 greased and floured loaf pans. Bake at 350° for 40 to 50 minutes. Remove from oven and cool on rack for 5 minutes, then turn out of pans and cool completely before slicing.

BROWN BREAKFAST BREAD
Hawthorne Inn (p. 170)

MAKES 2 loaves.

A spicy, moist and hearty bread. Makes excellent toast if any is left over for the next day.

¾ cup honey
¾ cup molasses
3½ cups whole wheat flour
2 tsp. baking soda
2 tsp. ginger
2 tsp. cinnamon
2 tsp. allspice
   dash salt
2 cups milk
2 Tbs. orange marmalade
1 cup raisins

Preheat oven to 350°F.
   Beat together the honey and molasses. Sift together the flour, baking soda, spices and salt; add to the honey and molasses and blend thoroughly. Beat in the milk and marmalade. Add the raisins, stir until all ingredients are well blended.
   Pour into 2 greased and floured bread pans. Bake at 350° for 45 minutes, or until done. Remove from pans and cool completely on racks before slicing.

General Hooker's House
Portland, Oregon

DURING THE CIVIL WAR, General Fighting Joe Hooker became famous not for the battles he won but for his casual acceptance of camp followers (who were called "Hooker's other army"), which thereby gave a new name to an old activity. When Lori Hall found this airy, mid-sized Victorian house, she was amused that the tree-lined street where it stands in a historic conservation district of Portland is called Hooker Street—named, like others in the area, for Civil War notables. Although General Hooker never even visited Portland, she decided to call her B&B General Hooker's House. (For good measure, she named her cat General Hooker.)

Stores, theatres and museums are an easy bus ride or brisk walk away. Duniway Park with its great jogging track is two blocks away, and Lair Hill Park, with public tennis courts, is just up the street. Although guests at General Hooker's House can see downtown Portland from the second-story roof deck, the neighborhood is old and sheltered. Downtown Portland has been described as a "model of urban development, a city that has returned itself to man, to a pedestrian way of life."

Guests at General Hooker's House are treated to a substantial continental-plus breakfast, served either in the dining room or, when weather allows, on the second-story roof deck with its fabulous view over the treetops to downtown Portland.

General Hooker's House Bed & Breakfast
125 SW Hooker
Portland, Oregon 97201
(503) 222-4435

Lori Hall

ONION-CHEESE BREAD

SERVES 6.

This delicious pan bread goes well with egg dishes. The crust is lumpy with onion and cheese, and it is always a well-received change from sweet breads and coffeecakes.

    3 Tbs. butter
1½ cups chopped onion
    2 cups flour
    3 tsp. baking powder
    1 tsp. salt
    2 Tbs. dried parsley
   ⅓ cup butter
    1 egg
    1 cup milk
   ½ cup sharp cheddar cheese, grated

Preheat oven to 425°F.
Heat the butter in a small skillet. Add the chopped onion and cook over low heat, stirring occasionally, for 10 minutes or until tender. Remove from heat.
In a separate bowl mix the flour, baking powder, salt, parsley and 2 tablespoons of the sautéed onions. Cut in the butter until mixture resembles coarse meal. Make a well in the center of this mixture, and pour the egg and milk (already beaten together) into it. Stir until moistened. Spread into a greased 8-inch-square baking pan. Spoon remaining onions over top and sprinkle with grated cheese. Bake at 425° for 30 minutes or until top is golden brown. Cut into squares and serve hot.

The sunny roof deck of General Hooker's House is hidden on the second floor (LEFT), while the charming Victorian angles are in plain view from the street (OPPOSITE).

Heart of the Hills Inn
Eureka Springs, Arkansas

BUILT IN 1890, Heart of the Hills has been lovingly restored to serve both as a Bed and Breakfast and as Jan Weber's home. Furnished with period antiques, the old homestead lies in the Eureka Historic District.

At the turn of the century, Eureka Springs, famous for its natural hot springs and mineral baths, was a popular resort for the well-to-do, as evidenced by the many elaborate Victorian houses and lavish public buildings. This charming town is now experiencing a renewed popularity, and the beautiful restoration of many of the buildings is a testament to the love the residents have for their town. Taking the four-block walk from Heart of the Hills to downtown Eureka Springs, passing many of these restored buildings along the way, is a pleasant morning's pastime. In addition to a good selection of shops and restaurants, this restored spa town has diverse museums to visit.

Jan serves a full gourmet breakfast on the porch when weather allows, or in the sunny breakfast room otherwise. The breakfast table is always decorated with fresh flowers from her garden.

Heart of the Hills Inn
5 Summit
Eureka Springs, Arkansas 72632
(501) 253-7468

Jan Jacobs Weber

POPPYSEED BREAD

MAKES 2 loaves.

Bread
3 cups flour
1½ tsp. baking powder
3 eggs, slightly beaten
2 cups sugar
1⅛ cups vegetable oil
1½ cups milk
¼ cup poppyseeds
1½ tsp. vanilla extract

Preheat oven to 350°F.
Combine the flour and baking powder in a bowl and set aside. In a separate bowl combine the eggs, sugar and oil and beat well. Add the flour mixture to the egg mixture and stir well. Add the milk, poppyseeds and vanilla and beat until smooth.

Pour into 2 greased and floured bread pans and bake at 350° for 45 minutes. Remove from oven and turn bread out onto cooling racks. Let the bread cool completely before glazing.

Glaze
¼ cup orange juice
¾ cup confectioners' sugar
½ tsp. vanilla extract

Combine all ingredients and mix thoroughly. Heat slightly until sugar dissolves. Remove from heat and cool slightly before pouring over the loaves.

To glaze the bread: When the loaves are completely cooled, placed in loaf pans, and prick the tops well with a toothpick. Pour the glaze over the bread and allow loaves to sit like this, soaking up the glaze for at least half an hour before removing from pans to serve. If you are not going to serve the bread until later, wrap in plastic wrap and refrigerate.

SOLDIERS BREAD
Strawberry Inn (p. 179)

MAKES 3 loaves.

Part of this recipe must be started a day ahead and allowed to stand overnight. The bread is baked in cans, and the cylindrical loaves are very pretty, with a good flavor and dense texture.

1½ cups raisins
  2 Tbs. butter
  2 cups hot water
  2 tsp. baking soda
  2 cups sugar
  1 tsp. cinnamon
  4 cups flour
  2 eggs
  1 tsp. vanilla
  1 cup chopped nuts

Preheat oven to 350°F.
   In a small bowl combine raisins, butter, hot water and baking soda. *Cover and let stand overnight.*
   Next morning combine the sugar, cinnamon and flour; set aside. In a large bowl beat together the eggs and vanilla. Add the flour mixture to this and beat well. Now stir in the raisin mixture and nuts, blending thoroughly. Pour the batter into three well-greased 1-lb. coffee cans. Bake at 350° for 60 minutes. Place the cans on a cooling rack and cool completely before removing the bottom of the can with a can opener. Push the loaf out of the can. Slice and serve with butter and cream cheese.

CORNBREAD
Murphy's B&B (p. 13)

SERVES 6 to 8.

Cornbread was always popular in my house when I was growing up, perhaps because of my father's Texas origins. Quick and easy to make, cornbread is an excellent accompaniment to eggs. I like it with eggs "over easy," and it's especially good served with avocado omelet (see page 80). Leftover cornbread can be used for bread crumbs and makes excellent stuffing for poultry.

1⅓ cups flour
  ⅔ cup cornmeal
  ⅓ cup sugar
  ½ cup cornstarch
  1 Tbs. baking powder
  1 tsp. baking soda
  1 tsp. salt
1⅓ cups buttermilk
  ¼ cup butter, melted and cooled
  2 Tbs. bacon fat, melted and cooled
  1 egg

Preheat oven to 350°F.
   In a large bowl combine the flour, cornmeal, sugar, cornstarch, baking powder, baking soda and salt; set aside. In a separate bowl beat together the buttermilk, butter, bacon fat and egg. Add the buttermilk mixture to the dry ingredients and stir just until moistened; do not overbeat. Pour batter into a greased 8-inch-square pan. Bake at 350° for 30 to 40 minutes. Cool on a rack, and when still warm cut into squares and serve.

COFFEE STRUDEL
Purple Mountain Lodge (p. 176)

MAKES 2 dozen.

Pastry
2 cups flour
1 cup butter
1 cup sour cream

To make the pastry: Combine the 3 ingredients well, knead, form into a ball and refrigerate overnight, wrapped in plastic wrap.

Filling
  ¾ cup apricot or cherry jam
  ½ cup raisins or currants
  ½ cup chopped nuts (walnuts or pecans)
1½ tsp. cinnamon
1½ tsp. sugar

Preheat oven to 350°F.
   Divide the dough into 3 parts. Roll out on a lightly floured board into a rectangular shape, approximately 8″ × 12″, about ¼″ thick. Spread each rectangle with one-third of the jam, sprinkle with one-third of the fruit and nuts and then sprinkle one-third of the cinnamon and sugar over all.
   Note: It may appear that you don't have enough filling. *You do.* When baking, the jam melts and spreads out.
   Starting with the long edge, roll up like a jelly roll and place on a greased cookie sheet. Bake at 350° for 20 minutes or until crust turns golden brown.
   Remove from oven, and let cool a few minutes. Cut diagonally into 1″ pieces and sprinkle with confectioners' sugar.
   Serve warm, or completely cooled.
   Note: You may freeze the unbaked strudel rolls, wrapped well in plastic wrap and foil. Defrost overnight in the refrigerator before baking.

L'ORANGE FROMAGE COFFEE PASTRY

The Heirloom (p. 91)

SERVES 6 to 8.

Pastry
1 cup butter
2 cups flour
2 Tbs. water
1 cup water
4 eggs
¾ tsp. almond extract

Glaze
⅓ cup slivered almonds
1 3-oz. pkg. of cream cheese
1 tsp. grated orange peel
¾ cup confectioners' sugar
1 Tbs. orange juice

Garnish
⅓ cup slivered almonds

Preheat oven to 400°F.

To make the pastry: Cut ½ cup of the butter into 1 cup of the flour until crumbly. Add 2 Tbs. water and mix until pastry holds together. Pat or roll out into a 10-inch circle on a cookie sheet. In a saucepan, combine 1 cup water with the remaining butter. Bring to boil and add remaining flour. Stir until dough forms a ball; remove from heat. Add the eggs, one at a time, and beat well. Beat in the almond extract. Spread this evenly over the pastry circle. Bake at 400° for 30 to 45 minutes.

While the pastry is baking, make the glaze. Put all ingredients in a mixing bowl and beat well.

When the pastry is done, remove from oven and cool on a rack for 10 minutes. Drizzle with glaze, and sprinkle with almonds. Serve warm, or completely cooled.

ICE CREAM STRUDEL

The Bells Bed & Breakfast (p. 9)

SERVES 12.

A rich breakfast pastry that immediately became a favorite in my house, this looks impressive yet is really quite simple to make. Note that the dough must be made a day in advance. If you only have a few breakfast guests, just bake one of the 3 strudel rolls; wrap the other 2 individually in plastic wrap and then foil, and freeze. Defrost in the refrigerator overnight before baking.

Dough
1 cup butter, softened
1 cup vanilla ice cream
2 cups flour

Filling
3 Tbs. sugar
1 tsp. cinnamon
⅔ cup preserves (apricot, strawberry, marmalade or the like)
1 cup cornflakes, crushed
1 cup raisins
1 cup chopped walnuts

To make the dough: Cut the butter into small pieces and mix with the ice cream. A food processor is best for this job. Add the flour and blend until smooth. *Form into a ball, wrap in plastic wrap, and refrigerate overnight.*

To make the filling: Mix together the sugar and cinnamon; set aside.

Divide the chilled dough into thirds. On a lightly floured board roll out to ⅛" thickness, in a rectangular shape, approximately 8 inches by 12 inches. Using one-third of all the filling ingredients spread each rectangle with preserves, sprinkle with cinnamon mixture, then with cornflake crumbs, raisins and nuts. Starting with the long edge, loosely roll up like a jellyroll. Place on a greased cookie sheet, seam-side down.

Bake at 350° for 25 to 30 minutes. Cool on a rack and sprinkle with confectioners' sugar. Slice diagonally into 1-inch sections. Serve slightly warm, or completely cooled.

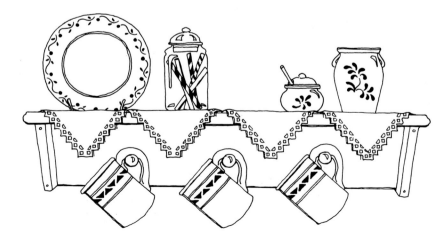

Yeasted Rolls, Breads & Pastries

COTTAGE CHEESE PAN ROLLS 201
Barnard–Good House

STICKY-TOP CINNAMON
ROLLS 201
Murphy's B&B

ENGLISH MUFFIN LOAVES 202
The Carlisle House Inn

BRIOCHE 203
Maple Lodge

CINNAMON BREAD 204
Phoenix House

CRUMPETS 204
*The English House Bed &
Breakfast*

PORTUGUESE EGG BREAD 204
Caverly Farm & Orchard B&B

SOURDOUGH RAISIN BREAD 205
Toccoa River Hideaway

SOURDOUGH CHOCOLATE
ALMOND BREAD 205
Toccoa River Hideaway

HONEY WHEAT BREAD 206
The Campbell Ranch Inn

PECAN NUT ROLL 207
Barrow House

CREAM CHEESE SWEET BREAD 208
River Haven Bed & Breakfast

PRUNE-FILLED TEA RING 209
Adams Inn

ANGEL BISCUITS 209
The Carriage House

The North Shore, as Bostonians call it, sweeps northward from Boston to Cape Ann, where the aptly named town of Rockport is located. Here the Inn on Cove Hill (see page 151) was built in 1791.

Manor House
The Inn at Norfolk

Amy Salcavik.

MANY OTHERWISE PROFICIENT cooks have convinced themselves that baking with yeast is mysterious and difficult. There is no doubt that making yeasted breads is more time-consuming than preparing unyeasted or quickbreads. With a little practice and understanding, however, anyone can master baking with yeast. The results are worth the effort — there is nothing so heavenly as the aroma of yeasted goods baking.

Yeast is a living culture. The first step in making yeasted breads is usually to dissolve the yeast in warm water. The water or other liquid should be warm but not hot, about 80° to 110°F. If the water is not warm enough, the yeast will not grow; if the water is too hot, the yeast will die; either way the bread will not rise. Understanding this factor is the basic step in working with yeast.

Most yeasted breads require rising time, which is the second step in working with yeast. Kneading is the third important step. Place the dough, formed into a ball, on a lightly floured surface, and using the heels of your hands, push the dough down and away. Fold the elongated dough back on itself and keep repeating this movement. Once you've done this a few times you will develop a rhythm, with the heels of your hands pushing the dough and your fingers folding the dough. Lean your weight right into the dough, and don't be afraid to give it a really good pounding. As you knead, you will feel and see the dough change. When you begin it is sticky, but as you knead, it becomes smooth and elastic. It stops absorbing flour from your work surface and begins to hold its own shape. Some recipes tell you to knead dough for ten minutes, others say "knead until the dough is smooth and elastic." Don't neglect to knead the dough sufficiently; dough that has been insufficiently kneaded makes bread that is too dense and coarse. Once you understand these basics of breadmaking, all you need is practice. The more you work with yeast, the better you will get.

Because baking with yeast is time-consuming, I like to make double or triple batches and freeze the unbaked loaves or rolls to be used later. It doesn't take much more time to make a triple batch of Sticky-Top Cinnamon Rolls, for instance, than it takes to make a single batch, once you've decided to spend an afternoon baking. Many of these pastries are easy to freeze, and such information is included with the recipes.

COTTAGE CHEESE PAN ROLLS
Barnard–Good House (p. 14)

MAKES 18 rolls.

1 pkg. yeast
½ cup warm water (110°)
1 cup cottage cheese
1 egg
⅛ cup fresh dill weed, chopped
3¾ cups flour
2 tsp. baking soda
1 tsp. salt
1 Tbs. sugar
2 Tbs. firm butter

In a 2-cup measuring cup dissolve yeast in water. Stir; set aside.

In a blender or food processor, mix cottage cheese and egg until smooth. Add the dill weed and process briefly.

Combine 3¼ cups of the flour with the baking powder, baking soda, salt and sugar. Cut in the butter until a crumbly mixture is formed. Add the cheese mixture and the dissolved yeast. Stir well.

Turn dough out onto a lightly floured board and knead until smooth and satiny, adding the remaining flour as needed to prevent sticking. Place the dough in a large, lightly oiled bowl. Then remove the dough, turn it over, and put back in the bowl so that all sides have a light coating of oil. Cover and let rise about 30 minutes. Punch dough down and divide into 18 equal parts. Shape into smooth balls. Place the rolls in a baking pan and let rise until almost double, about 1 hour. *At this point you may cover the rolls with plastic wrap and refrigerate overnight.*

When ready to bake, brush with a wash of beaten egg and water. Bake at 350° for 25 minutes. Cool briefly on a rack. Serve hot.

STICKY-TOP CINNAMON ROLLS
Murphy's B&B (p. 13)

MAKES about 24 rolls.

Rolls
2 pkgs. dry yeast
1½ cups milk
2 eggs
1 cup butter or shortening, melted
1 cup sugar
1 tsp. salt
1 Tbs. cinnamon
6–8 cups flour
1 cup raisins
¼ cup butter, melted
½ cup sugar
2 Tbs. cinnamon

Sticky Topping
1 cup brown sugar
½ cup honey
4 Tbs. butter
½ cup chopped pecans

Scald the milk and pour into a large bowl; allow to cool to lukewarm, then dissolve the yeast in it. Beat in the eggs, butter, sugar, salt, cinnamon and enough flour to make a stiff batter. When the mixer will no longer handle the dough, turn out onto a floured board and knead, adding flour as needed, until the dough is smooth and elastic. Cover the dough with a dry dishtowel, and let rise for 20 minutes.

Make the sticky topping, combining all ingredients in a saucepan. Heat, stirring, until the butter melts. Spread over the bottom of two 9″ × 13″ baking pans.

Divide the dough in half and roll each half out to a rectangle about 12″ × 18″, ½″ thick. Brush the rectangles with the melted butter and sprinkle with the cinnamon sugar. Distribute the raisins over the dough. Starting with the *long* edge of the dough, roll up like a jelly roll.

Using a sharp serrated knife, cut the roll into 2-inch sections, being careful not to flatten the dough. Place the rolls with the spiral design facing up and down in the prepared baking pans, spacing the rolls about ¾″ apart. See drawing below.

Cover with plastic wrap and refrigerate overnight, (or at least 8 hours) before baking. At this point the rolls may also be frozen. If you freeze the rolls, defrost them in the refrigerator overnight before baking.

Bake uncovered at 350° for 20 to 30 minutes. When done, *immediately* invert on to a serving plate. The sticky topping will be very hot; let cool a few minutes before serving.

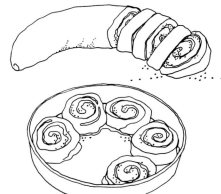

OPPOSITE: *The Manor House (see page 171) in Norfolk, Connecticut, is only a few miles south of the Massachusetts line in the foothills of the Berkshires.*

The Carlisle House Inn
Nantucket, Massachusetts

BUILT IN 1765, the Carlisle House Inn has been carefully restored to add modern conveniences while still maintaining the charm of old Nantucket.

Thirty miles off the coast of Massachusetts, Nantucket Island offers a warm and gentle climate from a very early spring through a late and lingering summer and autumn. With nearly fifty miles of beaches and with open exposures at all points of the compass, Nantucket is unsurpassed for water activities. Once the whaling capital of the world, Nantucket is also home to a popular whaling museum. Everywhere visitors can enjoy the tree-lined cobblestoned streets, roofs and fences covered with climbing roses, magnificently preserved buildings, a spectrum of museums, galleries, theatres and special exhibits, as well as many fine restaurants and specialty shops all within walking distance of one another.

Guests at the Carlisle House are served an elegant continental breakfast in the sun-dappled morning room.

The Carlisle House Inn
26 North Water Street
Nantucket, Massachusetts 02554
(617) 228–0720

Peter C. Conway

ENGLISH MUFFIN LOAVES

MAKES 2 loaves.

This makes marvelous, crusty loaves. Slice thick and toast; serve with unsalted butter and a selection of jams and jellies. You'll love the flavor and chewy, moist texture.

2 pkgs. yeast
6 cups flour
1 Tbs. sugar
2 tsp. salt
¼ tsp. baking soda
2 cups milk
½ cup water
   handful cornmeal

Combine the yeast with 3 cups of the flour, the sugar, salt and baking soda. Heat milk and water until very warm, and add to dry mixture, beating well. Add the rest of the flour, and stir well, making a stiff batter.

Grease 2 standard-size loaf pans and sprinkle with some of the cornmeal. Spoon the batter into the pans and sprinkle cornmeal on tops of loaves.

Cover and let rise for 45 minutes.

Bake at 400° for 25 minutes. Remove loaves from pans immediately and place on cooling racks. Cool completely before slicing and toasting.

Reflecting the charm of old Nantucket, an island lying thirty miles off Cape Cod, is the Carlisle House Inn, built in 1765.

Maple Lodge

Blowing Rock, North Carolina

LOCATED IN THE HEART of the Blue Ridge Mountains, Blowing Rock has been a popular vacation spot for many years. Maple Lodge offers guests quiet rooms furnished in antiques in the heart of Blowing Rock. Guests are within walking distance of the hamlet's arts, crafts and curio shops, filled with the work of mountain artisans. Miles of mountain trails for hiking or horseback riding are nearby, as is excellent golfing.

Guests at Maple Lodge enjoy a deluxe continental breakfast on the sun porch, with its view of the garden and the hummingbirds that feed there. Breakfast might include homemade nut breads, brioche, cinnamon rolls or muffins, accompanied by jams, butter and cream cheese, juice, fruit, granola and other cereal, coffee, tea and hot chocolate.

Maple Lodge
Sunset Drive
P.O. Box 1120
Blowing Rock, North Carolina 28605
(704) 295-3331

Marilyn and Ray Latham

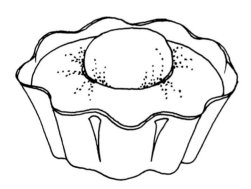

ABOVE *Set a small ball of dough in center.*

BELOW *Just before baking.*

BRIOCHE

MAKES 12 large brioches.

- ¾ cup water
- ½ cup milk
- ½ cup butter
- 3½–4 cups bread flour
- 1 pkg. dry yeast
- 1 tsp. salt
- ⅓ cup sugar
- 3 eggs plus 1 egg yolk (reserve egg white)
- 1 Tbs. sugar

Heat the water and milk to 110° or 115°. Add the butter and remove from heat. In a separate bowl combine 1 cup flour, yeast, salt and sugar. Add warmed liquid mixture and beat well for a couple of minutes. Slowly add eggs, and extra egg yolk, one at a time, beating well after each addition. Add ¾ cup of flour; beat at high speed 1 minute. Gradually add enough flour to make stiff batter (not too stiff).

Let rise in warm place until doubled (about 45 minutes). *Punch down, place in a covered bowl, and let rise in refrigerator overnight.*

Place the dough on a lightly floured surface and shape into the traditional brioche shape: make a roll from a large piece of dough. Place each in an individual brioche tin or an oversized muffin tin. Indent center and brush indentation with water. Set a small ball of dough into it (see illustration). This recipe makes 12 very large brioches. Let rise in a warm, draft-free place for about 30 minutes. Beat the reserved egg white with 1 Tbs. sugar and brush on top of each.

Bake at 350° for about 20 minutes. Serve hot with butter, jams and jellies.

CINNAMON BREAD

Phoenix House (p. 32)

MAKES 3 loaves.

Bread
6½–7 cups flour
2 pkgs. dry yeast
2 cups milk
¼ cup sugar
¼ cup butter
2 tsp. salt
3 eggs

Cinnamon sugar
1 cup sugar
4 tsp. cinnamon

Combine 3 cups of flour and the yeast. Place the milk, sugar, butter and salt in a saucepan and heat, stirring, until warm but not hot. Add to the flour and yeast; mix well. Add the eggs and beat thoroughly. Add as much of the rest of the flour as you can, stirring the batter with a wooden spoon, until it is too stiff to stir. Turn out onto a lightly floured board and knead until smooth and elastic, 5 to 8 minutes. Place in a lightly oiled bowl, turning so all sides are oiled. Cover with a towel and let rise in a warm, draft-free place until double in bulk, about 1 hour.

Combine the cinnamon and sugar; set aside. Punch down the dough and divide into 3 parts. On a lightly floured surface, roll each third into a rectangle about 8" × 14". Spritz with a little water and then sprinkle with cinnamon sugar. Beginning with a narrow end (8"), roll up the dough. Seal the edges and ends. Place in greased loaf pans, seam-side down. *At this point you may cover with plastic wrap and refrigerate overnight.* When ready to bake, let the loaves rise until double, about 45 minutes (1 hour if they have been refrigerated).

Bake at 350° for 35 to 45 minutes. Cool on a rack. Brush the tops with melted butter for a soft crust.

CRUMPETS

English House Bed & Breakfast (p. 94)

MAKES 8 to 10 crumpets.

1 cup milk
1 cup water
1½ Tbs. yeast
4 cups flour
¼ tsp. baking soda
1 tsp. salt

Mix the milk and water and warm it (do not permit it to become hot). Add the yeast and stir until it is dissolved; add the flour. Beat well for 5 minutes. Cover and leave in a warm place for 1 hour.

Dissolve the soda and salt in a teaspoon of warm water, and add to the batter. Beat well; cover and set in a warm place for 45 minutes to rise.

Heat a lightly oiled griddle to medium hot. Grease some crumpet rings (egg rings are fine), and place on the griddle to heat them. Spoon in enough batter to fill each ring halfway. Cook over medium heat until the top is set (the top will be dry and full of holes). Gently turn the crumpets over to allow the undersides to dry. When the crumpets have a light, golden color and are dry inside, place on a cooling rack and remove the rings. Serve immediately with butter or use them later—toasted and served with butter and jam.

PORTUGUESE EGG BREAD

Caverly Farm & Orchard Bed & Breakfast (p. 216)

MAKES 3 loaves.

Bread
1 pkg. yeast
2 cups warm milk
½ cup butter
1 tsp. honey
2 tsp. salt
3 cups flour
2 eggs, beaten
1 cup honey
4½–5½ cups flour

Egg Wash
1 egg yolk
1 Tbs. water

In a large bowl dissolve the yeast in the warm milk. Add the butter, honey, salt and 3 cups of the flour; beat well. Cover and let stand in a warm place for 2 hours.

Beat in the eggs and honey; add the remaining flour until a stiff batter forms. Turn out onto a floured board and knead the dough, adding more flour until the dough is smooth and elastic. Divide the dough into 3 parts.

To shape the loaves: Roll each section out to a cylinder about 8 to 10 inches long. Holding both ends, twist the dough, and form into a crescent shape. If you prefer, divide each third into 3 strips. Gently braid the dough, sealing the ends.

To make the egg wash: Beat the ingredients together well.

Place the loaves on a greased cookie sheet. Cover with a towel and let rise until double in bulk, about 1½ hours. Before baking brush the loaves with the egg wash. Bake at 375° for 30 to 40 minutes. Cool on a rack.

SOURDOUGH RAISIN BREAD

Toccoa River Hideaway (p. 86)

MAKES 8 loaves.

Starter
9 cups white flour
8½ cups lukewarm water
3 cups sugar
5 cups brown raisins
1 pkg. yeast

Place flour in a large porcelain bowl. Slowly add water, beating mixture until smooth with no lumps. Add the sugar, raisins and yeast; blend well. Cover with plastic wrap and allow to sit in a warm place at least 8 hours or until bubbly. The mixture should have a sour, winy smell. Stir mixture down and remove 1 cup for this recipe. Store the rest in a loosely covered container in the refrigerator. If you do not intend to make bread within the next week, the starter can be frozen. Allow to thaw completely before

using. If a film of alcohol forms at the top of the starter, pour off before using.

Sourdough Raisin Bread
8 cups white flour
4 cups whole wheat flour
2 Tbs. salt
1¼ tsp. ground ginger
2½ tsp. ground cloves
5 tsp. ground cinnamon
1 cup sourdough starter
1 cup oil

Reserve two cups of the white flour for flouring your work surface and hands. Combine the rest of the flours, salt and spices in a large bowl and mix until thoroughly combined. Add the starter and oil and mix well, using your hands much as you would when making meatloaf. Cover and leave in a warm place for 2 hours.

After 2 hours, remove the dough to a floured work surface and knead thoroughly for 10 minutes, repeatedly flouring hands and work surface to prevent sticking. This dough is sticky, and you must be sure that you add no more than the 2 cups reserved flour during kneading. A useful trick is to scrape your work surface to remove the dough that has stuck to it. Return these scrapings to the dough.

After kneading, form dough into a large flattened ball; dust with flour and place on a floured surface. Allow to rest 20 minutes. Cut into 8 equal parts. Knead each portion briefly and form into loaves. Place in oiled loaf pans and allow to rise until doubled in bulk, about 1 hour. Bake at 350° for 35 to 45 minutes or until top is brown. Brush tops with milk and remove from pans. Cool on a rack.

SOURDOUGH CHOCOLATE ALMOND BREAD

Toccoa River Hideaway (p. 86)

MAKES 8 loaves.

Starter
9 cups white flour
7½ cups water
3 cups sugar
1 pkg. yeast

Follow the starter directions given above for Sourdough Raisin Bread.

Sourdough Chocolate Almond Bread
12 cups white flour
1 tsp. salt
1 cup sourdough starter
1 cup oil
1 Tbs. almond extract
2½ cups semi-sweet chocolate morsels

Reserve two cups of the flour for flouring your work surface and hands. Combine the rest of the flour and salt in a large bowl and mix until thoroughly combined. Add the starter, oil, almond extract and chocolate morsels and mix well, using your hands much as you would when making meatloaf. Cover, and leave in a warm place for 2 hours.

Follow the directions for Sourdough Raisin Bread (above) for kneading and baking.

VARIATIONS

Sourdough Apple Bread
Follow the directions for Sourdough Chocolate Almond Bread, but in place of the chocolate pieces and almond extract substitute 2½ cups chopped dried apples that have been soaked in hot water for 2 hours and drained.

Sourdough Whole Wheat Bread
Follow the directions for the recipe above, using half whole wheat and half white flour. Omit the apples.

The Campbell Ranch Inn
Geyserville, California

FROM ITS HILLTOP LOCATION, the Campbell Ranch Inn affords views of the surrounding vineyards of Sonoma County. The ranch itself sprawls over thirty-five acres.

Nearby, there are wineries to visit, excellent restaurants to satisfy the appetite and quaint towns to explore. Lake Sonoma is four miles away, offering boating, swimming and fishing.

Guests can easily spend the day right at the ranch, where there are a tennis court, swimming pool and horseback riding.

In the morning, a full breakfast is served on the terrace, where guests can enjoy the view.

The Campbell Ranch Inn
1475 Canyon Road
Geyserville, California 95441
(707) 857–3476

Mary Jane and Jerry Campbell

BELOW: *The Campbell Ranch Inn offers fine views of the Sonoma County landscape.*

OPPOSITE: *Crocheted doilies, china and silver enhance the fine cuisine at Barrow House.*

HONEY WHEAT BREAD

MAKES 6 small loaves or 3 standard-size loaves.

Guests take these little loaves with them to have later with cheese on their wine-tasting tours.

1½ cups boiling water
 1 cup rolled oats
 ¾ cup honey
 3 Tbs. butter
 2 tsp. salt
 1 pkg. dry yeast
 2 cups lukewarm water
 1 cup 7-grain cereal
 3 cups whole wheat flour
 4 cups white flour

Pour boiling water over the oats; let stand 30 minutes. Add honey, soft butter and salt. Mix well. Dissolve the yeast in the warm water and stir into the oats mixture. Add the 7-grain cereal and the whole wheat flour. Mix well. Then add the white flour to make a medium soft dough. Turn onto a floured board. Knead for 10 minutes, until smooth and elastic. Place dough in greased bowl. Grease top and cover with a towel. Let rise 1 hour. Then turn out of bowl and knead again. Divide the dough into six equal portions. Shape into small loaves and place in six greased 5" × 3" × 2" loaf pans. Place the pans on a large cookie sheet, cover with a towel and let rise until double in size, about an hour. Place (uncovered) in 400° oven and bake for 5 minutes; lower heat to 350° and bake for 25 to 30 minutes longer, until loaves sound hollow when tapped. Turn out of pans and place on cooling racks. Brush tops with melted butter. Serve warm.

Barrow House

St. Francisville, Louisiana

TWENTY-FIVE MILES NORTH of Baton Rouge lies the little town of St. Francisville, which has the largest concentration of antebellum plantation houses in Louisiana open daily for touring. Barrow House— built in 1809 and listed on the National Register of Historic Places— lies on historic Royal Street in the heart of this lovely town. Shirley and Lyle Dittloff have prepared a cassette walking tour of St. Francisville's historic district, including Barrow House, and offer it free to their guests. Making St. Francisville seem like a jewel in a lovely setting, the surrounding countryside consists of rolling hills dotted with ancient live oaks.

Believing that food is an important feature of their B&B, the Dittloffs serve many regional Creole and Cajun dishes. Breakfast is served in the formal dining room, a beautiful room with a marble fireplace and French doors opening onto the front gallery, where the table is set with china and sterling silver. The entire house, in fact, is furnished with antiques from the 1860s.

Barrow House
524 Royal Street, P.O. Box 1461
St. Francisville, Louisiana 70775
(504) 635–4791

Shirley and Lyle Dittloff

PECAN NUT ROLL

MAKES 24 pieces.

Very light and buttery, this pastry is a confection.

  1 pkg. yeast
  1 tsp. sugar
  ¼ cup warm water
  2 cups flour
    dash salt
  ¾ cup butter, cut into pieces
  2 eggs, separated
  ½ cup sugar
  1 tsp. vanilla
  ¼ cup chopped pecans
    confectioners' sugar for dusting

Preheat oven to 375°F.

Combine yeast and 1 tsp. sugar in a small bowl with the warm water. Let stand for 15 minutes. Using a pastry cutter or food processor, mix the flour, salt and butter until crumbly. Add the egg yolks and the yeast mixture and beat until the dough forms a ball. Cover and set aside.

In a bowl, beat the egg white until frothy. Add the sugar, a little at a time, and beat until the egg whites are stiff. Add the vanilla.

Divide the dough in two, and on a lightly floured board roll out into 9″ × 13″ rectangles. Spread the egg-white mixture over the dough, leaving a half-inch space around the edges. Sprinkle with the pecans, and starting with the long edge roll up like a jelly roll. Transfer to a greased baking sheet, seam side down. Make a quarter-inch slit down the center of each roll. Bake at 375° for 25 minutes. Cool on a rack and dust generously with confectioners' sugar. Cut into 1-inch sections before serving.

River Haven Bed & Breakfast

White Pigeon, Michigan

THE ST. JOE RIVER flows past the garden at River Haven Bed & Breakfast. A lifetime ago, the same river flowed past the long-vanished St. Joe Orphanage where Jim Pressler grew up. Now retired, Jim and Blanche Pressler find great satisfaction in running a Bed & Breakfast.

White Pigeon is a rural town, made up mostly of corn, soybean and dairy farms. It's close to Shipshewana, Indiana, where the famous Shipshewana flea market is held, and just twelve miles from Goshen, Indiana, home of the Mennonite College. Amish and Mennonite crafts are available at many stores in the area — handmade furniture, quilts, baskets and the like. Among Jim Pressler's friends is an Amish furniture-maker who made many of the pieces at River Haven. Sometimes Jim takes guests to his shop to see him at work.

As they eat breakfast, guests at River Haven B&B enjoy a view across the flower garden to the river. They can enjoy watching the ducks coming up onto the lawn and the hummingbirds at the window feeder. According to Blanche Pressler, "A pretty table is as important as good food. We use our best dishes, including antiques, nice table covers and fresh flowers." Blanche also loves to bake (sometimes getting up as early as 3:00 AM to start, but being careful not to wake anyone) and says guests love the aroma of yeasted goods drifting up to their rooms in the morning. The full breakfast includes coffee or tea; a choice of juices; a fruit dish; a home-baked item like coffeecake, cinnamon rolls or bread; a choice of eggs or French toast; bacon, sausage or sugar-cured ham; fried potatoes and homemade jam or apple butter from Amish friends. Blanche and Jim join guests at the end of breakfast for coffee and conversation.

River Haven Bed & Breakfast
9222 St. Joe River Road
White Pigeon, Michigan 49099
(616) 483-9104

Jim and Blanche Pressler

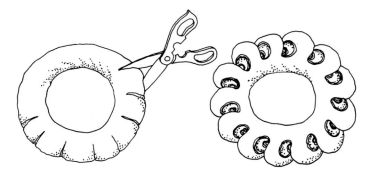

Preparing a Prune-filled Tea Ring for baking (see page 209).

CREAM CHEESE SWEET BREAD

MAKES 4 loaves.

This pretty and delicious pastry is partially made a day in advance and refrigerated overnight.

Bread
1 cup sour cream
½ cup sugar
½ cup butter, melted
1 tsp. salt
½ cup water, warm
2 pkgs. yeast
2 eggs
4 cups flour

Filling
2 8-oz. pkgs. cream cheese
1 egg
⅛ tsp. salt
¾ cup sugar
1 tsp. almond extract

Glaze
2 cups confectioners' sugar
8 tsp. warm milk
½ tsp. vanilla

Heat sour cream over low heat; stir in sugar, butter and salt. Remove from heat. In a small bowl dissolve the yeast in the warm water. Add the dissolved yeast to the sour cream mixture and stir. Beat in the eggs. Gradually add the flour and beat well. *Cover the bowl with plastic wrap and refrigerate overnight.*

The next day, make the filling by combining all the ingredients in a mixing bowl and beating well.

Note: You may substitute vanilla extract for the almond, or 1 tsp. grated lemon or orange zest mixed with 1 tsp. of lemon or orange juice.

(continued on next page)

CREAM CHEESE SWEET BREAD
(continued)

Divide the dough into 4 equal sections. On a lightly floured board roll each section out to an 8″ × 12″ rectangle. Spread each rectangle with filling. Roll each up like a jellyroll, starting with the long edge. Place the loaves on a greased cookie sheet, seam side down. Cut several slits in the top with scissors. Set in a warm, draft-free place and let rise about 1 hour. Bake at 375° for 15 to 20 minutes.

Remove bread from oven and cool briefly before frosting with the glaze. If desired, you may sprinkle snippets of maraschino cherries and chopped nuts such as pecans, walnuts or almonds over the glaze while it is still soft. Serve warm or completely cooled.

To make the glaze: Place all the ingredients in a blender and process until smooth. If necessary, refrigerate until the frosting is stiff enough to use. You should just be able to pour and spread this over the pastry; if it is too runny, it will run off the pastry, and make it soggy.

PRUNE-FILLED TEA RING
Adams Inn (p. 174)

SERVES 12.

Pastry
½ cup warm water
1 cake yeast
½ cup scalded milk
3 Tbs. shortening
2 Tbs. sugar
1½ tsp. salt
1 egg
3 cups flour

Filling
1 cup stewed pitted prunes, drained and chopped
¼ tsp. cinnamon
1 Tbs. lemon juice
¼ cup sugar
⅛ tsp. salt

Glaze
4 tsp. warm milk
1 cup confectioners' sugar
¼ tsp. vanilla

Dissolve the yeast in the warm water. In a separate bowl add the shortening to the scalded milk. Stir in the sugar and salt. Now add the yeast mixture and beat. Beat in the egg. Stir in the flour. Cover and let stand for 15 minutes.

Next, to make the filling, combine all ingredients in a saucepan over medium-high heat and cook until thick. Remove from heat and set aside to cool.

To assemble, on a lightly floured board, roll the dough to a 12″ × 14″ rectangle. Spread with cooled prune mixture; starting with the long edge, roll up like a jelly roll and place on a greased baking sheet, seam side down. Join ends together to form a ring. Using scissors, cut deep slits about 1 inch apart, cutting almost to center of ring, and turn each piece on its side, cut edge up with the spiral showing (see illustration, page 208). *At this point you may cover the ring with plastic wrap and refrigerate overnight.* Bake in the morning, or continue with the following steps.

Let rise until double in bulk (about 45 minutes). Bake at 350° for 30 minutes.

To make the glaze, place all ingredients in a blender and blend well.

When tea ring is done, remove from oven and place on cooling rack. Let cool for 10 minutes and then frost with the glaze. Serve warm or completely cooled.

ANGEL BISCUITS
The Carriage House (p. 30)

MAKES 36 biscuits.

1 pkg. dry yeast
3 Tbs. lukewarm water
5 cups flour
1 tsp. baking soda
3 tsp. baking powder
2 tsp. sugar
1½ tsp. salt
1 cup butter
3 cups buttermilk

Preheat oven to 400°F.

Dissolve yeast in warm water. In a large bowl sift together all dry ingredients. Cut in the butter, beat in the buttermilk and then add the yeast mixture. Combine well. Turn out onto a lightly floured board and knead for a minute or two. Roll the dough out to ½″ to ¾″ thickness. Cut with a biscuit cutter and place on an ungreased cookie sheet. Brush the tops with melted butter. Bake at 400° for 12 to 15 minutes. Serve hot.

Note: The unbaked biscuits may be covered and refrigerated overnight and baked the next morning or frozen until ready for use.

Jams, Jellies & Sauces____

FROZEN STRAWBERRY JAM   213
Hynson Tourist Home

SAND PLUM JAM   214
Harrison House

SOUTHERN FIG PRESERVES   215
St. Charles Avenue Home

RASPBERRY JAM   216
Caverly Farm & Orchard B&B

APRICOT-PINEAPPLE JAM   217
The 1859 Guest House

PRICKLY PEAR JELLY   218
Raford House

HOT PEPPER JELLY   219
Hedgerow B&B

APPLE BUTTER   220
The Jackson Street Inn

CAROL'S HOMEMADE
MUSTARD   221
Meramec Farm Stay B&B

MARTHA MURPHY'S
MARVELOUS MELBA SAUCE   221
Murphy's B&B

CRÈME FRAICHE   221
Phoenix House

LAKE DISTRICT LIME ICE   221
Gardner House

RHUBARB JAM   222
Palmer's Chart House

LEMON BUTTER   223
Radcliffe Cross

LEMON CURD   224
Briar Rose

LEMON CURD   225
1837 Bed and Breakfast

Built in 1818, the Gardner House in Wakefield, Rhode Island, is furnished throughout with antiques (see page 150).

MAKING JAM BASICALLY consists of combining fresh fruit with sugar, and cooking the mixture. A chemical reaction takes place, releasing pectin from the fruit to bind with the sugar, forming a jell. Some of these recipes call for the addition of bottled pectin, others do not. If you want to make jams without using bottled pectin, I recommend *Preserves Chez Madelaine* by Madelaine Bullwinkle. It is full of good recipes and plenty of basic information on making jams and jellies.

To make jams and jellies, you need fresh, good-quality fruit; granulated sugar; a large, heavy copper-bottomed saucepot; a jelly thermometer; a jelly strainer and jelly bag; a wide-mouth funnel for filling the jars; a good stainless-steel ladle, and a collection of jam and jelly jars. A large kettle bath for processing the jars of jam and jelly is good to have too.

Don't limit your use of jams and jellies to toast, muffins, biscuits and scones. You can serve them with pancakes and waffles or make jam tarts for afternoon tea. Even if you make a batch that comes out too runny, you can use it as an ice cream topping. A jar of a homemade jam, jelly or sauce with a ribbon tied around the neck also makes a wonderful present any time of the year. If you are not already a jam-maker, I hope this section will inspire you to venture into this most satisfying of kitchen endeavors.

Hynson Tourist Home

Easton, Maryland

THE EASTERN SHORE is the name Marylanders give to the finger of their state that stretches downward to the east of the Chesapeake Bay. Here, in historic Easton, is the Hynson Tourist Home and the country's oldest Quaker Meeting House. Wildlife and bird sanctuaries in the area are of interest to the naturalist. The location is also convenient to Washington, D.C., a city with an inexhaustible selection of things to see and do. Historic St. Michaels is also nearby.

Guests at the Hynson Tourist Home enjoy true hospitality and a home-cooked breakfast that always includes homemade jams.

Hynson Tourist Home
804 Dover Road
Easton, Maryland 21601
(301) 822–2777

Nellie R. Hynson

FROZEN STRAWBERRY JAM

MAKES about 4 cups.

Nellie Hynson recommends this for its fresh taste—the strawberries are not cooked. For this reason, the jam tends to be thinner than cooked jam, making it very good over ice cream.

    1 qt. strawberries
    4 cups sugar
    ¾ cup water
    1 box Sure-Jell Pectin

Wash and hull the strawberries. In a large pan thoroughly crush fruit 1 layer at a time until fine. Mix strawberries and sugar; let stand 10 minutes.

Combine water with Sure-Jell in a saucepan. Bring to a full boil, and boil 1 minute, stirring constantly. Pour this into the crushed fruit and stir for 3 minutes. Ladle quickly into sterilized freezer jars to about ½ inch from top. Cover at once with lid. Let stand about 24 hours, then store in freezer. Defrost overnight before using; once opened, keep refrigerated.

OPPOSITE: *The Williams House in Hot Springs, Arkansas* (see page 66), *is an imposing mansion of brick and of stone quarried in the Ozarks.*

Harrison House
Guthrie, Oklahoma

FROM ITS DARK SATIN WOOD to its shimmering brass fixtures, period wallpapers and curtains, to its exquisite antiques, Harrison House has been renovated with loving care. This bed & breakfast inn actually encompasses four buildings, all erected in 1898, located in the historic district of Guthrie.

Guthrie, Oklahoma's first state capital, offers a wide variety of activities for the visitor. The town promotes itself as "America's largest, most complete Victorian restoration." Nearby, authentic western ranches offer horseback riding, hayrides and cookouts. Guests may also want to visit Guthrie's Oklahoma Territorial Museum, a tribute to the men and women who first settled the area. A championship 36-hole PGA golf course, Cedar Valley Golf Course, is nearby, as is the Scottish Rite Temple, the largest and most magnificent Masonic temple in the world. Excellent shopping and dining are within walking distance of Harrison House.

Guests enjoy a continental breakfast served in the parlor. It features fresh coffee, a selection of baked goods, juice and, of course, Sand Plum Jam. Most guests have never even heard of sand plums, but once they try the jam, they want to take a few jars home with them.

Harrison House
124 West Harrison
Guthrie, Oklahoma 73044
(405) 282–1000

Phyllis Murray

SAND PLUM JAM

MAKES about 3 pints.

Sand plums grow wild in the countryside around Guthrie, Oklahoma. They are small, about the size of bing cherries, and have a tart, unusual flavor. They grow on small trees in thickets. In Guthrie, sand plums are so popular and special that the town holds an annual sand plum festival from mid-June to mid-July.

5 cups plum pulp
2 Tbs. lemon juice
1 pkg. pectin (Sure-Jell Pectin is good)
7 cups sugar

To make the plum pulp: Gather about ½ gallon sand plums. Boil with 1 cup water until soft. Press through a jelly colander for pulp.

Mix all ingredients in a large, heavy saucepan. Bring to a rolling boil. Boil hard for 2 minutes, stirring constantly. Pour into sterilized jelly jars and seal.

St. Charles Avenue Home
New Orleans, Louisiana

A TYPICAL NEW ORLEANS-STYLE wood-frame house, the St. Charles Avenue Home was built in the mid-1800s. The "first" floor sits well above street level, with a double flight of steps leading up to the front door. Located in a former plantation community on the outskirts of New Orleans, the house is close to antiques shops, restaurants and the Audubon Park and Zoo. A streetcar conveniently passes the house on its run to and from the heart of downtown New Orleans, famous for its jazz, fine and diverse cuisine and noteworthy architecture.

Guests here are served a continental breakfast featuring homemade biscuits and jams, such as Southern Fig Preserves, before setting off to explore the city.

St. Charles Avenue Home
Bed & Breakfast, Inc.
c/o P.O. Box 52257
New Orleans, Louisiana 70152–2257
(504) 525–4640

Hazell Boyce

SOUTHERN FIG PRESERVES

MAKES 4 cups.

This rich jam makes an excellent present.

7 cups fresh whole figs
3 cups sugar
  juice of 1 lemon

Combine the whole figs, sugar and lemon juice in a large saucepan. Stir and cook until the sugar is dissolved and the juice is as thick as desired (use a jam thermometer if you are unfamiliar with jam-making). Pour the preserves into sterilized jars; cap and store.

Especially good served with fresh, hot biscuits.

LEFT: *The St. Charles Avenue Home reflects the serenity of its New Orleans neighborhood; but thanks to that miracle of technology, the trolleycar, visitors can easily reach the downtown area.*

OPPOSITE: *With the Oklahoma land rush, the town of Guthrie sprang up almost overnight. Much of the old town (including the four buildings that comprise Harrison House) has survived. Today it has been restored—right down to the brick sidewalks—as one of the largest tourism centers in the country.*

Caverly Farm and Orchard B&B
St. Louis, Missouri

DESPITE ITS mailing address, this century-old farmhouse lies just outside St. Louis, making this a pleasantly rural location for both business and pleasure travelers. Many guests at Caverly Farm come to the area to do business in St. Louis but prefer to stay outside the city.

David and Nancy Caverly not only grow many of the fruits and vegetables they serve at breakfast, they also keep bees and harvest their own honey. Nancy cooks with it as much as possible, and always makes it available at breakfast, along with a selection of homemade jams and jellies. Guests here enjoy a full breakfast, served in the dining room at a table set with antique china and fresh flowers from Nancy's garden.

Caverly Farm and Orchard B&B
St. Louis, Missouri

David and Nancy Caverly
c/o Bed & Breakfast of St. Louis
1900 Wyoming St.
St. Louis, Missouri 63122
(314) 965–4328

Mike Warner

RASPBERRY JAM

MAKES about 1½ pints.

The Caverlys make this jam from their own raspberries. If you have the space in your yard and the right growing conditions, you can do it too. A wonderful treat, raspberries can be used in many ways. I, too, grow my own, and find they are much better than the store-bought variety. They're also much less expensive!

4 cups fresh raspberries
3 cups sugar

Combine the raspberries with the sugar in a large saucepan. Cook over high heat, stirring constantly until a jelly thermometer reads 230° to 240°, the soft ball stage. Ladle into sterilized jars and seal.

The 1859 Guest House
Bridgton, Maine

THE AREA SURROUNDING The 1859 Guest House is delightful to visit any time of year. In the winter it offers downhill and cross-country skiing. There are eight lakes in the area offering ice skating, boating, fishing and swimming. This is also a lovely region for viewing fall foliage, and shopping for antiques is a pleasant pastime any time of the year. Eleven miles away from the 1859 Guest House is the "largest free-standing boulder in the world"; the view from the top takes in the White Mountains and surrounding lakes, towns, woods and meadows.

A retired physician, Dr. William Zeller is an avid clock collector. He has over one hundred clocks and is happy to show his collection to guests.

A full breakfast is usually served in the formal dining room decorated with antiques; but occasionally breakfast is served in the kitchen with a fire crackling in the fireplace.

The 1859 Guest House
60 South High Street
Bridgton, Maine 04409
(207) 647–2508

William and Mary Zeller

APRICOT-PINEAPPLE JAM

MAKES 4 cups.

This is a colorful, pretty jam. Known to some people as Christmas Jam, it makes a lovely present. Quick and easy to make, and tasty too!

1 box dried apricots
1 20-oz. can crushed pineapple
6 cups sugar
12 maraschino cherries, coarsely chopped
1 package Certo pectin
¼ cup lemon juice
1 Tbs. butter

Cut the apricots into small pieces with scissors, removing any hard stems, and place in a bowl. Add two cups of water and let stand for at least 4 hours. Place softened apricots in large, heavy pot and add the other ingredients. Mix well. Place over high heat and bring to full rolling boil stirring constantly. Boil 10 minutes to prevent floating fruit. Ladle into sterilized jars and seal.

Raford House
Healdsburg, California

A SONOMA COUNTY historical landmark, the Raford House was built in the 1880s. Renovated by the hosts and decorated and furnished in period style, it has become a charming Bed and Breakfast. A large front porch overlooks vineyards and orchards, and grassy patios on either side of the house bloom with color from flower beds and more than one hundred rose bushes.

The Raford House is close to many fine wineries, restaurants and historical points of interest. The Russian River offers a nearby opportunity for swimming, canoeing and sun-bathing. There are good bike roads to Healdsburg and Windsor from this area.

A light breakfast of warm rolls, breads, jams and jellies, as well as fruit and coffee or tea, is served in the formal dining room.

The Raford House
10630 Wohler Road
Healdsburg, California 95448
(707) 887-9573

Alan Baitinger

PRICKLY PEAR JELLY

MAKES 6 cups.

This is one of the many award-winning jellies made at Raford House, with blue ribbons from both the Sonoma County Fair and the Sonoma County Harvest Fair. Besides the Prickly Pear Jelly, Raford House also makes jellies from several varieties of grapes, including Zinfandel and Pinot Noir, and a jam from wild blackberries. All fruit used comes from Raford House property.

Prickly Pear Jelly has a beautiful coral color and a delicate flavor that reminded me of rose-hip jelly. Even though I live in New England, I was able to get prickly pears at the local produce market. The fruit is called prickly pear or cactus pear. Ask your grocer.

        5 lbs. cactus pears
     ½ cup water
    1½ pkgs. dry pectin
        6 cups sugar
     ½ cup lemon juice

Cut pears in half. Scoop out meat. Place the meat in a large pot, add water and simmer 10 minutes; don't boil. Press out juice through a strainer; add lemon juice. Run through jelly bag; repeat at least 4 times, adding another layer of cloth each time.

Pour the strained juice (you should have about 4 cups) into a large pot and add the pectin. Bring to a boil. Add sugar and boil hard while stirring for exactly 2 minutes. Remove from heat and pour into sterilized jelly jars. Seal and cool.

Hedgerow B&B
Kingston, Rhode Island

LOCATED JUST one-half mile from the University of Rhode Island campus, Hedgerow B&B is a large colonial-style house set on extensive grounds that include lawns and gardens, a lily pond, a patio and a tennis court. Named for the dense, clipped, eight-foot hedges that enclose the back yard and give it a marvelous sense of privacy, Hedgerow offers a good base for the business or pleasure traveler alike. The large, comfortable rooms are furnished with an attractive mix of antiques and contemporary pieces.

The historic town of Kingston has a main street lined with restored antique houses, many dating from the eighteenth century. Some of New England's best beaches are just five miles away. The area is also known for antiques shops and art galleries. Newport is only twenty minutes away, Providence just thirty. Other popular day trips include Mystic Seaport and Block Island—the ferry for Block Island leaves from Narragansett, six miles away. With its proximity to the University of Rhode Island, Hedgerow affords the visitor access to a variety of cultural events, such as concerts, plays, lectures and art exhibits.

Guests at Hedgerow are served a full breakfast in the formal dining room. In the afternoon, tea or wine is available either in the living room or on the patio overlooking the gardens, depending on the season. Jim and Ann Ross are happy to help visitors plan excursions and get the most out of a stay in Rhode Island.

Hedgerow B&B
1747 Mooresfield Road
P.O. Box 1586
Kingston, Rhode Island 02881
(401) 783–2671

Jim and Ann Ross

HOT PEPPER JELLY

MAKES about 3 pints.

This is served with cream cheese and crackers as an afternoon hors d'oeuvre at Hedgerow B&B.

 ¼ cup chopped hot peppers (red and green—with seeds)
 ¾ cup chopped sweet bell peppers (red and green)
 1½ cups apple cider vinegar
 6½ cups sugar
 1 bottle Certo pectin

Place the peppers and vinegar in a blender and chop. Pour into a saucepan, add the sugar, and bring to a boil. Stir and simmer for 5 minutes. Remove from the heat and let sit for 2 minutes. Stir in the Certo. Ladle into sterilized jars and seal.

OPPOSITE: *Surrounded by palm trees, Raford House sits on a mountaintop in the Sonoma Valley, heart of the California wine country.*

LEFT: *Hedgerow B&B, with its carefully tended plantings, is at its best in the springtime when flowering shrubs and trees are in full bloom. At any time of year, its tall hedges insure privacy.*

Jackson Street Inn
Janesville, Wisconsin

THIS BIG, GRACIOUS turn-of-the-century house is surrounded with beautifully landscaped grounds and gardens. The interior features such fine appointments as a glass prism chandelier, brass lighting fixtures, oak cross-beam ceilings, leaded beveled-glass windows, intricately carved oak paneling and marble mantelpieces over the fireplaces.

The inn is within walking distance of Old Town Janesville, with the Lincoln-Tallman Restorations and Museums, Mercy Hospital and Medical Center, and a national historical area in Courthouse Park containing more than a hundred registered homes. Known as the city of many parks, Janesville also has three excellent golf courses. Nearby Lake Koshkonong is popular for boating and fishing. Other scenic attractions of southern Wisconsin are within easy driving distance; and Madison, the state capital, can be reached in less than an hour.

A full breakfast is served in the cozy dining room or on the screened porch overlooking the gardens. Breakfast might include a fruit salad of bananas and kiwi, orange juice, fresh coffee, banana-nut bread, blueberry pancakes with maple syrup or peach marmalade and sausage patties. The Sesslers grow their own apples, rhubarb, black raspberries and strawberries.

Jackson Street Inn
210 S. Jackson Street
Janesville, Wisconsin 53545
(608) 754-7250

Bob and Ilah Sessler

APPLE BUTTER

MAKES 4 pints.

"We frequently use apples, as we have 4 trees that bear exceedingly well. This recipe for apple butter is a favorite here," say Bob and Ilah Sessler. I agree; this makes the best apple butter I've ever had.

    3 qts. sweet apple cider
    8 lbs. well flavored apples
2 ½ cups firmly packed brown sugar
1 ½ tsp. ground cloves
2 ¼ tsp. ground cinnamon
1 ¼ tsp. ground allspice
  ½ tsp. salt

Reduce cider to 1 ½ qts. by cooking over moderate heat. Quarter and core the apples (do not peel) and add to cider. Cook until the apples are tender, stirring frequently. Work apple mixture through sieve or food mill to remove peels.

Return puree to kettle. Add sugar, spices and salt. Cook, stirring constantly (this scorches easily) until very thick.

Pack into sterilized jars and seal. This also can be frozen well.

The Jackson Street Inn makes an excellent headquarters from which to explore Janesville, one of the best-preserved old towns in southern Wisconsin and home of the Lincoln-Tallman Restorations and Museum.

CAROL'S HOMEMADE MUSTARD
Meramec Farm Stay B&B (p. 124)

MAKES 6 to 7 pints.

Carol Springer makes big batches of this mustard and finds many uses for it. It's needed to make the glaze for her baked ham recipe (see page 124); she also uses it in potato salads, on sandwiches and put up in pretty bottles as Christmas presents. She says this basic recipe may be varied by adding different herbs (such as tarragon, dill or thyme) to give each batch a unique flavor. A fresh sprig of your favorite herb may be placed in the jar, adding an artistic touch to the package.

3 cups dry mustard
1½ cups sugar
¾ cup brown sugar
1 cup flour
10 eggs
5 cups cider vinegar

In a large bowl mix together the mustard, sugars and flour. Beat the eggs, and add to the mustard mixture. Whisk in the vinegar. Pour into a large saucepan and cook over medium heat, whisking constantly, until sufficiently thickened, about 5 to 10 minutes.

Pour into sterilized jars and seal.

MARTHA MURPHY'S MARVELOUS MELBA SAUCE
Murphy's B&B (p. 13)

MAKES about 1 pint.

3 cups fresh raspberries
1½ cups sugar
1 Tbs. lemon juice

In a large saucepan mash the raspberries and heat over medium-high heat, stirring, until the fruit is just barely hot and has mostly separated from the seeds. Remove from the heat and pour through a fine-mesh stainless-steel strainer into a bowl. Most of the juice will pour right through, but there will be a large mass of seeds and pulp left in the strainer. Using a stainless-steel spoon, force the rest of the fruit pulp through the strainer, leaving the seeds behind. Try to get as much of the raspberries as possible. Discard the seeds.

Return the mixture to the saucepan, add the sugar and lemon juice and heat over medium-high heat, stirring constantly. When the mixture comes to a boil, immediately lower the heat; cook until the mixture starts to thicken. You may use a jelly thermometer if you wish; bring the temperature to just below the soft ball stage.

I do not use a thermometer when I make this; I just go by eye. If you cook this too long it will turn to jelly, which is fine—you can serve it with toast. If you don't cook it long enough it will be too runny, more like a juice than a sauce, and you will have to return it to the heat and cook again. Once you've made it successfully, you'll have your own technique down pat.

Pour into sterilized jars and seal. Store in the refrigerator.

CRÈME FRAICHE
Phoenix House (p. 32)

MAKES 2 cups.

This is a delicious topping for fruit dishes. It is especially good with fresh cherries, pitted of course. At Phoenix House, they like to serve it over fresh strawberries sprinkled with a little brown sugar.

1 cup heavy cream
1 cup sour cream

Whisk together the heavy cream and the sour cream. Cover with plastic wrap and let stand in a warm spot in kitchen for up to 24 hours, or until very thick. Whisk the mixture again, and spoon into a jar. Cover and refrigerate overnight or until thoroughly chilled before using. Will keep for up to 2 weeks.

LAKE DISTRICT LIME ICE
Gardner House (p. 150)

MAKES about 2 cups.

½ cup plus 1 Tbs. sugar
1½ cups water
¾ cup fresh lime juice
grated zest of 2 large limes

Make a syrup by dissolving sugar in water over medium heat. Bring to boil and simmer 5 minutes. Remove from the heat, cool slightly and mix in the lime juice and grated zest. *Pour into metal ice tray and freeze overnight.* When mixture is frozen, place in a food processor to make a slush; then freeze until needed.

This is especially good as a topping for fresh summer fruit, such as melon, berries or peaches.

Palmer's Chart House
Deer Harbor, Washington

ORCAS ISLAND lies in Washington Sound between Seattle and Vancouver. It is reached by ferry or an eight-passenger plane from Seattle. Palmer's Chart House is a waterfront home with a magnificent view of Deer Harbor. Sheer rock bluffs crowned with firs drop into the clear waters, and a constant parade of yachts in the sound adds to the beauty of the setting. Guests can enjoy this view from the house or its deck or from the deck of the 33-foot yacht, *Amante*, which the Palmers own and charter. The house itself is surrounded with flower and vegetable gardens and a lawn sloping down to the water.

Following a restful night where peace and quiet prevail, guests at Palmer's Chart House enjoy a full breakfast in the morning. Whether served indoors or (weather permitting) on the deck, the view of the harbor is breathtaking.

Palmer's Chart House
Box 51
Deer Harbor, Orcas Island, Washington 98243
(206) 376–4231

Majean and Don Palmer

RHUBARB JAM

MAKES 4 cups.

At Palmer's Chart House, this is served as a jam for hot biscuits, or as a topping for ice cream. It's made from rhubarb the Palmers grow.

  6 cups raw rhubarb, chopped
4½ cups sugar
  1 pint raspberries
  2 packages unflavored gelatin

Mix the rhubarb and sugar in a large saucepan. Crush and strain the raspberries; add the juice to the rhubarb. Let stand overnight.

Bring to a boil, and stirring constantly, boil for 12 minutes. Remove from the heat and stir in the gelatin.

Pour into a container for freezing. Cover tightly and freeze until ready to use.

Defrost overnight before serving.

Radcliffe Cross

Chestertown, Maryland

BUILT ABOUT 1725 and surrounded by century-old boxwood plant-ings, Radcliffe Cross is a stately brick house, set back on a well groomed lawn and approached by a long, curving drive. The in-terior's most striking feature is a unique hanging spiral staircase that rises from the large center hallway to the third floor. Fireplaces in each of the rooms and original pine floors add to the charm of the old manor. The furnishings are antique.

Chestertown is in an historic area of Maryland's Eastern Shore, known for its restored colonial houses and its abundance of antiques shops. Just a few miles away is the Intracoastal Waterway that con-nects eastern Maryland to western Maryland. The many protected estuaries in this area make it an ideal spot for bird watchers and naturalists.

Guests are served a full breakfast that might include ham and eggs au gratin, hot biscuits, juice and fresh coffee. Another favorite menu is fresh fruit in season, baked omelet garnished with bacon, oatmeal muffins with lemon butter, apple tart and coffee.

Radcliffe Cross
Quaker Neck Road
Chestertown, Maryland 21620
(301) 778-5540

Dan and Marge Brook

LEMON BUTTER

MAKES 1 pint.

This recipe is a childhood favorite of Marge Brook. She especially likes to serve it with hot oatmeal muffins. Make this a day ahead to allow the butter to chill thoroughly before serving.

> 3 eggs
> 1½ cups sugar
> 1 Tbs. butter
> grated zest and juice of 2 lemons

Beat eggs, add remaining ingredients. Cook in double boiler until thickened — about 10 minutes. Chill. Serve with hot muffins.

LEFT: *Radcliffe Cross lies on the Eastern Shore of Maryland, that delicate finger of land that stretches down to the east of the Chesapeake Bay. The shore is a flat area of quiet inlets and colonial mansions not often to be seen from the main roads.*

OPPOSITE: *Hand-hewn beams and ancient brickwork, uncovered during restoration, create a warm backdrop to the breakfast table at Barrow House (see page 207).*

Briar Rose
Boulder, Colorado

THIS TURN-OF-THE-CENTURY HOUSE is in a city set in the foothills of the Rockies. Visitors come to this area to ski in the winter, hike in the summer and enjoy the scenic beauty that this Rocky Mountain location offers at all times. The University of Colorado has a campus here, making Briar Rose a good location for the business or pleasure traveler alike.

A continental-plus breakfast is served in either the dining room, on the porch, or in the guest's room. It includes homebaked goods, yogurt with fresh fruit, juice and coffee or tea.

Briar Rose
2151 Arapahoe Avenue
Boulder, Colorado 80302
(303) 442-3007

Emily Hunter and Kit Riley

LEMON CURD

MAKES 1 quart.

Use to fill your favorite pastry shells (baked) or your favorite crepes or to spread on toast or muffins.

- 12 eggs, beaten well
- juice of 6 lemons
- 1 Tbs. grated lemon zest
- 1 cup butter
- 3 cups sugar

Put all ingredients in a double boiler over medium heat and stir with a whisk continuously until thickened, about 30 minutes. Pour into sterilized jars, using a knife in the jar to disperse the heat, and cool on a counter. When cooled, cover tightly and refrigerate. Keeps well for 2 weeks.

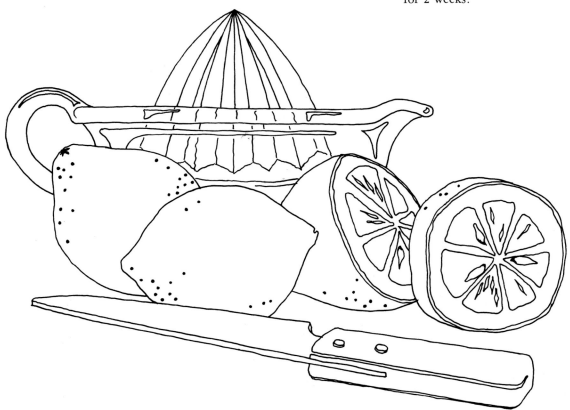

1837 Bed & Breakfast
Charleston, South Carolina

BUILT BY A PROSPEROUS cotton planter to house his family and his horses, the 1837 Bed & Breakfast lies in the heart of historic Charleston, believed by many to be the most beautiful city in the United States. The area abounds with spacious townhouses built by sea island planters in the early 1800s. Guests can walk from here to the shops, restaurants, parks and other attractions. Furnished with antiques, 1837 House still has its original red cypress wainscoting, cornice moldings and wide heart-of-pine floors.

A full gourmet breakfast is served in the formal dining room, where the tables are set with linen and china. While classical music plays, guests may be offered a breakfast of creamed eggs on puff pastry with a cream sauce, homemade fruit-breads, juice and coffee or tea.

1837 Bed & Breakfast
126 Wentworth Street
Charleston, South Carolina 29401
(803) 723-7166

Sherri Dunn

LEMON CURD

MAKES 5 cups.

"Excellent spread on scones and breads, especially our Apple Nut Bread," says SHERRI DUNN.

    1 cup fresh-squeezed lemon juice
    7 Tbs. grated lemon zest
    2 cups sugar
    ½ cup butter
    8 eggs, lightly beaten

Combine lemon juice, zest, sugar and butter in top of double boiler. Heat, stirring, until sugar is dissolved and all ingredients are smooth. Add lightly beaten eggs to the lemon mixture and whisk together. Continue cooking, whisking constantly, until mixture is thick. Remove from heat, pour into sterilized jars, cool and store.

The beautiful old fireplace surround and the plank floors at the 1837 B&B are set off by an ornamental firescreen. A deco chandelier is reflected in the mirror.

Afternoon Tea: Sandwiches & Sweets

CURRIED CHICKEN TEA
SANDWICHES 229
Carolina House

RADISH TEA SANDWICHES 229
Britt House

OLIVE TEA SANDWICHES 229
Britt House

CUCUMBER BACON TEA
SANDWICHES 230
Carolina House

GINGIES 231
Britt House

SCOTCH SHORTBREAD
COOKIES 231
The Parsonage 1901

SHORTBREAD 231
*The English House Bed &
Breakfast*

EXCELLENT GINGERSNAPS
WITH APRICOT CHEDDAR
SPREAD 232
Carolina House

LEMON BARS 232
Britt House

WALNUT DREAM BARS 232
Britt House

PRIDE OF IDAHO COOKIES 233
Greenbriar Bed & Breakfast Inn

PINEAPPLE BARS 234
Nuuanu B&B

COCONUT-MACADAMIA
NUT BARS 235
Pukalani B&B

PECAN SQUARES 236
The Frederick Fitting House

ENGLISH GINGERBREAD 236
The Heartstone Inn

HERSHEY BROWNIES AND
ICING 236
Bridgeford Cottage

SPICE CAKE 237
The Parsonage 1908

OLD-FASHIONED WHITE
CAKE 238
Oak Square

OLD-FASHIONED NUT CAKE 238
Oak Square

GRAHAM CRACKER CRUMB
FRUITCAKE 239
June's Bed & Breakfast

SOUR CREAM RAISIN PIE 240
Cedar Knoll Farm

GRANNY SMITH APPLE
BUTTER TART 240
Toccoa River Hideaway

ALMOND PEAR TART 241
Carter House

CHESS PIE À LA WATSON 241
Murphy's B&B

APPLE PHILO TART 242
Carter House

APPLE RAISIN NUT TART 242
Greenbriar Bed & Breakfast Inn

PEAR PIE 243
Britt House

APPLE ALMOND TART 243
Carter House

PRUNE TART 244
Barnard–Good House

MAPLE MOUSSE TARTLETS 244
Carolina House

CREAMY CHOCOLATE
TARTLETS 245
Carolina House

PEACH MELBA TART 245
Murphy's B&B

CHOCOLATE PECAN PIE 246
The Victorian Inn

MAKES-ITS-OWN-CRUST
CHERRY COBBLER 247
The Bells Bed & Breakfast

LEMON PIE 247
The Frederick Fitting House

CLA FOUTIS 248
*The Rogers House Bed
& Breakfast*

APPLE CRISP 248
Britt House

RICE PUDDING 248
The Bells Bed & Breakfast

STRAWBERRY SHORTCAKE 249
Longswamp Bed & Breakfast

FRESH BERRY COBBLER 250
RoyAl Carter House

DIVINITY CANDY 251
Borgman's Bed & Breakfast

SOUTHERN PRALINES 252
St. Charles Avenue Home

OLD-FASHIONED SYLLABUB 252
Oak Square

*Tea is an afternoon ritual at Britt House
(see page 16) in San Diego, California,
where the table is laid with a variety of
delicacies.*

$\mathcal{A}$FTERNOON TEA IS intended as a break from the business of the day, an interlude of relaxation and reflection over a cup of steaming tea—and incidentally, a chance to lessen late-afternoon hunger pangs with a snack. The foods served at tea are traditionally scones, biscuits, crumpets (accompanied by sweet butter and an assortment of jams); small sandwiches of cucumber, watercress, deviled meat and the like; and tarts, cakes and cookies. Afternoon tea can be formal or casual—there are many ways to serve it.

It should be no surprise to learn that the most important thing you need to know about serving afternoon tea is how to make tea properly. Always start with a clean teapot, fresh water and good tea. Fill a kettle with fresh, cold water and put it over high heat to bring the water to a boil. While waiting for the water to boil, fill the teapot with very hot tap water. It is better still to fill it with boiling water although this means bringing the kettle to a boil twice. This step "scalds" the pot and helps keep the tea hot while it brews. Just before the kettle reaches a boil, empty the teapot and put in the tea. Loose tea is best; use one teaspoon per cup of water. Have the teapot near the stove so that *as soon as the water begins to boil* you can pour it into the teapot. Letting the water boil drives out oxygen and produces flat-tasting tea. Stir the tea once, put the lid on the pot, and let it sit for five minutes. The tea is now ready to be poured, either through a strainer directly into teacups or (also through a strainer) into a second scalded teapot. The purpose of the second teapot is to prevent the tea from getting too strong if it must stay in the pot very long. If you serve tea from the pot in which it was brewed, you can add additional boiling water to the pot after you have poured the first round of tea. This practice helps prevent the tea from becoming too strong, keeps the tea hot and gives you more tea. Either method is fine—using one teapot or two. You will develop your own preference. Hot tea should be accompanied by a small pitcher of milk, a bowl of sugar, lemon wedges and honey.

Popular during the warm months, iced tea is offered as an alternative to hot tea by most of the B&Bs that serve an afternoon tea. Make iced tea exactly as you would make hot tea (skipping the step of scalding the teapot), but make the tea somewhat stronger—it will be diluted by the melting ice in the glass. When the tea has brewed, pour it into a container with a tight lid (so it doesn't pick up any flavors or odors) and refrigerate for at least a few hours. I always keep a large jug of tea in the fridge during the summer. Every morning while I make coffee I also make a pot of tea for the iced tea jug. As soon as the tea is ready, I add it to what's left of the cold tea, and by afternoon it's thoroughly chilled. Earl Grey, Lapsang Souchong, Irish Breakfast and Black Currant tea are some of my favorites iced, but any good black tea that you enjoy hot will also be good chilled. Serve iced tea in tall glasses filled with ice and garnish with a lemon ring or mint leaf. Provide iced tea spoons, sugar and lemon wedges.

CURRIED CHICKEN TEA SANDWICHES
Carolina House (p. 230)

MAKES about 24 open-faced tea sandwiches.

A savory accompaniment to an afternoon tea tray. As with all tea sandwiches, the leftover scraps of bread can be used for bread pudding, stuffing, bread crumbs or bird food.

Filling
2 cups finely chopped cooked breast of chicken
⅔ cup drained crushed pineapple
½ cup finely chopped celery
⅓ cup mayonnaise
⅓ cup finely chopped toasted slivered almonds
1 Tbs. curry powder
1½ tsp. sugar
1½ tsp. lemon juice
¼ tsp. salt
⅛ tsp. white pepper

Bread
24 slices white bread

Garnish
Major Gray chutney
bunch of fresh watercress

In a large bowl combine all the ingredients and blend well. Cover and refrigerate for one hour.

Using a high-quality, fine-textured bread, cut the slices into rounds (a biscuit cutter works well for this). Spread each round *lightly* with a little mayonnaise, and then with the chicken spread.

Garnish each round with a small dab of chutney and a watercress leaf. Serve immediately.

RADISH TEA SANDWICHES
Britt House (p. 16)

MAKES about 12 open-faced tea sandwiches.

These have a hot flavor that goes well with sweet tea or tart lemonade. The bread for these sandwiches is homemade at Britt House.

1 bunch of radishes (8 to 10), grated
½ tsp. salt
½ cup unsalted butter, softened
½ cup mayonnaise
3 fresh chive stems, chopped
1 Tbs. fresh parsley, chopped
pinch of fresh dill, chopped
dash of paprika
dash of pepper

12 slices white bread

Grate the radishes into a large bowl; add the salt and let sit for 30 minutes. Drain (the salt draws out the liquid) and squeeze with paper toweling.

In a separate bowl combine the butter, mayonnaise, herbs and spices; blend well. Add the radishes and combine thoroughly.

Remove the crusts from the bread and cut into 3-inch squares. Spread with the radish mix. Serve immediately.

Note: If desired, these sandwiches can be topped with slices of bread that have been cut into special, smaller shapes with miniature cookie cutters.

OPPOSITE: *At the Carriage House in Laguna Beach, California, the courtyard between the two flanking pavilions is an ideal place for afternoon tea (see page 30).*

OLIVE TEA SANDWICHES
Britt House (p. 16)

MAKES about 12 open-faced tea sandwiches.

A popular and easy afternoon tea sandwich. At Britt House, all afternoon tea sandwiches are made from homemade bread.

1 cup pitted black or green olives, finely chopped
2 stalks celery, finely chopped
½ cup butter, softened
3 fresh chive stems, chopped
1 Tbs. fresh parsley, chopped
pinch of fresh dill, chopped
¼ tsp. curry powder
dash of paprika
dash of pepper

12 slices white bread

In a large bowl combine all ingredients and mix together well.

Remove the crusts from the bread and cut into 3-inch squares. Spread with the olive mix. Serve immediately.

Note: If desired, these sandwiches can be topped with slices of bread that have been cut into special, smaller shapes with miniature cookie cutters.

Carolina House
Houston, Texas

THIS LARGE, GRACIOUS BRICK HOUSE represents the fulfillment of a dream for Carol Maupin. After thirty-five years in the hospitality business, she finally has her own B&B. Ms. Maupin studied under Helen Corbitt, who taught Texans what really fine American food was all about. She went on to plan parties for a king, two presidents and many celebrities, including Julia Child.

The vastness of Houston offers much for the visitor to see and do. The Fine Arts Museum of Houston is just across the street from the Contemporary Arts Museum. Bayou Bend, the estate of Ima Hogg, whose father was the first governor of Texas, features antique furnishings, as well as magnificent gardens. Sam Houston Park is of interest to history buffs, and the Houston Zoo is one of the best in the Southwest.

Houston also has a lively theatre district, with cultural events that include ballet, symphony and opera, as well as a variety of stage productions. In the summer there are musicals under the stars at the Miller Outdoor Theatre. The Galleria, one of the first large indoor shopping centers built, is anchored by an ice-skating rink and features merchandise from all over the world. NASA, the space agency, is just a short drive away.

Guests at Carolina House are treated to superbly prepared and presented food. The day begins with coffee, choice of juice and the morning paper all delivered to guest's rooms an hour before breakfast. Depending on the weather and a guest's preference, a full breakfast can be served in the formal dining room, in the wicker-furnished sun room or on the brick patio.

Carolina House
802 Hyde Park
Houston, Texas 77006
(713) 522–3102

Carol Maupin

CUCUMBER BACON TEA SANDWICHES

MAKES about 24 open-faced sandwiches.

These are tasty and traditional for afternoon tea. They should be—the recipe comes from Carol Maupin, who has been in charge of menu planning for some of the Neiman-Marcus tea rooms.

Filling
1 8-oz. pkg. cream cheese
2 small cucumbers—peeled, seeded and finely chopped
1 small red onion, finely chopped
3 slices of bacon—cooked crisp and crumbled
3 Tbs. fresh parsley, chopped
2 Tbs. mayonnaise
¼ tsp. lemon juice
    salt and white pepper to taste

Bread
24 slices white bread

Garnish
1 small cucumber, washed but unpeeled, thinly sliced
1 Tbs. fresh parsley, chopped

In a large bowl whip the cream cheese until smooth. Stir in the cucumbers, onion, bacon, parsley, mayonnaise and lemon juice. Season to taste with salt and white pepper.

Using a high-quality, fine-textured bread, cut the slices into rounds (a biscuit cutter works well for this). Spread each round *lightly* with a little mayonnaise, and then with the cucumber spread.

Garnish each round with a thin half-round of cucumber and sprinkle on a little fresh parsley. Serve immediately.

GINGIES
Britt House (p. 16)

MAKES about 48 cookies.

A spicy cookie made special by the icing. The batter should be made a day in advance.

Cookies
⅓ cup butter
1 cup brown sugar
1½ cups molasses
½ cup water
1 egg
6 cups flour
1 tsp. salt
1 tsp. each: allspice, ginger,
    cloves, cinnamon
2 tsp. baking soda
3 Tbs. water

Icing
1 cup confectioners' sugar
¼ tsp. salt
½ tsp. vanilla
2 Tbs. cream
1 egg white

In a large bowl combine the butter, sugar and molasses; beat well. Beat in the cold water and egg. In a separate bowl sift together the flour, salt and spices. Add to molasses mixture and mix well. Dissolve the baking soda in the 3 Tbs. water; add to batter and beat well.

Chill the batter thoroughly for at least 6 hours. When ready to bake, roll the dough out to ½" thick. Cut with round cookie cutter and place on greased cookie sheet. Bake at 350° for 15 minutes or until no imprint remains when touched with a finger.

Cool on a rack.

While the cookies are cooling, make the icing. Combine all ingredients and beat well. Spread over top of cooled cookies.

SCOTCH SHORTBREAD COOKIES
The Parsonage 1901 (p. 22)

MAKES 90 cookies.

These rich, buttery cookies are served with afternoon tea at the Parsonage 1901. This recipe will make a large batch of batter; it can be frozen before baking, and the baked cookies can be stored indefinitely in an airtight container.

2 cups butter
2 cups confectioners' sugar
2 tsp. vanilla
½ tsp. salt
4½ cups flour
1 pkg. (12 oz.) butterscotch chips
    confectioners' sugar for dusting

Preheat oven to 350°F.

Cream together the butter and sugar. Beat in vanilla and salt. Gradually stir in the flour. Dough will be stiff. Work in the butterscotch chips (use your hands if necessary). Using a melon baller make 1-inch balls and place 2 inches apart on an ungreased baking sheet. Flatten with fork to 1½ inches. Bake at 350° for 15 minutes. Remove from oven and place on a cooling rack. While warm, sprinkle with confectioners' sugar.

SHORTBREAD
The English House Bed and Breakfast (p. 94)

MAKES about 24 bars.

These are served with afternoon tea at the English House. A rich, buttery treat.

1 cup butter
1½ cups superfine sugar
1 cup cornstarch
2 cups flour
½ tsp. vanilla extract

Preheat oven to 325°F.

Cream together the butter and sugar until they are light and fluffy. Combine the cornstarch and flour; add to the butter and sugar slowly, beating well. Lastly add the vanilla and blend in thoroughly.

Press the batter into a 9" × 13" jellyroll pan and prick all over with a fork. Bake at 325° for about 30 minutes, or until pale gold. Place the pan on a cooling rack, and score the shortbread into bars while still hot. Allow to cool completely in the pan before cutting into bars and removing. Store in an airtight container.

EXCELLENT GINGERSNAPS WITH APRICOT CHEDDAR SPREAD

Carolina House (p. 230)

MAKES about 48 cookies.

Gingersnaps
1 cup sugar
2 cups flour
½ tsp. salt
1 tsp. baking soda
1 tsp. cinnamon
1 tsp. ginger
½ tsp. cloves
¾ cup shortening
¼ cup molasses
1 egg, slightly beaten
   sugar for coating unbaked
   cookies

Preheat oven to 350°F.

In a large bowl combine the sugar, flour, salt, soda and spices; blend thoroughly. Cut in the shortening until the mixture resembles coarse meal. Add the molasses and egg; stir until well-blended.

Shape the dough into 1-inch balls, and roll them in sugar. Place on an ungreased cookie sheet; flatten each ball with the tines of a fork. Bake at 350° for 10 minutes. Remove the cookies from the baking sheet and transfer to a cooling rack immediately. Cookies will firm quickly as they cool.

Serve the gingersnaps while still warm, with the Apricot-Cheddar Spread on the side as a topping for the cookies.

Apricot-Cheddar Spread
½ lb. grated sharp cheddar cheese
1½ cups finely chopped dried
   apricots
2 Tbs. finely chopped Major
   Gray chutney
2 Tbs. mayonnaise
6 Tbs. sour cream
2 Tbs. finely chopped pecan
   pieces

In a large bowl combine the cheese with the apricots. In a separate bowl beat together the chutney, mayonnaise, sour cream and pecans. Add to the cheddar mixture and blend well. Serve with warm gingersnaps.

LEMON BARS

Britt House (p. 16)

MAKES about 24 bars.

Crust
2 cups flour
½ cup powdered sugar
1 cup butter

Filling
4 eggs
2 cups sugar
⅓ cup lemon juice
¼ cup flour
½ tsp. baking powder

Preheat oven to 350°F.

To make the crust: Combine the flour, sugar and butter together thoroughly. Pat into greased 9" × 13" pan. Bake at 350° for 15 to 25 minutes or until golden.

To make the filling: Combine eggs, sugar and lemon juice and beat well. In a separate bowl mix other ingredients; add to egg mixture and combine well.

Pour over the baked crust. Return to oven and bake at 350° for an additional 25 to 30 minutes.

Cool thoroughly on a rack, then cut into bars. Sprinkle generously with powdered sugar.

WALNUT DREAM BARS

Britt House (p. 16)

MAKES about 24 bars.

Crust
2 cups flour
1 cup butter

Filling
4 eggs
3 cups brown sugar
2 tsp. vanilla
¼ cup flour
½ tsp. baking powder
¼ tsp. salt
1½ cups flaked coconut
1 cup chopped walnuts

Icing
¼ cup butter
3 cups powdered sugar
6 tsp. orange juice
2 tsp. lemon juice

Preheat oven to 350°F.

To make the crust, cut the butter into the flour until crumbly. Press into a greased 9" × 13" pan. Bake at 350° for 15 minutes.

While the crust is baking, make the filling: Beat together the eggs and sugar. Add the vanilla. In a separate bowl combine the flour, baking powder and salt. Add to the egg mixture and blend well. Stir in the coconut and walnuts. Pour the filling over the baked crust and bake for another 20 minutes. When done, remove from oven and place on a cooling rack.

While the bars are cooling make the icing: Beat icing ingredients together until creamy. If necessary, chill the icing for a while to stiffen it to spreading consistency. When the bars are completely cooled, spread with the icing.

If desired, sprinkle a few chopped walnuts on top for decoration.

Greenbriar Bed and Breakfast Inn
Coeur d'Alene, Idaho

GREENBRIAR BED AND BREAKFAST Inn is the only brick house in Coeur d'Alene and the only house to be listed in the National Register of Historic Places. Built in 1908 as a private residence, it was later enlarged as a boarding house—some say a fancy bordello. The interior reflects the elegance of 1908 when it was built—winding mahogany staircases, arched passages and windows, high ceilings and hand-crafted cabinetry. It is furnished with a heterogeneous collection of antiques.

After breakfast, guests can relax on the porch, rent a bicycle (Greenbriar even has a bicycle built for two) or a canoe, or visit beautiful Lake Coeur d'Alene, just four blocks away. Thirty miles long, the lake is known as one of the most pristinely beautiful in the country. It is used for fishing, canoeing, swimming and sailboarding. Coeur d'Alene has a dinner-dance boat that departs each evening in summer, and the town is also known for its summer theatre. In the winter months the skiing is excellent.

The menu for the four-course breakfast at Greenbriar changes every day. Kris McIlvenna, who also runs the Greenbriar Gourmet Catering business, believes that the menus must be special, never commonplace, and says, "We emphasize the quality of the food as a major feature of the inn."

Greenbriar Bed & Breakfast Inn
315 Wallace
Coeur d'Alene, Idaho 83814
(208) 667–9660

Kris McIlvenna

PRIDE OF IDAHO COOKIES

MAKES about 36 cookies.

1 cup vegetable shortening
1 cup firmly packed light brown sugar
1 cup granulated sugar
2 eggs
2 cups sifted all-purpose flour
1 tsp. baking powder
1 tsp. baking soda
¼ tsp. salt
1 tsp. vanilla
1 tsp. brandy flavoring
1 cup flaky coconut
1 cup chocolate chips
½ cup chopped nuts of your choice
3 cups quick-cooking rolled oats

Preheat oven to 350°F.
Cream together shortening and sugars. Beat in eggs. In a separate bowl sift flour with baking soda, baking powder and salt. Stir into creamed mixture and add vanilla and brandy flavoring; mix well. Stir in coconut, chocolate chips, nuts and oats. Roll into 1½-inch balls and space them 2½ inches apart on a greased cookie sheet. Using a glass, flatten balls onto sheet until cookie dough is about ¼-inch thick. Bake at 350° for 8 to 10 minutes or until pale brown. Remove to wire racks and cool.

A striking feature of Greenbriar is the huge second-story window with its arched clerestory.

Nuuanu B&B
Honolulu, Oahu, Hawaii

NESTLED IN NUUANU VALLEY, Nuuanu B&B offers a private location set in lush tropical surroundings. From the deck, guests enjoy views of a tropical rain forest, a rushing stream and beautifully landscaped gardens. The hosts, who are part Hawaiian, are happy to help visitors get the most out of their stay.

Famous for Waikiki Beach, the island of Oahu offers much more to see and do. The Punchbowl Memorial, the National Memorial Cemetery of the Pacific, where more than twenty thousand servicemen are buried, is an important stop for most visitors. The Aloha Tower in the Port of Honolulu provides an excellent view of Honolulu, Pearl Harbor and the entire south coast of Oahu. Some of the important museums here include Iolani Palace, Academy of Arts (famous for its collection of Asian arts), Mission House Museum, Bishop Museum (giving an interesting look at Polynesian culture), and Queen Emma's Summer Palace. The Foster Botanical Gardens are home to trees found nowhere else in the islands. On Mondays, the Farmers Market in Honolulu is a good place for visitors to take in local color and buy local produce at prices much lower than those in the supermarkets. The drive east of Honolulu, past Hanauma Bay, around the point past Sandy Beach and then on to Waimanalo is considered one of the most scenic in all Hawaii. The expansive beaches on the north shore are unrivaled.

Guests at Nuuanu B&B enjoy a continental breakfast on the deck, where they can listen to the morning songbirds.

Nuuanu B&B
c/o Bed & Breakfast Hawaii
Box 449
Kapaa, Hawaii 96746
(808) 822–7771

Evie Warner

PINEAPPLE BARS

MAKES about 24 bars.

Hawaii is the country's premier producer of pineapples. A delicious treat, this recipe makes a wonderful afternoon tea item.

1½ cups flour
 1 tsp. baking powder
 ½ tsp. baking soda
1½ cups sugar
 1 cup chopped walnuts
 4 eggs
 ½ cup butter, melted and cooled
 ¾ cup crushed pineapple, well drained
    confectioners' sugar for dusting

Preheat oven to 350°F.

In a large bowl combine the flour, baking powder, baking soda, sugar and walnuts; set aside. In a separate bowl beat the eggs with the butter. Blend in the pineapple. Add the pineapple mix to the dry ingredients and blend thoroughly. Pour into a greased 9″ × 13″ baking pan and bake at 350° for 20 to 30 minutes. Cool on a rack. Sprinkle with confectioners' sugar and cut into squares.

OPPOSITE: *On special occasions at Murphy's B&B (page 13), a silver tea service that has been in the family for generations is put to use.*

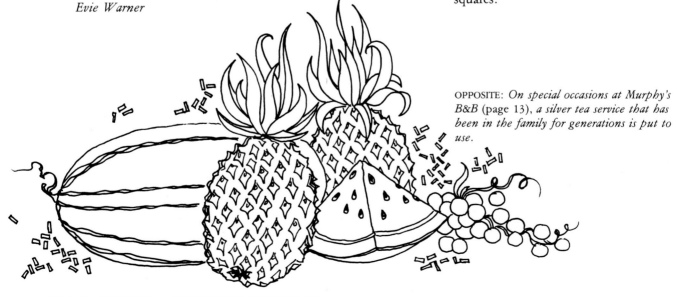

Pukalani B&B
Pukalani, Maui, Hawaii

JUST A FIFTEEN-MINUTE drive from Kahului, Pukalani is an excellent headquarters for seeing all of Maui. Built near the beautiful Pukalani Golf Course, this new B&B is beautifully furnished and landscaped. The host's hobby is woodworking, which is evident throughout the house.

Lying on the slopes of Haleakala, which rises up to a little over ten thousand feet, Pukalani is one of several small towns and communities that make up an area known as "upcountry Maui." This is the farming and ranching area of Maui, famous for the expensive Maui onion. The area is also known for protea, a unique flowering shrub, and for many of the carnations and orchids used in making leis. There is even a winery here, Tedeschi Winery, which is known for its pineapple wine and is beginning to produce grape wine. The beaches of Paia attract windsurfers from all over the world, and Maui's many other beautiful beaches offer excellent swimming and sunbathing.

Guests at Pukalani B&B are served a continental breakfast on the deck or patio.

Pukalani B&B
c/o Bed & Breakfast Hawaii
Box 449
Kapaa, Hawaii 96746
(808) 822–7771

Evie Warner

COCONUT-MACADAMIA NUT BARS

MAKES about 20 bars.

Two products for which Hawaii is famous—the coconut and the delectable macadamia nut—are combined in this recipe to make a rich and delicious cookie bar.

```
1 cup butter
1 cup sugar
2 tsp. vanilla
3 eggs
2 cups + 2 Tbs. flour
½ tsp. baking powder
¼ tsp. salt
¾ cup light brown sugar
1 cup flaked coconut
1 cup chopped macadamia nuts
```

Preheat oven to 350°F.
In a large bowl cream together the butter and the granulated sugar. Beat in 1 teaspoon of the vanilla and 1 egg. Blend in 2 cups of the flour, combining thoroughly. Spread the batter evenly in a greased 9" × 13" baking pan. Bake at 350° for about 30 minutes.

While the bottom layer of the bar is baking, make the top layer by combining the 2 tablespoons of flour, baking powder and salt in a small bowl; set aside. In a large bowl beat together the remaining 2 eggs and 1 teaspoon of vanilla until the eggs are thick and lemon-colored. Add the flour mixture and blend well. Stir in the coconut and macadamia nuts.

When the initial 30-minute baking time is up, spread the coconut mixture over the bottom layer of the bar while it's still hot. Return the pan to the oven and continue baking at 350° for another 30 minutes. Cool on a rack, and cut into bars.

PECAN SQUARES

The Frederick Fitting House
(p. 103)

MAKES about 24 squares.

Thin, buttery, crunchy and just sweet enough, these are perfect served with tall glasses of strong iced tea.

1 cup butter, soft
1 cup sugar
1 egg, separated
1 tsp. vanilla
2 cups flour
1 cup pecans, chopped

Preheat oven to 375°F.

Cream together the butter and sugar until smooth and light. Beat in the egg yolk, vanilla and flour until well mixed. Pat evenly into a greased 9″ × 15″ jellyroll pan.

Beat the egg white slightly and brush over the dough. Sprinkle the pecans evenly on top and lightly press them into the dough. Bake at 375° for 15 to 18 minutes or until golden brown. Cool on a rack, and when partially cooled score to cut into small squares. Cool completely before removing from pan and serving. Store in an airtight cookie jar.

ENGLISH GINGERBREAD

The Heartstone Inn (p. 160)

SERVES 6 to 8.

This gingerbread is dense and spicy, filling the house with a wonderful aroma while it bakes. May be served at breakfast, afternoon tea or dessert.

½ cup softened butter
½ cup sugar
1 egg, beaten
2½ cups all-purpose flour
1½ tsp. baking soda
1 tsp. cinnamon
1 tsp. ground ginger
½ tsp. ground cloves
½ tsp. salt
1 cup dark molasses
1 cup hot water

Preheat oven to 350°F.

Cream together the butter and sugar in a large mixing bowl; beat until light and fluffy. Add the beaten egg and mix well. In a separate bowl combine the dry ingredients. Set aside. In another bowl mix together the molasses and hot water. Alternately mix the molasses and the dry ingredients into the creamed mixture. Mix well.

Spoon the batter into a greased 9″ × 9″ × 2″ baking pan. Bake at 350° for 40 minutes. Cool on a rack before cutting into squares.

Serve warm or cold with a dollop of whipped cream.

HERSHEY BROWNIES & ICING

Bridgeford Cottage (p. 58)

MAKES 12 brownies.

"My guests love these brownies with a glass of cold milk for their bed-time snack," says NYLA SAWYER.

Brownies
1 cup sugar
½ cup butter
4 eggs
1 1-lb. can Hershey's chocolate syrup
1 cup flour
1 cup walnuts, chopped

Icing
1⅓ cups confectioners' sugar
6 Tbs. butter
6 Tbs. milk
½ cup chocolate chips

Preheat oven to 350°F.

To make the brownies: Cream together the sugar and butter. Add the eggs and chocolate syrup and combine well. Stir in the flour. Add the nuts. Pour into a greased 9″ × 13″ pan and bake at 350° for 30 minutes. When done, remove from oven and place on cooling rack. When cool, frost with icing.

To make the icing: Combine sugar, butter and milk and bring to a boil over medium-high heat, stirring constantly. Boil for 1 minute. Remove from heat and stir in chocolate chips. Beat well until smooth. Spread over the cooled brownies.

The Parsonage 1908
Holland, Michigan

THIS INVITING OLD HOUSE in the arts-and-crafts tradition was built in 1908 as a church parsonage. The oak woodwork and leaded glass windows reflect the period, and the antique furnishings complete the picture. The Parsonage, which has been a private residence since 1973, is located in a quiet residential neighborhood.

Holland, Michigan, home of the famous Holland Tulip Festival, is situated on the shores of Lake Michigan and beautiful Lake Macatawa. It is within easy driving distance of Chicago, Detroit and Traverse City.

The Parsonage Bed and Breakfast is owned and operated by a mother and daughter. Multitalented and energetic, they have taken on as their latest venture making and marketing their trademarked, handmade B&B flags, which they hope will "become the identity symbol for B&Bs and inns across the U.S." A continental breakfast is served to guests either in the formal dining room or on the outdoor garden patio.

The Parsonage 1908
6 East 24th
Holland, Michigan 49423
(616) 396–1316

Bonnie Verwys and Wendy Westrate

SPICE CAKE

MAKES 1 bundt cake.

This is a dense, spicy, substantial cake, especially good in fall or winter. It is perfect for afternoon tea or breakfast. "Frosting is not necessary for this cake. Its special charm is its old-time spicy flavor, which should not be drowned out in a flood of flavored frosting," say the hosts of the Parsonage 1908.

1½ cups brown sugar
½ cup butter
2 eggs
2 cups flour
1 tsp. baking soda
½ tsp. cinnamon
½ tsp. nutmeg
½ tsp. ground clove
½ cup buttermilk
1 cup chopped walnuts
1 cup raisins

Preheat oven to 350°F.

Cream together the sugar and butter. Beat in the eggs. In a separate bowl sift together the flour, baking soda and spices. Beat the flour and buttermilk alternately into the creamed sugar mixture. When well blended, stir in the nuts and the raisins.

Pour into a greased and floured bundt pan. Bake at 350° for 40 to 60 minutes or until done. Remove from oven and place on a rack to cool for 5 minutes before turning out of pan to continue cooling. When the cake is turned out of the pan, sift confectioners' sugar over the top. Very good served warm or cold.

The hostesses of the Parsonage 1908 take pride in utilizing their talents in this delightful house built in the arts-and-crafts style.

OLD-FASHIONED WHITE CAKE

Oak Square (p. 158)

MAKES a 3-layer 9-inch cake.

A beautiful, sweet, "simple" cake. Its delicate almond flavor immediately made me think of good Southern cooking. This is a tea-time favorite at Oak Square, where it is served with Old-Fashioned Syllabub and hot or cold spiced tea.

1 cup butter
2 cups sugar
9 egg whites
3 cups flour
1 tsp. baking powder
1 cup milk
1 tsp. almond extract

Preheat oven to 350°F.

Cream the butter with 1 cup of the sugar. In a separate bowl beat the egg whites with 1 cup sugar. Set aside. Sift flour and baking powder together and add alternately with the milk to the creamed butter mixture. Mix in the almond extract, add the beaten egg whites and fold in thoroughly.

Pour into 3 greased and floured 9-inch cake pans and bake at 350° for 30 minutes.

Cool briefly on racks before turning out of pans. Cool completely before frosting. Frost with Boiled Icing (recipe follows).

Boiled Icing
3 egg whites
3 cups sugar
1½ cups water

Beat the egg whites until stiff. Cook the sugar and water until they reach the "soft ball" stage (use a candy thermometer). Remove from heat and beat into the stiff egg whites. The frosting will be very glossy and soft. *Do not overbeat,* as this will make the frosting lose its glossy look and become dry and hard.

OLD-FASHIONED NUT CAKE

Oak Square (p.158)

MAKES 1 large bundt cake or 2 loaves.

Dense and delicious, this is an old Mississippi recipe, very popular there. It is a tea-time favorite at Oak Square, where it is served with Old-Fashioned Syllabub and hot or cold spiced tea.

4 cups flour
2 tsp. baking powder
2 tsp. nutmeg
1 cup butter
2 cups + 5 Tbs. sugar
6 eggs, separated
½ cup whiskey
1½ cups applesauce
½ lb. candied cherries
1 lb. dried mixed fruits, chopped
2 cups pecans

Preheat oven to 300°F.

Sift together the flour, baking powder and nutmeg. Stir in half the nuts and fruit. In a separate bowl cream the butter and 2 cups of sugar. Beat in the egg yolks. Stir in the flour mixture and whiskey alternately. Add applesauce and the rest of the nuts and fruit; stir well. Beat the egg whites with 5 Tbs. sugar until stiff peaks form. Fold the egg whites into the batter.

Pour into a large, greased tube pan or 2 loaf pans. Place a large pan of water on the lowest rack in the oven. Place the cake on the center rack and bake at 300° for about 60 minutes. Remove the pan of water and continue to bake for another 60 minutes, or until brown and dry. Remove from oven and cool on a rack. Cool completely before serving.

June's Bed & Breakfast

Tucson, Arizona

WITH TOWERING MOUNTAINS in the background, June's Bed & Breakfast looks down on the city of Tucson. The beautiful backyard contains a pool and a patio, which guests are welcome to use.

Guests at June's are in Tucson for business as often as for pleasure. There are a number of stables and ranches in the area where horses can be rented for trail riding. The rodeo is always popular, as is hiking in the beautiful red hills. For visitors seeing it for the first time, the desert itself is a special experience. Shops with Western wear entice many, and handcrafted Indian jewelery of silver and turquoise is available at local shops and boutiques.

June Henderson serves a continental breakfast of fruit juices, muffins and assorted breads, fresh fruit in season, assorted jams and jellies and a choice of coffee, tea or hot chocolate. June loves running a B&B—"We enjoy the world-wide scan our guests give us," she says.

June's Bed & Breakfast
3212 W. Hooaday Street
Tucson, Arizona 85746
(602) 578-0857

June Henderson

GRAHAM CRACKER CRUMB FRUITCAKE

SERVES 10 to 12.

This cake is a beautiful nut-brown color with a thick, glossy crust on top. It's not too sweet, and the fruit and nuts add great flavor and texture. Perfect with afternoon tea.

    1 1-lb. box of Graham crackers
 1 ½ cups brown sugar
    3 tsp. baking powder
  ½ tsp. salt
    1 tsp. vanilla
    3 eggs
 1 ¼ cups milk
    1 cup raisins
    1 cup nuts, broken coarsely
    1 cup chopped dates

Preheat oven to 350°F.

Crush the Graham crackers. Add the brown sugar, baking powder and salt; stir well. Beat in the vanilla, eggs and milk. Stir in the raisins, nuts and dates. Mix ingredients together well. Pour into a greased 10-inch springform pan. Bake at 350° for about 60 minutes. Loosen and remove sides of pan and cool on a rack.

OPPOSITE: *Tea is served daily in the parlor at Gingerbread Mansion.*

LEFT: *A bouquet of wild Narragansett roses fills an antique Limoges bowl on a sideboard at Murphy's B&B (see page 13).*

SOUR CREAM RAISIN PIE

Cedar Knoll Farm (p. 24)

MAKES 1 pie.

"This is an old Midwest farm recipe handed down through my grandmother and mother. I find my B&B guests love a thin sliver of pie with their after-breakfast coffee," says Mavis Christensen.

Pie Crust (makes 2)
2½ cups flour
1 cup lard
1 tsp. salt
⅓ cup icy water

Filling
3 egg yolks
1 egg white
1 cup sugar
1 cup sour cream
½ tsp. cinnamon
½ tsp. cloves
pinch of nutmeg
½ cup seeded raisins

Preheat oven to 350°F.

To make the crust: In a large bowl mix the flour, lard and salt with a pastry cutter until well mixed. Stir in the icy water and mix with a fork. Divide dough in half, and roll out on a lightly floured board. Because you need only one crust for this recipe, you can freeze the other for use later. To freeze pie crusts: Wrap dough well in plastic wrap and foil, and store in freezer on cookie sheet. Defrost before lining pie plate.

Note: According to Mavis Christensen, "The lard is a must for the pie crust. I can't tell you how many batches of pastry I threw away when I was mastering the technique of pie crust as a young bride. When using a top crust, brush with a thin coating of milk and sprinkle with granulated sugar before baking. People even eat the edges."

To make the filling: Beat egg yolks and egg white until fluffy; then add sugar, sour cream, spices and raisins. Pour into an unbaked 9" pie crust and bake at 350° for 50 minutes, or until custard sets.

GRANNY SMITH APPLE BUTTER TART

Toccoa River Hideaway (p. 86)

MAKES 1 12-inch tart

A delicious, rich tart, this is always a hit at afternoon tea. At Toccoa River Hideaway they make this tart using their own homemade apple butter.

Crust
1¼ cups flour
6 Tbs. butter
2 Tbs. shortening
2 Tbs. ice water
1 egg white

Filling
6 Granny Smith apples
1 pint apple butter
1 Tbs. sugar

To make the crust: Using a food processor or pastry cutter, cut the butter and shortening into the flour until the mixture is crumbly. Add the ice water and blend just until the dough holds together. Form the dough into a ball, wrap in plastic wrap, and refrigerate for 30 minutes. Then roll out on a lightly floured board to about ¼-inch thickness, and fit it into a 12-inch tart pan. Beat the egg white and brush on the inside of the pastry. Cover and refrigerate while you prepare the filling.

To make the filling: Peel, core and thinly slice the apples. Spread the apple butter in the tart shell. Arrange the apple slices in a circular pattern over the apple butter, and sprinkle with the sugar.

Bake at 450° for about 25 minutes, or until the apples are slightly browned. Place on a rack and cool completely before serving.

ALMOND PEAR TART
Carter House (p. 34)

SERVES 8.

In this rich tart, the flavor of the roasted almonds is distinct and well complemented by the taste of creamy, ripe pear. Well suited for breakfast or afternoon tea.

Pastry
1 ¼ cups flour
½ cup butter, chilled
1 egg
1 Tbs. sugar

Filling
¾ cup sliced, toasted almonds
½ cup sugar
2 Tbs. butter
1 egg
1 firm pear

To make the pastry dough: Process flour, butter, egg and sugar in a food processor until mixture forms a ball. Roll out on a lightly floured board to line a 9-inch tart pan, or pat dough into a 9-inch tart pan. Chill pastry while you make the filling.

To make filling: In a food processor or blender, process the almonds and sugar until well blended. Then add butter and the egg, and process mixture until it is smooth and creamy. Spread the mixture into prepared crust.

Peel pear and slice lengthwise into eight sections (cut off any fragments of core). Fan pear sections over the filling.

Bake at 375° for 20 to 25 minutes, or until golden brown. Remove from oven and cool on a rack. Sift powdered sugar over top; serve completely cooled.

CHESS PIE À LA WATSON
Murphy's B&B (p. 13)

SERVES 8 to 12.

This is an old family recipe, and I have loved it ever since I was a child. According to my Aunt Margaret, it originated with her Aunt Mabel, a Texas farm wife, where it showed up for both breakfast and dessert. During the B&B season, I serve this with afternoon tea. It is also a wonderful recipe for Thanksgiving and Christmas.

Pie Crust
1 ½ cups flour
¾ cup shortening
1 Tbs. lemon juice
2–4 Tbs. ice water

Filling
1 cup raisins
½ cup butter
1 cup chopped walnuts
1 cup sugar
1 Tsp. vanilla
3 eggs

To make the pie crust: Using a pastry fork or food processor, cut the shortening into the flour until the mixture is crumbly. Add the lemon juice and enough of the ice water to just form a ball. Wrap in plastic wrap and refrigerate for 30 minutes. Roll out on a lightly floured board to about ¼" thickness. Line a pie plate, trim any excess, and crimp the edges. Cover and refrigerate until ready to fill and bake.

Place the raisins in a small saucepan and add just enough water to cover. Bring the mixture to a boil; pour off the liquid and set the raisins aside to cool. While the raisins are still warm, add the butter (cut into small pieces) and stir gently. Stir in the sugar and vanilla. In a separate bowl beat the eggs well. Add to the raisin mixture and blend thoroughly. Pour into the unbaked pie shell, and bake at 350° for 35 to 40 minutes. Cool on a rack.

APPLE PHILO TART

Carter House (p. 34)

MAKES 9-inch tart.

A beautiful tart, with its puffy golden pastry dusted with confectioners' sugar. Can be served at breakfast or afternoon tea.

Topping
2 apples, peeled, cored and sliced
2 Tbs. butter
2 Tbs. sugar
   dash of nutmeg

Filling
¾ cup toasted hazelnuts
½ cup sugar
2 Tbs. butter
1 egg

Pastry
6 sheets philo
¼ cup unsalted butter, melted
   and cooled

Preheat oven to 325°F.
   Sauté the apples in the butter until just tender; stir in the sugar and nutmeg. Set aside.
   To prepare filling, put sugar and hazelnuts in a food processor and process until well blended. Next add the butter and the egg, and process until smooth and creamy. Set aside.
   Place the first sheet of philo in a 9-inch tart pan and brush with some of the melted butter. Continue in this fashion until you have used all the sheets of philo. The sheets will hang over the edges of the tart pan. Do not trim.
   Spoon the hazelnut filling into tart pan and then arrange sautéed apples on top. Fold philo sheets over the top and brush with melted butter.
   Bake at 325° for 25 minutes or until golden brown. When done, remove from oven and place on cooling rack. Sift powdered sugar over top and cool slightly or completely before serving.

APPLE RAISIN NUT TART

Greenbriar Bed & Breakfast Inn (p. 233)

SERVES 8 to 10.

Pastry
2 cups flour
   pinch salt
½ cup butter
¾ cup sugar
2 egg yolks

Filling
1 lb. cooking apples
¼ cup sugar
   juice of 1 lemon
   pinch of cinnamon
⅓ cup raisins
½ cup ground almonds or walnuts
½ cup ground hazelnuts or walnuts

Topping
3 Tbs. apricot or raspberry jam
3 Tbs. honey
3 Tbs. Kirsch or brandy

Sift flour and salt into large bowl. Cut in butter, add sugar and egg yolks, and mix until blended. Form into a ball, wrap in plastic wrap, and chill for 30 minutes. Cut in half and roll out on a lightly floured board. Fit into a 10-inch springform pan. Spoon in filling. Top with remaining dough, rolled out.
   To make the filling: Peel, core and slice the apples; then combine with the other ingredients, blending well.
   Bake at 400° for 30 minutes. While tart is baking, make the topping by combining ingredients over medium heat in a saucepan. Pour warm topping over the cooled tart. Cool the glazed tart well before slicing to serve.

PEAR PIE
Britt House (p. 16)

SERVES 8.

This rich, creamy, delicious pie is an excellent way to use pears. My guests have enjoyed this at both breakfast and afternoon tea.

Crust
1½ cups flour
2 Tbs. sugar
½ cup butter
3 Tbs. cold water

Filling
3 eggs
⅓ cup flour
1 cup sugar
1 tsp. almond extract
¼ cup melted butter
3 large pears, peeled, cored and sliced

To make the crust: Combine the flour and sugar. Cut in the butter until it is well incorporated. Add the cold water, 1 tablespoon at a time, and mix together until a ball forms. Wrap and chill for at least 30 minutes. Place chilled dough on a lightly floured board and roll out. Use it to line a 9-inch pie tin.

Combine eggs, flour, sugar, almond extract and butter; beat well. Pour into the unbaked pie shell. Arrange pears in spokes radiating from the center. Bake at 375° for 15 minutes, and then at 350° for 25 to 35 minutes or until the custard under the pears is firm.

Remove from oven and cool on a rack. Cool completely before serving.

Tea in season at Murphy's B&B (page 13). OPPOSITE: *Hot tea with scones for chilly weather.* RIGHT: *Summertime tea with lemonade accompanied by zucchini bread.*

APPLE ALMOND TART
Carter House (p. 34)

MAKES a 9-inch tart.

Crust
1¼ cups flour
½ cup butter
1 egg
2 Tbs. sugar

Filling
¾ cup sliced, toasted almonds
½ cup sugar
2 Tbs. butter
1 egg
1 apple (Granny Smith or other good baking apple)

Glaze
¼ cup strained apricot jam
2 Tbs. Triple Sec Liquor

To make the crust: Place ingredients in a food processor and process until dough forms a ball. Roll out on a lightly floured board, and line a 9-inch tart pan with dough. Place tart pan on a cookie sheet and chill while you make the filling.

To make the filling: In a food processor or blender, process the almonds and sugar until blended. Add butter and the egg, and process until smooth and creamy. Spoon filling into prepared crust. Peel and core the apple; slice into ⅛-inch slices to produce apple circles and rings. Arrange the apple slices in a circular pattern on top of filling.

Bake at 375° for 20 to 25 minutes, or until golden brown. While the tart is baking, prepare the glaze by mixing the ingredients in a small bowl.

When tart is done, place on a cooling rack and cool for 15 minutes before brushing the top with the glaze. Cool completely before serving.

PRUNE TART

Barnard–Good House (p. 14)

SERVES 8 to 10.

This is a not-too-sweet tart, perfect for afternoon tea. Since it calls for dried and frozen fruit, it can be made when fresh fruit is not available.

Pastry
½ cup plus 1 Tbs. butter
2 cups minus 2 Tbs. flour
⅓ cup sugar
1 egg
3 Tbs. ice water

Filling
30 pitted prunes
2 cups warm water
2 Tbs. Armagnac
1½ cups heavy cream
2 large eggs
2 large egg yolks
⅓ cup sugar
¼ tsp. nutmeg
¼ tsp. cinnamon
1 package frozen raspberries
   (16 oz.), thawed
   fresh mint for garnish

To make the crust: Cut the butter ter into the flour and sugar until it resembles a coarse meal. Beat the egg and mix it into the flour along with the water. Form the dough into a ball, wrap in plastic wrap and refrigerate for 30 minutes. Roll the chilled dough out on a lightly floured board to about quarter-inch thickness. Line a 10-inch tart pan with the pastry. Trim the edges, and prick the bottom and sides with a fork. Place on a cookie sheet and freeze for 15 minutes while the oven is heating to 425°. Line the pastry with aluminum foil and fill with pie weights. Bake at 425° for 10 minutes, then remove the foil and weights and bake for an additional 5 minutes. Cool thoroughly on a rack before filling.

To make the filling: Soak the prunes in the warm water and Armagnac for 30 minutes. Drain and discard liquid; cut the prunes in half and arrange over the bottom of prepared (baked and cooled) pastry crust.

Beat together the cream, eggs, egg yolks and sugar. Pour the mixture over the prunes. Sprinkle with nutmeg and cinnamon.

Place the tart pan on a cookie sheet and bake at 300° until the top is lightly browned and firm to the touch, about 40 minutes.

While the tart is baking, crush the raspberries and push through a strainer to remove the seeds. This will be a sauce for the tart.

Place the baked tart on a wire rack to cool. The tart is best served slightly warm. Serve each slice with a little raspberry sauce and garnish with mint.

MAPLE MOUSSE TARTLETS

Carolina House (p. 230)

MAKES 24 tartlets.

A creamy confection as suitable for dessert as for afternoon tea.

24 baked tartlet shells
4 egg yolks
¾ cup maple syrup
¼ tsp. nutmeg
¼ tsp. ginger
¼ tsp. pumpkin pie spice
2 cups heavy cream, whipped
½ cup finely ground pecans

Using your favorite pastry recipe, make 24 tartlet shells, bake and cool.

In a medium size bowl beat the egg yolks until light. In the top of a double boiler heat the syrup; when the syrup is very hot, stir in the egg yolks and spices. Continue cooking and whisking the mixture until thickened. Transfer to a bowl and allow to cool. While the mixture cools, whip the heavy cream in a large bowl. Fold the cooled maple mixture into the whipped cream.

Place 1 teaspoon of finely ground pecans in the bottom of each tartlet, shaking to distribute evenly over the bottom of the pastry. Spoon in the filling. Top each tartlet with an even sprinkle of ½ teaspoon ground pecans. Serve immediately.

CREAMY CHOCOLATE TARTLETS

Carolina House (p. 230)

MAKES 24 tartlets.

A rich and creamy delight. Although the filling for this recipe is quickly prepared, the elegant results will make your guests think otherwise.

Pastry
24 baked tartlet shells

Filling
3 ounces semisweet chocolate
1 ounce unsweetened chocolate
1 ½ tsp. instant coffee
1 ½ Tbs. cognac
2 cups heavy cream
¼ cup honey

Garnish
whipped cream
rolls of shaved semisweet
    chocolate

Using your favorite pastry recipe, make 24 tartlet shells, bake and cool.

In a double boiler melt the chocolate. Stir in the instant coffee and cognac; remove from heat, transfer to a large bowl and cool slightly.

In a large bowl whip the cream; beat in the honey. Fold this into the chocolate mixture. Cover and chill thoroughly.

Spoon the chocolate mixture into the tartlet shells, top with a small dollop of whipped cream and a few rolls of shaved chocolate. Serve immediately.

PEACH MELBA TART

Murphy's B&B (p. 13)

MAKES a 9-inch tart.

This is one of my favorite summer recipes, and it's always a hit. We grow our own raspberries, and the flavor of the raspberry glaze with ripe peaches is heavenly. I serve this at breakfast or afternoon tea and for dessert.

4 large ripe peaches
2 cups water
1 cup sugar
    zest of ½ lemon
1 ½ cups milk
2 Tbs. cornstarch
¼ cup sugar
½ tsp. vanilla
¼ cup melba sauce (page 221)
1 baked 9-inch tart shell
    (page 243)

To make the filling: Cut the peaches in half, going through the stem end, and remove the pits. In a saucepan combine the water and 1 cup sugar, and bring to a boil. Stir, reduce to a simmer, and add the peaches and lemon peel. Simmer, partially covered, for 5 to 10 minutes. The peaches should be just tender, not soft. If the syrup does not completely cover the peaches while poaching, turn them over halfway through the process. Using a slotted spoon, remove the peaches from the syrup and let cool on a plate, skin side up. When cool enough to touch, pinch the skin and pull it off (it should slip off easily; if not, the peaches were not poached long enough). Cover with plastic wrap and refrigerate. Discard the syrup.

In a small bowl mix the cornstarch, ¼ cup sugar, and a little of the milk to make a smooth paste. In a saucepan scald the rest of the milk. Then whisk in the cornstarch mixture and continue to cook over medium high heat, stirring constantly, until thickened. Remove from heat and stir in the vanilla. Cover and chill.

To assemble the tart: Spread the cooled custard over the bottom of the baked and cooled tart shell. Slice the chilled peaches in sections about ½-inch and arrange symmetrically, fanning out in a circle from the center, over the custard. Brush the melba sauce over the fruit, covering the tart completely, including any custard that shows. Chill for one hour before serving.

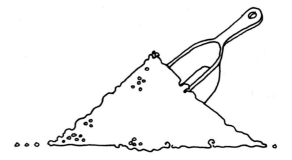

The Victorian Inn

Port Huron, Michigan

BUILT IN 1896, the Victorian Inn is an outstanding example of Queen Anne–style architecture. After its careful restoration by the Petersons and the Secorys, the old house was included on the state register of historic places in 1983. Some of its special features include exquisite woodwork, leaded glass windows, period furnishings and Victorian decor.

Port Huron is home to the beautiful Bluewater Bridge, linking the United States with Canada. Just an hour's drive north of Detroit, the town is also known for its Museum of Arts and History, Fort Gratiot Lighthouse (the first lighthouse on the Great Lakes), and an historic district of restored buildings from the nineteenth century. The St. Clair River, which flows into Lake Huron, is lively with boat traffic of all sorts; this busy shipping channel is also popular for leisure craft.

Guests are served a full breakfast in the elegant dining room. "All of our food is prepared with utmost care, in our own kitchen, with an attention to detail that was the order of the day in a bygone era," says Vicki Peterson.

The Victorian Inn
1229 Seventh Street
Port Huron, Michigan 48060
(313) 984-1437

Ed and Vicki Peterson
Lew and Lynn Secory

CHOCOLATE PECAN PIE

MAKES 1 pie.

Pastry
1⅓ cups flour
1 Tbs. sugar
½ tsp. salt
½ cup butter
½ tsp. lemon juice
3½ Tbs. ice water

Filling
5 ounces bittersweet chocolate
1 cup + 2 Tbs. sugar
½ cup butter
1 cup light corn syrup
4 eggs
¼ cup creme de cacao
2 cups pecan halves
1 cup whipping cream, whipped
   for topping

To make the crust: In a large bowl combine the flour, sugar and salt. Cut the butter into pats, and using a pastry fork or food processor mix the butter into the flour until it resembles coarse meal. Mix the lemon juice and water together and add to the flour mixture. Mix just until the dough forms a ball. Wrap the dough in plastic wrap and refrigerate for 30 minutes. On a lightly floured board roll out the chilled dough to quarter-inch thickness. Line a 10-inch pie plate with the dough, cover and refrigerate for 20 minutes. While the pie shell is in the refrigerator, heat the oven to 425°. Line the pastry shell with foil and fill with metal pie weights or dried beans. Place on a cookie sheet, and bake for 10 to 12 minutes. The pastry should be set but not brown. While the pie shell is baking, prepare the filling.

(continued on next page)

CHOCOLATE PECAN PIE
(continued)

Using a food processor, combine the chocolate and sugar until the chocolate is finely chopped. Place the butter and corn syrup in a small saucepan and heat until the butter is melted. Pour the melted butter-corn syrup into the food processor with the chocolate mixture and blend well. Add the eggs and crème de cacao. Blend just until the eggs are incorporated. Gently stir in the pecans.

When the pie shell has baked for 10 to 12 minutes, remove it from the oven, and *lower the oven temperature to 350°*. Remove the foil and weights, and pour the filling into the warm pastry shell. Return to the oven, placed on a cookie sheet, and bake at 350° for 60 minutes. If the crust starts to become too brown during the baking, cover the edge with foil. Cool on a rack. Serve garnished with a dollop of whipped cream.

MAKES-ITS-OWN-CRUST CHERRY COBBLER
The Bells Bed & Breakfast
(p. 9)

SERVES 6.

This is one of those dessert items that are served at breakfast at The Bells. It's marvelous for breakfast or dessert.

    2 cups sugar
    1 egg
    ½ cup milk
    ¾ cup flour
    1 tsp. baking powder
    1 Tbs. butter
    1 16-oz. can tart, red, pitted
      cherries, undrained

Preheat oven to 425°F.

Combine ½ cup of the sugar with the eggs, milk, flour and baking powder. Beat well and spread in bottom of a greased 1½-quart baking dish.

Combine the remaining 1½ cups sugar with the cherries in a saucepan and stir over medium-high heat until the mixture boils. Carefully pour the fruit mixture over the batter. Bake at 425° for 25 to 30 minutes.

This is best if served immediately. Serve with a splash of heavy cream.

LEMON PIE
The Frederick Fitting House
(p. 103)

MAKES 1 pie.

A creamy, lemony pie, perfect for afternoon tea on a hot summer day. Serve with tall glasses of strong iced tea.

    1 unbaked crust
    1½ cups sugar
    1 Tbs. cornstarch
    1 Tbs. flour
    3 eggs
    ¼ cup butter, melted
    ¼ cup lemon juice
    2 Tbs. grated lemon rind
    ¼ cup milk

Make a pie crust (page 241), and line a 9-inch pie plate. Cover and chill while making the filling.

Preheat oven to 375°F.

Mix together the sugar, cornstarch and flour. In a separate bowl beat the eggs, butter, lemon juice, lemon rind and milk. Pour into the dry ingredients and beat well. Pour into unbaked crust. Bake at 375° for 30 to 40 minutes. Cool thoroughly on a rack before serving.

OPPOSITE: *With its ornate, tufted and carved American renaissance parlor suite, the Victorian Inn lives up to its name.*

CLA FOUTIS
*The Rogers House Bed &
Breakfast (p. 23)*

SERVES 6.

A rich apple dish that is not too
sweet, this is appropriate as a fruit
dish at breakfast, or as a dessert
item.

 4 golden delicious apples
 5 Tbs. butter
 ⅔ cup sugar
 2 eggs
 ½ cup milk
 3 tsp. vanilla
 ½ cup flour

Preheat oven to 475°F.

Peel, core and thinly slice the
apples. Arrange them in a greased
pie pan, overlapping, 2 layers thick.
In a bowl cream together the butter
and sugar. Beat in the eggs. Add
the milk and vanilla, beating well.
Last, mix in the flour. Spoon the
batter over the apples and bake at
475° for 10 minutes. Lower the
oven temperature to 350° and continue baking for an additional 30
minutes. Cool on a rack for at least
10 minutes before serving. Serve
warm or cooled.

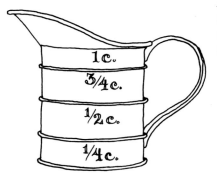

APPLE CRISP
Britt House (p. 16)

SERVES 8.

I have often served this for dessert,
but I discovered that many B&Bs
serve apple crisp for breakfast. This
excellent version can be served any
time.

 Filling
 6 tart apples
 2 Tbs. lemon juice
 ½ cup sugar
 ½ tsp. cinnamon
 ½ cup water

 Topping
 1 cup flour
 1 cup firmly packed brown sugar
 1⅔ cups rolled oats
 2 Tbs. dry milk
 1 tsp. cinnamon
 1 tsp. ginger
 ¾ cup butter

Preheat oven to 350°F.

Peel, core and thinly slice the
apples. In a large bowl combine
them with the lemon juice, sugar,
cinnamon and water. Distribute
evenly over the bottom of a greased
9" × 13" pan.

To make the topping, combine
all ingredients except the butter.
Then cut in the butter until the
mixture is crumbly. Sprinkle over
top of apples.

Bake at 350° for 30 minutes.
Place on a cooling rack to cool
slightly before serving. Serve warm,
topped with whipped cream, ice
cream or heavy cream.

RICE PUDDING
*The Bells Bed & Breakfast
(p. 9)*

SERVES 6.

An old-fashioned dessert, this is
served at breakfast at The Bells.

 ¼ cup rice, uncooked
 ½ cup raisins
 1 cup water
 4 eggs
 ⅔ cup sugar
 2 cups milk
 1 tsp. vanilla
   cinnamon

Preheat oven to 350°F.

Combine the rice, raisins and
water in a saucepan and bring to a
boil. Simmer for 10 minutes. Drain
well and set aside. In a large bowl
beat together the eggs, sugar, milk
and vanilla. Add the rice mixture
and combine thoroughly.

Pour into a greased 1½ quart casserole dish. Sprinkle with a little
cinnamon. Set the casserole into a
pan of hot water in the oven and
bake at 350° for 1 hour. Bring to
room temperature before covering
and refrigerating. Chill and serve
with heavy cream.

Longswamp Bed & Breakfast
Mertztown, Pennsylvania

LOCATED ON five acres, Longswamp B&B is a stately old house with portions dating from 1740. In 1860, Colonel Trexler enlarged the big old farmhouse, creating an imposing structure. The second-story verandah—with its hanging begonias, comfortable rockers and peaceful view of the yard—is a wonderful place to read and relax.

Antiques and Amish handicraft shops, riding stables and lush rolling farmland abound along the country roads here. In winter, the nearby ski area offers trails for all levels of proficiency.

Elsa Dimick is also a professional caterer, and her full breakfasts include homemade jams, jellies and breads. The Dimicks grow their own blueberries, strawberries, raspberries and rhubarb, as well as a variety of vegetables, herbs and flowers. These also appear at breakfast as the seasons dictate. In spring, Elsa may serve asparagus quiche, rhubarb cobbler or strawberry shortcake. During fine weather, breakfast is served on the patio; in the cooler months the setting is the 1740 "summer kitchen," with its inviting fireplace.

Longswamp Bed & Breakfast
Box 26
Mertztown, Pennsylvania 19539
(215) 682–6197

Elsa and Dean Dimick

STRAWBERRY SHORTCAKE

SERVES 6.

This is true strawberry shortcake. Most people are used to a spongecake, and call it shortcake. This is sometimes served for breakfast at Longswamp B&B; it is so rich that coffee and juice are the only accompaniments.

1	quart fresh strawberries
¾	cup confectioners' sugar
1	pint whipping cream

Shortcake Biscuits

4	cups flour
6	tsp. baking powder
1	tsp. salt
2	Tbs. sugar
¼	tsp. nutmeg
⅔	cup oil
1½	cups milk
2	eggs

Clean, hull and quarter the berries. Place in a large bowl; cover with the confectioners' sugar and toss. Cover with plastic wrap and refrigerate.

While the berries are chilling, make the biscuits. While the biscuits are baking, whip the cream.

To make the biscuits: In large bowl mix together the flour, baking powder, salt, sugar and nutmeg. In a separate bowl beat the oil, milk and eggs; pour over dry ingredients. Mix lightly, only enough to moisten.

Drop by large spoonfuls onto a greased baking sheet to make 6 large biscuits. Bake at 450° for 10 minutes. Watch bottoms so they don't burn. When sufficiently cool to handle, split in half and butter generously. Top with berries and whipped cream.

RoyAl Carter House
Ashland, Oregon

A BUNGALOW-STYLE HOUSE dating from 1909, the RoyAl Carter House is located in a town and surrounding area that offer much for the visitor to see and do. Nearby Lithia Park is a lovely place, offering a hundred acres of paths for strolling and jogging, with both duck ponds and its famous Oriental Garden. The Shakespeare Festival held in Ashland every summer attracts theatre lovers from across the country. There are also open-air performances of ballet and concerts in the band shell during the summer every Monday, Wednesday and Friday night.

This area is also known for its natural hot springs; Jackson Hot Springs is two miles away. Both a national forest and the lower portion of the Cascade Mountain Range are a few miles from Ashland. At 7,525 feet, Mt. Ashland offers excellent skiing in the winter. Lake Emigrant is six miles away, and Crater Lake — North America's deepest lake, famous for its clear and intense blue water — is forty miles away.

According to Alyce and Roy Levy, "From evening theatre to morning tea, we offer you a delightfully unique holiday experience. Breakfast is served in the traditional dining room or patio garden."

RoyAl Carter House
514 Siskiyou Blvd.
Ashland, Oregon 97520
(503) 482-5623

Alyce and Roy Levy

FRESH BERRY COBBLER

SERVES 8.

A delicious summer treat made with fresh berries.

Filling
1 cup raspberries
3 cups blackberries
1 cup sugar
3 Tbs. cornstarch
¼ cup fruit juice (white grape juice or apple juice)

Topping
2 cups flour
3 tsp. baking powder
½ tsp. salt
4 Tbs. sugar
⅔ cup milk
3 Tbs. melted butter

Preheat oven to 400°F.

To make the filling: Combine berries and sugar. Put in 9" × 14" Pyrex dish and place in 400° oven for 10 minutes.

While berries are in oven, mix the cornstarch and juice together. When you remove the berries from the oven, stir in the cornstarch mixture and mix well.

To make the topping: Mix the flour, baking powder, salt and sugar together. Then stir in milk and melted butter; beat well.

Spoon the dough onto the prepared berry mixture and bake at 400° for 20 minutes, or until top is golden brown.

Cool on a rack, slightly, before serving.

Borgman's Bed & Breakfast
Arrow Rock, Missouri

THE EMPHASIS IS on comfort in the warm, homey atmosphere of this century-old house located in historic Arrow Rock. Founded in 1829, Arrow Rock is historically interesting as the beginning of the Santa Fe Trail, an important trading route in the mid 1800s. The town was also home to American artist George Caleb Bingham, noted for his portrayal of frontier life and scenes on the Missouri River. His home, now open for tours, can be seen on a walking tour that includes six other fascinating buildings in town. In summer, the famous Lyceum Theatre presents musicals, comedies and dramas in a restored church that seats two hundred. Although home to only eighty-two permanent residents, Arrow Rock has enough restaurants, antiques shops and craft boutiques to accommodate eighty- to a hundred-thousand visitors who pass through every year. The Missouri River flows right past the town, and Arrow Rock State Park is a few miles down the road.

Guests at Borgman's Bed and Breakfast can walk just about anywhere they'd want to go in town. If they don't feel like going anywhere, there's always the comfortable porch swing in which to while away the day. In the morning a family-style breakfast is served in the kitchen, consisting of freshly baked breads, juice or fruit and coffee or tea. "Come, enjoy Arrow Rock. We do," say Kathy and Helen Borgman.

Borgman's Bed and Breakfast
Arrow Rock, Missouri 65320
(816) 837–3350

Kathy and Helen Borgman

DIVINITY CANDY

MAKES about 24 candies.

This is an old-fashioned Southern confection. Guests at Borgman's Bed and Breakfast find a plate of this homemade candy in their room.

  4 egg whites
  ½ tsp. cream of tartar
  4 cups sugar
  1 cup water
  1 cup white corn syrup
  1 tsp. vanilla

Have egg whites at room temperature. Beat until foamy; add cream of tartar and beat until stiff.

Place the sugar, water and corn syrup in a saucepan. Stirring constantly over medium-high heat, bring the mixture to 250°F (use a candy thermometer). Carefully add half the hot syrup to the egg whites, beating constantly.

Heat the rest of the syrup mixture to 280°. Again beat egg white mixture as you slowly add the rest of the boiled syrup mixture. Add vanilla and mix well.

Let the mixture sit until it cools, beating occasionally. It will lose its glossy look. Drop by tablespoonfuls onto a cookie sheet covered with waxed paper. Allow to harden.

OPPOSITE: *Heavy overhanging eaves and overscale porch columns are hallmarks of the bungalow style. The RoyAl Carter House is a typical American house from the years just before World War I.*

LEFT: *A bed of flowers is one more "bed" feature of many American B&Bs.*

SOUTHERN PRALINES

St. Charles Avenue Home

(p. 215)

MAKES 2 dozen.

This candy is a treat as is or broken over vanilla ice cream.

1 cup white sugar
1 cup brown sugar
½ cup condensed milk
¼ cup butter
2 cups pecans
1 tsp. vanilla

Combine all ingredients except the vanilla in a saucepan and place over medium-high heat. Stirring constantly, bring the mixture to a boil and cook for 3 to 5 minutes. Remove from the heat and stir in the vanilla. Beat for one minute. Spoon out on waxed paper. When hardened, wrap individually in waxed paper.

OLD-FASHIONED SYLLABUB

Oak Square (p. 158)

SERVES 6.

In colonial days syllabub was served the way ice cream is served today. Recipes appear in cookbooks of the early eighteenth century. This recipe for syllabub is Martha Lum's favorite, a teatime specialty at Oak Square where it is served with old-fashioned nut cake and old-fashioned white cake. Serve with hot or cold spiced tea.

1½ cups milk
3 eggs
¾ cup sugar
½ tsp. salt
3 cups light cream
2 cups sweet white wine

Scald milk. Meanwhile, beat the eggs with the sugar and salt. Gradually add hot milk to egg mixture, and cook in a double boiler, stirring constantly until mixture thickens. Cool. Whisk in the light cream and wine, and chill again. Spoon into custard cups or stemmed glasses. Serve cold.

Metric Conversion Tables

Liquid and Dry Conversion

The following table will help you convert from the conventional designations of teaspoons, tablespoons and cups to ounces or to the metric system with the nearest convenient equivalents:

Conventional		Ounces	Metric
Liquid			
1	tsp.	1/16	5 ml
2	tsp.	1/3	10 ml
1	Tbs.	1/2	15 ml
1/2	cup	4	125 ml
1	cup	8	250 ml (.25 l or 2.5 dl)
2	cups	16	500 ml (.5 l)
4	cups	32	1 liter (approx.)*
Butter, Shortening, Cheese			
1	Tbs.	1/2	15 gm
1/2	cup	4	115 gm
1	cup	8	225 gm
Granulated Sugar			
1	tsp.	1/6	5 gm
1	Tbs.	1/2	15 gm
1/4	cup	1 3/4	60 gm
1/3	cup	2 1/4	75 gm
1/2	cup	3 1/2	100 gm
2/3	cup	4 1/2	130 gm
3/4	cup	5	150 gm
1	cup	7	200 gm
Flour			
1	Tbs.	1/4	8.75 gm
1/4	cup	1 1/4	35 gm
1/3	cup	1 1/2	45 gm
1/2	cup	2 1/2	70 gm
3/4	cup	3 1/2	105 gm
1	cup	5	140 gm

*To be more exact 4 1/3 cups = 1 liter, 4 cups = 1 liter less 1 dl.

Conversion to Centigrade

Oven temperatures in this book are given in the Farenheit (F) scale. If your oven thermostat is calibrated in the centigrade (celsius) scale, you can use the following table to convert to the proper settings.

Farenheit Scale	Centigrade (Celsius) Scale
160	71
212	100
221	105
225	107
230	121
300	149
302	150
350	177
375	190
400	205
425	218
475	246
500	260
525	274
550	288

Featured B&Bs by State

To find a description of each B&B and the recipes included in this book, see the Index of B&Bs.

ALABAMA

Mentone Bed & Breakfast
P.O. Box 284
Mentone, AL 35984
(205) 634–4836
Amelia Brooks

ALASKA

Crondahl's Bed & Breakfast
626 5th Street
Juneau, AK 99801
(907) 586–1464
Judy Crondahl

Magic Canyon Ranch Bed & Breakfast
40015 Waterman Road
Homer, AK 99603
(907) 235–6077
Carrie Reed

Pat Wilson's Bed & Breakfast–Valdez
3346 Eagle, P.O. Box 442
Valdez, AK 99686
(907) 835–4211
Patricia Wilson

ARIZONA

Dierker House
423 West Cherry
Flagstaff, AZ 86002
(602) 774–3249
Dorothea Dierker

June's Bed and Breakfast
3212 West Holladay Street
Tucson, AZ 85746
(602) 578–0857
June Henderson

Guests departing from Hersey House (page 54) look back over glowing beds of marigolds.

ARKANSAS

Bridgeford Cottage
263 Spring Street
Eureka Springs, AR 72632
(501) 253–7853
Ken and Nyla Sawyer

Heart of the Hills Inn
5 Summit
Eureka Springs, AR 72632
(501) 253–7468
Jan Jacobs Weber

The Heartstone Inn
35 Kingshighway
Eureka Springs, AR 72632
(501) 253–8916
Bill and Iris Simantel

Oak Tree Inn
Vinegar Hill, 110 W.
Heber Springs, AR 72543
(501) 362–7731
Freddie Lou Lodge

Singleton House Bed & Breakfast Inn
11 Singleton
Eureka Springs, AR 72632
(501) 253–9111
Barbara Gavron

Williams House Bed & Breakast Inn
420 Quapaw
Hot Springs National Park, AR 71901
(501) 624–4275
Mary and Gary Riley

CALIFORNIA

Britt House
406 Maple Street
San Diego, CA 92103
(619) 234–2926
Daun Martin

The Campbell Ranch Inn
1475 Canyon Road
Geyserville, CA 95441
(707) 857–3476
Mary Jane and Jerry Campbell

The Carriage House
1322 Catalina Street
Laguna Beach, CA 92651
(714) 494–8945
Dee Taylor

Carter House
1033 3rd Street
Eureka, CA 95501
(707) 445–1390
Mark and Christi Carter

Country House Inn
91 Main Street
Templeton, CA 93465
(805) 434–1598
Dianne Garth

Dunbar House, 1880
271 Jones Street
Murphys, CA 95247
(209) 728–2897
Bob and Barbara Costa

The Fleming Jones Homestead, 1883
3170 Newtown Road
Placerville, CA 95667
(916) 626–5840
Janice Condit

The Gingerbread Mansion
400 Berding Street
Ferndale, CA 95536
(707) 786–4000
Wendy Hatfield and Ken Torbert

Glendeven
Little River, CA 95456
(707) 937–0083
Janet de Vries

The Green Gables Inn
104 Fifth Street
Pacific Grove, CA 93950
(408) 375–2095
Claudia Long

The Heirloom
P.O. Box 322
Ione, CA 95640
(209) 274–4468
Melissande Hubbs

The Raford House
10630 Wohler Road
Healdsburg, CA 95448
(707) 887-9573
Alan Baitinger

COLORADO

Briar Rose
2151 Arapahoe Avenue
Boulder, CO 80302
(303) 442-3007
Emily Hunter and Kit Riley

The Dove Inn
711 14th Street
Golden, CO 80401
(303) 278-2209
Ken and Jean Sims

Elizabeth Street Guest House
202 East Elizabeth Street
Fort Collins, CO 80524
(303) 493-2337
John and Sheryl Clark

Fool's Gold
1069 Snowdon
Silverton, CO 81433
(303) 387-5879
Ann Marie Wallace

Holden House
1102 West Pikes Peak Avenue
Colorado Springs, CO 80904
(303) 471-3980
Sally and Welling Clark

Purple Mountain Lodge
P.O. Box 897
Crested Butte, CO 81224
(303) 349-5888
Dorothy Lockwood

River Song
P.O. Box 1910
Estes Park, CO 80517
(303) 586-4666
Gary and Sue Mansfield

CONNECTICUT

Eastover Farm B&B
P.O. Box 275
Bethlehem, CT 06751
(203) 266-5740
Erik and Mary Hawvermale

The Felshaw Tavern
Five Mile River Road
Putnam, CT 06260
(203) 928-3467
Herb and Terry Kinsman

The Fowler House
Plains Road, P.O. Box 432
Moodus, CT 06469
(203) 873-8906
Barbara & Paul Ally and
    Penny & Arnie Davidson

Manor House
Maple Avenue, P.O. Box 701
Norfolk, CT 06058
(203) 543-5690
Diane and Henry Tremblay

DELAWARE

O'Connor's Guest House B&B
20 Delaware Avenue
Rehobeth Beach, DE 19971
(302) 227-2419
Pat O'Connor

Small Wonder Bed & Breakfast
213 West Crest Road
Wilmington, DE 19803
(302) 764-0789
Dorothy Brill

DISTRICT OF COLUMBIA

Adams Inn
1744 Lanier Place, N.W.
Washington, D.C. 20009
(202) 745-3600
Nancy Thompson

FLORIDA

The Bailey House
28 7th Street South
Fernandina Beach, FL 32034
(904) 261-5390
Tom and Diane Hay

Casa de Solana
21 Aviles Street
St. Augustine, FL 32084
(904) 824-3555
Faye McMurry

1735 House
584 South Fletcher
Fernandina Beach
Amelia Island, FL 32034
David and Susan Caples

GEORGIA

The Marlow House
192 Church Street
Marietta, GA 30060
(404) 426-1887
Kathleen McDaniel

Toccoa River Hideaway
P.O. Box 300
Blue Ridge, GA 30513
(404) 632-2411
Charles Hay

HAWAII

Hilo B&B
c/o Bed & Breakfast Hawaii
P.O. Box 449
Kapaa, HI 96746
(808) 822-7771
Elvrine Chow

Nuuana B&B
c/o Bed & Breakfast Hawaii
P.O. Box 449
Kapaa, HI 96746
(808) 822-7771
Elvrine Chow

Pukalani B&B
c/o Bed & Breakfast Hawaii
P.O. Box 449
Kapaa, HI 96746
(808) 822-7771
Elvrine Chow

IDAHO

Greenbriar Bed & Breakfast Inn
315 Wallace
Couer d'Alene, ID 83814
(208) 667–9660
Kris McIlvenna

The River Street Inn
100 River Street West Ketchum
Sun Valley, ID 83353
(208) 726–3611
Ginny Van Doren

ILLINOIS

Aldrich Guest House
900 Third Street
Galena, IL 61036
(815) 777–3323
Judy Green

INDIANA

Green Meadow Ranch
Rt. 2, Box 592
Shipshewana, IN 46565
(219) 768–4221
Ruth and Paul Miller

Milburn House
707 East Vistula Street
Bristol, IN 46507
(219) 848–4026
Pauline Mihojevich

Morton Street Bed & Breakfast Homes
P.O. Box 775
Shipshewana, IN 46565
(219) 768–4391
Joel and Ester Mishler

IOWA

Robin's Nest
327 9th Avenue
Council Bluffs, IA 51503
(712) 323–1649
Dorothea Smith and Wendy Storey

Victorian Bed and Breakfast Inn
425 Walnut Street
Avoca, IA 51521
(712) 343–6336
Jan and Gene Kuehn

KANSAS

Bed 'n Breakfast–Still Country
Route 1, Box 297
Wakefield, KS 67487
(913) 461–5596
Pearl Thurlow

KENTUCKY

Old Talbott Tavern
107 West Stephen Foster
Bardstown, KY 40004
(502) 348–3494
Jim Kelley

LOUISIANA

Barrow House
524 Royal Street
St. Francisville, LA 70775
(504) 635–4791
Shirley and Lyle Ditloff

Madewood Plantation House
Highway 308
Napoleonville, LA 70390
(504) 369–7151
Keith and Millie Marshall

St. Charles Avenue Home
c/o Bed & Breakfast, Inc.
1360 Moss Street, P.O. Box 52257
New Orleans, LA 70152
(504) 525–4640
Hazell Boyce

Tree House in the Park
16520 Airport Road
Prairieville, LA 70769
(504) 622–2850
Fran Schmieder

MAINE

Bufflehead Cove Inn
Gounitz Lane, P.O. Box 499
Kennebunkport, ME 04046
(207) 967–3879
Harriet Gott

The Captain Jefferds Inn
Pearl Street, Box 691
Kennebunkport, ME 04046
(207) 967–2311
Warren Fitzsimmons

High Meadows Bed & Breakfast
Route 101
Eliot, ME 03903
(207) 439–0590
Elaine Raymond

Kenniston Hill Inn
Route 27
Boothbay, ME 04537
(207) 633–2159
Paul and Ellen Morissette

The 1859 Guest House
60 South High Street
Bridgton, ME 04009
(207) 647–2508
William and Mary Zeller

MARYLAND

Betsy's Bed & Breakfast
1428 Park Avenue
Baltimore, MD 21217
(301) 383–1274
Betsy Grater

Holland House
5 Bay Street
Berlin, MD 21811
(301) 641–1956
Jim and Jan Quick

Hynson Tourist Home
804 Dover Road
Easton, MD 21601
(301) 822–2777
Nellie Hynson

The Inn at Mitchell House
Box 329, R.D. 2, Tolchester Estates
Chestertown, MD 21620
(301) 778–6500
Jim and Tracy Stone

Radcliffe Cross
Quaker Neck Road
Chestertown, MD 21620
(301) 778–5540
Dan and Marge Brook

The Strawberry Inn
17 Main Street, Box 237
New Market, MD 21774
(301) 865–3318
Jane and Ed Rossig

MASSACHUSETTS

The Carlisle House Inn
26 North Water Street
Nantucket, MA 02554
(617) 228–0720
Peter Conway

The Hawthorne Inn
462 Lexington Road
Concord, MA 01742
(617) 369–5610
Gregory Burch and Marilyn Mudry

The Inn on Cove Hill
37 Mount Pleasant Street
Rockport, MA 01966
(617) 546–2701
John and Marjorie Pratt

MICHIGAN

Chaffin Farms
3239 West St. Charles Road
Ithaca, MI 48847
(517) 463–4081
Sue Chaffin

Hidden Pond Farm
P.O. Box 461
Fennville, MI 49408
(616) 561–2491
Edward X. Kennedy

The House on the Hill
Box 206, Lake St.
Ellsworth, MI 49729
(616) 588–6304
Julie Arnim

The Parsonage 1908
6 East 24th
Holland, MI 49423
(616) 396–1316
Bonnie Verwys and Wendy Westrate

The Pentwater Inn Bed & Breakfast
180 East Lowell Street
Pentwater, MI 49449
(616) 869–5909
Dick and Sue Hand

River Haven Bed and Breakfast
9222 St. Joe River Road
White Pigeon, MI 49099
(616) 483–9104
Jim and Blanche Pressler

The Stagecoach Stop
0–4819 Leonard Road West
Lamont, MI 49430
(616) 677–3940
Marcia Ashby

The Victorian Inn
1229 Seventh Street
Port Huron, MI 48060
(313) 984–1437
Ed and Vicki Peterson,
   Lew and Lynn Secory

MINNESOTA

Cantebury Inn Bed & Breakfast
723 Second Street S.W.
Rochester, MN 55902
(507) 289–5553
Mary Martin & Jeffrey Van Sant

Cedar Knoll Farm
Route 2, Box 147
Good Thunder, MN 56037
(507) 524–3813
Mavis Christiansen

MISSISSIPPI

Oak Square
1207 Church Street
Port Gibson, MS 39150
(601) 437–4350
Martha and William Lum

MISSOURI

Borgman's Bed and Breakfast
Arrow Rock, MO 65320
(816) 837–3350
Kathy and Helen Borgman

Caverly Farm and Orchard
c/o Bed and Breakfast of St. Louis
1900 Wyoming Street
St. Louis, MO 63122
(314) 965–4328
Mike Warner

LaFayette House
c/o Bed and Breakfast of St. Louis
1900 Wyoming Street
St. Louis, MO 63122
(314) 965–4328
Mike Warner

Little Piney Canoe Resort
c/o Bed and Breakfast of St. Louis
1900 Wyoming Street
St. Louis, MO 63122
(314) 965–4328
Mike Warner

Meramec Farm Stay
c/o Bed and Breakfast of St. Louis
1900 Wyoming Street
St. Louis, MO 63122
(314) 965–4328
Mike Warner

The Southern Hotel
146 South Third Street
Ste. Genevieve, MO 63670
(314) 883–3493
Mike and Barbara Hankins

MONTANA

The Voss Inn
319 South Willson
Bozeman, MT 59715
(406) 587–0982
Bruce and Frankee Muller

NEBRASKA

The Rogers House
2145 B. Street
Lincoln, NE 68502
(402) 476–6961
Nora Houtsma

NEVADA

Edith Palmer's Country Inn
South B Street
Virginia City, NV 89440
(702) 847-0707
Erlene Brown

Old Pioneer Garden
Unionville #79, NV 89418
(702) 538-7585
Mitzi Jones

NEW HAMPSHIRE

The Beal House Inn
247 West Main Street
Littleton, NH 03561
(603) 444-2661
Jim and Ann Carver

The Bells
P.O. Box 276
Bethlehem, NH 03574
(603) 869-2647
Bill and Louise Sims

The English House Bed and Breakfast
P.O. Box 162
Andover, NH 03216
(603) 735-5987
Gillian and Ken Smith

NEW JERSEY

Barnard–Good House
238 Perry Street
Cape May, NJ 08204
(609) 884-5381
Nan and Tom Hawkins

NEW MEXICO

Grant Corner Inn
122 Grant Avenue
Santa Fe, NM 87501
(505) 983-6678
Patrick and Louise Walter

NEW YORK

Fala Bed & Breakfast
East Market Street
Hyde Park, NY 12538
(914) 229-5937
Maryann Martinez

House on the Hill
Box 86
High Falls, NY 12440
(914) 687-9627
Shelly and Sharon Glassman

NORTH CAROLINA

Hillcrest House
209 Hillcrest Road
Chapel Hill, NC 27514
(919) 942-2369
James and Betty York

Maple Lodge
Sunset Drive
Blowing Rock, NC 28605
(704) 295-3331
Marilyn Latham

NORTH DAKOTA

Pleasant View
Box 211
Regent, ND 58850
(701) 563-4542
Marlys Prince

OHIO

The Frederick Fitting House
72 Fitting Avenue
Belleville, OH 44813
(419) 886-4283
Jo and Rick Sowash

The Inn on Kelleys Island
Kelleys Island, OH 43438
(419) 746-2258

Wal–Mec Farm
5663 State Route 204 NW
Thornville, OH 43076
(614) 246-5450
Anne and Paul Mechling

OKLAHOMA

Harrison House
124 West Harrison
Guthrie, OK 73044
(405) 282-1000
Phyllis Murray

OREGON

General Hooker's House
125 SW Hooker
Portland, OR 97201
(503) 222-4435
Lorry Hall

Hersey House
451 North Main Street
Ashland, OR 97520
(503) 482-4563
Gail Orell

The John Palmer House
4314 North Mississippi Avenue
Portland, OR 97217
(503) 284-5893
Mary Sauter

MacMaster House
1041 S.W. Vista Avenue
Portland, OR 97205
(503) 223-7362
Cecilia Murphy

Marjon Bed and Breakfast
44975 Leaburg Dam Road
Leaburg, OR 97489
(503) 896-3145
Countess Margaret Olga Von
  Retzlaff Haas

The RoyAl Carter House
514 Siskiyou Boulevard
Ashland, OR 97520
(503) 482-5623
Alyce and Roy Levy

PENNSYLVANIA

Barley Sheaf Farm
Box 10
Holicong, PA 18928
(215) 794-5104
Don and Ann Mills

Hollinger House Bed & Breakfast
2336 Hollinger Road
Lancaster, PA 17602
(717) 464–3050
Leon and Jean Thomas

Longswamp Bed and Breakfast
RD 2, Box 26
Mertztown, PA 19539
(215) 682–6197
Elsa and Dean Dimick

Spring House
Muddy Creek Forks
Airville, PA 17302
(717) 927–6906
Ray Hearne

RHODE ISLAND

Gardner House
629 Main Street
Wakefield, RI 02879
(401) 789–1250
Nan and Will Gardner

Hedgerow B&B
1747 Mooresfield Road
Kingston, RI 02881
(401) 783–2671
Ann and Jim Ross

Murphy's B&B
43 South Pier Road
Narragansett, RI 02882
(401) 789–1824
Kevin and Martha Murphy

Richards' Bed and Breakfast
144 Gibson Avenue
Narragansett, RI 02882
(401) 789–7746
Steven and Nancy Richards

Starr Cottage
68 Caswell Street
Narragansett, RI 02882
(401) 783–2411
Gail Charren

SOUTH CAROLINA

The Capers–Motte House
69 Church Street
Charleston, SC 29401
(803) 722–2263
Jessica Marshall

1837 Bed & Breakfast
126 Wentworth Street
Charleston, SC 29401
(803) 723–7166
Sherri and Richard Dunn

SOUTH DAKOTA

Skoglund Farm Bed & Breakfast
Route 1, Box 45
Canova, SD 57321
(605) 247–3445
Delores Skoglund

TENNESSEE

The Lowenstein–Long House
217 North Waldran
Memphis, TN 38105
(901) 274–0509
Martha W. Long

TEXAS

Carolina House
802 Hyde Park
Houston, TX 77006
(713) 522–3102
Carol Maupin

Hazlewood House
1127 Church Street
Galveston, TX 77550
(409) 762–1668
Pat Hazlewood

UTAH

Brigham Street Inn
1135 East South Temple
Salt Lake City, UT 84102
(801) 364–4461
Sandy Scott

The Pullman Inn Bed & Breakfast
415 South University Avenue
Provo, UT 84601
(801) 374–8141
Dennis Morganson

VERMONT

Maple Crest Farm
Box 120
Cuttingsville, VT 05738
(802) 492–3367
Donna Smith

VIRGINIA

The Catlin–Abbott House
2304 East Broad Street
Richmond, VA 23223
(804) 780–3746
Dr. and Mrs. William Abbott

WASHINGTON

The Beech Tree Manor
1405 Queen Anne Avenue North
Seattle, WA 98109
(206) 281–7037
Virginia Lucero

Log Castle Bed & Breakfast
3273 East Saratoga Road
Langley, WA 98260
(206) 321–5483
Jack and Norma Metcalf

Palmer's Chart House
Box 51
Deer Harbor, WA 98243
(206) 376–4231
Majean and Don Palmer

The Parsonage 1901
4107 Burnham Lane
Gig Harbor, WA 98335
(206) 851–8654
Sheila and Edward Koscik

WEST VIRGINIA

Countryside B&B
Box 57
Summit Point, WV 25446
(304) 725–2614
Lisa and Daniel Hileman

WISCONSIN

Jackson Street Inn Bed & Breakfast
210 South Jackson Street
Janesville, WI 53545
(608) 754–7250
Ilah and Bob Sessler

Phoenix House
1075 Highway F
Minocqua, WI 54548
(715) 356–3535
Odeen Prudhom

WYOMING

The Boyer YL Ranch
Box 24
Savery, WY 82332
(307) 383–7840
Winston and George Boyer

Ferris Mansion
607 West Maple
Rawlins, WY 82301
(307) 324–3961
Janice Lubbers

Savery Creek Thoroughbred Ranch
Box 24
Savery, WY 82332
(307) 383–7840
Joyce Saer

Spahn's Big Horn Mountain Bed
& Breakfast
P.O. Box 579
Big Horn, WY 82833
(307) 674–8150
Ron and Bobbie Spahn

Teton Tree House
Box 550
Wilson, WY 83014
(307) 733–3233
Chris and Danny Becker

B&B Reservation Agencies

Some of these agencies cover an entire state, and some cover a few states within a region. Such information is included below the name of the reservation service.

This list is supplied by
Bed & Breakfast Reservation Services
    World-Wide (A Trade Association)
P.O. Box 14797, Dept 174
Baton Rouge, LA 70898

with the exception of Bed & Breakfast of St. Louis.

ARIZONA

Mi Casa Su Casa Bed & Breakfast
(Arizona, Utah, California, New Mexico
    & Nevada)
P.O. Box 950
Tempe, AZ 85281
(602) 990–0682

CALIFORNIA

American Family Inn/Bed & Breakfast
    San Francisco
(Greater S.F. wine and gold country,
    Monterey & Carmel)
P.O. Box 349
San Francisco, CA 94101
(415) 931–3083

Bed & Breakfast of Southern California
1943 Sunny Crest Drive #304
Fullerton, CA 92635
(714) 738–8361

California Houseguests, Int'l., Inc.
(statewide)
18653 Ventura Blvd. #190 B
Tarzana, CA 91356
(818) 344–7878

Co-Host, America's Bed & Breakfast
P.O. Box 9302
Whittier, CA 90608
(213) 699–8427

Eye Openers B&B Reservations
(statewide)
P.O. Box 694
Altadena, Ca 91001
(213) 684–4428
(818) 797–2055

COLORADO

Bed & Breakfast Rocky Mountains
(Colorado, New Mexico & Utah)
P.O. Box 804
Colorado Springs, CO 80901
(719) 630–3433

Bed & Breakfast Vail/Ski Areas
(ski areas)
P.O. Box 491
Vail, CO 81658
(303) 949–1212

CONNECTICUT

Nutmeg Bed & Breakfast Agency
(statewide & specializing in executive
  relocation)
222 Girard Avenue
Hartford, CT 06105
(203) 236-6698

DELAWARE

Bed & Breakfast of Delaware (Assoc.)
(Delaware, Maryland & Pennsylvania)
Box 177, 3650 Silverside Road
Wilmington, DE 19810
(302) 479-9500

DISTRICT OF COLUMBIA

Bed 'n' Breakfast Ltd.
(Washington, DC, Maryland & Virginia)
P.O. Box 12011
Washington, DC 20005
(202) 328-3510

The Bed & Breakfast League / Sweet
  Dreams and Toast
(District of Columbia)
P.O. Box 9490
Washington, DC 20008
(202) 363-7767

GEORGIA

Bed & Breakfast Atlanta
(statewide)
1801 Piedmont Avenue #208
Atlanta, GA 30324
(404) 875-0525

HAWAII

Bed & Breakfast Hawaii
(statewide)
P.O. Box 449
Kapaa, HI 96746
(808) 822-7771
1-800-367-8047, ext. 339

Bed & Breakfast Honolulu
(all islands)
3242 Kaohinani Drive
Honolulu, HI 96817
(808) 595-7533
1-800-288-4666

Pacific-Hawaii Bed & Breakfast
(statewide—Oahu, Maui, Kauai &
  Island of Hawaii)
19 Kai Nani Place
Kailua, Oahu HI 96734
(808) 262-6026

IDAHO

Bed & Breakfast Travel Connections
  (Assoc.)
(Idaho, Montana, Washington &
  Canada)
5805 Pine Grove Drive
Coeur d'Alene, ID 83814
(208) 765-9090

ILLINOIS

Bed & Breakfast / Chicago, Inc.
P.O. Box 14088
Chicago, IL 60614
(312) 951-0085

Prairie Hospitality, Inc. (Assoc.)
(statewide)
P.O. Box 3035
Oak Park, IL 60303
(312) 386-8620

INDIANA

Bed & Breakfast / Indiana, Inc. (Assoc.)
(statewide)
P.O. Box 481
Nashville, IN 47448-0481
(812) 988-0733

Ohio Valley Bed & Breakfast
(Ohio, Kentucky & Indiana)
6876 Taylor Mill Road
Independence, KY 41051
(606) 356-7865

KANSAS

Bed & Breakfast Kansas City (Assoc.)
(Kansas & Missouri)
P.O. Box 14781
Lenexa, KS 66215
(913) 888-3636

LOUISIANA

Bed & Breakfast, Inc.
(New Orleans & Barbados)
1360 Moss Street, Box 52257
New Orleans, LA 70152-2257
(504) 525-4640
1-800-228-9711

Bed & Breakfast—Southern Comfort
  Reservation Service
(Louisiana, Mississippi, New Mexico &
  Acapulco)
2856 Hundred Oaks
Baton Rouge, LA 70808
(504) 346-1928
1-800-523-1181

MAINE

American / Vermont Bed & Breakfast
  Reservation Service
(statewide)
P.O. Box ONE
East Fairfield, VT 05448
(802) 827-3827

MARYLAND

Amanda's Bed & Breakfast
  Reservation Service
(Maryland, Virginia, Pennsylvania,
  Delaware, Washington, DC &
  West Virginia)
1428 Park Avenue
Baltimore, MD 21217-4230
(301) 225-0001

MASSACHUSETTS

Bed & Breakfast Agency of Boston
(Greater Boston & Cape Cod)
47 Commercial Wharf
Boston, MA 02110
(617) 720-3540

Bed & Breakfast Marblehead &
    North Shore
(Massachusetts, Vermont & New
    Hampshire)
P.O. Box 172
Beverly, MA 01915
(617) 921–1336

Berkshire Bed & Breakfast Homes
(Massachusetts & New York)
106 South Street
Williamsburg, MA 01096
(413) 268–7244

House Guests of Cape Cod
(Cape Cod, Nantucket & Martha's
    Vineyard)
Box 1881
Orleans, MA 02653
(617) 896–7053

MICHIGAN

Bed & Breakfast in Michigan
(statewide)
P.O. Box 1731
Dearborn, MI 48121
(313) 561–6041

MISSISSIPPI

Lincoln Ltd. Bed & Breakfast
Mississippi Reservation Service
(Mississippi, E. Louisiana, W.
    Alabama & S.E. Tennessee)
Dept. W., Box 3479
Meridian, MS 39303
(601) 482–5483

MISSOURI

Bed & Breakfast Kansas City (Assoc.)
(Kansas & Missouri)
P.O. Box 14781
Lenexa, KS 66215
(913) 888–3636

Bed & Breakfast of St. Louis
1900 Wyoming Street
St. Louis, MO 63122
(314) 965–4328

MONTANA

Bed & Breakfast Western Adventure
(Wyoming & Montana)
P.O. Box 20972
Billings, MT 59104
(406) 259–7993

Bed & Breakfast Travel Connections
    (Assoc.)
(Idaho, Montana, Washington &
    Canada)
5805 Pine Grove Drive
Coeur d'Alene, ID 83814
(208) 765–9090

NEW HAMPSHIRE

American/Vermont Bed & Breakfast
    Reservation Service
(statewide)
P.O. Box ONE
East Fairfield, VT 05448
(802) 827–3827

NEW JERSEY

Bed & Breakfast of New Jersey
(statewide)
Suite 132, 103 Godwin Ave.
Midland Park, NJ 07432
(201) 444–7409

NEW MEXICO

Bed & Breakfast Rocky Mountains
(Colorado, New Mexico & Utah)
P.O. Box 804
Colorado Springs, CO 80901
(719) 630–3433

Mi Casa Su Casa Bed & Breakfast
(Arizona, Utah, California, New Mexico
    & Nevada)
P.O. Box 950
Tempe, AZ 85281
(602) 990–0682

Bed & Breakfast of Santa Fe
(Santa Fe & statewide)
625 Don Felix
Santa Fe, NM 87501
(505) 982–3332

NEW YORK

At Home in New York
(Manhattan, Brooklyn, Queens &
    Staten Island)
P.O. Box 407
New York, NY 10185
(212) 956–3125

B&B Network of New York
134 W. 32nd St., Suite 602
New York, NY 10001
(212) 645–8134

Bed & Breakfast U.S.A., Ltd.
(New York, Massachusetts, Pennsylvania,
    Washington, DC & Florida)
P.O. Box 606
Croton-on-Hudson, NY 10520
(914) 271–6228

Bed & Breakfast Leatherstocking
    Reservation Service
(Central New York)
389 Brockway Road
Frankfort, NY 13340
(315) 733–0040

Blue Heron Bed & Breakfast Reservation
    Service (Assoc.)
384 Pleasant Valley Road
Groton, NY 13073
(607) 898–3814

Rainbow Hospitality Bed & Breakfast
(Western New York State & Southern
    Ontario, Canada)
758 Richmond Avenue
Buffalo, NY 14222
(716) 283–4794

OHIO

Ohio Valley Bed & Breakfast
(Ohio, Kentucky & Indiana)
6876 Taylor Mill Road
Independence, KY 41051
(606) 356–7865

OREGON

Pacific Bed & Breakfast Agency
(Oregon, Washington State & British
  Columbia)
701 N. W. 60th Street
Seattle, WA 98107
(206) 784–0539

PENNSYLVANIA

Bed & Breakfast of Philadelphia
(greater Philadelphia area)
P.O. Box 630
Chester Springs, PA 19425
(215) 827–9650

Bed & Breakfast of S.E. Pennsylvania
146 W. Philadelphia Avenue
Boyertown, PA 19512
(215) 367–4688

Bed & Breakfast Connections
(Philadelphia, Center City, Mainline
  & suburbs)
P.O. Box 21
Devon, PA 19333
(215) 687–3565

Guesthouses
(Pennsylvania, Delaware, New Jersey
  & Maryland)
RD 9
West Chester, PA 19380
(215) 692–4575

Pittsburgh Bed & Breakfast
(Southwestern Pennsylvania)
2190 Ben Franklin Drive
Pittsburgh, PA 15237
(412) 367–8080

RHODE ISLAND

Anna's Victorian Connection
(statewide)
5 Fowler Avenue
Newport, RI 02840
(401) 849–2489

Bed & Breakfast of Rhode Island
(Rhode Island, Massachusetts &
  Connecticut)
P.O. Box 3291-WW
Newport, RI 02840
(401) 849–1298

SOUTH CAROLINA

Historic Charleston Bed & Breakfast
43 Legare Street
Charleston, SC 29401
(803) 722–6606

TENNESSEE

Host Homes of Tennessee
(statewide)
P.O. Box 110227
Nashville, TN 37222–0227
(615) 331–5244

TEXAS

Bed & Breakfast Texas Style, Inc.
(Texas, Oklahoma, Mississippi,
  Georgia & London)
4224 W. Red Bird Lane
Dallas, TX 75237
(214) 298–8586

King William Bed & Breakfast Registry
(San Antonio & New Braunfels)
201 E. Rische
San Antonio, TX 78204
(512) 227–1190

UTAH

Bed & Breakfast Rocky Mountains
(Colorado, New Mexico & Utah)
P.O. Box 804
Colorado Springs, CO 80901
(719) 630–3433

Mi Casa Su Casa Bed & Breakfast
(Arizona, Utah, California, New Mexico
  & Nevada)
P.O. Box 950
Tempe, AZ 85281
(602) 990–0682

VERMONT

Vermont Bed & Breakfast
  Reservation Service
(statewide & New England)
P.O. Box ONE
East Fairfield, VT 05448
(802) 827–3827

VIRGINIA

Bensonhouse
(Williamsburg, Richmond & Northern
  Virginia; specializing in corporate
  relocation)
2036 Monument Avenue
Richmond, VA 23220
(804) 648–7560

Blue Ridge Bed & Breakfast
(Virginia, West Virginia, Maryland &
  Pennsylvania)
Rocks and Rills
Rt. 2, Box 3895
Berryville, VA 22611
(703) 955–1246

Guesthouses Bed & Breakfast, Inc.
(Charlottesville, Albemarle County
  & Luray)
P.O. Box 5737
Charlottesville, VA 22905
(804) 979–7264

WASHINGTON

Bed & Breakfast Travel Connections
  (Assoc.)
(Idaho, Montana, Washington &
  Canada)
5805 Pine Grove Drive
Coeur d'Alene, ID 83814
(208) 765–9090

Pacific Bed & Breakfast Agency
(Oregon, Washington & British
  Columbia)
701 N. W. 60th Street
Seattle, WA 98107
(206) 784–0539

WEST VIRGINIA

Blue Ridge Bed & Breakfast
(Virginia, West Virginia, Maryland &
    Pennsylvania)
Rocks and Rills
Rt. 2, Box 3895
Berryville, VA 22611
(703) 955-1246

WISCONSIN

Wisconsin Southern Lakes Bed &
    Breakfast Reservation Services (Assoc.)
P.O. Box 322
Fontana-On-Geneva Lake, WI 53125
(414) 275-2266

WYOMING

Bed & Breakfast Western Adventure
(Wyoming & Montana)
P.O. Box 20972
Billings, MT 59104
(406) 259-7993

B&B Guidebooks

Each guidebook in the following list contains an alphabetical state-by-state listing of B&Bs, annotated with descriptions of the accommodations, addresses and phone numbers, as well as other pertinent information such as special amenities, rates and activities available in each area. Illustrations in the books range widely; some have only a few black-and-white sketches, others are lavishly illustrated with color photographs. All the books contain B&B reservation agency listings. These books are commonly available for sale at bookstores, and most are updated every other year. Although this is a comprehensive list, it does not represent all the B&B guidebooks on the market. Visit your local bookstore or library to choose your own favorite.

Bernice Chesler. *Bed and Breakfast in New England.* Chester, Connecticut: The Globe Pequot Press. *Over 200 carefully selected B&Bs.*

Bernice Chesler. *Bed and Breakfast in the Mid-Atlantic States.* Chester, Connecticut: The Globe Pequot Press. *Over 200 carefully selected B&Bs.*

Phyllis Featherston & Barbara Ostler. *The Bed & Breakfast Guide.* Norwalk, Connecticut: National Bed & Breakfast Association. *Lists over 1,000 bed & breakfast homes in the United States and Canada.*

R. Gardner. *East Coast Bed and Breakfast Guide.* New York: Prentice Hall Press. *Over 100 B&Bs in New England and the Mid-Atlantic states.*

Pamela Lanier. *Bed & Breakfasts, Inns & Guesthouses.* Santa Fe, New Mexico: John Muir Publications. *Lists over 2,800 inns and over 10,000 private guesthouses in the United States and Canada.*

Toni Sortor. *American Bed & Breakfast.* Nashville, Tennessee: Rutledge Hill Press. *Lists nearly 4,000 bed & breakfasts throughout the United States, Canada, Puerto Rico and the Virgin Islands.*

Courtia Worth. *West Coast Bed and Breakfast Guide.* New York: Prentice Hall Press. *Over 100 B&Bs in California, Oregon and Washington.*

B&B Index

NOTE: Roman type indicates a recipe from the B&B, *italic* identifies the B&B description and **boldface** shows the location of an illustration.

A

Adams Inn, 174, *174,* **174,** 189, 191, 209
 Pumpkin-Cranberry Nut Bread, 189
 Prune-Filled Tea Ring, 209
 Special Dried Apricot Fruit Cake, 174
 Zucchini Pineapple Loaf, 191
Aldrich Guest House, 48, **74,** *98,* **98**
 Sausage Breakfast Casserole, 98
 Sour Cream Pancakes, 48

B

Bailey House, The, 182, *182,* **182,** 188, 193
 Banana Bread, 182
 Date Nut Bread, 193
 Pumpkin Bread, 188
Barley Sheaf Farm, 25, *25,* **25,** 180
 Grapefruit Ambrosia, 25
 Peach Bread, 180
Barnard–Good House, 14, *14,* **14,** 37, 112, 129, **138,** 201, 244
 Apple Cider Soup, 37
 Cottage Cheese Pan Rolls, 201
 Prune Tart, 244
 Shellfish Crepe Pie, 112
 Sweet Potato Pancakes, 129
 Tom's Treat II, 14
Barrow House, 3, 113, 207, *207,* **207, 222**
 Cajun Crabmeat Filo Pastries, 113
 Pecan Nut Roll, 207
Beal House Inn, The, 155, *155,* **155, 164**
 Popovers, 155
Bed n' Breakfast-Still Country, 47, *47,* 117
 Pearl's Homemade Sausage, 117
 Pearl's Prize-Winning Pancake Mix, 47
Beech Tree Manor, 111, *111,* **111**
 Eggs Pacifica, 111
Bells Bed & Breakfast, The, **6–7,** 9, *9,* **9,** 33, 72, 88, 89, 117, 125, 197, 247, 248
 Baked Ham and Cheese Sandwich, 89
 Blintz Casserole, 72
 Chipped Beef and Egg Bake, 88

Bells Bed & Breakfast *(continued)*
 Ice Cream Strudel, 197
 Makes-Its-Own-Crust Cherry Cobbler, 247
 Orange Julius, 9
 Rice Pudding, 248
 Sausage & Wild Rice, 117
 Scrubbed & Tubbed, Boiled, Baked, & Glazed Oranges, 33
 Tennessee Gravy & Biscuits, 125
Betsy's Bed & Breakfast, 157, *157,* **157**
 Betsy's Biscuits, 157
Borgman's Bed & Breakfast, 251, *251*
 Divinity Candy, 251
Boyer YL Ranch, 82, *82*
 South-of-the-Border Scrambled Eggs, 82
Briar Rose, 224, *224*
 Lemon Curd, 224
Bridgeford Cottage, 58, *58,* **58,** 104, 156, 236
 Apple Fritters, 58
 Bridgeford Biscuit Mix,156
 Hershey Brownies and Icing, 236
 Zucchini Crescent Pie, 104
Brigham Street Inn, 149, *149,* **149**
 Bran Muffins, 149
Britt House, 16, *16,* **16,** 180, **226–227,** 229, 231, 232, 243, 248
 Apple Crisp, 248
 Gingies, 231
 Hot Chocolate Mix, 16
 Hot Spiced Cider, 16
 Irish Soda Bread, 180
 Lemon Bars, 232
 Olive Tea Sandwiches, 229
 Pear Pie, 243
 Radish Tea Sandwiches, 229
 Walnut Dream Bars, 232
Bufflehead Cove Inn, The, 63, *63,* **63**
 Green-Apple Stuffed French Toast, 63

C

Campbell Ranch Inn, The, 206, *206,* **206**
 Honey Wheat Bread, 206
Canterbury Inn, 36, *36,* **36**
 Norwegian Fruit Soup, 36
Capers–Motte House, The, 21, *21,* **21,** 137, 156
 Aunt Marte's Cheese Straws, 137
 Cream Cheese Biscuits, 156
 Grapefruit with Strawberries, 21

Captain Jefferds Inn, **2,** 15, *15,* **15,** 80, **162**
 Hot Mulled Wine, 15
 Zucchini Frittata, 80
Carlisle House Inn, The, 109, 202, *202,* **202**
 Crab Quiche, 109
 English Muffin Loaves, 202
Carolina House, 229, 230, *230,* 232, 244, 245
 Cucumber Bacon Tea Sandwiches, 230
 Curried Chicken Tea Sandwiches, 229
 Creamy Chocolate Tartlets, 245
 Excellent Gingersnaps with Apricot Cheddar Spread, 232
 Maple Mousse Tartlets, 244
Carriage House, The, 30, *30,* **30,** 209
 Angel Biscuits, 209
 Hot Spiced Fruit, 30
Carter House, **18,** 34, *34,* **34,** 35, **35, 42,** 88, 112, 129, 136, 148, 241, 242, 243
 Almond Pear Tart, 241
 Apple Almond Tart, 243
 Apple Philo Tart, 242
 Baked Apples in Carmel Sauce, 35
 Eggs Jerusalem in an Orange Champagne Sauce, 88
 Morning Carrots, 136
 Morning Glory Muffins, 148
 Morning Potatoes, 129
 Pears Poached in Wine Sauce, 34
 Smoked Salmon Egg Crepes, 112
Casa de Solana, 62, *62,* **62**
 Lost Bread, 62
Catlin–Abbott House, The, 99, *99,* **99**
 Catlin–Abbott Breakfast Bake, 99
Caverly Farm and Orchard B&B, 204, 216, *216*
 Portuguese Egg Bread, 204
 Raspberry Jam, 216
Cedar Knoll Farm, 24, *24,* **24,** 132, 240
 Golden Fruit Cup, 24
 Lima Bean Casserole, 132
 Sour Cream Raisin Pie 240
Chaffin Farms B&B, 145, *145,* **145**
 Blueberry Muffins, 145
Country House Inn, 52, *52,* **52**
 Apple Pancake, 52
Countryside B&B, 187, *187,* **187**
 Countryside's Apple Bread, 187
Crondahl's Bed & Breakfast, 45, 142, *142,* **142**
 Banana Bran Muffins, 142

Crondahl's B&B *(continued)*
Sourdough Hotcakes, 45

D

Dierker House, 134, *134,* **134**
Rellenos Dierker House, 134
Dove Inn, The, 65, *65,* **65,** 81
Apple French Toast with Cottage
Cheese, 65
Garden Scramble, 81
Dunbar House, 1880, 10, *10,* **10,** 132,
169, 173
Bacon-and-Cream-Topped Tomatoes,
132
Buttermilk Poppyseed Cake, 169
Orange Julius Spritzer, 10
Pumpkin Apple Cake, 173

E

Eastover Farm B&B, 185, *185,* **185**
Lemon Layer Loaf, 185
Edith Palmer's Country Inn, 153,
153, **153**
Pumpkin Muffins, 153
1859 Guest House, The, 141, 217, *217*
Apricot-Pineapple Jam, 217
Maine Blueberry Muffins with
Topping, 141
1837 Bed & Breakfast, 188, 225,
225, **225**
Apple Nut Bread, 188
Lemon Curd, 225
Elizabeth Street Guest House, 57, *57,* 84
Dutch Babies with Apples, 57
Scotch Eggs, 84
English House Bed and Breakfast, The,
94, *94,* **94,** 109, 204, 231
Crumpets, 204
English House 24-Hour Soufflé, 94
Kedgeree, 109
Shortbread, 231

F

Fala Bed & Breakfast, 83, *83*
Fresh Vegetable & Herb Omelet, 83
Felshaw Tavern, 146, *146,* **146**
Felshaw Tavern Bran Muffins, 146
Ferris Mansion, 177, *177,* **177,** 193
English Morning Cake, 177
Grape Nut Bread, 193
Fleming Jones Homestead, The, 81,
122, *122,* **122**
Baked Herb Cheese Eggs, 81
Herbed Sausage Cheese Balls, 122

Fool's Gold, 159, *159*
Scones, 159
Fowler House, The, 64, *64,* **64,** 148, 184
Dover Toast, 64
Dr. Fowler's Muffins, 148
Lemon Yogurt Bread, 184
Frederick Fitting House, The, 103,
103, **103,** 152, 172, 173, 189, 192,
236, 247
Almond Tea Bread, 192
Cranberry Nut Bread, 189
Fresh Apple Walnut Cake, 172
Lemon Pie, 247
Pecan Squares, 236
Raisin-Filled Coffeecake, 173
Sausage-Filled Crepes, 103
Sweet Potato Muffins, 152

G

Gardner House, 150, *150,* **150,** 161,
210–11, 221
Cranberry-Apple Muffins, 150
Dad's Scotch Scones, 161
Lake District Lime Ice, 221
General Hooker's House, **186,** 194,
194, **194, 195**
Onion-Cheese Bread, 194
Gingerbread Mansion, 183, *183,* **183,**
184, 188, 189, **238**
Harvest Apple Cake, 188
Pumpkin Gingerbread, 189
Valerie's Sour Cream Banana Bread,
183
Very Lemony Lemon Bread, 184
Glendeven, 31, *31,* **31,** 168
Baked Apples, 31
Coffeecake Glendeven, 168
Grant Corner Inn, **8,** 14, 49, 154,
154, **154**
Cranberry Banana Frappé, 14
Jalapeño Cheese Muffins, 154
Pumpkin Raisin Pancakes, 49
Green Gables Inn, The, 135, *135,* **135**
Baked Mushrooms, 135
Green Meadow Ranch, 147, *147,* **147**
Bran Muffins, 147
Greenbriar Bed & Breakfast Inn, 233,
233, **233,** 242
Apple Raisin Nut Tart, 242
Pride of Idaho Cookies, 233

H

Harrison House, 214, *214,* **214**
Sand Plum Jam, 214
Hawthorne Inn, 170, *170,* 180, 193

Hawthorne Inn *(continued)*
Brown Breakfast Bread, 193
Morning Cake Delight with
Topping, 170
Pear Breakfast Cake, 180
Hazlewood House, 97, *97,* **97**
Texas Hazlewood Quiche, 97
Heart of the Hills Inn, 148, 195, *195*
Bran Pineapple Muffins, 148
Poppyseed Bread, 195
Heartstone Inn, The, 84, 132, 160,
160, **160,** 161, 236
British Broiled Tomatoes, 132
English Currant Buns, 161
English Gingerbread, 236
Scotch Eggs, 84
Welsh Country Scones, 160
Hedgerow B&B, 219, *219,* **219**
Hot Pepper Jelly, 219
Heirloom, The, 91, *91,* **91,** 197
Aunt Marie's Cheese Soufflé, 91
L'Orange Fromage Coffee Pastry, 197
Hersey House, 5, 33, 45, 54, *54,* **54,**
80, 96
Avocado Omelet, 80
Baked Pears Hersey, 33
Egg Soufflé, 96
Gingerbread Pancakes, 45
Puffed Pear Pancakes, 54
Quiche Lorraine, 96
Hidden Pond Farm, 123, *123*
Ham Loaf with Mustard Sauce, 123
High Meadows Bed and Breakfast,
143, *143*
Blueberry Muffins, 143
Hillcrest House, 60, *60,* 156
Buttermilk Biscuits, 156
Hillcrest House Waffles, 60
Hilo B&B, 186, *186*
Mango Bread, 186
Holden House, 102, *102,* **102**
Crepe Cups, 102
Holland House, 13, 70, *70,* **70**
Coffee Mocha Continental, 13
Night-Before French Toast Casserole,
70
Hollinger House, 40, *40,* **40**
Baked Oatmeal, 40
House on the Hill, 73, *73,* **73**
Cheese Blintzes, 73
House on the Hill, The, 26, *26,* **26**
Michigan Sesquicentennial Fruit and
Yogurt, 26
Hynson Tourist Home, 213, *213*
Frozen Strawberry Jam, 213

I

Inn at Mitchell House, The, 69, 130, *130*, **130**, 169
  Christel's Apple Cake, 169
  Dover Potatoes, 130
  Super French Toast à L'Orange, 69
Inn on Cove Hill, 141, 144, 151, *151*, **151**, **198–199**, 210211
  Banana Muffins, 141
  Moist Bran Muffins, 144
  Orange Buttermilk Muffins, 151
Inn on Kelley's Island, The, 101, *101*, **101**
  Reuben Brunch Casserole, 101

J

Jackson Street Inn, The, 220, *220*, **220**
  Apple Butter, 220
John Palmer House, The, 71, *71*, **71**, **106–107**
  Blueberry Crepes, 71
June's Bed & Breakfast, 239, *239*
  Graham Cracker Crumb Fruit Cake, 239

K

Kenniston Hill Inn, 28, *28*, **28**, 69
  Ellen's Blueberry Delight, 28
  Peaches-and-Cream French Toast, 69

L

Lafayette House, 96, 100, *100*, 184, 192
  Butter Pecan Bread, 192
  Marmalade Bread, 184
  Sausage and Egg Brunch Casserole, 100
  Sausage Mushroom Quiche, 96
Little Piney Canoe Resort, 29, *29*, 49
  Sautéed Apples, 29
  Three-Grain Griddle Cakes, 49
Log Castle, 55, *55*, **55**
  Cottage Cheese Hotcakes, 55
Longswamp Bed & Breakfast, 61, 249, *249*
  Pumpkin Waffles, 61
  Strawberry Shortcake, 249
Lowenstein–Long House, The, 118, *118*, **118**
  Sausage & Grits Casserole, 118

M

MacMaster House, 93, *93*, **93**
  Brunch Egg Casserole, 93

Madewood Plantation House, 11, *11*, **11**, 33, **114–115**
  Mimosas, 11
  Pumpkin Madewood LaFourche, 33
Magic Canyon Ranch, 110, *110*
  Magic Canyon Quiche, 110
Manor House, 61, 96, **126–127**, 170, 171, *171*, **200**
  Orange Waffles, 61
  Poached Eggs with Lemon-Chive Sauce, 96
  Rhubarb Coffeecake, 171
Maple Crest Farm, 46, *46*, **46**, 169
  Buttermilk Pancakes with Blueberries, 46
  Cinnamon Coffeecake, 169
Maple Lodge, 203, *203*
  Brioche, 203
Marjon Bed & Breakfast, 56, *56*, **56**
  Aebleskivers, 56
Marlow House, 120, *120*, **120**
  Sausage Bake, 120
Mentone Bed & Breakfast, 121, *121*, **121**, 136
  Artichoke Squares, 136
  Oktoberfest Sausage, 121
Meramec Farm Stay B&B, 124, *124*, 137, 221
  Baked Country Ham with Mustard Glaze, 124
  Baked Garlic Cheese Grits, 137
  Carol's Homemade Mustard, 221
Milburn House B&B, 50, *50*, 141
  Banana-Praline Muffins 141
  Oatmeal Pancakes, 50
Morton Street Bed & Breakfast, 12, *12*, **12**
  Cranapple Tea, 12
Murphy's B&B, 13, *13*, **13**, 22, 45, **47**, 61, 85, 109, 113, **118**, **123**, 125, **143**, 152, 192, 196, 201, 221, 241, 245
  Applesauce Oatmeal Muffins with Maple Glaze, 152
  Buttermilk Pancakes, 45
  Chess Pie à la Watson, 241
  Chocolate Tea Bread, 192
  Chocolate Waffles, 61
  Cornbread, 196
  Corned Beef Hash, 125
  Eggs Benedict, 85
  Finnan Haddie, 113
  Lemonade, 13
  Lobster Newburg, 113
  Lobster Quiche, 109
  Martha Murphy's Marvelous Melba Sauce, 221

Murphy's B&B *(continued)*
  Peach Melba Tart, 245
  Sticky-Top Cinnamon Rolls, 201

N

Nuuanu B&B, 234, *234*
  Pineapple Bars, 234

O

O'Connor's Guest House B&B, 84, 190, *190*, **190**
  Carrot-Pineapple Bread, 190
  Egg Strata, 84
Oak Square, 137, 158, *158*, **158**, 238, 252
  Cheese Grits, 137
  Old-Fashioned Nut Cake, 238
  Old-Fashioned Syllabub, 252
  Old-Fashioned White Cake, 238
  Southern Buttermilk Biscuits, 158
Oak Tree Inn, The, 144, 175, *175*, **175**
  Oak Tree Coffeecake, 175
  Oak Tree Granola Muffins, 144
Old Pioneer Garden, 49, 131, *131*, **131**
  Fruit Pancakes, 49
  Potato Pancakes, 131
Old Talbott Tavern, 90, *90*, **90**
  Sausage Soufflé, 90

P

Palmer's Chart House, 129, 136, 222, *222*
  Bleu Cheese Mushrooms, 136
  Parmesan Potatoes, 129
  Rhubarb Jam, 222
Parsonage 1908, The, 237, *237*, **237**
  Spice Cake, 237
Parsonage 1901, The, 22, *22*, 231
  Favorite Fruit Sundae, 22
  Scotch Shortbread Cookies, 231
Pat Wilson's Bed & Breakfast-Valdez, 167, *167*, 168
  Blueberry Coffeecake, 167
  Sour Cream Vanilla Coffeecake, 168
Pentwater Inn Bed & Breakfast, 67, *67*, **67**
  Skiers French Toast, 67
Phoenix House, 32, *32*, 89, 204, 221
  Apple Compote, 32
  Cinnamon Bread, 204
  Crème Fraiche, 221
  Ham and Cheese Soufflé, 89
Pleasant View B&B, 78, *78*
  Fancy Egg Scramble, 78

Pukalani B&B, 235, *235*
  Coconut-Macadamia Nut Bars, 235
Pullman Inn B&B, The, 17, *17*, **17**,
    117
  Hot Christmas Wassail, 17
  Walnut Sausage Rolls, 117
Purple Mountain Lodge, 176, *176*, 196
  Coffee Strudel, 196
  Oatmeal Cake, 176

R

Radcliffe Cross, 89, 223, *223*, **223**
  Ham and Eggs au Gratin, 89
  Lemon Butter, 223
Raford House, 218, *218*, **218**
  Prickly Pear Jelly, 218
Richards' B&B, 72, 87, *87*, **87**, 108
  Blueberry-Sauced Blintzes, 72
  Eggs Florentine, 87
River Haven Bed & Breakfast, 208, *208*
  Cream Cheese Sweetbread, 208
River Song, 53, *53*, **53**
  Baked Apple Pancake, 53
River Street Inn, The, 105, *105*, **105**, 172
  Apple Raisin Coffeecake, 172
  Italian Spinach Pie, 105
Robin's Nest Inn, 79, *79*, **79**, 104
  Cheesy Scrambled Eggs in Puffy
    Shell, 79
  Hot Chicken Salad Crepes, 104
Rogers House B&B, 23, *23*, **23**, 81, 248
  Cla Foutis, 248
  Galliano Fruit Cups, 23
  Jana's Käse und Eieer, 81
RoyAl Carter House, 250, *250*, **250**
  Fresh Berry Cobbler, 250

S

St. Charles Avenue House, 215, *215*,
    215, 252
  Southern Fig Preserves, 215
  Southern Pralines, 252
Savery Creek Thoroughbred Ranch,
    59, *59*
  Outlaw Waffles, 59
1735 House, The, 181, *181*, **181**
  Sour Cream Cinnamon Loaves, 181
Singleton House, 178, *178*, **178**
  Cous Cous Cake, 178
Skoglund Farm B&B, 48, *48*, **48**
  Swedish Pancakes, 48
Small Wonder B&B, 38, *38*, **38**, 39, **39**
  Homestyle Granola Cereal, 39
  Hot Apple Cereal, 38
Southern Hotel, The, 37, 95, *95*, **95**
  Banana Bisque with Cinnamon
    Croutons, 37
  Miss Dodie's Eggs, 95
Spahn's Big Horn Mountain Bed &
    Breakfast, 77, *77*, **77**
  Creamy Scambled Eggs, 77
Spring House, 133, *133*, **133**
  Corn Fritters, 133
Stagecoach Stop, The, 92, *92*, **92**
  Cheese Soufflé, 92
Starr Cottage Inn, 41, *41*, **41**
  Breakfast Parfait, 41
Strawberry Inn, The, 179, *179*, **179**, 196
  Soldier's Bread, 196
  Strawberry Bread, 179

T

Teton Tree House, 165, *165*, **165**, 191
  Swedish Buttermilk Coffeecake, 165
  Zucchini Bread, 191
Toccoa River Hideaway, 86, *86*, **86**,
    205, 240
  Eggs Paula, 86
  Granny Smith Apple Butter Tart, 240
  Sourdough Chocolate Almond
    Bread, 205
  Sourdough Raisin Bread, 205
Tree House in the Park, **50**, 51, *51*, **51**
  Pancakes Supreme, 51

V

Victorian Bed & Breakfast Inn, 68, *68*, **68**
  French Toast Puff, 68
Victorian Inn, The, 37, 246, *246*, **246**
  Chocolate Pecan Pie, 246
  Summer Fruit Soup, 37
Voss Inn B&B, The, 27, *27*, **27**, 80
  Fried Nectarines, 27
  Voss Inn Baked Eggs, 80

W

Wal–Mec Farm, 144, 166, *166*,
    166–167, 191
  Raisin Bran Muffins, 144
  Sour Cream Coffeecake, 166
  Zucchini Bread, 191
Williams House B&B, 66, *66*, **66**,
    85, **212**
  Baked Toast Almondine, 66
  Eggs Benedict, 85

General Index

This index does not include the B&Bs listed in this book; an index for them can be found on page 266.

A

Aebleskivers, 56
Almond(s)
  Tea Bread, 192
  Apple Tart, 243
  Baked Toast Almondine, 66
  Pear Tart, 241
  Sourdough Chocolate Almond
    Bread, 205

Almond Pear Tart, 241
Almond Tea Bread, 192
Angel Biscuits, 209
Apple(s)
  Almond Tart, 243
  Baked, 31
  Baked with Caramel Sauce, 35
  bread, 187, 188
  Butter, 220
  Christel's Apple Cake, 169
  Cla Foutis, 248
  Cider Soup, 37
  Compote, 32
  Cranberry-Apple Muffins, 150

Apple(s) *(continued)*
  Crisp, 248
  Dutch Babies with Apples, 57
  French Toast with Cottage Cheese, 65
  Fritters, 58
  Granny Smith Apple Butter Tart, 240
  Green-Apple Stuffed French Toast, 63
  Harvest Cake, 188
  Hot Apple Cereal, 38
  Hot Spiced Fruit, 30
  Nut Bread, 188
  Oktoberfest Sausage, 121
  pancake, 51, 53, 52
  Pumpkin Apple Cake, 173

Apple(s) *(continued)*
   Philo Tart, 242
   Raisin Coffeecake, 172
   Raisin Nut Tart, 242
   Sautéed, 29
   Sourdough Bread, 205
   Walnut Cake, 172
Apple Almond Tart, 243
Apple Butter, 220
Apple Cider Soup, 37
Apple Compote, 32
Apple Crisp, 248
Apple French Toast with Cottage
   Cheese, 65
Apple Fritters, 58
Apple Nut Bread, 188
Apple Pancake, 52
Apple Philo Tart, 242
Apple Raisin Coffeecake, 172
Apple Raisin Nut Tart, 242
Applesauce
   Oatmeal Muffins with Maple Glaze,
      152
   Old-Fashioned Nut Cake, 238
   Pearl's Prize-Winning Pancake Mix, 47
Applesauce Oatmeal Muffins with
   Maple Glaze, 152
Apricot(s)
   Blintz Casserole, 72
   Coffee Strudel, 196
   Cheddar Spread, 232
   Ice Cream Strudel, 197
   -Pineapple Jam, 217
   Special Dried Apricot Fruitcake, 174
Apricot-Pineapple Jam, 217
Artichoke(s)
   Eggs Jerusalem in an Orange
      Champagne Sauce, 88
   Squares, 136
Artichoke Squares, 136
Aunt Marie's Cheese Soufflé, 91
Aunt Marte's Cheese Straws, 137
Avocado(s)
   Omelet, 80
   Texas Hazlewood Quiche, 97
Avocado Omelet, 80

B

Bacon
   -and-Cream-Topped Tomatoes, 132
   Brunch Egg Casserole, 93
   Cheesy Scrambled Eggs in a Puffy
      Shell, 79
   Crepe Cups, 102
   Cucumber Bacon Tea Sandwiches, 230
   Garden Scramble, 81

Bacon *(continued)*
   how to cook, 116
   Lima Bean Casserole, 132
   Quiche Lorraine, 96
   Voss Inn Baked Eggs, 80
Bacon-and-Cream-Topped Tomatoes,
   132
Baked Apples, 31
Baked Apples in Caramel Sauce, 35
Baked Apple Pancake, 53
Baked Country Ham with Mustard
   Glaze, 124
Baked Garlic Cheese Grits, 137
Baked Ham and Cheese Sandwich, 89
Baked Herb Cheese Eggs, 81
Baked Mushrooms, 135
Baked Oatmeal, 40
Baked Pears Hersey, 33
Baked Toast Almondine, 66
Banana(s)
   Aebleskivers, 56
   Bisque with Cinnamon Croutons, 37
   bread, 182, 183
   Cranberry Banana Frappé, 14
   Favorite Fruit Sundae, 22
   Golden Fruit Cup, 24
   muffins, 142
   Pancakes, 45
   -Praline Muffins, 141
   serving suggestions, 20
Banana Bisque with Cinnamon
   Croutons, 37
Banana Bran Muffins, 142
Banana Bread, 182
Banana Muffins, 141
Banana-Praline Muffins, 141
Bar Cookies
   Coconut-Macadamia Nut, 235
   Lemon, 232
   Pecan, 236
   Pineapple, 234
   Shortbread, 231
   Walnut Dream, 232
Betsy's Biscuits, 157
Biscuits
   Angel, 209
   Betsy's, 157
   Bridgeford Mix, 156
   buttermilk, 156, 158
   Cream Cheese, 156
   Strawberry Shortcake, 249
   Tennessee Gravy and, 125
   tips on making, 140
Blackberry(ies)
   Fresh Berry Cobbler, 250
Bleu Cheese Mushrooms, 136
Blintz Casserole, 72

Blintzes
   Blueberry-Sauced, 72
   Casserole, 72
   Cheese, 73
   tips on making, 44
Blueberry(ies)
   Buttermilk Pancakes with, 46
   coffeecake, 167, 175
   Cous Cous Cake, 178
   Crepes, 71
   Ellen's Blueberry Delight, 28
   Galliano Fruit Cups, 23
   Michigan Sesquicentennial Fruit and
      Yogurt, 26
   muffins, 141, 143, 145
   Outlaw Waffles, 59
   -Sauced Blintzes, 72
Blueberry Coffeecake, 167
Blueberry Crepes, 71
Blueberry Muffins, 143, 145
Blueberry-Sauced Blintzes, 72
Bran Muffins, 147, 149
Bran Pineapple Muffins, 148
Bread(s), unyeasted
   almond, 192
   apple, 188
   banana, 182, 183
   Brown Breakfast, 193
   Carrot-Pineapple, 190
   chocolate, 192
   cranberry, 189
   Date Nut, 193
   Grape Nut, 193
   Irish Soda, 180
   lemon, 184, 185
   Mango, 186
   Marmalade, 184
   Onion-Cheese, 194
   Peach, 180
   pecan, 192
   Poppyseed, 195
   pumpkin, 188, 189
   Soldier's, 196
   Sour Cream Cinnamon, 181
   zucchini, 191
Bread(s), yeasted
   Brioche, 203
   cinnamon, 204
   English Muffin Loaves, 202
   Honey Wheat, 206
   Portuguese Egg, 204
   Sourdough, 205
Breakfast Parfait, 41
Bridgeford Biscuit Mix, 156
Brioche, 203
British Broiled Tomatoes, 132
Brown Breakfast Bread, 193

Brownies, 236
Brunch Egg Casserole, 93
Buns
    English Currant, 161
Butter
    Apple, 220
    Lemon, 223
Butter Pecan Bread, 192
Buttermilk Biscuits, 156
Buttermilk Pancakes, 45
Buttermilk Pancakes with Blueberries, 46
Buttermilk Poppyseed Cake, 169

C

Cajun Crabmeat Filo Pastries, 113
Cake(s)
    Graham Cracker Crumb, 239
    Old-Fashioned Nut, 238
    Old-Fashioned White, 238
    Spice, 237
Coffeecake(s)
    apple, 169, 172, 173
    blueberry, 167, 175, 178
    buttermilk, 165, 169
    cinnamon, 168, 169
    English Morning, 177
    Dried Fruit, 174
    Morning Cake Delight with
        Topping, 170
    Oatmeal, 176
    Pear, 180
    poppyseed, 169
    Pumpkin Apple, 173
    raisin, 172, 173
    Rhubarb, 171
    Sour Cream, 166
Candy
    Divinity, 251
    Southern Pralines, 252
Carol's Homemade Mustard, 221
Carrot(s)
    Eggs Jerusalem in an Orange
        Champagne Sauce, 88
    Morning, 136
    Morning Glory Muffins, 148
    -Pineapple Bread, 190
Carrot-Pineapple Bread, 190
Catlin-Abbott Breakfast Bake, 99
Cereal
    Baked Oatmeal, 40
    Breakfast Parfait, 41
    Homestyle Granola, 39
    Hot Apple Cereal, 38
Champagne
    Mimosas, 11
    sauce, 88

Cheese
    Artichoke Squares, 136
    Aunt Marte's Straws, 137
    Baked Mushrooms, 135
    Bleu Cheese Mushrooms, 136
    British Broiled Tomatoes, 132
    Excellent Gingersnaps with Apricot
        Cheddar Spread, 232
    Grits, 137
    Herbed Sausage Balls, 122
    Jalapeño Muffins, 154
    Lima Bean Casserole, 132
    Onion Bread, 194
    Parmesan Potatoes, 129
    Rellenos Dierker House, 134
Cheese and eggs
    Aunt Marie's Soufflé, 91
    baked, 80, 81
    Brunch Casserole, 93
    Catlin-Abbott Breakfast Bake, 99
    Eggs Florentine, 87
    Egg Soufflé, 96
    Egg Strata, 84
    English House 24-Hour Soufflé, 94
    Fancy Egg Scramble, 78
    Fresh Vegetable & Herb Omelet, 83
    Garden Scramble, 81
    Ham and Eggs au Gratin, 89
    Ham and Cheese Soufflé, 89
    Jana's Käse Und Eieer, 81
    Miss Dodie's Eggs, 95
    quiche, (see Quiches)
    Reuben Brunch Casserole, 101
    Sausage & Egg Brunch Casserole, 100
    Sausage-Filled Crepes, 103
    Sausage Breakfast Casserole, 98
    Sausage Soufflé, 90
    Scrambled Eggs in a Puffy Shell, 79
    Scotch Eggs — Elizabeth St., 84
    soufflé, (see Soufflés)
    Zucchini Frittata, 80
Cheese, cottage
    Apple French Toast with, 65
    Blintz Casserole, 72
    Blueberry Crepes, 71
    Cheese Blintzes, 73
    Hot Cakes, 55
    yeasted rolls, 201
Cheese, cream
    Biscuits, 156
    Blintz Casserole, 72
    Cajun Crabmeat Filo Pastries, 113
    Creamy Scrambled Eggs, 77
    Green-Apple Stuffed French Toast, 63
    L'Orange Fromage Coffee Pastry, 197
    Oak Tree Coffeecake, 175
    Sausage-Filled Crepes, 103
    Sweet Bread, 208

Cheese, ricotta
    Blueberry-Sauced Blintzes, 72
    Dr. Fowler's Muffins, 148
    Green-Apple Stuffed French Toast, 63
Cheese Blintzes, 73
Cheese Grits, 137
Cheese Soufflé, 92
Cheesy Scrambled Eggs in Puffy Shell, 79
Cherry(ies)
    Apricot-Pineapple Jam, 217
    Buttermilk Pancakes, 45
    Coffee Strudel, 196
    Makes-Its-Own-Crust Cobbler, 247
    Norwegian Fruit Soup, 36
    Old-Fashioned Nut Cake, 238
Chess Pie à la Watson, 241
Chicken
    Curried Chicken Tea Sandwiches, 229
    Hot Chicken Salad Crepes, 104
Chipped Beef and Egg Bake, 88
Chocolate
    Coffee Mocha Continental, 13
    Creamy Tartlets, 245
    Sourdough Almond Bread, 205
    Hershey Brownies and Icing, 236
    Hot Chocolate Mix, 16
    Pecan Pie, 246
    Tea Bread, 192
    Waffles, 61
Chocolate chips
    Pride of Idaho Cookies, 233
Chocolate Pecan Pie, 246
Chocolate Tea Bread, 192
Chocolate Waffles, 61
Christel's Apple Cake, 169
Cider
    Apple Butter, 220
    Apple Cider Soup, 37
    Hot Spiced, 16
Cinnamon
    Bread, 204
    Sticky-Top Cinnamon Rolls, 201
    Coffeecake, 169
    croutons, 37
    Sour Cream Cinnamon Loaves, 181
Cinnamon sticks
    Cranapple Tea, 12
    Hot Christmas Wassail, 17
    Hot Mulled Wine, 15
    Hot Spiced Cider, 16
    Hot Spiced Fruit, 30
Cinnamon Bread, 204
Cinnamon Coffeecake, 169
Cla Foutis, 248
Cocoa, 16
Coconut
    Breakfast Parfait, 41

Coconut *(continued)*
    Favorite Fruit Sundae, 22
    Grapefruit Ambrosia, 25
    Homestyle Granola Cereal, 39
    -Macadamia Nut Bars, 235
    Morning Glory Muffins, 148
    Pride of Idaho Cookies, 233
Coconut-Macadamia Nut Bars, 235
Coffee
    how to prepare, 8
    Mocha Continental, 13
Coffee Mocha Continental, 13
Coffee Strudel, 196
Coffeecake Glendeven, 168
Cookies
    bar, (see Bar Cookies)
    Gingersnaps, 232
    Gingies, 231
    Pride of Idaho, 233
    Scotch Shortbread, 231
Corn Fritters, 133
Cornbread, 196
Corned Beef
    Hash, 125
    Reuben Brunch Casserole, 101
Corned Beef Hash, 125
Cornmeal
    bread, 196
    Fruit Pancakes, 49
Cottage Cheese Hotcakes, 55
Cottage Cheese Pan Rolls, 201
Countryside's Apple Bread, 187
Cous Cous Cake, 178
Crab Quiche, 109
Crabmeat
    Cajun Crabmeat Filo Pastries, 113
    Quiche, 109
    Shellfish Crepe Pie, 112
Cranapple Tea, 12
Cranberry(ies)
    -Apple Muffins, 150
    Cranapple Tea, 12
    Cranberry Banana Frappé, 14
    Hot Spiced Fruit, 30
    Nut Bread, 189
    Pumpkin-Cranberry Nut Bread, 189
Cranberry-Apple Muffins, 150
Cranberry Banana Frappé, 14
Cranberry Nut Bread, 189
Cream Cheese Biscuits, 156
Cream Cheese Sweet Bread, 208
Creamy Chocolate Tartlets, 245
Creamy Scrambled Eggs, 77
Crème Fraiche, 221
Crepe(s)
    basic recipe, 72
    Blueberry, 71

Crepe(s) *(continued)*
    Blueberry-Sauced Blintzes, 72
    Cheese Blintzes, 73
    Cups, 102
    egg, 71, 112
    Hot Chicken Salad, 104
    Sausage-Filled, 103
    Shellfish Crepe Pie, 112
    Smoked Salmon Egg Crepes, 112
Crepe Cups, 102
Crumpets, 204
Cucumber and Bacon Tea Sandwiches, 230
Curried Chicken Tea Sandwiches, 229
Currant(s)
    Baked Apples, 31
    Buns, 161
    Norwegian Fruit Soup, 36
    Scones, 159
    Welsh Country Scones, 160

D

Dad's Scotch Scones, 161
Date(s)
    Chocolate Tea Bread, 192
    Graham Cracker Crumb Fruitcake, 239
    Nut Bread, 193
Date Nut Bread, 193
Dill
    Cottage Cheese Pan Rolls, 201
Divinity Candy, 251
Dover Potatoes, 130
Dover Toast, 64
Dr. Fowler's Muffins, 148
Dutch Babies with Apples, 57

E

Egg(s)
    baked, 80, 81
    Benedict, 85
    Baked Ham and Cheese Sandwich, 89
    Brunch Casserole, 93
    Chipped Beef and Egg Bake, 88
    crepes, 71
    Crepe Cups, 102
    Florentine, 87
    Ham and Eggs au Gratin, 89
    how to prepare, 76
    Jana's Käse und Eieer, 81
    Jerusalem in an Orange Champagne Sauce, 88
    Miss Dodie's Eggs, 95
    omelet, (see Omelets)
    poached, 85, 86, 96
    Paula, 86

Egg(s) *(continued)*
    Reuben Brunch Casserole, 101
    Sausage Breakfast Casserole, 98
    Sausage and Egg Brunch Casserole, 100
    scrambled, 77, 78, 79, 81, 82
    Scotch, 84
    soufflé, (see Soufflés)
    Strata, 84
    with Lemon-Chive Sauce, 96
    with shrimp, 111
Egg Soufflé, 96
Egg Strata, 84
Eggs Benedict, 85
Eggs Florentine, 87
Eggs Jerusalem in an Orange Champagne Sauce, 88
Eggs Pacifica, 111
Eggs Paula, 86
Ellen's Blueberry Delight, 28
English Currant Buns, 161
English Gingerbread, 236
English House 24-Hour Soufflé, 94
English Morning Cake, 177
English Muffin Loaves, 202
Excellent Gingersnaps with Apricot Cheddar Spread, 232

F

Fancy Egg Scramble, 78
Favorite Fruit Sundae, 22
Felshaw Tavern Bran Muffins, 146
Finnan Haddie, 113
Feta Cheese
    Eggs Florentine, 87
Figs
    Preserves, 215
Filo
    Apple Tart, 242
    Cajun Crabmeat Pastries, 113
Finnan Haddie, 113
French Toast
    Apple with Cottage Cheese, 65
    Baked Almondine, 66
    Dover Toast, 64
    Green-Apple Stuffed, 63
    Lost Bread, 62
    Night-Before Casserole, 70
    Peaches-and-Cream, 69
    Puff, 68
    Skiers, 67
    Super à L'Orange, 69
French Toast Puff, 68
Fresh Apple Walnut Cake, 172
Fresh Berry Cobbler, 250
Fresh Vegetable & Herb Omelet, 83

Fried Nectarines, 27
Frozen Strawberry Jam, 213
Fruit Pancakes, 49

G

Galliano
    sauce, 23
Galliano Fruit Cups, 23
Garden Scramble, 81
Gingerbread
    English, 236
    Pancakes, 45
    Pumpkin, 189
Gingerbread Pancakes, 45
Gingies, 231
Gingersnaps
    Gingies, 231
    with Apricot Cheddar Spread, 232
Golden Fruitcup, 24
Graham Cracker Crumb Fruit Cake, 239
Grand Marnier
    Super French Toast à L'Orange, 69
Granny Smith Apple Butter Tart, 240
Granola
    Breakfast Parfait, 41
    Homestyle Granola Cereal, 39
    Oak Tree Granola Muffins, 144
    Felshaw Tavern Bran Muffins, 146
Grape Nut Bread, 193
Grape Nuts cereal
    Bread, 193
Grapefruit
    Ambrosia, 25
    serving suggestions, 20
    with Strawberries, 21
Grapefruit juice
    Wassail, 17
Grapefruit Ambrosia, 25
Grapefruit with Strawberries, 21
Green-Apple Stuffed French Toast, 63
Grits
    Baked Garlic Cheese, 137
    Cheese, 137
    and sausage, 118, 120

H

Haddock
    Finnan Haddie, 113
    Kedgeree, 109
Ham
    and Cheese Soufflé, 89
    and Eggs au Gratin, 89
    Baked Ham and Cheese Sandwich, 89
    Baked with Mustard Glaze, 124
    Egg Soufflé, 96

Ham (continued)
    Loaf with Mustard Sauce, 123
Ham and Cheese Soufflé, 89
Ham and Eggs au Gratin, 89
Ham Loaf with Mustard Sauce, 123
Harvest Apple Cake, 188
Herbed Sausage Cheese Balls, 122
Hershey Brownies and Icing, 236
Hillcrest House Waffles, 60
Homestyle Granola Cereal, 39
Honey
    Breakfast Parfait, 41
    Cous Cous Cake, 178
    Favorite Fruit Sundae, 22
    Homestyle Granola, 39
    Portuguese Egg Bread, 204
    Wheat Bread, 206
Honey Wheat Bread, 206
Hors d'Oeuvres
    Artichoke Squares, 136
    Aunt Marte's Cheese Straws, 137
    Baked Mushrooms, 135
    Bleu Cheese Mushrooms, 136
    Cajun Crabmeat Filo Pastries, 113
    Herbed Sausage Cheese Balls, 122
Hot Apple Cereal, 38
Hot Chicken Salad Crepes, 104
Hot Chocolate Mix, 16
Hot Christmas Wassail, 17
Hot Mulled Wine, 15
Hot Pepper Jelly, 219
Hot Spiced Cider, 16
Hot Spiced Fruit, 30

I

Ice Cream
    Old-Fashioned Syllabub, 252
    Strudel, 197
Ice Cream Strudel, 197
Icing
    boiled, 238
    brownies with, 236
    cookie with, 231
    glaze for pastry, 197, 208, 209
    maple glaze, 152
    orange/lemon, 232
Irish Soda Bread, 180
Italian Spinach Pie, 105

J

Jalapeño(s)
    Cheese Muffins, 154
    Hot Pepper Jelly, 219
Jalapeño Cheese Muffins, 154

Jam(s)
    Apricot-Pineapple, 217
    Frozen Strawberry, 213
    Raspberry, 216
    Rhubarb, 222
    Sand Plum, 214
    Southern Fig Preserves, 215
Jana's Käse und Eieer, 81
Jelly(ies)
    Hot Pepper, 219
    Prickly Pear, 218

K

Kedgeree, 109

L

Lake District Lime Ice, 221
Lemon(s)
    Bars, 232
    bread, 184, 185
    Butter, 223
    Curd, 224, 225
    Layer Loaf, 185
    Lemonade, 13
    Pie, 247
Lemon Bars, 232
Lemon Butter, 223
Lemon Curd, 224, 225
Lemon Layer Loaf, 185
Lemon Pie, 247
Lemon Yogurt Bread, 184
Lemonade, 13
Lima Bean Casserole, 132
Lime(s)
    Ice, 221
    Tom's Treat II, 14
Lobster
    Newburg, 113
    Quiche, 109
    Shellfish Crepe Pie, 112
Lobster Newburg, 113
Lobster Quiche, 109
L'Orange Fromage Coffee Pastry, 197
Lost Bread, 62

M

Macadamia nut(s)
    bars, 235
Magic Canyon Quiche, 110
Maine Blueberry Muffins with Topping,
    141
Makes-Its-Own-Crust Cherry Cobbler,
    247

Mango Bread, 186
Maple
    glaze, 152
    Mousse Tartlets, 244
Maple Mousse Tartlets, 244
Marmalade
    Bread, 184
    Dr. Fowler's Muffins, 148
Marmalade Bread, 184
Martha Murphy's Marvelous Melba
    Sauce, 221
Melba Sauce, 221
Melon(s)
    Favorite Fruit Sundae, 22
    serving suggestions, 20
    Summer Fruit Soup, 37
    topping for, 221
Michigan Sesquicentennial Fruit and
    Yogurt, 26
Mimosas, 11
Miss Dodie's Eggs, 95
Moist Bran Muffins, 144
Molasses
    Brown Breakfast Bread, 193
    cookies, 231, 232
    English Gingerbread, 236
    Felshaw Tavern Bran Muffins, 146
    Gingerbread Pancakes, 45
Morning Cake Delight with Topping,
    170
Morning Carrots, 136
Morning Glory Muffins, 148
Morning Potatoes, 129
Muffins
    Applesauce Oatmeal with Maple
        Glaze, 152
    banana, 141, 142
    blueberry, 141, 143, 145
    bran, 142, 144, 146, 147, 148, 149
    Cranberry-Apple, 150
    Dr. Fowler's, 148
    granola, 144
    Jalapeño Cheese, 154
    Orange Buttermilk, 151
    Pumpkin, 153
    Raisin Bran, 144
    Sweet Potato, 152
    tips on making, 140
Mushroom(s)
    Baked, 135
    Bleu Cheese, 136
    Catlin-Abbott Breakfast Bake, 99
    Chipped Beef and Egg Bake, 88
    Fancy Egg Scramble, 78
    Hot Chicken Salad Crepes, 104
    Sausage and Wild Rice, 117
    Sausage Mushroom Quiche, 96

Mustard
    Carol's Homemade, 221
    glaze, 124
    sauce, 123

N

Nectarine(s)
    Fried, 27
Night-Before French Toast Casserole, 70
Norwegian Fruit Soup, 36
Nuts (see Almonds, Macadamia nuts,
    Pecans, Walnuts)

O

Oak Tree Coffeecake, 175
Oak Tree Granola Muffins, 144
Oatmeal
    Baked, 40
    Cake, 176
    granola, 39, 41
    muffins, 152
    pancakes, 47, 50, 51
Oatmeal Cake, 176
Oatmeal Pancakes, 50
Oktoberfest Sausage, 121
Old-Fashioned Nut Cake, 238
Old-Fashioned Syllabub, 252
Old-Fashioned White Cake, 238
Olive Tea Sandwiches, 229
Omelet(s)
    Avocado, 80
    Fresh Vegetable & Herb, 83
Onion-Cheese Bread, 194
Orange(s)
    baked, 33
    beverages, 9, 10, 11, 14, 17
    Buttermilk Muffins, 151
    Favorite Fruit Sundae, 22
    French toast, 69
    frosting, 232
    glaze, 195
    Golden Fruit Cup, 24
    pastry, 197
    Waffles, 61
Orange Buttermilk Muffins, 151
Orange Julius, 9
Orange Waffles, 61
Outlaw Waffles, 59

P

Pancake(s)
    Aebleskivers, 56
    apple, 52, 53
    Blueberry, 46

Pancake(s) (continued)
    buttermilk, 45, 46
    cornmeal, 49
    Cottage Cheese, 55
    Dutch Babies with Apples, 57
    Fruit, 49
    Gingerbread, 45
    Oatmeal, 50
    Pearl's Prize-Winning Mix, 47
    Puffed Pear, 54
    Pumpkin Raisin, 49
    Sour Cream, 48
    Sourdough, 45
    Supreme, 51
    Swedish, 48
    Three-Grain, 49
    whole wheat, 47, 49, 51
Pancakes Supreme, 51
Parmesan Potatoes, 129
Pastry(ies)
    Cajun Crabmeat, 113
    Coffee Strudel, 196
    Cream Cheese Sweet Bread, 208
    Ice Cream Strudel, 197
    L'Orange Fromage, 197
    Pecan Nut Roll, 207
    pie crust, 241
    Prune-Filled Tea Ring, 209
    quiche, 109
    Walnut Sausage Rolls, 117
Peach(es)
    -and-Cream French Toast, 69
    Bread, 180
    Breakfast Parfait, 41
    Fruit Pancakes, 49
    Galliano Fruit Cups, 23
    Melba Tart, 245
    serving suggestions, 20
    Summer Fruit Soup, 37
Peach Bread, 180
Peach Melba Tart, 245
Peaches-and-Cream French Toast, 69
Pear(s)
    Almond Tart, 241
    Baked, 33
    Breakfast Cake, 180
    Pie, 243
    Poached in Wine Sauce, 34
    Puffed Pancakes, 54
Pear Breakfast Cake, 180
Pear Pie, 243
Pearl's Homemade Sausage, 117
Pearl's Prize-Winning Pancake Mix, 47
Pears Poached in Wine Sauce, 35
Pecan(s)
    Banana-Praline Muffins, 141
    Butter Pecan Bread, 192

Pecan(s) (continued)
    Chocolate Pecan Pie, 246
    Maple Mousse Tartlets, 244
    Nut Roll, 207
    Old-Fashioned Nut Cake, 238
    Southern Pralines, 252
    Squares, 236
    Sticky-Top Cinnamon Rolls,
      201
Pecan Nut Roll, 207
Pecan Squares, 236
Pepper(s)
    Hot Pepper Jelly, 219
    Jalapeño Cheese Muffins, 154
    Morning Potatoes, 129
    Rellenos Dierker House, 134
Pie(s)
    Chess, 241
    Chocolate Pecan, 246
    crust, 241
    Italian Spinach, 105
    Lemon, 247
    Pear, 243
    quiche, (see Quiches)
    Shellfish Crepe, 112
    Sour Cream Raisin, 240
    tart, (see Tarts)
    walnut and raisin, 241
    Zucchini Crescent, 104
Pineapple
    Apricot Jam, 217
    Bars, 234
    Bran Muffins, 148
    Carrot Bread, 190
    Tom's Treat II, 14
    Zucchini Loaf, 191
Pineapple Bars, 234
Poached Eggs with Lemon-Chive
    Sauce, 96
Popovers, 155
Poppyseed
    Bread, 195
    coffeecake, 169
Poppyseed Bread, 195
Portuguese Egg Bread, 204
Potato(es)
    Dover, 130
    Morning, 129
    Pancakes, 131
    Parmesan, 129
    Sweet Potato Pancakes, 129
Potato Pancakes, 131
Preserves
    jam, (see Jam)
    Southern Fig, 215
Prickly Pear Jelly, 218
Pride of Idaho Cookies, 233

Prune(s)
    Norwegian Fruit Soup, 36
    Tart, 244
    Tea Ring, 209
Prune Tart, 244
Prune-Filled Tea Ring, 209
Pudding
    Rice, 248
Puffed Pear Pancake, 54
Pumpkin(s)
    Apple Cake, 173
    Bread, 188
    cooked, 33
    -Cranberry Nut Bread, 189
    Gingerbread, 189
    Madewood LaFourche, 33
    Muffins, 153
    Raisin Pancakes, 49
    Waffles, 61
Pumpkin Apple Cake, 173
Pumpkin Bread, 188
Pumpkin-Cranberry Nut Bread, 189
Pumpkin Gingerbread, 189
Pumpkin Madewood LaFourche, 33
Pumpkin Muffins, 153
Pumpkin Raisin Pancakes, 49
Pumpkin Waffles, 61

Q

Quiche(s)
    Crab, 109
    crust, 109
    Lobster, 109
    Lorraine, 96
    salmon, 110
    Texas, 97
    Sausage Mushroom, 96

R

Radish Tea Sandwiches, 229
Raisin(s)
    Apple Raisin Coffeecake, 172
    Apple Raisin Nut Tart, 242
    Bran Muffins, 144
    Chess Pie, 241
    -Filled Coffeecake, 173
    Morning Glory Muffins, 148
    Norwegian Fruit Soup, 36
    Pumpkin Madewood LaFourche, 33
    Pumpkin Pancakes, 49
    Rice Pudding, 248
    Soldier's Bread, 196
    Sour Cream Pie, 240
    Sourdough Bread, 205
    Sticky-Top Cinnamon Rolls, 201

Raisin Bran Muffins, 144
Raisin-Filled Coffeecake, 173
Raspberry(ies)
    and blueberry parfait, 26
    Fresh Berry Cobbler, 250
    Jam, 216
    Melba Sauce, 221
    Outlaw Waffles, 59
    Peach Melba Tart, 245
Raspberry Jam, 216
Rellenos Dierker House, 134
Reuben Brunch Casserole, 101
Rhubarb Coffeecake, 171
Rhubarb Jam, 222
Rice
    Apple Cider Soup, 37
    cakes, 86
    Pudding, 248
    Sausage and Wild, 117
Rice Pudding, 248

S

Salmon
    crepes, 112
    quiche, 110
Sand Plum Jam, 214
Sandwiches
    Baked Ham and Cheese, 89
    Cucumber Bacon, 230
    Curried Chicken, 229
    Olive, 229
    Radish, 229
Sauce(s)
    Bearnaise, 86
    Bechemel, 112
    caramel, 35
    Crème Fraiche, 221
    Eggs Benedict, 85
    Hollandaise, 85
    lemon-chive, 96
    Lime Ice, 221
    mushroom, 89
    mustard, 123
    raspberry, 221
Sauerkraut, 121
Sausage
    and Egg Brunch Casserole, 100
    and Grits Casserole, 118
    and Wild Rice, 117
    Bake, 120
    Breakfast Bake, 99
    Breakfast Casserole, 98
    crepes, 103
    Herbed Cheese Balls, 122
    homemade, 117
    Italian Spinach Pie, 105

Sausage (continued)
  Oktoberfest, 121
  quiche, 96
  Scotch Eggs, 84
  Soufflé, 90
  Tennessee Gravy and Biscuits, 125
  Walnut Rolls, 117
Sausage Bake, 120
Sausage Breakfast Casserole, 98
Sausage and Egg Brunch Casserole, 100
Sausage and Grits Casserole, 118
Sausage and Wild Rice, 117
Sausage-Filled Crepes, 103
Sausage Mushroom Quiche, 96
Sausage Soufflé, 90
Sautéed Apples, 29
Scones, 159
  Dad's Scotch, 160
  Welsh Country, 160
  Fool's Gold, 159
  tips on making, 140
Scotch Eggs, 84
Scotch Shortbread Cookies, 231
Scrubbed & Tubbed, Boiled, Baked &
  Glazed Oranges, 33
Shellfish Crepe Pie, 112
Shortbread, 231
Shrimp
  Eggs Pacifica, 111
  Shellfish Crepe Pie, 112
Skier's French Toast, 67
Smoked Salmon Egg Crepes, 112
Soldier's Bread, 196
Soufflé(s)
  cheese, 91, 92
  Egg, 96
  English House 24-Hour, 94
  Ham and Cheese, 89
  Sausage, 90
Soup
  Apple Cider, 37
  Banana Bisque, 37
  Norwegian Fruit, 36
  Summer Fruit, 37
Sour Cream
  Baked Eggs, 80
  Cinnamon Loaves, 181
  Coffeecake, 166
  Crème Fraiche, 221
  Ellen's Blueberry Delight, 28
  English House 24-Hour Soufflé, 94
  Pancakes, 48
  Raisin Pie, 240
  Sausage-Filled Crepes, 103
  Vanilla Coffeecake, 168
Sour Cream Cinnamon Loaves, 181

Sour Cream Coffeecake, 166
Sour Cream Pancakes, 48
Sour Cream Raisin Pie, 240
Sour Cream Vanilla Coffeecake, 168
Sourdough
  Apple Bread, 205
  Chocolate Almond Bread, 205
  Hotcakes, 45
  Raisin Bread, 205
  Whole Wheat Bread, 205
Sourdough Chocolate Almond Bread,
  205
Sourdough Hotcakes, 45
Sourdough Raisin Bread, 205
South-of-the-Border Scrambled Eggs, 82
Southern Buttermilk Biscuits, 158
Southern Fig Preserves, 215
Southern Pralines, 252
Special Dried Apricot Fruit Cake, 174
Spice Cake, 237
Spinach
  Eggs Florentine, 87
  Fresh Vegetable & Herb Omelet, 83
  pie, 105
Sticky-Top Cinnamon Rolls, 201
Strawberry(ies)
  Bread, 179
  Galliano Fruit Cups, 23
  Jam, 213
  Shortcake, 249
  with grapefruit, 21, 25
Strawberry Bread, 179
Strawberry Shortcake, 249
Summer Fruit Soup, 37
Super French Toast a L'Orange, 69
Swedish Buttermilk Coffeecake, 165
Swedish Pancakes, 48
Sweet Potato Muffins, 152
Sweet Potato Pancakes, 129
Syllabub, 252

T

Tart(s)
  Almond Pear, 241
  Apple Almond, 243
  Apple Filo, 242
  Apple Raisin Nut, 242
  Creamy Chocolate, 245
  Granny Smith Apple Butter, 240
  Maple Mousse, 244
  Peach Melba, 245
  Prune, 244
Tea
  Cranapple, 12
  how to prepare, 228

Tennessee Gravy and Biscuits, 125
Texas Hazlewood Quiche, 97
Three-Grain Griddle Cakes, 49
Tomato(es)
  Bacon-and-Cream-Topped, 132
  British Broiled, 132
Tom's Treat II, 14

V

Valerie's Sour Cream Banana Bread, 183
Very Lemony Lemon Bread, 184
Voss Inn Baked Eggs, 80

W

Waffles
  Chocolate, 61
  Hillcrest House, 60
  Outlaw, 59
  Orange, 61
  Pumpkin, 61
Walnut(s)
  Apple Compote, 32
  Apple Nut Bread, 188
  Apple Walnut Cake, 172
  Chess Pie, 241
  Date Nut Bread, 193
  Dream Bars, 232
  Pride of Idaho Cookies, 233
  Sausage Rolls, 117
Walnut Dream Bars, 232
Walnut Sausage Rolls, 117
Wassail, 17
Welsh Country Scones, 160
Wine
  Hot Mulled, 15

Y

Yogurt
  Baked Oatmeal, 40
  Breakfast Parfait, 41
  fruit and, 26
  Lemon Bread, 184

Z

Zucchini
  breads, 191
  pie, 104
  with eggs, 80
Zucchini Bread, 191
Zucchini Crescent Pie, 104
Zucchini Frittata, 80
Zucchini Pineapple Loaf, 191